MY TRADE

Andrew Marr was born in Glasgow. He graduated from Cambridge University and has enjoyed a long career in political journalism, working for the *Scotsman*, the *Independent*, *The Economist*, the *Express* and the *Observer* before being appointed as the BBC's political editor in May 2000. He is also the presenter of *Start the Week*. Andrew Marr's broadcasting includes series on contemporary thinkers for BBC 2 and Radio 4, and political documentaries for Channel 4 and BBC *Panorama*. He has had major prizes from the British Press Awards, the Royal Television Society and Bafta, among others. He lives in London.

Andrew Marr

MY TRADE

A Short History of British Journalism

PAN BOOKS

First published 2004 by Macmillan

First published in paperback 2005 by Pan Books
an imprint of Pan Macmillan Ltd
Pan Macmillan, 20 New Wharf Road, London N1 9RR
Basingstoke and Oxford
Associated companies throughout the world
www.panmacmillan.com

ISBN 0 330 41192 6

A CIP catalogue record for this book is available from
the British Library.

Typeset by SetSystems Ltd, Saffron Walden, Essex
Printed and bound in Great Britain by
Mackays of Chatham plc, Chatham, Kent

This book is for Jackie,

love of my life,

and in memory of

my friend, mentor and hero,

Tony Bevins

Contents

Acknowledgements

I would like to thank all the very many friends and BBC colleagues who gave so generously time and thought to help me; the staff of the London Library; all those I interviewed but did not quote; and my family. In particular I would like to thank my agent, Ed Victor, who brought a thin idea to a fat conclusion – he usually advocates fat to thin; Philippa Harrison, who reorganized many thoughts, hacked at solecisms and helped me reduce a vastly longer manuscript to the current volume; and to Andrew Kidd, my editor at Macmillan, for his great good humour and patience.

Preface

You cannot hope
to bribe or twist,
thank God! The
British journalist.

But, seeing what
the man will do
unbribed, there's
no occasion to.

Humbert Wolfe, 'The British Journalist'

The British journalist is not altogether popular. National newspaper circulation is falling and has been for a very long time. Some of the best-known papers are in the worst circulation trouble – the *Financial Times* at one end of the market, and the *Daily Mirror* at the other. Some local papers do all right, but the decline has spread well beyond what we used to call Fleet Street. Editors have tried all sorts of tricks. Broadsheets have adopted the strident fusing of opinion and reporting that the tabloids pioneered. There has been aggressive price-cutting; all manner of special offers; ever more flamboyant front page 'puffs'; giveaway copies in hotels and trains; folding one paper as a free gift inside another; even changing the size of newspapers. As the first broadsheet to cut down to tabloid format, the *Independent* bucked the trend and won a good sales increase, using its front page to campaign for centre-left causes almost as vigorously as the *Daily Mail* had been doing from the right.

But overall, looking at the national newspaper market as a whole, the tricks have not worked. What has been going wrong? It isn't lack of talent. The trade employs many of the best writers in Britain. Papers as distinct as the *Guardian* and *Daily Mail* are brilliantly designed, far better than they were twenty or thirty years ago. Above all, we live in a news-driven world: from Baghdad to Westminster, from cannibal trials in Germany to the sex lives of the British royals, from global warming to Africa's AIDS pandemic, there is not exactly a shortage of stories. Throughout the centuries commentators and foreign visitors have expressed astonishment at Britain's love affair with news; we still buy and read far more papers than any other European country and we still have a national press that is infinitely more varied and lively than that of America. For decades people have claimed the love affair is about to end. For decades they have been proved wrong. But today's sales figures are grim: it makes you wonder if something is wrong with what journalists actually do, day in, day out.

Beyond the raw circulation figures there is a great, unfolding argument about the ethics, working habits and produce of British reporters. For BBC employees, it has been particularly acute because of the anger-mottled drama that followed the Iraq War, in which a government-employed scientist, David Kelly, killed himself after being exposed as the source of a story on the *Today* programme that had sent Downing Street into a fury. The inquiry by Lord Hutton into those events was tough on the processes and behaviour of the BBC, which has been regarded by most people as a trusted source. During a dreadful few hours it cost the Corporation both its chairman Gavyn Davies and its popular director-general Greg Dyke. Many journalists felt that there had been a culture clash between the world of public life and the world of journalism; that Lord Hutton had been harsh and unsympathetic to the trade generally; and that a single mistake on a single programme, albeit an influential one, had been used to condemn the practices of a whole profession. ('But that's *exactly* how you treat *us* every day of the week!' reply politicians.)

The issue of trust in journalism cannot be shrugged off. The Hutton process shone a light on customs and practices that many other journalists find hard to defend. Was it all right to rely on a single source when making a serious allegation? (As a Westminster journalist, I do it all the time, and have done for twenty years.) How full and accurate are one's notes at the time supposed to be? (Many reporters these days do not have reliable shorthand – or any shorthand.) Is it fair to use anonymous quotes from people who won't identify themselves to attack others? (Probably not; but without this, half of the news in newspapers would vaporize.) When TV and radio journalists are broadcasting to millions of people, should we write down all the important bits beforehand, rather than simply speaking off the cuff? (It would be safer, particularly on dangerous stories. But be warned: such reporting sounds so wooden you might feel yourself forced to switch the radio off.) Many of the reporters slouched at the back of the courtroom watching the BBC's Andrew Gilligan trying, vainly, to explain himself to QCs and Lord Hutton, wondered how their own practices would stand up to that kind of examination. How good are their sources, really? How often do they inflate the importance of a source? Or buff up a quote? Or call back to double-check that the source stands by what was said in a brief surreptitious encounter?

Nor was the Gilligan affair, which wrought such damage on the BBC, a one-off disaster. Eminent US newspapers have suffered from the scandal of reporters caught simply making up stories – the most damaging being the *New York Times*'s sacking of Jayson Blair in 2003. In Britain, a reporter for Sky News killed himself after being sacked for faking a report that seemed to be showing a cruise missile being fired from a British submarine. Regular doses of hype, sloppy reporting and uncorrected mistakes have long marked British newspapers, despite the attempts by the best of them to use readers' ombudsmen and regular corrections to improve their standing.

Yet Britain has a tradition of raucous press freedom, and for good reasons. Historically, it has often been the derided and marginal-seeming figures who were right, and the smug majority which turned out to be wrong. Whether it was Claud Cockburn's mimeographed anti-appeasement news-sheet of the 1930s, *The Week*, which saw the real diplomatic story of Nazi advance more clearly than *The Times*; or Andrew Morton's much-derided inside story of the disastrous marriage of Charles and Diana, which proved the 'experts' fools, the British have good reason to thank 'irresponsible' journalism. Whisper it softly, but there are still those in the darker corners of Whitehall and Westminster who feel that even Andrew Gilligan, whatever his faults, was far more right than he was wrong.

What are my qualifications for writing about British journalism? This book is decidedly not a memoir but I have used episodes in my career so far as jumping-off points for larger arguments and burrowings into the origins of the trade. Michael Frayn wrote a novel about Fleet

Street in which one of the characters said: 'A journalist's finished at forty, of course.' I am now forty-five. I have been a trainee hack, a general reporter, a sub-editor, a parliamentary reporter, a political journalist, a radio presenter, a broadsheet and a tabloid columnist, a hilariously inexperienced newspaper editor, an author of books, a maker of TV documentary and interview series and am now, as the BBC's political editor, a television reporter. I have not been a sports reporter or written about dogs and fashion – yet – but I do sometimes write about a guinea pig. I have, in short, done many jobs in modern journalism. On the way I've been a near-alcoholic in Scotland, the disloyal 'friend' of ministers and prime ministers, engaged in savage and surreal boardroom rows and learned what to do when the TV camera lights go out and a piercing whistle blows the newsreader's question out of an oversized ear. I've worked with heroes and liars, haggled with proprietors and learned many of the dirty tricks of one of the dirtiest trades in the land.

I didn't decide to become a journalist. I stumbled into journalism. I'd done the requisite English degree, played politics, drawn cartoons and learned how to smoke sixty cigarettes a day without being sick. I'd started a PhD, washed dishes and been turned down for a job in a second-hand bookshop. Despite having a first-class degree and having read an unfeasibly large number of books, it began to dawn on me that I couldn't actually *do* anything. I couldn't sing, act, tell jokes, play any musical instrument, hit, kick or catch a ball, run for more than a few yards without panting, speak another language, or assemble things without them falling apart immediately. I was a scientifically illiterate innocent with the entrepreneurial instincts of a thirteenth-century peasant and the iron determination of a butterfly. Journalism seemed the only option.

Even then, it was a little intimidating. At university there had been lean young men and handsome women with urgent faces who were always too busy to speak and rarely smiled, except 'ironically', and who phoned diary items to newspapers in London. They took the student newspaper seriously. They could type. Unlike me, they didn't spend most of their time on marches supporting an (ungrateful) working class, or drinking. One has ended up as the editor of the *Financial Times*. Another is a distinguished foreign correspondent for the *Sunday Times*.

At the opening of the eighties, there was the beginning of a rush to the City but journalism was the favoured option of would-be intellectuals too dim or greedy to stay in academia. One of the early stars of my time returned a year after leaving to interview me about a rebellion then going on in the Cambridge English faculty, and which *Panorama*, to which he was 'attached', thought might be interesting for a short film. He arrived at the pub we had arranged to meet in wearing a trench coat. If he didn't actually have a trilby with a paste card reading 'press' stuck in one side of it, the effect was the same. We'd known each other slightly – well. enough to be on Christian-name terms. 'Robert Harris – BBC – *Panorama*,' he said, holding out his hand without a flicker of a smile. 'Hi, Robert,' I replied. I thought he was a complete prick. Then I thought, almost instantaneously, and that's *exactly* the kind of complete prick I want to be, too.

In those days, the BBC offered several dozen traineeships every year. Since broadcasting was only speaking and therefore did not involve learning to type, it seemed a more attractive option than trying to get a newspaper job. On the train down to London I read *The Economist* – well, several pages of it at least. I already had a thorough knowledge of current affairs, being an avid reader of various international Marxist magazines, the *New Left Review* and *Radical Philosophy*. Though I wore a second-hand tweed jacket and a wool tie to show how grown-up I was, I carefully pinned on my most important badges – my Anti-Nazi League badge, my CND badge in blue and yellow and my Eastern European Solidarity Campaign badge to show that I was also interested in current affairs. Oh yes, and I had an orange beard.

In London we were greeted at an office in Portland Place opposite Broadcasting House by friendly enough but very old men in their thirties – some even in their forties. We were asked to dictate various texts into a microphone, carefully written to be hard to read, and we were questioned about politics and current affairs. I found it all very easy. So easy in fact, that I had a couple of pints at lunchtime to relax myself before the main afternoon interview. It was very hot. With time in hand and heavily dressed, I then went for a rest in Regent's Park. I lay down. It was really *very* hot. I fell asleep. My interview was at 3 p.m. I woke at 2.59 p.m. I sprinted back to Portland Place and arrived, bright red (to go with the orange beard), bathed in sweat, with my mind a complete blank. After three or four questions from a panel of interviewers I noticed that they were talking very slowly and smiling in a kindly, reassuring fashion.

'What would you like – to – do – at – the B-B-C?' asked a lady. *That* was a very interesting, very difficult question and I sat silently for more than a minute wondering about it, smiling back to show I was friendly too.

'Would – you – like – to – be – a – sports – reporter?' asked a man.

I thought about this for a long time. 'Yes,' I said.

The lady perked up a bit. 'Are you interested in sport?'

I pondered that in silence for a very long time, too. 'No,' I said.

They thanked me and smiled very kindly. Mysteriously, I did not become a BBC trainee.

Luckily for me, a real journalist pulled out of a training place on a course for the *Scotsman* newspaper and one of my many begging letters came up trumps. I was invited to Edinburgh for an interview. I clambered onto the overnight sleeper from King's Cross. In second class, in those days, one shared a sleeping compartment. Mine was already half occupied by a substantially built, dark-bearded Scot wearing nothing but his underpants, heavily tattooed and smoking. He looked me up and down. 'Good,' he finally said, 'I wasn't the kind of poof who went' – he put on a squeaky English voice – ' "Ooh, I say, do you mind if I get some sleep?" ' And he pulled out a cardboard box of beer cans and a duty-free carton of cigarettes. Some eight hours later, unshaven, entirely drunk at breakfast time and smelling like a homeless kipper, I arrived for my interview at the *Scotsman*.

It was perfect preparation. I would fit in well. The *Scotsman* building is today an upmarket hotel for style-conscious Americans and Scandinavians but then it was still in its oily, grimy prime – one of the great Edwardian newspaper buildings, part castle, part factory. It still had the remains of a dovecote on the roof for messenger pigeons. The sandstone building, which stands high above Edinburgh's Waverley Station, glaring down from the city's Old Town, was constructed on the principle that the highest and most abstract parts of the business took place at the top and as you descended, floor by floor, the physical side took over. So on the highest floor, originally, there would have been the board of directors. Then, four yards below, came the editor and the editorial writers, austere liberals and home-rulers all. Then the newsroom. Then sub-editors and so on down and down, until you came to the Linotype operators and the intoxicating sweet stench of newsprint and the rumble and heat of the presses. Eventually, as originally designed, the freshly printed, cut, folded and rolled-up parcels of newspaper would fall out of the building's stone anus into a waiting railway truck – the line actually went into the basement of the building – and be whisked across Scotland hot for the breakfast tables of lawyers, GPs and ministers of the kirk. It was the kind of building a clever child might have designed and hugely satisfying to work in.

On that chill morning, shaking with nerves, I shaved around my stubbly beard in the BR loos, filled myself with coffee and reported for my interview. The newsroom was a huge, dingy place, apparently full of huge, dingy men. Everybody was smoking, which was reassuring. Nothing else was. It was like nowhere I'd ever been or seen before. My English degree, my half-digested politics, my 'posh' voice – none of these things would be any use here. Along the walls were desks piled with yellowed old newspapers. Communal desks stretched to a kind of top desk, or top table, where a row of fat, angry-looking men were barking into phones. Hardly anyone there had had a university education. The news editor, George Barton, was a solidly built, intimidating man, the sergeant major of the news operation, whose snarls, barks and dressings down would dominate the next year or two. The previous year's trainee, a defiant woman called Melanie Reid, warned me that George's habit was to patrol up and down the room behind the reporters as they hammered away on their East German-surplus typewriters. Each story was typed on three thin sheets of paper, with two sheets of carbon paper between them. The top copy went to the news desk, the second to the sub-editors and the third you kept on a metal spike by your desk. George would stop behind a trainee and stand silently as one did one's best with the white fish catch from Peterhead or a missing car in Aberfeldy. Then he would reach over with one brawny arm and, without uttering a word, remove the paper from the typewriter, scrumple it into a ball in front of the trainee's face, throw it over his shoulder and – wordlessly – carry on walking. You knew you were getting better when he allowed you to finish the paragraph before he destroyed it. For someone who'd recently been writing 3,000-word essays on symbolism in late modernist poetry, it was a rude wake-up call. Even Melanie sometimes collapsed in floods of tears.

After an initial suspicious grilling by the news editor, I was led through to meet the editor himself. In those days, editors of the *Scotsman* were approached through a sequence of oak-panelled rooms. Names of previous editors were inscribed in gold paint around the antechamber. My first editor, Eric Beattie Mackay, was a remote and awesome figure, famous throughout the Scottish newspaper industry. He was a wiry, depressive-looking man with a shock of white hair and a taciturn manner, to look at not unlike Corporal Fraser from *Dad's Army*. Like Fraser, he was unrelentingly pessimistic. Unlike Fraser, he had a group of subordinate colleagues who seemed to spend a lot of time in muttering huddles trying to work out what he meant by the snorts and head shakings. I was ushered through. At first all I could see was the leather soles of his shoes. He was lying flat in his chair, his feet on his large Edwardian desk, staring at the ceiling, his glasses tipped up his forehead. He said nothing. I said nothing. It was a profound, contemplative nothing. It went on for some time. Eventually I coughed. He suddenly swung upright. Scarily intelligent eyes stared at me for a moment in apparent surprise. He asked what the dickens I thought I was doing. Aghast, I stuttered that I was there about a traineeship. He knew *that*, he said. He wasn't *stupid*. 'Laddie, I asked you, why?' Again, I stuttered. I had – ah – that is I wanted to – I believed in – well, – quality journalism – and the *Scotsman* . . .

At this point, Mackay's chair crashed backwards and he sprung to his feet like a jackknife, striding to the huge bow window that looked down over Edinburgh towards Princes Street and its morning rush-hour crowds. He waved an arm.

'Quality journalism! Quality journalism? Laddie, no one out there is interested in quality journalism. D'you not understand? It's *over*. It's all over . . .' He walked back, sat down and slowly returned to the horizontal, staring at the ceiling again. 'Hmph. Quality journalism . . .' he muttered. Then he said, '*Still* . . .' And that was it. After a few more moments of silence, I slowly backed out. Waiting for me was the managing editor, a large, pink-faced, anxious-looking man. Had I got the job, he asked. I replied honestly, that I hadn't the faintest clue. Well, what had the editor said? I repeated the conversation as accurately as I could. 'Hmm,' said the managing editor, 'that was an interesting one.' He called in the deputy editor and they talked together. Then, while I was sent to wait, one of them went in to find out. The editor was apparently surprised at my reaction. Of course I'd got the job. What kind of a *fool* was I?

So the first and most important door to a life in journalism opened. Twenty years ago it was a much more ordered trade. Under rules agreed between the main newspaper groups and the National Union of Journalists, hardly anyone was allowed to start in Fleet Street. Everyone had to pass exams set by the National Council for the Training of Journalists and then work for at least two years in a provincial newspaper. Various newspaper groups had training schemes. The *Wolverhampton* and *Sheffield Stars* had one. The Mirror Group had a centre in Plymouth. And Thomson Regional Newspapers, which in those days owned the *Scotsman*, as well as papers such as the *Chester Chronicle*, the *Aberdeen Press & Journal* and the *Newcastle Journal*, had its training centre in the middle of Newcastle upon Tyne where I was fortunate enough to be sent for training. It was known to all as 'the Brownlee Academy' after John Brownlee, a larger-than-life cigar-chewing newspaper musketeer and lifelong press romantic who ran it. Brownlee believed that to be a journalist was the greatest luck in the world and exuded wicked glee at the stunts and dirty tricks a proper hack must learn. By then I'd taught myself to touch-type, but in Newcastle we learned shorthand – still, in my view, invaluable to anyone in journalism – and libel law, and how to report court cases, and newspaper terminology and the structure of local government.

More than that, we were taught how to get a simple local story: we were sent off to local villages and outlying suburbs of Newcastle and told not to come back until we had half a dozen publishable stories for the evening paper, the *Chronicle*. That meant slowly scrubbing away any natural shyness, banging on vicars' doors, stopping shopkeepers and pleading with councillors for anything – anything. Stray dog? Upset at the Guild? Oldest villager? Proud parents of footballer? We learned the soon-to-be-useless skill of removing the voicebox from a public telephone so that a rival couldn't phone his story back – this being several years before mobile phones arrived. We were told to bribe publicans to put 'out of order' signs on the bar phone and encouraged to call rivals with misleading train times – the field craft of a vanished era.

Back at work in Edinburgh, I found myself an unwilling bit player in a long-running drama about class. In essence, middle-class university children were stealing what had been a male, school leavers' trade. I was hardly the first. Sir Peregrine Worsthorne, for example, was sent as a graduate experiment to the *Glasgow Herald* immediately after the war. He had rather sweetly misunderstood newspaper terminology and thought he was being offered the job of deputy editor, rather than trainee sub-editor, the lowest of the low. The natives, naturally, were unfriendly. He sent most of his time making them tea. The social tragi-comedy being enacted on the newsroom floor of the *Scotsman* when I arrived there thirty years later was not fundamentally different. Rather as in the army, experienced and sceptical working-class men were knocking the ignorance out of milksops. In a way, George Barton and thousands like him were the staff sergeants to the witless second lieutenant of adjectives that, at twenty, I was.

I survived as a journalist only because of other people. There were people like Arthur Macdonald, a business reporter on the *Scotsman* who kept a sardonic and bloodshot but essentially friendly eye on what I was up to. One day, I was called and given a scoop by an entrepreneur who said he had discovered a technique for pressing waste paper into a substance that could in turn be used to build yacht hulls. He had glossy brochures and was about to employ hundreds of people at Portree in Skye. I met him in Glasgow and produced a laudatory feature for the next day's paper. It was a front page story on the business section, my first. Flushed with success the next morning, I took a call from a local Skye reporter up there, a man working for the *West Highland Free Press*. Och, he just wanted to check up, he said – to be sure – that I did know about the fraud charges. The what? Och, yes, at Portree Sheriff Court . . . and my contact left the country. I froze. There may have been literal beads of sweat. Arthur, who was keen on what he would describe as 'a modest refreshment' in the local pub, was watching me silently. As I contemplated the destruction of my career, he gently cheered me up and bought me a beer. Mind you, from then on, whenever he thought I was getting just a little bumptious he would quietly start to whistle 'The Skye Boat Song'. Ever since, when I've made some awful howler, when I've been leaping to conclusions yet again, I hear it still.

I have had great editors – Mackay turned out to be one – and generous colleagues of all kinds. My own journalistic hero, though, to whom this book is dedicated, was a reporter. Tony Bevins was the wild man of political journalism when I finally arrived in London in the mid-1980s. He looked like a silver-haired Buddy Holly and he believed passionately that governments were generally up to no good, and could be tracked down and exposed if you looked carefully enough through the official papers. He was often right. He had a piratical streak and when the *Independent* was formed, Bevins was made its political editor. More experienced colleagues from other newspapers warned me repeatedly to have nothing to do with him. 'Bevins is – completely – mad,' said Jim Naughtie, and most people seemed to agree. So as soon as he offered me a job I signed up and started the happiest time of my working life. Tony Bevins wrote a savage book about journalism of his own. *Ratpack* attacked the corruption of political journalism by cur-like reporters and bullying bosses, of whom, having worked for papers including the *Sun*, *Mail* and *Times*, he'd known a few. It was completely unpublishable: one publisher told Tony he had never come across any manuscript with so many libels on every page. At their wild dinner parties Bevins and his wife Mishtu entertained many hacks and politicians and stirred up Westminster horribly. They died suddenly and unexpectedly two years ago. I miss Bevins every day.

Now I turn round, and find I've been doing this strange apology for a proper job for more than twenty years, still in it years longer than Michael Frayn advises. I'm quite young, really, but quite a lot of my other journalistic heroes and friends have died – cancer, heart attacks, liver failure. Others have moved on to become novelists or businessmen. Somehow, somewhere along the road, journalists stopped being shabby heroes, confronting arrogant power, and became sleazy, pig-snouted villains. I don't know when it happened, or why: this book is partly my attempt to find out. Has something turned rotten in the state of journalism or is that only what all ageing hacks believe?

For that is what I am. In seventeenth-century England, the 'Tribe of Ben' became the chosen collective description of playwrights and poets who looked back to Ben Jonson as their national hero and father figure. For all journalists, it is his near-namesake Sam Johnson who is the tribal chief, if only because of his dictum 'only a blockhead writes, except for money'. (Below that, in letters of gold, we should remember two of his other remarks – that 'A man may write at any time, if he set himself doggedly to it' and, equally pertinent to modern journalism, 'round numbers are always false'.) The Tribe of Sam is now vast. We come in all shapes and sizes, good, bad, decent, disreputable, drunk, sober, male and female. This book is idiosyncratic and mottled. It misses out friends, enemies, large areas of journalism about which I know nothing and feuds I feel have gone on too long already. But it is this hack's attempt to tell the story of British journalism.

To write this, I have read half a library's worth of books, floated on a sea of old newspapers and interviewed very many people. Just occasionally, I have had to rely on my memory, which worries me: when one goes back to check the facts, it is astonishing how frequently one finds them in an impossible or unfamiliar arrangement. But that too is part of this book. We are the story-telling mammal and we constantly reshape the world into narratives which make psychological sense to us. Journalists just get paid for doing it. Many of the names of the people who have helped me so much appear in what follows. I thank them all. The mistakes are mine, as they always have been.

The paperback edition of this book is in most respects identical to the hardback edition. The trends identified have not changed, though *The Times* is now fully tabloid. In most cases, circulations are even lower. I have made a handful of minor corrections brought gleefully to my attention by 'friends' and by friends. The main change is that I have added an index. I left one out of the first edition hoping this would spur idle and time-pressed colleagues to actually read the book. But almost every reviewer protested. They cannot all be wrong and I have succumbed. For those who want to dig deeper into some of the modern stories told here, there are many excellent formal histories, most recently Roy Greenslade's account of post-war newspapers. The structure of this book is straightforward: it begins with two chapters looking at the social history of British journalism, little written about, and the history of news. There follow more specific chapters about political journalism, editing, broadcast journalism, foreign correspondents and columnists, concluding with a general survey of the state of the trade.

1

The Snobs and the Soaks

'The journalist requires to be a man or woman of sound physique ... journalism is no profession for the delicate in health and the physical weakling ... Perhaps the most desirable quality in a journalist is that he should be a good mixer, a sociable soul – The solitary, the exclusive, the scholarly recluse, the boorish, self-opinionated dogmatist, the bigot, the pedant, the snob – none of these will find themselves at home in the world of journalism.'

Teach Yourself Journalism, 1951[1]

'Every journalist who is not too stupid or full of himself to notice what is going on knows that what he does is morally indefensible. He is a kind of confidence man, preying upon people's vanity, ignorance and loneliness, gaining their trust and betraying them without remorse . . .'

Janet Malcolm[2]

Who are Journalists?

What kind of people are they? Have they always been roughly the same, from the slither and stink of Grub Street 300 years ago to the smooth hum of a modern national newspaper office? No, clearly not. Even in my time they have changed. In 1980 I joined a world which was overwhelmingly male and lower middle class. The typical journalist seemed to be a cheery middle-aged man having trouble at home, who drank pretty freely, had a constant inch of cigarette jammed between his fingers, the nails of which were blunt and damaged from years of ill-treating typewriters. Now there are regiments of women, snappily dressed, without discernible alcohol problems, well-educated,

with sharp smiles and sharper elbows. The men are sometimes
teetotallers who keep fit and dress stylishly. They have beliefs which
go beyond the sacred duty of lunch. But below the social shifts
are deeper questions. Are there particular psychological types who are
drawn to the trade? Are journalists as much born as made? A shuffle
through the history of journalism, which is still an under-researched
area, does suggest there are messages about us which everyone who
reads a paper, or watches a TV news bulletin would benefit from
hearing.

For instance, reporters have often been volunteer exiles, people
who have left a secure working-class or professional world in order to
live a more precarious and interesting life. In the very early days, this
might mean gossip writers who had fallen out of polite or aristocratic
society – because of sex, gambling, drink – and had to live on their
wits. Grubs not butterflies. Later it meant working-class boys who
struggled out of respectable and thrifty families to a louche, drunken
Fleet Street. Also, I have been fascinated by the number of times in a
journalist's autobiography, or in conversation, that fatherlessness
comes up. And anyone who reads about or watches journalists' lives
must be struck by our unreliability as partners – not all of us,
obviously, but many of us. Nor do journalists have high self-esteem as
a class. The passing-on of information that somebody, somewhere,
does not want to see published is not a popular business. Devour the
gossip; spit out the gossip monger.

It is often said that journalists as a class are less respected than any
group except estate agents and politicians; but it isn't as simple as that.
According to a poll by YouGov in 2003, it depends upon who you
work for. There are said to be some 70,000 journalists working in
Britain, though with so many freelance and part-time people it is hard
to be sure. Among them journalists for BBC News, ITV News and
Channel 4 News are trusted greatly – by 81 per cent of those asked,
just below family doctors and above head teachers in a 'trust index'.
Broadsheet journalists were trusted by 65 per cent. Local journalists
were trusted by 60 per cent. Journalists working for the *Daily Mail* and
Daily Express were trusted by 36 per cent but people working for the
'red-top' tabloids were indeed down there with estate agents at just
16 per cent. This is illogical and out of date. But overall, 'hacks' are seen

as characteristically venal, untrustworthy and prurient. Is there something in the trade and the people it attracts which makes us like this?

Certainly, British journalism is not a profession. Over the years many people have tried to make it one. In the United States they have mostly succeeded. There, every year, tens of thousands of journalism graduates are turned out in a sophisticated production process – *squish, gloop, plonk,* journalist! *Squish, gloop, plonk* journalist! They are taught about the technical skills and the ethics, the heroes of American journalism and its theory. In the process they are moulded and given a protective gloss of self-importance. They have Standards and, in return, they get Status. In Britain, it isn't like this at all. Journalism is a chaotic form of earning, ragged at the edges, full of snakes, con artists and even the occasional misunderstood martyr. It doesn't have an accepted career structure, necessary entry requirements or an effective system of self-policing. Outside organized crime, it is the most powerful and enjoyable of the anti-professions. No country in the world has been as journalism-crazed as Britain. Yet, broadly, we do not respect the people who deliver us the very thing we ache for.

People get into journalism by mistake; or via some obscure trade magazines, or through writing pornography, or family connections. There are well-known journalists today who got in by starting as telephonists, printers or secretaries. Others, the winged ones, floated in from Oxbridge colleges straight to *The Economist* or *Financial Times*. Yet others had, besides their talents, the happy good fortune to be brought up in journalistic dynasties – to be a Coren, Lee-Potter, Lawson, Dimbleby, Wintour, Carvel or Dacre.

However they got in, the vast majority are journalists because of an irresistible, scratchy need. People will sit for years in local newspaper offices cold-calling the police and hospitals, try desperately to stay awake in local council planning or water and sewerage meetings, write about garden ornament design, accountancy vacancies for trade journals, and sit being bellowed at by drunken old news editor tyrants. And in the end many fail. We fail sideways; we go off and do something with easier hours and better pay, such as becoming a press officer or public affairs consultant for a company or public body. Or we fail upwards, discovering that we have a greater talent for writing novels, plays or film scripts, and then the good things of life, from

mossy rectories to first-class plane seats and daughters who know what
Verbier is, fall softly into our laps. Or we ... just plain, ordinary,
everyday damn-it-can't-pay-the-bills fail. But for those who want to
be journalists, the wanting, the urgent desperation to be a hack is the
only thing that really matters.

   What is a journalist? Answer: anyone who does journalism. Journalism includes people who think of themselves as part of a noble elite of
truth-seekers and secular priests. It includes drunks, dyslexics and some
of the least trustworthy, wickedest people in the land. The innocent
newspaper reader is not forewarned. To distinguish quality, readers
use brands, not bylines. And of course bylines don't have bracketed
descriptions after them saying rascal, or liar. The reader doesn't know
who pretends to make the necessary phone calls, but never bothers; or
that this one hates Tories and always writes them down; or that she is
so unreliable her stories are patched together by sub-editors from Press
Association copy after she's gone home. Different papers do have
different cultures, and carry some kind of reader guarantee. But today
newspaper cultures are blurred, and there is a far less clear distinction
between broadsheet journalists and tabloid hacks than the people who
responded to that poll supposed. People move easily between papers
and between papers and telly. But, like plumbing or selling fish, there
are certain skills without which it's very hard to be a journalist –
though it's a fair bet that there are more journalists who can't write
shorthand or who don't understand libel law than there are fishmon-
gers who cannot gut a mackerel.

   One cheap way of answering the 'What is a journalist?' question,
which has held many real journalists in thrall, is that a journalist is
someone who looks and behaves like a journalist. This is a boy thing,
mainly, though a few great female journalists, Martha Gellhorn or Ann
Leslie, have a certain unmistakable and raffish style. More often, it's
all those tens of thousands of men who thought that rumpled suits,
battered trilbies, chain-smoking, a whisky habit and a lifetime's avoid-
ance of responsibility were the thing itself, and not merely life-stylistic
quirks around it. The memoirs of journalists are reeking and rancid
with this romanticism, the smell of cologne and Senior Service cigarettes mingled with damp ink and hot collars.

   The lifestyle and image that people want from a job is the magnetic
force that draws in some, and repels others. It can shape what the job,

the '-ism' comes to be. Journalists often choose long hours and insecurity as the entry price for a certain lightness of being. This in turn has made journalism able to stand outside established authority – the world of rank, predictability, professionalism and deference. It is why the term 'responsible journalism' should be shunned. Responsible to whom? The state? Never. To 'the people'? But which people, and of what views? To the readers? It is vanity to think you know them. Responsible, then, to some general belief in truth and accuracy? Well, that would be nice.

Some say that journalists are people who attempt to search out the truths about the world around them, and then inform the societies they inhabit. Certainly 'finding out' is pretty central to everyone's notion of journalism. Journalists do need a certain native nosiness, an urgent, itchy curiosity, or more than that, the ability to spot a 'story' in a mass of apparently random facts. But where does that leave the people writing about lawnmowers, or cheap wine offers, or even columns about their lovers? How many people who call themselves journalists have ever – in their entire careers – really found out *anything* much?

That's not necessarily their fault. In a complicated, developed society, much of the most important finding out can only be done by people with sharper, narrower skills – microbiologists, meteorologists, opinion pollsters and market analysts, whose discoveries journalism simply passes on in a more popular (and generally distorted) form. Is a journalist who is told a piece of malice-tinged gossip by a politician and passes it on, unchecked, 'finding out'? Or a journalist who notes down football scores? Most journalism is second-hand retailing, a link in a chain. Rather than discoverers, a more honest description might be a kind of postal service for events. Certainly, you can define a journalist as someone who passes on: a compulsion to blab and spill secrets is one of the very few things everyone in journalism would agree is essential. But the truth is, 'What is a journalist?' is one of those questions to which there is no answer. Journalists have a blurred social status, a foggy range of skills, an ill-defined purpose and a ludicrously romantic haze where a professional code would normally be.

Early Journalists

The prehistory of modern journalism shows that it has been a ragged and confusing trade all the way through. As early as the 1620s there had been the corantos – as in 'current', as in 'current affairs' – which were semi-regular bulletins of news from the Continent, picked out from similar papers there and translated without comment into English. Reporting London news was simply too dangerous. They could run up to eight pages in length; were constantly being suppressed and then tolerated by the Crown; and were popular enough for their printers to be satirized by Ben Jonson. The first anonymous hacks were the ancestors of the news agencies, picking up and passing on overseas information.

The largest group of early writers who wrote for themselves and published weekly, sometimes daily, fare were the dissenting pamphleteers of the seventeenth century. By Cromwell's Commonwealth, according to one estimate, 30,000 pamphlets and journals with a political motive were being published in a single year. Were they journalists? The pamphleteers didn't think of themselves as reporters in a modern sense but as partisan political players, and often religious bringers of Truth and Enlightenment. They bear a passing resemblance to today's more splenetic columnists, though during the Civil War they took greater risks. As both Crown and parliament marshalled their arguments, a school of savage, satirical political writing grew up. Nothing feeds the hunger for news quite like war. And it is then, for the first time, that we meet journalists, of a kind. In evolutionary terms, they may be *Homo habilis* to our *Homo sapiens*, but the gait and glance of the eyes are familiar. Among those whose names we know were John Berkinhead and Marchmont Nedham, a former secretary and a former school usher, both in their twenties, born poor, both abusive, unreliable and for hire.

After the war, under Cromwell's Commonwealth, the press was dull and censored. With the Royalist Restoration, more publications returned but were also censored, by the thoroughly unpleasant Roger L'Estrange. Born in the year Shakespeare died, L'Estrange was a former spy. He is sometimes called the first journalist. In fact he is the origin of all journalism's ill-wishers. He published a pamphlet calling for the severest measures against not only printers and authors but also 'letter-founders, and the smiths and joiners that work upon presses, with the stitchers, binders, stationers, hawkers, mercury women, pedlars, ballad-singers, posts, carriers, hackney coachmen, boatmen and mariners' who might distribute uncensored writing. As a reward for proposing a system of censorship that was only finally achieved in Stalin's Russia, Charles II appointed L'Estrange as England's official censor, with his own army of snoops and spies to hunt down unlicensed journalists and printers.

In principle, L'Estrange was against the idea of any public news-papers at all, 'because I think it makes the Multitude too Familiar with the Actions and Counsels of their Superiours . . . and gives them, not only an Itch, but a kind of Colourable Right and License, to be meddling with the government'. But London was hungry for news and when the printers were stopped, people would simply hand write newsletters and circulate them. L'Estrange compromised by producing two official newspapers: the *Intelligencer* on Mondays and the *News* on Thursdays. Samuel Pepys, the greatest private reporter of his day, thought the early editions of the *Intelligencer* very dull. So did everyone else. Then the plague arrived in London, and the court removed itself promptly to Oxford where the courtiers feared they were infected, with something even deadlier than dullness. So in 1665 the *Oxford Gazette*, the first official newspaper that we would recognize as such, appeared – to L'Estrange's fury. As the court moved back to the capital, the paper moved too and its name was soon changed to the *London Gazette*. Crammed with adverts, full of court and official news, anonymously written, it is hardly a good read, but it was all the frustrated citizens of England were officially allowed. For the final years of Charles's reign were characterized by a brutal war against dissenting journalists, such as Henry Care, which was resolved in the Court's favour.

However, the Glorious Revolution of 1688 opened the floodgates. The arrival of a coffee-house culture, where party politics, Whigs against Tories, began to be played out, marks the real start of informed public opinion. And for public opinion there must be journalists too. The theatre, and the world of pamphlets, and newsbooks, meant there was already a sub-class of educated but poor writers looking for work. The term 'Grub Street' had been used to describe the poets and scribblers who lived there as early as the 1630s, but it was only by the 1690s that many of them could earn a living from professional news writing. News-sheets began to appear, not only in London but quickly in provincial cities too, publishers printing them off in the streets around St Paul's and other cathedrals. One man would be editor, publisher and collector of facts. He would have touts and tip-off merchants at court, in the early financial markets of the coffee and chocolate houses, and at Westminster. The printers' names survive on mastheads – Robert Walker of Seacoal Lane; Abel Roper the Warwick-shire printer, in business at a saddler's shop in Middle Temple; Joanna Brome of the Gun by St Paul's, and many more. These printers were mostly general publishers, turning out pamphlets, cheap books and ballads as well as newspapers, and they were in the business of selling information about public appointments, and aristocratic gossip, some of it as scandalous as anything in today's tabloid papers – murderous duels, bizarre sexual tastes, hidden pregnancies.

By the early 1700s there was a real newspaper market in London. The *Courant*, the first daily paper, with a circulation of 800 a day, struggled against another eight rivals, including the *London Gazette*. Few Londoners could read and many of the 500 or so coffee and chocolate houses kept the papers to be read out loud. They were curiously intimate. Some, for instance, like Ichabod Dawks' *News-Letter* made a point of leaving some space blank for personal news, which could then be written in and posted on to friends and relatives in the country. Others are full of the village gossip of London, impenetrable to anyone not living within the radius of a few streets. Would we recognize those early eighteenth-century efforts as newspapers now? They were full of political propaganda, unchecked, unlikely rumour and filthy gossip . . . so the answer is yes. But they were stilted and episodic and, to the modern eye, pretty hard to read. For the most part, this is still journalism without named or full-time journalists.

But even in these early days, there are flickerings of what will follow. It took one writer of genuine genius, the tradesman's son, government spy, novelist and traveller Daniel Du Foo, also known as Defoe, to create a journalistic style that lasted. He wrote excellent, clear, uncluttered, reporterly English full of relatively short sentences of plain description. Defoe's longest work was not *Robinson Crusoe* or *Moll Flanders*. It was his own newspaper, the *Review*, which did the secret bidding of his Tory ministerial masters and was published from 1704 to 1713. Like many later journalists, he came into journalism as a radical and found that survival involved getting in with the powerful. But he wrote for many other papers too including the best-regarded London paper of the time, the *Post-Man*, owned by a French exile Jean de Fonvive – so you could say that British journalism starts with a pro-government hack writing for a foreign proprietor.

Yet Defoe understood, as no one before him seems to have done quite so clearly, that the news business would only thrive if the public developed a basic trust in its sources and truthfulness. He attacked his rival news-sheets and reported that journalistic lying was so widespread in London that it was 'the Jest of the Town' with neighbours asking one another: 'What is the Lye of the Week? Or what is the Lye *Courant* for the Day?' Defoe was as vehemently attacked for lying himself yet he had the right end of the stick; and it is interesting that the coffee-sippers of the early 1700s seem to have been at least as sceptical about their daily papers as Londoners are three centuries later. Defoe was frustrated and puzzled by the torrent of nonsense published by his rivals and by the public's ability to laugh at how easily and regularly they were fooled by false news . . . and then to go out and buy the same scandal-sheet the next week, too. Here again, not much has changed. He came to believe in the need for a regulated press, not a censored or government-run press, but one where a certain ethical commitment to the truth was required. In that he was way ahead of his time.

But above all, Defoe was a *reporter*: he believed in going and seeing with his own eyes. He wanted to hear witnesses with his own ears. He was a perpetual motion machine, who travelled and wrote down and interviewed. It didn't mean he resolved to be impartial, but it did mean he was telling, not just arguing. Some of his most influential and vivid reporting, for instance, was carried out for the *Post-Boy* while he was in Edinburgh. He was actually there as a spy for the London government, watching the riots in the streets and the debates in the Scottish parliament as it prepared to vote itself into extinction. Defoe was a passionate believer in the coming union. But the reports he sent back were eyewitness ones, not only of the Scottish debates, but of that year's Scottish corn crop, and house fires in Edinburgh, and horse races. Later, after the two countries were joined, Scottish industry had a very hard time, and there was much bitterness. We know about this because of Defoe's reporting: he went back and recorded the bad, as well as the good. While in Scotland, as a spy, he was in real danger. But he had the reporter's instinct. He just wanted to be there. And he had the priceless journalist's tool – shorthand – again, way ahead of his time. Later as an editor, where he was passing on information, Defoe generally gave some indication of his source – and when he received anonymous tip-offs, he was suspicious, and let it be known: 'The Gentleman who sent a Letter sign'd R.P. is desir'd to send some Authentick Proof of the Fact in his Letter.'

Like Defoe, the few stars of early journalism tended to be outsiders who forced themselves up, partly because they were articulate and partly because they were desperate. Defoe came from a poor dissenting family – his father sold wax for candles. Jonathan Swift sneered at him for being low-born and addressing his work to the barely literate London rabble. But though there were well-born writers doing a form of opinion-forming genteel journalism, such as Addison and Steele, they were not characteristic of the young trade. Those collecting and passing on the stories were more often disreputable and marginal figures – people like the wicked vicar Henry Bate; the scandal-raking Captain Edward Topham; the champion hoaxer Theodore Hook, and early female gossip-traders such as the notorious Mrs Manley and Eliza Heywood of the *Female Spectator*.

According to the editor of Pope's *Grub Street Journal*, by 1730 there was a class of 'Collectors' who were paid to 'furnish materials for the Dayly Papers' and would scour the villages and suburbs for titbits – just as I and my friends were taught to do in Newcastle 250 years on. Pope also pointed out that since they were paid according to the length and number of their stories 'it is no wonder that so few of them are true'. We know some journalists' real names but they wrote under a wild and confusing thicket of pseudonyms – Scandalosissima Soundrelia, Novellus Scandalus, Abednego Simpleton, Mr Nibble-news and Verbosus Enthusiasticus. They were not all Londoners. The weekly *Worcester Postman* was going as early as 1690. Overseas travellers wrote back letters, clerks were paid to send details of court gossip and the printer himself might collect lists of animal prices. By the 1750s there were regular papers in Liverpool, Manchester, Nottingham, Coventry, Birmingham, Exeter, Sherborne, Salisbury, Lewes, Bristol, Canterbury,

Reading, Ipswich, Cambridge, Oxford, Stamford, Leicester, Leeds, Hull, York, Newcastle, Worcester and Derby.

They were effectively small business start-ups, edited and run by their printers, the capital coming from a wide range of more traditional trades, from distilling to wig making. Where, as in Northampton in 1722, two papers were in competition, it was severe and savage. Robert Raikes and William Dicey, publishing the *Mercury*, had the following to say about their unfortunate rival James Pasham and his upstart *Northampton Journal*: he was a noisy animal, possessed of a 'thick and stupid Crannium' whose initial newspaper was nothing more than 'his first Parcel of Bum-fodder'. These papers were certainly rough and ready: the news was generally printed in the order it arrived, and if organized, then merely into news from the Continent, America, London and so on. Relatively little local news initially appeared, presumably because in small towns everyone knew it long before the once- or twice-weekly local paper appeared.[3]

Back in London, William Perry, the son of an Aberdeen carpenter, and an early owner of the *Morning Chronicle*, founded in 1769, was the first person in Britain to become rich from newspapers. Thomas Gurney, who founded *Hansard*, was an East Anglian watchmaker. He did well, too. The founder of *The Times* in 1785, John Walter, was a former coal merchant and bankrupted insurance underwriter who went into newspapers as an offshoot from a failed printing experiment. Captain Topham founded the *World*, a grandly named paper, simply because he wanted to puff the attractions of his mistress, who was appearing on stage in Drury Lane. Both newspapers and advertising were very heavily taxed in the eighteenth century and it was hard to turn an honest penny. The solution was simply to flip dishonest ones instead. Many early editors and reporters, picking up stories about the rich and famous, then simply sold them back again at a tariff, taking bribes not to print what they had learned. Another option was taking money from government ministers or rich Opposition politicians who would pay to spread their views. It is hard to maintain any sense of dignity when you are scrabbling for bribes and writing to order. Sir Walter Scott told his son-in-law as late as 1829 that to be connected with any newspaper would be 'a disgrace and degradation. I would rather sell gin to poor people and poison them in that way.'[4]

There are famous names whom we could include as early journalists – as mentioned already, Samuel Johnson, for his rewriting and reimagining of parliamentary speeches before direct reporting was allowed, is one; John Wilkes, the journalistic hero of the age, who will be considered later in relation to politics and journalism, is another. Most novelists we remember, including Fielding and Richardson, also wrote for newspapers. So did Boswell. In general, though, we are talking about literary essays or rambles, not news. The few inspiring figures tend to be political radicals or idealists who used the power of the press to assault authority – Wilkes in his epic fight with parliament, Hazlitt, and William Cobbett, the greatest political journalist after Defoe. Cobbett was like Defoe in being an outsider, the son of a Surrey farm labourer. He was like him in his anger and in running his own paper, the *Political Register*. He was like him in falling foul of the government, imprisoned and financially smashed for attacking the flogging of local Cambridgeshire soldiers by German mercenaries. He was also like him in his use of English which, along with Hazlitt's, hugely influenced the development of newspaper writing in the twentieth century. (Cobbett, however, was not at all like Defoe in his prejudices and beliefs. He was a passionately anti-Whig, xenophobic defender of Old England against her modern and reformist enemies, his superb contempt for high finance and political corruption mingled with a less than superb contempt for machinery and Jews.)

Toiling alongside the few remembered geniuses were hundreds of forgotten names, the victims of an era when bylines hadn't been thought of, a struggling class of educated craftsmen, clerks and professionals down on their luck begging a pittance from the first printer-proprietors. Journalists were sneeringly described in the aristocratic *London Review* of 1835 as a class still degraded and sinking: 'the conduct of our journals falls too much into the hands of men of obscure birth, imperfect education, blunt feelings and coarse manners, who are accustomed to a low position in society, and are contented to be excluded from a circle in which they have never been used to move'. From the first British journalism was brutally divided into classes of winners and losers: a small crust of the brilliant and famous, and a thin, turbulent porridge of sub-literary desperation roiling below it. And that would not change. But the general exclusion of journalists from the class of the powerful was about to change dramatically.

How Journalists First Became Powerful

To put it crudely, the Victorians did four things which made Britain the newspaper-mad nation it remains even today. They cut the taxes and lifted the legal restraints which had stopped papers being profitable; they introduced machinery to produce them in large numbers; they educated a population to read them; and they developed the mass democracy that made them relevant. 'The press' in the sense of a great national force had arrived. Leaving behind the rough sexual equality of the coffee houses, and rubbing noses with men in power, journalism moved up in the world. It was not always a pretty sight.

The stamp duty on papers had kept the entrepreneurs who were making fortunes from iron, steam and railways away from the newspaper business – paying all that tax to the government made it simply too expensive and risky to bother with. The ferocious laws of criminal libel and censorship imposed during and after the wars against Napoleon had also made journalism a little too dangerous for all but the few bravest or most desperate souls. The second generation of provincial papers were relatively small-scale operations, with an editor and a handful of sub-editors plus reporters. Since bylines were still virtually unknown, it can be hard to identify the individuals who made up the trade in early Victorian newspapers, unless they happened to come under a literary spotlight. One of the most influential dailies, now almost forgotten, did because it was founded by Charles Dickens ten years before stamp duty was abolished. The *Daily News* started publication in January 1845 as a liberal, but high-quality daily. It had a staff of around thirty editors, sub-editors, critics and reporters – fourteen of the latter, including Hazlitt's son and a future famous QC, sitting in their own room, where they wrote with steel-nib pens the stories they had gathered in streets, meetings and from arriving ships. Within a year the paper was making waves, proudly declaring that 'the newspaper is the intellectual life of the nineteenth century, the great agent of modern civilisation'. Dickens soon gave up the *Daily News* to return to novels and his journalism is only now being fully appreciated once more for its brilliance. But in the wider picture of early Victorian journalism, the significance of Dickens, and indeed Thackeray, is that they bring a kind of glamour and status to the trade that was lacking before. The place where literature touches reporting is special and valuable: and the presence of some of the cleverest literary stars of the 1840s and 1850s in the newspaper world gave early newspapermen a better sense of themselves. The *Daily News* was full of people who lived on the border between literature and hacking – Douglas Jerrold, a printer's son, former Royal Navy officer, self-educated playwright and hack; Harriet Martineau, the blistering anti-slavery campaigner who churned out six long articles a week; Mark Lemon, son of Jewish pub owners and failed dramatist, who became the first editor of *Punch*, and many more.

The abolition of newspaper stamp duty in 1855 was the break-through moment. It came after decades of campaigning for an end to 'taxes on knowledge', both from radicals and conservative reformers who thought that education and information would keep the rising working class from revolution. From this moment on, journalism throughout Britain becomes a recognizable trade and not simply a hobby or character flaw. The cosmopolitan literary crowd of early Victorian journalism quickly needed constant reinforcements from the classes below.

One characteristic career shows the shift. Thomas Catling started at the *Cambridge Chronicle* aged just eleven, employed to remove the damp sheets of freshly printed paper from the press. The *Chronicle*, carried through the streets of Cambridge in washing baskets, sold some two thousand copies, and boasted a reporter of its own. At fourteen, for a pittance, Catling decided to try London instead and got a job as a journeyman printer at *Lloyd's*. His memory of the job in 1854 offers a rare glimpse of the hard life of early newspaper offices:

> The machines left the type in a fearful condition, so that many weary hours had to be devoted to washing it with the strongest pearlash or potash procurable. Dirt mingling with ink caked the letters together . . . Journeymen were content to wait about all day on the chance of getting a night's work. Public-houses were of necessity their chief resort, affording amusement as well as shelter – cards, bagatelle, skittles . . .

Checking copy for mistakes led him to get a part-time education, and then a job as a sub-editor when one fell ill and died. Catling then took advantage of the high-mindedness or sloth of *Lloyd's* theatre critic, who refused to send in a review on the grounds that nothing in London that week was worth reviewing, and was promptly sacked. Catling advanced through the new world of London journalists' clubs and learned the tricks of reporting. Whether the job was watching a hanging, checking up on a society dinner, discovering the condition of Jack the Ripper's victims, trying to arm-twist Gladstone into writing an article, or, later, watching Oscar Wilde hear himself pronounced guilty, Catling would go in person, even after he became the editor of the weekly. By the time he finally retired, after fifty-two years on the paper, Catling was a rather grand social figure, who had dined with the Prince of Wales and been received by an American president. He was lucky in his trajectory but not unique and looked back wryly to the 1840s when a Glasgow paper had warned that journalism was a disastrous and impoverishing trade: 'Reader!' said the *Glasgow National*, 'Have you yet fixed upon a profession? If not, never once think of becoming an editor. Beg, take a pedlar's pack, keep lodgers, take up a school, set up a mangle, take in washing. For humanity's sake, and especially for your own, do anything rather than become a newspaper editor.'

The next great Victorian innovation, in journalism as everywhere else, was the appliance of science. They invented or imported new printing presses and technologies such as the railway and the telegraph, which spread news faster round the country. The first speech to be telegraphed was by Queen Victoria in 1849 but the real exploitation of the telegraph started in the 1860s, when the *Scotsman* was the first paper to install its own wires to London, capable of transmitting 30,000 words of news each evening. *The Times* quickly installed a line to Paris and soon a basic principle of news, which is that it should be new, could be applied almost everywhere in Britain. Leapfrogging improvements in the quality of paper, printing presses and Linotype setting machines made it possible to print far more copies far faster. The paper itself changed and today's wood-pulp paper arrived in the 1880s. The machines coming in from America made the physical process of 'composing' or arranging the letters and lines of metal infinitely quicker – and at least one, the Linotype, was still going when I started in journalism. Finally, railways hugely speeded up distribution, helping spread the 'national' press to the big urban populations of the north too. Today's highly centralized British media can be blamed, in part, on the railways. From very early on, special trains were organized to bring edition after edition of the London papers to most of the country – even to Scotland where they were not needed.

Altogether, mid-Victorian Britain was undergoing a media technology revolution unlike anything that followed until the new technologies of the past twenty-five years, with full colour web offset printing and photocomposition and the Internet. But the final Victorian achievement made the 1870s a more auspicious and generous time for journalism than the 1970s ever were. The Education Act and the arrival of an almost universally literate population – by 1888, literacy was up to 97 per cent which may be higher in English than it is now – produced a boom in readership that gave the press a political power the early Victorians would never have dreamt it could wield. A survey in 1867 concluded that the working man with his penny newspaper 'is by its aid a man of fuller information, better judgement and wider sympathies than the workman of thirty years back who had to content himself with gossip and rumour, and whose source of information as to public events was the well-thumbed weekly newspaper of the public house'.[5] By the 1870s one has the impression of a teeming new trade, still ill-paid but rampantly competitive and ingenious in supplying an insatiable market for news and novelty. When trains pulled in at stations and emptied out their commuters and travellers in the 1870s, the floors and seats were left piled high with crumpled and discarded papers. The print-mad people had arrived.

But if profits, technology and education made British journalism grow big, politics made it matter. For as the franchise widened, in great circles, throughout the century, drawing in ever wider numbers of voters, the politicians needed these new newspapers to get their messages across to the new voters. It was an intensely, sometimes violently, political age in which speeches and manifestos were eagerly read and argued over. Journalists came in from the cold, and posh journalists appeared for the very first time.

Something of the change in status that Victorian journalists enjoyed can be found in the novels of Thackeray and Trollope. In Thackeray's *Pendennis*, written in bursts during the 1840s, Thackeray tells the story of the setting up of a (fictional) *Pall Mall Gazette*. It is launched with a wildly overwritten prospectus, hinting untruthfully at high political contacts declaring 'The Statesman and the Capitalist, the Country

Gentleman and the Divine, will be amongst our readers, because our writers are amongst them – the *Pall Mall Gazette* is written by gentlemen for gentlemen.' The reality is described later, as the paper's sub-editor, Jack Finucane, works with his paste and scissors, stealing news:

> With an eagle eye he scanned all the paragraphs of all the newspapers which had anything to do with the world of fashion over which he presided. He didn't let a death or a dinner-party of the aristocracy pass without having the event recorded . . . It was a grand, nay, a touching sight for a philosopher to see Jack Finucane, Esquire, with a plate of meat from the cookshop and a glass of porter from the public-house, for his meal, recounting the feasts of the great, as if he had been present at them; and in tattered trousers and dingy shirt-sleeves, cheerfully describing and arranging the most brilliant *fêtes* of the world of fashion.

Move on just a few years and contrast that with Trollope's depiction of the journalist Tom Towers in his first Barsetshire novel, *The Warden*, in 1855. Towers is a remarkably up-to-the-minute creation based on Delane, who we will meet shortly; and his *Jupiter* is *The Times*. Towers lives in a luxurious apartment at the lawyers' chambers, the Temple, surrounded by a fine library, with a painting by Millais, and overlooking a lawn which stretches down to the Thames. The equivalent today would be a riverside penthouse, decorated with Britart. His newspaper has awesome power in politics and public life, terrifying bishops and able to crush dukes with a single column: 'Britons have but to read, obey and be blessed. None but fools doubt the wisdom of the *Jupiter*: none but the mad dispute its facts.' Towers is a malign, frightening force in Trollope's world.

> He loved to sit silent in a corner of his club and listen to the loud chattering of politicians, and to think how they were all in his power – how he could smite the loudest of them, were it worth his while to raise his pen for such a purpose . . . Each of them was responsible to his country, each of them must answer if inquired into, each of them must endure abuse with good humour, and insolence without anger. But to whom was he, Tom Towers, responsible? No one could insult him; no one could inquire into him . . .

This is so exactly how politicians and others today see editors such as Paul Dacre, of the *Daily Mail*, that one has to shake one's head and remember it was written 150 years ago. Only a few years divided that novel from Thackeray's more louche and rackety journalists; but although these divisions are never as clear in real life, the jump from outsiders to insiders was really happening in mid-Victorian London.

The Rise of the Political Hack

The most important names in mainstream Victorian journalism were the men who made *The Times*. Its first owner, as we have seen, was a bribe-taking former insurance and coal merchant. But his son, also called John Walter, made a point of hiring Oxford and Cambridge graduates, gentlemen whom he paid well and treated almost as guests in his office, where they sat down to dinners of venison, beef and turbot. *The Times*'s first great editor, William Barnes, a friend of radicals and romantic poets,[6] kept himself anonymous as he built up the paper's extraordinary network of contacts across London and the Continent. He infuriated and influenced politicians of all parties, and was courted by them. He left one of the best early descriptions of the case for violently aggressive journalism, particularly in this rainy island. Newspaper writing, he said, was like brandy: 'John Bull, whose understanding is rather sluggish – I speak of the majority of readers – requires a strong stimulus. He consumes his beef and cannot digest it without a dram; he dozes composedly over his prejudices which his conceit calls opinions; and you must fire ten-pounders at his densely compacted intellect before you can make it comprehend your meaning . . .'[7]

Barnes died relatively young, at fifty-five, from overwork and drink – a journalistic model in more ways than one – and was succeeded by John Delane, who got the job partly through family connections. Delane is still the most famous editor of *The Times* and it was under him that the High Victorian version of the paper became the thundering voice of the British Establishment. A workaholic, whose wife became mad and who shunned his home, Delane developed a wide range of political and social contacts, which allowed him to reach deep into the inner thinking of successive governments. He called his socializing 'swelling' and was a good enough journalist to remain mentally an outsider: 'I have the bad taste not to greatly admire the society of Dukes and Duchesses, and a nearer acquaintance with the stuff out of which "great men" are made certainly does not raise one's opinion either of their honesty or capacity.'[8]

His working day reflected the late deadlines of Victorian newspapers. According to the paper's official history, 'He remained in bed until shortly before luncheon, turning that meal into breakfast. He generally reached Printing House Square at 10.' Then Delane would instruct his leader writers, read up to 200 letters sent in each day for publication and revise, by hand, the whole text of the paper. We can picture him in his white top hat and surging whiskers picking his way home through the quiet streets of the Victorian capital, the first light coming up on Wren's steeples, leaving his paper with its revelations as a ticking political bomb behind him. He rarely left *The Times* office before 5 a.m. and famously claimed to have seen more sunrises than any man alive. Delane picked up so much inside material that one Whig leader, Lord Russell, told Queen Victoria it was 'mortifying, humiliating and incomprehensible'.[9] In his later years – he retired in 1877 – *The Times* was accused of being the real government of Britain. Everyone, including prime ministers and the queen herself, protested and tut-tutted about Delane's power. And everyone courted him and everyone read his paper.

The *Times*'s leader writers were generally Old Etonians and Oxbridge types, with impressive educational records; but there were loucher characters too. The paper had on its staff characters like General Eber, a Hungarian freedom fighter, and Henri Stefan Opper de Blowitz, swathed in furs and cigar smoke, a man who sounds like someone out of Thackeray's wilder fantasies but who was in fact a diplomatic correspondent, interviewing Bismarck and scooping half the embassies of Europe partly by the expedient tactic of sleeping with the statesmen's wives. Most famously of all, there was William Howard Russell, an Irishman from a struggling family, whom we will meet later.

Over at the *Daily Telegraph*, meanwhile, they had George Augustus Sala. Lucky them: Sala was in many ways Britain's first modern newspaper star, a real roving reporter as we understand the term. Later in life, when he was famous throughout Europe and America for his *Telegraph* reports, Sala happily boasted: 'I have forced myself on the public. I have dragged myself up. I have *compelled* the world to listen to me.' It was not an exaggeration. Sala sprang from an almost ludicrously colourful but impoverished family which included male dancers, Prussian gentry, an Italian cardinal and at least one female tightrope-walker. At times he experienced dreadful poverty, wandering through London's clubland, peering in at the dining-room windows and drooling as he watched luckier men eat, or walking behind cigar smokers to sniff their second-hand smoke. His means of subsistence included a growing stream of hack journalism for Charles Dickens's periodical *Household Words*.

One hot August night in 1851 Sala was locked out of his home and when his cleaning woman let him in the next day, he sat down to write an account of his evening, 'The Key of the Street', which a friend persuaded him to send to the great Dickens, who liked it. Sala's early essay in journalism can still be read, entirely anonymous, in bound copies of *Household Words*. And it still reads well. It made Sala's name. At times a little elaborate, even overwritten in the mid-Victorian style, it was as racy and detailed as Dickens's writing itself. We move from a cheap fourpence-a-night flophouse ('. . . the smell of the bugs, Ugh! – the place was alive with them. They crawled on the floor – they dropped from the ceiling – they ran mad races on the walls!') to a fire in Soho and then to a bench in St James's Park where he meets a young tramp, half-naked with neither shoes nor socks, who mutters 'hard lines, mate'. By early morning, Sala is briefly tempted by a so-called coffee from a stall ('burnt beans, roasted horse-liver and refuse chicory'), avoids some genuinely dangerous pubs frequented by muggers, whose sideline is strangling their victims, to finish his night slumped over a copy of the *Sun* newspaper – no relation – in a coffee house until dawn breaks. 'The Key of the Street' has more than a whiff of George Orwell's reportage as a tramp in the 1930s and it is not hard to see why it impressed not only Dickens, but also Thackeray and a clutch of London editors.

So Sala finally found his trade and began his career as a paid reporter. During the course of a long working life, he reported from Russia, America during the Civil War, Austria, Italy, North Africa, Spain, Australia and Mexico. He was arrested as a spy in France, asked to stand for parliament (he refused), narrowly escaped death when a boiler on Brunel's *Great Eastern* exploded, and became a great Victorian celebrity. Stupidly, soon after his night-time walk, Sala fell out with Dickens, and was hired by the cheap and disreputable, newly founded *Daily Telegraph*, for whom he wrote for over thirty-seven years. Like many hacks to come, Sala assumed munificent expenses. He is said to have returned one day to the *Telegraph*'s office and written out a chit, 'To expenses in Persia – £3,000.' When an accounts clerk nervously asked if perhaps he could have a little more detail, Sala grabbed a pen and wrote simply: 'To arsing and buggering about in Persia – £3,000.' He was good value, in the sense of churning out hundreds of thousands of words, but it came at another kind of price, too. Sala's prose was rarely as fresh as it is in his early street essay. With the hot breath of daily deadlines on his neck, he became, like so many overworked hacks, long-winded.

It was the era of self-important, prolix, arch English, the original 'journalese', and Sala's biographer claims Sala was, more than anyone else, responsible for a time when 'your smart reporter did not speak of coffee, for instance, but of the fragrant berry of Mocha. Blood, of course, was the crimson stream of life, a dog's tail his caudal append-age, and the oyster . . . the succulent bivalve.'[10] Sala himself admitted that in order to fill up the paper, 'I made as much as I could of what I knew. I was impatient, dogmatical, illogical and could be, myself, from time to time, aggressive and abusive.'[11] Blather and abuse remain, today, the stand-ins for scores of columnists churning out too many words. As George Orwell complained half a century later, this intro-duced a profound insincerity into English: 'A mass of Latin words falls upon the facts like soft snow, blurring the outlines and covering up all the details . . . When there is a gap between one's declared aims, one turns as it were instinctively to long words and exhausted idioms, like a cuttlefish squirting out ink.' I like to think of Sala as the grandest, happiest cuttlefish of all.

Like many modern journalists, Sala lived high on the hog during his good years. By the age of forty he was earning the rough equivalent of a £200,000 salary today, but was unable to manage his finances, and died poor. Like later followers, he worked on his image, always wearing bright white waistcoats and scarlet ties (think of Robin Day, or the battered-trilby-and-raincoat brigade). He travelled abroad with a revolver, corkscrew and dress suit and in 1871 gave his own assessment of what a good reporter needed: 'to speak half a dozen different languages with tolerable fluency; to have visited or resided in most parts of the habitable globe . . . to be a good cook, a facile musician, a first-rate whist-player, a practised horseman, a tolerable shot, a ready conversationalist, a freemason, a philosopher, a moderate smoker – and a perfect master of the art of packing'. Who could resist journalism after reading that? Sala was not only famous in his lifetime, but remained a great figure of memory in Edwardian Fleet Street and was still being quoted by hacks in bars in the 1950s and 1960s. He forms part of the DNA of the modern British journalist's self-image, even though hardly anyone remembers his name today. His exuberant lifestyle, financial chaos, boasting, competitiveness and tricks are part of much that is romantic and attractive in the journalistic myth.

Victorian journalists are not distant relatives of today's trade. They are its fathers. Dickens, Jerrold, Lemon, Barnes, Russell, Eber and Catling, as well as Sala, were outsiders, who struggled with early poverty and setbacks and who fought for their later fame and power. A high proportion – and this holds good for a wider sample – came from immigrant or Irish families. Most of them led undisciplined and occasionally riotous private lives, yet worked fanatically hard at their profession. They tended to be clubbable, boastful, short-tempered and bad with money. They began as radicals and mostly – not all – ended up as conservative patriots. And, of course, they were becoming more powerful. Where once, in the time of Hazlitt and Cobbett, and the early Dickens, political journalism was idealistic, angrily throwing stones at unreformed power, it began to become the writing of journalists who knock at power's door, and are let in. Next, journalism starts to become a power itself, a force to be reckoned with, flattered but resented.

The Overreachers

The warning signs had been there with Delane. But as Victorian democracy was spread from the rich to ever-wider classes of householders, so journalists became their essential intermediaries. What had really kept journalism down in the previous century was a lack of self-respect and confidence amongst journalists. This was changing. Quite a few provincial editors and Fleet Street writers went into the Commons as MPs themselves. Many were given honours and considered themselves to be the social equals of dukes and members of the Cabinet. As the century wore on, politicians had to win the ear of editors to get their views across. It was the power, as politicians from Burke to Churchill complained, of the middleman. Shrewd politicians picked this up quickly. Lord Palmerston worked so closely with supportive newspapers he was widely suspected of actually writing their articles about him. According to the definitive account of the period, 'Lord Rosebery had a stable of journalists whom he kept nearly as well groomed as his stable of horses.'[12] Disraeli's journalistic dabbling was constant and famous. Gladstone blamed his fall from power in 1874 entirely to losing the support of the pro-Liberal *Daily News*.

By late Victorian times, the leading papers employed a select band of top-hat-wearing and self-important political writers. They were a cadre of perhaps a hundred professional leader writers, recruited directly from the universities, paid well (up to £1,000 a year in the 1870s, a good middle-class income then) and regarded with jealousy and dislike by ordinary hacks. Most journalists, of course, were not like this. The leading reporters of Victorian London, as opposed to the political commentators, were rarely university educated and had few delusions of power: 'they belonged not to the swell West End Clubs but instead haunted the City taverns, the Cheshire Cheese, the Cock, the Edinburgh Castle, which used to remain especially open for them late into the night ... men of little social ambition ... the rootless product of an expanding society'.[13] A surprising proportion were Irish or Scottish – by one guess at the time, three-quarters of London reporters were – and many were alcoholics. But the general status of the trade was being pulled up by politics.

Soon journalists began to overreach themselves. The most stunningly successful and colourful late-Victorian editor was undoubtedly W. T. Stead, the bearded, blazing-eyed and riotously sexual editor of first the *Northern Echo* and later, more notoriously, *The Pall Mall Gazette*, which he turned from a staid political newspaper into a massively influential campaigning organ. A passionate evangelical Christian from the north of England, Stead made the empire crackle with his opinions. He drove the government into reforms of the Royal Navy; was heavily responsible for Gladstone's disastrous decision to

send General 'Chinese' Gordon to Khartoum; campaigned coura-
geously against the Boer War; and helped promote the first Hague
peace conference, as he became increasingly worried about a war of
the European powers. He believed that 'the English race, like Jews and
Romans even more, has a world wide mission to civilise, colonise,
Christianise, conquer, police the world and fill it with an English-
speaking, law-abiding Christian race'.

Stead's journalism used frank sensationalism in style and layout.
He was a great user of multi-deck headlines and other American-style
innovations which looked to later Victorian eyes as lurid as the
extremes of tabloid style can seem today. His importance is that he
was the first to show how sensationalism allied to campaigns could
change the country's politics. He could whip up crowds, scare Gladstone and humble the Admiralty . . . and he did not apologize for any
of it. He campaigned against slum housing in London as effectively as
Dickens in his day, achieving great reforms where traditional higher-
minded campaigners failed. Most famously, he campaigned against the
vile sex trade in girls – some as young as eight. *The Pall Mall Gazette*'s
offices were besieged by readers desperate for the latest instalment and
Stead's achievement was to get the female age of consent raised to
sixteen. But in doing so, he paid money to a mother, got caught in a
journalistic sleight of hand, and was imprisoned for three months.

Characteristically, Stead seems to have thoroughly enjoyed prison,
conducting himself as a latter-day Christian martyr and prophet. An
unabashed believer in what he called government by journalism,
he understood that newspaper power would become rampant in the
century ahead. In 1886 he said:

> I am but a comparatively young journalist, but I have seen
> Cabinets upset, Ministers driven into retirement, laws repealed,
> great social reforms initiated, Bills transformed, estimates remod-
> elled, programmes modified, Acts passed, generals nominated,
> governors appointed, armies sent hither and thither, war pro-
> claimed and war averted, by the agency of newspapers.[14]

He went down with the *Titanic*: his trade kept rising.

Politicians, naturally, saw dangers here and tried to repel it, but by
the end of the First World War, the interweaving of newspaper

power and political power had become dangerously intense, and 'the pressman when he calls on a Cabinet Minister ... is likely as not to find tea laid on for him, cigars at his elbow, carefully selected liqueurs on the sideboard, while the information he is in search of is freely poured out, of course more or less diluted or sweetened according to taste'.[15]

Literary Journalism

Literary reviewers are a class apart. They are fundamentally different from the reporting or editing hack. It could be argued they barely belong in this book at all. They wrote weekly articles, at great speed; but their spread of learning and wisdom was far beyond what you would expect from a newspaperman. I suppose that including reviewers in a book about journalism is a bit like including T. S. Eliot in a book about banking. Still, even if they are our grander second cousins, they need to be mentioned. Their genealogy being different, I have grouped their family history here, and kept it short.

The first and best of the great reviews was started by a Scottish lawyer with deep literary and intellectual interests and a savage pen. Francis Jeffrey's *Edinburgh Review* came out four times a year, and reached an audience of some 50,000, ranging from most of the serious thinkers of Britain to overseas subscribers such as Napoleon. He intended to educate and reform public life, by reviewing everything worth knowing about, from politics to poetry, science to agriculture, geography to the classics. This fantastically ambitious attempt to tell the intelligent readers about all of life, and in doing so make them better people, has been described as a kind of progressive 'spilt religion'. Jeffrey was seen by his enemies as an ayatollah of the Enlightenment and his power was enormous: when an early poem of Byron's got a bad notice in the *Edinburgh*, the poet contemplated suicide and downed three bottles of claret. (This, it has to be said, was not an entirely unusual Byronic response to life's little upsets.)

The *Edinburgh* was followed by the *Quarterly Review*, the *Nineteenth Century*, and many other rivals, giving an outlet for writers of the quality of Coleridge, Sydney Smith, Macaulay, Trollope and Carlyle. The *Westminster Review* was edited by the great philosopher

of utilitarianism John Stuart Mill, and later by George Eliot. In that
great blizzard of printed paper that was Victorian Britain, a host of
others followed – *The Academy, John O'London's Weekly*, the *Fortnightly
Review*. The seriousness of the great Victorian quarterlies passes down
to later flavours of spilt religion, such as the socialism of Sidney and
Beatrice Webb's *New Statesman* – which also tries to educate its readers
in everything from world affairs and industrial economics to the
modern novel. One of the things the reviews did for journalism was
to open it up for university professors; young literary writers, struggling with their first books; and the host of serious amateur Victorian
and Edwardian intellectuals – the travelling clergymen, the multilingual
colonial administrators, and the politicians who studied Greek coins
in their spare time. They did part of the job that upmarket radio
programmes and late-night TV reviews do now, providing a platform
for the country's intellectual conversation. The most successful literary
journalists are famous independently of newspapers through their
books and lectures – Ruskin, Matthew Arnold, and later George
Bernard Shaw, even George Orwell, who despite being a star member
of the National Union of Journalists never worked a day in a newspaper
office in his life.

The penury and graft of book reviewing in the old Fleet Street is a
theme that echoes through scores of memoirs of Edwardian and early
twentieth-century London. From the late 1930s comes this brutal
assessment by a reporting journalist:

> There is … nothing so appalling as being a specialist. There
> are in Fleet Street book reviewers who look tired and faded.
> They have a bowed air. They look frail as moths. One man
> I know reads twenty books a week. He is never without a
> book. He walks with one under his arm. He reads at every meal.
> He sleeps barely five hours a night. He rarely talks. His mind
> is absolutely doped … He is as much to be pitied as the
> mechanic who performs one tedious operation on a machine for
> his living.[16]

Book reviewing is still a hard, underpaid, hamster-wheel of a life.

The original professor-hack of modern times, who churns out
newspaper pieces to order and boosts his or her income massively,
was A. J. P. Taylor. He reached a mass audience through papers and

later television, earning the envy and contempt of toffee-nosed historians who could not or would not do the same. David Starkey and John
Casey, a donnish don from Cambridge who cranks out 'why, oh why?'
hand-wringing pieces for the *Daily Mail*, are modern equivalents.
Simply put, if newspapers require fast writing and some historical
knowledge, then universities have, and always will have, people who
can meet the demand . . . and are relatively underpaid, and willing.
The emergence of Superdon, with huge book contracts, television
series and regular columns, making more money than novelists or film
writers, is only the latest evolutionary step in a trend which started in
arguments about romantic poetry conducted with quill pens 200 years
ago. In its way, reviewing helped elevate the profession, too, so that
there seemed to be a shimmering blur between the writing of grand
novels, or holding chairs in ancient universities, and the inky, grubby
business of writing for newspapers for money. Some of the most
influential and famous journalist role models of all turn out to be
people who were really more literary than journalistic. George Orwell
and Evelyn Waugh, opposites in most things, had more influence on
the way journalists see themselves than any ordinary news reporter
has had.

Getting In: Local Papers and the Rise of the Modern Reporter

But what of them? Even as the political grandee journalists of Edwardian London were stretching out for their brandies and enjoying their
new status, and New Grub Street was filling up with would-be essayists
and reviewers from Oxbridge, real journalism was being seized from
below. The vast growth of the press saw weeklies, evening dailies and
then daily morning papers spring up across Britain, not only in the
great merchant and industrial cities – but in hundreds of dormitory
towns and suburbs whose sense of themselves was based around a
local paper. It was an age of local pride which modern Britain has at
least half forgotten. The great carved and marbled halls of newspaper
offices in the largest cities mimicked the libraries and town halls
being raised at the same time. Almost everywhere soon had its 'local
rag'. Servicing them required tens of thousands of reporters and fast
word-slashing subs; so a rising trade gave a bright, glittering opening

to sharp, literate, working-class boys trying to avoid a lifetime as a clerk or shop assistant.

Competition in the cities produced a steady spiral in pay, making journalism a practical option for people who wanted respectability. In the 1870s local journalists were still often earning less than brick-layers or rural schoolteachers.[17] In the sticks, journalists' status was low. Merely being involved in newspapers could get you excluded from local clubs. So the toughest then went to the national papers and began to change the whole atmosphere of the trade.

One young recruit, later a *Daily Mail* editor, Tom Clarke, arrived in Fleet Street at the turn of the twentieth century and described the leading men of the *Mail* then in words that could have been used for scores of other papers: 'Few of them could be accused of soft-heartedness or sentimentality. Most of them had come up from near the bottom by sheer hard work, and that had left an ineradicable hardness of character. Scarcely one among them had had time or money to go to university . . .'[18] They had been recruited young from school, because they were paid by age and no one wanted to waste money on twenty-something newcomers when you could get a fresh, hyperactive and nervous teenager.

The earliest mass training scheme was introduced, based on the indenture system. By 1931, little had changed in this almost wholly male world:

> The apprenticeship begins in a small town or suburban newspaper office upon the payment of a variable premium. The lad is bound for three or five years to undertake every job from sweeping out the reporters' room to delivering letters and gazing at dead bodies in mortuaries. He receives in return barely enough to pay for his bus fares and lunches. At the end of the apprenticeship, on a test not of merit but of years, he is entitled to a union-maintained minimum wage . . . which at least ensures him the right to live.[19]

The atmosphere of servant-and-master is well caught by a 1939 apprenticeship agreement for sixteen-year-olds: '. . . the apprentice . . . shall not gamble with cards or dice and shall not play at unlawful games or frequent taverns but in all things he shall demean and behave himself towards the masters as a good and lawful apprentice ought to do'.[20] It sounds more like joining a medieval monastery than a modern office.

It was a start that would have been familiar to thousands, including the 'three Cs' of British journalism in the middle of the twentieth century: Hugh Cudlipp, generally regarded as its greatest all-round journalist; James Cameron, its greatest reporter; and Arthur Christiansen, its greatest editor.

Cudlipp was the son of a rotund, gregarious commercial traveller in the Welsh valleys and had two brothers who were both journalists. For a while, all three were national newspaper editors at the same time. Hugh was brought up in a scrimping working-class family and was an early intellectual rebel at school. He left at fourteen, and in 1927 began as indentured trainee at the tiny *Penarth News*, learning to hang around with undertakers to get death notices; to write up local football matches, church events and Scout news; and even to review a local musical society's rendition of Handel's *Messiah* – a work he knew nothing of, had to look up in a local library, and reported by the successful expedient of recording the name of every singer. When that paper, with its circulation of 3,000, eventually failed, Cudlipp went to the Cardiff *Evening Express* and then to Blackpool, where he used every stunt and wheeze in the book to get scoops about travelling circuses, naughty vicars and the like. He was just eighteen when he made it to Fleet Street as a sub-editor on the *Evening Chronicle* and was a full-grown editor three years after that. Cudlipp edited like a god, wrote like an angel and was an irascible, hard-drinking, trilby-wearing icon to a generation; his life is brilliantly described, however, in many other books, including his own.

Some years earlier, Arthur Christiansen, editor of the *Daily Express* in its golden years, had followed a similar path. The son of a struggling shipwright, he left school at sixteen and he started in 1920 at the tiny *Wallasey and Wirral Chronicle*, whose office was much like that of Cudlipp's *Penarth News* – ten by fifteen feet, with a floor covered with rotting linoleum and two tables covered with old newspapers, a single book and the local street directory. He had been advised to do anything to get into newspapers, even scrubbing the steps. He rose through the Liverpool papers like a rocket and reached Fleet Street as a valued London editor aged just twenty. But, unlike Cudlipp, who had loved

the romance and wickedness of his Blackpool reporting, Christiansen
loathed that side of the trade. His first reporting mission, a characteristic job for a novice, involved gathering details of the death of a local
churchman from his widow. Later he wrote:

> I hated this side of newspaper work. I hated calling at the homes
> of the bereaved in train disasters and the like . . . I hated pushing
> people around as reporters must sometimes do . . . I was frightened
> of tipping witnesses in case I gave them too much or distressed
> them by giving them nothing at all. I hated being in the 'ring' of
> shorthand reporters that evening newspapers employ for the pur-
> pose of getting important speeches quickly to the printer . . . those
> old cuttings bring memories of fright, nausea, hot embarrassment
> and near-failure.[21]

He found his natural world to be the office, the page layout and the
headline, where he turned out to be a 'sub' of genius, with a natural
eye for making pages look exciting and other people's prose read well.

James Cameron was by contrast in lifelong revolt against what he
called the 'imbecile thralldom of the office'. Both his parents died from
drink and his father had been an unsuccessful lawyer who wrote
sensational and sentimental stories for D. C. Thomson newspapers.
Cameron left school at seventeen and joined the Manchester office of
the Scottish-owned Weekly News, 'filling paste-pots and impaling the
other daily newspapers on the file' before getting his start in Dundee
and Glasgow. Arriving in London, he found he hated the whole
business of working as a sub-editor: 'I loathed every day of my absurd
looking-glass life, working through the noisy hours of darkness, drinking desultorily through the brief day that is a newspaper sub's only
contact and relationship with the rest of the world . . .'[22] Spurning this
existence he became instead perhaps the greatest foreign correspondent
of his age.

These boys from poor families, far from London, missing college
and working like maniacs to reach Fleet Street in their twenties,
starting in local papers, are characteristic of twentieth-century national
newspaper journalism, which produced a particular kind of reporter.
For many decades indentured trainees joined an intensely male, local
undersea world of booze and broken marriages, rollicking with its own

myths and demons from behind undistinguished shop fronts with
frosted glass in the main street, looking like the local solicitor's office,
or the insurance salesman's.

And at these small papers, responsibility often came incredibly
early, since the smallest ones could have a staff of just two or three.
Sir Bernard Ingham, later Margaret Thatcher's famous press secretary,
found himself in sole charge of the *Hebden Bridge Times* at nineteen
years old working a seven-day week.

> I threw myself into writing at least 15 columns a week – a good
> 15,000 words – sub-editing the whole of the editorial matter and
> writing the headlines; writing the leader column which required
> me to pontificate with all the wisdom of my nineteen years on
> matters of concern to the people of Calder Valley; supplying the
> theatrical criticism which the Hebden Bridge Little Theatre and
> other groups read so closely; identifying the lead story and front-
> page material; providing rudimentary layout sketches for the
> front and, if possible other pages . . . and not least bringing order
> to the coverage of sport by personally laying out the page, putting
> the type into the forme and locking it up.[23]

Even today, though the hot metal finale to Ingham's account is out of
date, there are hundreds of local paper editors who do a lot of their
own reporting, subbing and layout and feel themselves, rightly, much
more rounded professionals than their higher-paid London rivals.

Generations were brought up to know that an incorrect birth date,
or name spelling, or church gala receipt, would mean a red-faced, irate
reader rapping at the door that morning; a casually brutal assessment
of the local amateur dramatic group by a young hack struggling to
remember his English teacher's sarcasms would be swiftly punished
with a poked umbrella; an unfair write-up of the rugby league game,
focusing too much on the brothers' tackling deficiencies, would mean
a grumble when the pint was poured. Lacking this direct response
from their readers, reporters who have emigrated to London or other
national centres are readier to behave more recklessly, even dishon-
estly, than they would at home. J. B. Priestley, the novelist and
journalist who started in Bradford at around the time that Cudlipp
was getting going in Blackpool, described the case for local journalism
as he remembered it there, when

with three newspapers, working at full steam, we had our own
Fleet Street. We had our own news, gossip, literary, dramatic,
musical criticism. I have always suspected that the provincial
journalists of those days had more fun than the London stars, for
most of them did a bit of everything and they were somebodies
in the town. They did not disappear into a huge Fleet Street
machine every morning, to be shot out into private life every
evening at Richmond or Streatham. They were members of a
community, and scribbled in our midst.[24]

The competitive liveliness of industrial towns with three competing
serious papers is long gone, but local journalists are still 'somebodies'
on their patch and are still part of a community.

Here is one of the greats of British journalism fifty years later,
the Sunday Times man Phillip Knightley, on his first grounding at the
Lismore Northern Star, a paper in northern New South Wales:

The idea of interviewing someone on the telephone never
occurred to us – we went out and met people face to face. We
were part of the community. We knew everybody and everybody
knew us. If I got someone's second initial wrong, they would
stop me on the street to complain. If I got the whole story
wrong, I would never hear the end of it ... you could not use
your privileged access as a journalist to come into their lives,
suck them dry, and then leave again. You had personal and civic
responsibilities.[25]

A rite of passage for all young provincial journalists is known as the
death knock – going and knocking on the door of a house which has
just lost a family member, preferably in horrific or embarrassing
circumstances. At my Newcastle course we were taught the art of
charming and sympathizing one's way across the doorstep, and the
absolute necessity, while taking notes, of trying to remove, preferably
but not necessarily by agreement, any photos of the bereaved from
the mantelpiece. The job of getting these stories can be a horrible,
soiling experience which puts people off reporting for life. One of
my fellow trainees on that course, Fiona Anderson, who now works
for the BBC in London, started by reporting for the local paper in
Kettering and had a very similar reaction to Christiansen sixty years
earlier: 'I had to do one story about an old guy who was decapitated

by a lorry, and I told the editor and subs that the police hadn't told his family what happened to him.' She thought the grisly details had been left out of the newspaper, but as soon as she was out of the office, they were put straight back in again; she had to go and 'doorstep' the bereaved family the following morning:

> I arrived just after the paperboy had dropped the paper on the mat, and it was all there. His wife was saying, 'But I didn't know *that* happened' and I . . . well, basically, I just made her a cup of tea. Then there was a house fire with three kids in hospital. I think two died overnight and I had to go round and bang on their door the next morning and I felt like a piece of shit. Then one of our printers had a son who was killed in a car crash and again I had to go round . . . it was all too close and I just had to get out.

Barry Norman's experience of doorstepping was less harrowing. He had landed up at the tabloid daily the *Sketch*, a paper he clearly loathed, as a trainee gossip writer, and he didn't excel. He recalled, for example, being sent to interview a fox-hunting peer, whose wife had run away with the master of foxhounds:

> His Lordship answered the door, which threw me a bit because I'd been expecting a butler. 'Who are you?' he asked. I told him. 'What do you want?' I told him that too, in a faltering sort of way – 'Well, you know, your wife and the master of foxhounds . . . gone off together . . . I was just wondering what you . . .'
>
> 'What the hell's it got to do with you?' he said and right away he had me. I was stuck for an answer, knowing perfectly well that his marital unhappiness had nothing to do with me or the prurient readers of the *Daily Sketch*. I was mumbling something about letting him put his side of the story when he slammed the door in my face. I couldn't blame him; I'd have done the same.[26]

The story could serve as a morality test about intrusive, but interesting, journalism. Norman solved his dilemma by telling his news desk that he was continuing to harass the cuckolded aristocrat, while actually sitting in a local café doing a newspaper crossword. It was a good human answer, and bad journalism.

The other thing that reporters quickly discover is that much of the work is frankly dull. In the 1930s one reporter bluntly described his trade thus: 'The reporter on more than ninety per cent of the world's newspapers is merely a creature of routine, he is sent to police courts, inquests, council meetings, chamber of commerce lunches, vicarage fetes, hospital galas, and makes notes until his arm is stiff ... The reporter becomes an automaton. There is no scope for individuality. And the papers prove appalling conglomerations of unrelieved dullness.'

While you could make the same arguments today, local journalism continues to be redeemed by local accountability. However, as Priestley went on, shrewdly, to point out, when hacks migrate to London, things change:

> I have never been able to understand how London editors contrive to know what their readers want, because they never meet any of their readers, never exchange a word with them. They are no more in touch with the actual public than are Grand Lamas. They must base their judgements on statistics, which are notoriously misleading, or on their correspondence, which may be the work of half-wits.

When Fleet Street was Fleet Street

There must be a hundred books about or set in old Fleet Street, the 'Street of Ink' or the Street of Shame, or the Street of Adventure, and the ultimate target of tens of thousands of locally taught journalists throughout the twentieth century. Again and again one reads of the shaking, heaving pavements as the great presses roared underfoot through the evening and night; of the honking of lorries fighting to deliver newsprint, or take away fresh papers; of the sharp smell of ink in the air; and the feuds carried out over cheap wine or whiskies in the back rooms of heaving pubs; and long-forgotten 'characters' and no longer funny practical jokes. For a century the street was a classless Illyria, a fantasy territory where eccentric Old Etonians, chippy Welsh grammar-school boys, Mancunian crime reporters, Eastern European Marxists and angry Australians on the make could rub shoulders, and where the conventions of middle-class London life were temporarily suspended. No other country had a little press republic quite like Fleet

Street, its uniqueness partly due to the chance of printing concerns congregating by the sewer-like Fleet River, which then became a boozy haven conveniently sandwiched between the City and Westminster.

There was money about, helped by the rise of the National Union of Journalists. Formed in 1906, following the new National Union of Teachers, the NUJ had idealistic and socialist origins; but its breakthrough came courtesy of the brilliant monster and ultimate press baron Lord Northcliffe, founder of the *Daily Mail* and the *Daily Mirror*, and owner of *The Times*. When, in 1911, a survey revealed widespread low pay amongst journalists, Northcliffe wrote to the NUJ saying that since, during the past twenty years, journalism had risen from being 'a humble, haphazard and badly paid occupation to a regular profession' and new machinery had made 'the work less arduous but more nerve exhausting . . . it is incumbent that journalists should unite for the obtaining of longer annual holidays and better pay'. He contemptuously rejected other newspaper proprietors' proposals for banding together to keep wages down: 'We are rolling in money,' he famously told them, 'and it is time to disgorge to the staff.' By 1951 the NUJ combined with the employers to form the National Council for the Training of Journalists (NCTJ) and finally put the trade on the kind of semi-professional footing Northcliffe had hoped for. By the mid-1960s it had achieved a more or less complete closed shop in newspaper journalism and imposed extraordinarily detailed pay agreements.

So, as the century went on, the people arriving in Fleet Street expected decent money. Though there were plenty of posh types, particularly among the leader writers, there was a strong prejudice in favour of practical reporters who'd learned the craft on local papers. George Blake, the novelist and hack, said that between the wars most of the English journalists in Fleet Street came from Manchester (which was a huge newspaper centre in its own right, and remained so until the late 1960s when there were nearly 700 newspaper journalists working for national papers there), Hull, Sheffield and Newcastle. He also pointed out that 'Irishmen abound, and many who hope to be accounted Irishmen . . . Scotland has proportionately the highest representation among those who nightly deal with blue pencils and flimsies [the thin paper copies, marked by carbon, of stories] in the harsh light of the globes above the sub-editorial tables.'[27] Characteristically, they would have got to Fleet Street in their twenties and would fight to stay there until their sixties, though very many died before that of drink, cancer or despair. Because of the long hours of the typical working week, many would be unmarried when they arrived in London, living in lodgings and only moving out to the better suburbs in their thirties or forties, when they had made enough to marry. They would learn, if they hadn't already, to falsify expenses claims as petty cash. A high proportion would divorce and remarry, often several times.

Fleet Street, a great cluster of head offices, was first a subs' world. The biggest division in journalism is between natural reporters and natural 'subs'. It is a flesh and bone thing. The history of journalism is littered with awed accounts of men who could tame torrents of sloppy, incoherent copy and turn them into clear, clean stories. It is a great talent, and any writer who has been corrected by a great sub knows it. But it can come at a human cost. There's a sense of insecurity, an edgy defensiveness to life's natural subs, the result of clambering up and down a ladder of other people's ignorance and errors. So much sloppy writing, third-rate thinking, self-indulgent prose and looming deadlines can sour your view of life forever. Take Peter Eastwood, for many years the real power behind the *Daily Telegraph*'s news pages and described as the most hated man ever to work for that paper. In a hotbed of Oxbridge firsts and Tory intellectuals, Eastwood was a grammar-school boy from Yorkshire. The paper's historian says of him that 'On paper he was magic, with humans a disaster. One sub-editor of the day described his arrival at the *Telegraph* as "like putting a tiger into a children's play-pen" and said his whole history on the paper was "littered with corpses".'[28] But he turned out a great newspaper. Subs are more inclined to be learned, to hold strong political and religious opinions, and to be either morose or ferocious; and they *never* get out of the office.

It is hard now to recreate the atmosphere of mid-twentieth-century news gathering. The trade was more competitive than today. There were more evening papers in particular, right across urban Britain as well as London, all selling directly onto the street against one another, all looking for the half-inch of advantage a scoop or a slightly better-written story would bring them. A scoop could mean a promotion and extra money, so people fought for them. They reminisce about tricks which seem half-insane today: how you would call a friend on a rival paper and arrange to take the 8.10 a.m. train together for a story, knowing that the fast train, which you were on, actually left at 7.30 a.m. 'The Street' itself meant a hugely competitive journalism, since successful reporters and editors could literally cross the road and move from one job to the next, as they rose and others fell. Many of the older reporters I've talked to moved jobs many times between rival papers. Each move brought them a few extra pounds a week. This was a firing culture as well as a hiring one. If you missed an angle you would be bawled out by your news editor, of whom you were frightened because he chucked out reporters every month. Christiansen records that most of those he sacked took it on the chin, with 'a wry, puzzled smile, a philosophical shrug of the shoulders, a quip about the notice period money paying off a few debts' and a friendly handshake. But not all of them: 'With one man who said he was going to throw himself over Blackfriars Bridge, I had to be tough and tell him that I would pay him a fiver if he gave me the time of the event so that the paper could publish a good picture.'

The old technology meant that domestic news reporters of the fifties and sixties spent more time getting out of their offices and then getting their stories back. The roving reporters, or 'firemen', of the major papers fanned out across Britain in packs, securing phones and rooms and buying up local knowledge. One crime reporter described arriving in a small Welsh town for a murder trial in 1960 like this:

> The telephone exchange is usually the first to feel it. Within a few hours operators are snowed under with long-distance calls . . . Then the hotels feel it. Managers, receptionists and house-keepers magically conjure up more accommodation than the brochures ever listed. Hall porters and housemaids struggle with spare mattresses and chefs get hysteria. Taxi drivers find a sudden boom on their hands and people who are used to a normally quiet town, stop in the main street and stare at the passing excitement. Soon everything is cosy. Reporters who have never been within a hundred miles of the place before, settle in like old inhabitants. Policemen, who at first viewed so many strange faces with cautious suspicion, nod and pass the time of day. Shopkeepers show a kindly interest and learn to reach for the right brand of tobacco before they are asked . . .[29]

Foreign 'firemen' moved around like a seedy flock of familiar vultures too. Christopher Hitchens, who went on to become a famous controversialist based in the US, recalls his early days at the *Daily Express* when it was still a Beaverbrook paper.

> Was it true that the standby slogan of the *Express* foreign desk, for any hack stumbling onto a scene of carnage and misery, was 'Anyone here raped and speaks English?' I regret to say that it was. Is it true that an *Express* scribe in some hellhole, his copy surpassed by a *Daily Mail* man who had received an honourable flesh-wound, received a cable: 'Mail Man shot. Why you unshot?' I never saw the cable itself . . .[30]

He had, though, seen a fine and wholly fictitious front page confected by a hack who had missed a world-shaking event. Were there any high principles in old Fleet Street?

For great journalists need to have principles, as well as luck and all the talents, and Fleet Street produced no reporter of the international status of Woodward and Bernstein. The nearest was James Cameron, who resigned twice on a point of principle. The first time was in 1950 in protest at a smear campaign linking the Labour Cabinet minister John Strachey and the atom bomb spy Klaus Fuchs. The second came when he was working at the *Picture Post* – outraged by the refusal of the paper's owners to publish a front page public appeal to the United Nations that Cameron and his editor Tom Hopkinson had planned denouncing the excesses of the British and US-backed Synghman Rhee regime in South Korea. Hopkinson was fired and Cameron resigned. He then went to the *News Chronicle* where he campaigned for nuclear disarmament and was still on its staff when it folded in 1960 – a sad moment which Cameron memorably described as being caused by 'a simple thrombosis . . . an active circulation impeded by clots'.

As a foreign correspondent, initially for Beaverbrook's *Daily Express* in its post-war glory years, criss-crossing the world watching atom bomb tests, war in Korea, visiting the Empire as it dissolved itself and watching the new powers of the modern world, in Washington and Moscow, Cameron became a hero to a younger generation of journalists, partly for his writing style but also for his commitment, his anger and his principles too. His influence on British journalists, particularly foreign correspondents, of the sixties and seventies was analogous to Sala's on Edwardian journalists and we shall meet him again later.

Cameron was one of the stars who attracted new post-war journalists, along with the heroes of wartime journalism, and the new fame of the broadcasters. More assertive, professionally proud and militant people came into the trade. By the 1960s the journalists' union had insisted on all new reporters doing three years outside Fleet Street, though journalists who arrived before the bar fell included William Rees-Mogg, Robin Day and Alasdair Milne. The *Financial Times* and the *Observer* held out, and took their own people direct from university. So for a while did the *Guardian*, while based in Manchester, recruiting famous journalists such as Neal Ascherson, George Gale and Anthony Howard direct from Oxbridge. Others, like Nicholas Tomalin (regarded as one of the finest journalists in the world when he was killed, aged forty-one, on the Golan Heights), had the luck to walk into a national title.

Inspired by these examples, there was a press of ambitious university-educated people determined to find a way straight into Fleet Street. It was the beginnings of a class takeover. As the well-educated middle classes realized that journalism could be a high-earning and high-status job, they started to swipe it back from the working classes. The chain-smoking Welshmen and northerners, the Scots and the Mancunians, found themselves employing, then being elbowed out by, smoother characters who felt more at home in the age of irony, national decline and TV satire. Televisual Oxbridge men, playwrights and sardonic Australians began to arrive.

The ambivalence of this period is well caught by one of the only two novels about journalism universally regarded as truly great, Michael Frayn's *Towards the End of the Morning*, first published in 1967 (the other being Evelyn Waugh's *Scoop*, of which more later). Frayn had gone straight from university to the *Guardian* and was a near-contemporary of Tomalin's. In his novel, a valediction to the Fleet Street of backyard offices and long liquid lunches, Frayn plays off the distance between a feature editor, the underemployed Dyson, who gets a chance to show off on a commercial TV show, and the ancient Eddy Moulton. Moulton is a speaking version of the Fleet Street myth-making of the twenties and thirties:

'I knew Stanford Roberts,' he said. 'But then I knew most of them. Walter Belling, Stanley Furle, Sir Redvers Tilley – you name them, I knew them ... I was in the Feathers the night Sandy MacAllister punched Laurence Uden on the nose for saying that Stanford Roberts had been drunk at poor old Sidney Cunningham's funeral.'[31]

So Moulton's stories wind on and on, entirely ignored by his younger university-educated colleagues. Eventually, stricken by remorse, Dyson decides to take old Eddy down to the pub and 'listen, really listen, while old Eddy disinterred one man's life from the dust of time ...' But then he looks across the office and realizes that he's too late. While he has been thinking, Eddy has died.

Intellectuals

Even before the middle-class putsch in journalism, one group stood out from the world of, originally working-class, self-made men: the intellectuals. I mean intellectual in the continental sense of people of ideas who change society's direction by the force of their thinking. Britain is a famously unintellectual country, or said to be, but there have been at least two obvious eruptions of serious political intellectualism in modern British newspapers. The first came during and after the Second World War when the country turned to the left. Although the journalist-intellectuals who helped that happen worked in different places including the BBC and *The Times*, the centre of the movement was David Astor's *Observer* in the 1940s and 1950s.

His reign started with a coup. J. L. Garvin, the editor employed by David Astor's father after he bought the *Observer*, had the same sort of semi-mythical status in late Edwardian England as Harry Evans had half a century later. Astor, burning with anti-Nazi idealism, had been changed for life by his friendship with the heroic German conspirator Adam von Trott, strangled after the failed plot on Hitler's life. He regarded Garvin as an antediluvian, pro-appeasement relic of failed policies. He deposed him and set about creating the paper which would set the tone for much of the post-war settlement. It was an early champion of Beveridge's welfare state, and by far the most vigorous British voice for decolonization as the empire was wound up after the war. Far more open to continental influences than other British journals, Astor's paper was dominated by Eastern European intellectuals – Isaac Deutscher, Sebastian Haffner, Arthur Koestler, E. F. Schumacher – and by public school- and Oxbridge-educated progressives, including Orwell, Patrick O'Donovan, Michael Davie, Neal Ascherson and Philip Toynbee. They were read, and followed, by a generation of socialist politicians who began as journalists – Michael Foot, a Beaverbrook man and the moving spirit of *Tribune* in its glory days; Richard Crossman of the *New Statesman*; Tom Driberg of the *Express*.

The second moment for journalist-intellectuals came some thirty years later when Britain reacted against the world the first lot had helped shape, and moved sharply back to the right in the 1970s and 1980s. This included people like Peter Jay and Samuel Brittan on the economic side, who spread the gospel of monetarism from Chicago, and others like Peter Utley and Maurice Cowling, dealing with the role and philosophy of the state. Their causes were smaller government; the need to take on the trade unions; and the importance of the (British) nation state in a world of Brussels federalists and Irish republicanism. As with any successful group of intellectuals they influenced, and were influenced by, politicians – Margaret Thatcher, Keith Joseph and Nigel Lawson (himself a financial journalist and magazine editor before he became a Tory minister). They dominated the opinion pages of key newspapers, in particular *The Times*, *The Economist* and the *Daily Telegraph*; they lunched, dined, lectured and debated, and they had the infinite satisfaction of helping underpin a government that carried through many of their ideas. But intellectuals, once disappointed, make irreconcilable enemies. Much of the most bitter criticism of Labour leaders from Wilson to Blair came from the disappointed journalist-intellectuals of the left; and when Margaret Thatcher finally fell, rightist intellectuals turned their anger and disappointment on her successors, to equally deadly effect.

What now remains? Not much. The *Spectator* is the last survivor of a tradition of political periodicals on the right, but tends to avoid the heavyweight. On the left, the *New Statesman* has about half its rival's sales but, shorn of any connection to today's more right-wing Labour Party, has barely a shred of its old influence. The journal

Prospect offers long, well-written and mentally provocative reads. *The Economist* has on its staff several people whose brains are so huge they find it hard to keep their necks straight; it is the last survivor of the truly ideological newspaper, whose staff remain anonymous and subordinate to, in its case, pure free-market liberalism. The *London Review of Books*, which has come out twice-monthly since 1980, tries to keep alive the English essay, as practised in the great nineteenth-century journals. While some of its contributors work for newspapers, few could honestly be described as journalists; they are, rather, the upmarket 'media dons' from humanities departments in universities. Across daily and Sunday journalism, there are many clever and politically engaged writers. There are neo-conservatives, Old Tories, Liberals and even some socialists. But in terms of real intellectuals, visibly rethinking our world and drawing the allegiance of tens of thousands, I think there are none left. Environmentalism, anti-globalism, the Blairite 'third way' and 'compassionate conservatism' have failed to produce the flaming public writers who emerged from earlier struggles. The intellectual only comes into his or her own at a turning point, when there is a hunger for explanations and a readiness to rethink old assumptions. Perhaps today's conditions are not yet appropriate.

Journalism's Private Class System

There are two ways to be seriously posh in journalism: you can become the editor of a great newspaper, or you can get out. Getting out often means becoming a novelist, which is today regarded as 'nice' or 'proper' for an ambitious person, rather as joining the colonial service or a 'good' merchant bank used to be. Robert Harris, John Lanchester, Andrew O'Hagan and Philip Hensher are current examples of this form of trade escapology. They could be top-drawer journalists. Now they dabble in it. Editors? The most influential editorial chairs are those of the *Daily Mail, The Times, Financial Times*, the *Daily Telegraph, Sun, Mirror*, and *Guardian*. With the exception of the *Guardian*, which retains a whiff of non-conformist restraint, these jobs bring great riches – salaries ranging from around £300,000 to more than twice that, plus share options. Charles Moore, former editor of the *Telegraph*, is the nearest of any of them to being properly posh, the son of an active Liberal politician, and an Old Etonian, whose career took off through the Thatcher years and whose economically dry, Eurosceptic views, impeccably expressed, took him to the editorial chair of the *Spectator* before the daily title. He is a tall, elegantly dressed fox-hunter currently writing Margaret Thatcher's official biography. Reversing the expected order of things, the editor of the *Sun*, Rebekah Wade, is a favoured insider at Downing Street, while Robert Thomson, the editor of *The Times* is an Australian interloper who seems to disdain the social and political cachet his job once had. Alan Rusbridger at the *Guardian* has friends in politics but is no part of the Downing Street 'set' either. Piers Morgan, though partly educated at a private school, has made himself a political outsider at the *Mirror*, disdaining the flattery or menaces of Downing Street.

There is a rival journalistic aristocracy to the newspaper editors: the star writers and broadcasters. They may be mercenaries, but they are flattered and coddled by those they 'serve'. It is a little like the artists for hire in Renaissance Europe. The best columnists are hugely prized by their editors, though there is no evidence I have ever seen that the loss of a writer visibly moves circulation at all. It is a master–servant relationship but one in which the servant's power comes from his involvement in the wider world, while the master's power is institutional; because institutions wither and the world does not, the servant is sometimes stronger than the master. The more powerful the paper or programme, the more powerful the editor; the less its prestige, the less his, also. If in doubt, follow the money: star columnists, such as Simon Jenkins and Matthew Parris of *The Times* and Richard Littlejohn at the *Sun*, are paid more than some national newspaper editors. The same goes for the big-name radio and TV performers, who with their agents can beat editors, nominally above them, in the salary stakes. The best opinion writers are able to live a swanky metropolitan lifestyle, buying fine art and living in large houses, sending their children to private school and taking several foreign holidays a year. And a few, a very few, top journalists are earning salaries that would be regarded as good even in the City. There is a television reporter on close to £500,000 a year, and at least one tabloid columnist on about the same. There is a broadsheet writer on £300,000.

If the stars form the upper crust of modern journalism, the well-doing middle classes are the section editors, the specialist reporters and the rest of the columnists. In London, you can live a pretty good life as a moderately successful journalist, but the penalty is hard work. On salaries ranging from £50,000 to three times that, the bourgeoisie of the keyboard-battering classes know that the pyramid narrows sharply once you get to your forties. New work is harder to come by; the hot breath of keen, hyperactive people in their twenties and thirties fans your neck. For the editors of magazines, weekly supplements and daily newspaper sections, it's all about grit and reliability – the professionalism that churns out plausible ideas and finds plausible, affordable writers for them while keeping strictly to budget. Personnel management, cash flow and office politics loom large; chances for promotion to a real editor's chair narrow, then vanish. It is not a bad life, though the hours and commuting to out-of-town industrial sites are hardly glamorous.

For writers, the challenge is different. It takes dogged discipline to continue producing well-written, fresh-seeming (the emphasis on seeming) material, week in, week out, for decade after decade especially as the economics and management of modern newspapers trap writers in offices and don't push them out enough to stumble across new ideas or people. The specialists – the political editors, the theatre and film critics, the sports writers – can carry on quietly improving, like vintage wines, deepening their knowledge and contacts all the time. Some of the most acute writers on science, education and business are journalists in their forties, fifties and sixties who have stayed the course and stayed interested. It is a perilous life, though, since younger editors, casting around for ways to demonstrate their potency, are always tempted to cull their elders and betters. (I've done it myself.) Rather as with senior teachers, who keep a school going, yet are never able to advance in salary beyond a certain level without turning bureaucrat, the good and seasoned writers, who are not stars but who give a newspaper its heft and gravity, often have a wry and disappointed air. Journalism is not a young person's trade in the way football or option trading are; but it has a bias that way.

Next, the middle-middle classes. Local newspaper editors and seasoned reporters who have done thirty years covering their own patch can be found everywhere in Britain, their motivation often a world away from the careerist scramble of London journalism. Anyone who has lived without a local paper quickly comes to realize how important they are; a community which has no printed mirror of itself begins to disintegrate. To be a local journalist is to accept relatively low pay – there are plenty of men and women in their middle years who will never earn more than £30,000, yet count themselves lucky to be doing something they love among people they know. But in London and the big cities, the people on lower salaries are mostly the young struggling to rise, working long hours as sub-editors or general reporters, hoarding their cuttings and sending off for some of the scores of award schemes, hoping to be noticed. And a high proportion of the people who come into the trade in their teens or early twenties, exit again two decades later, taking up jobs in PR, or switching to teaching, media training or a variety of small business wheezes. Today the original recruiting ground, provincial and local journalism, is in serious trouble. Mergers, the pressure of free newspapers and technology are all hitting the number and interest of the jobs on local papers. The pay gap too has widened hugely. A specialist on a national newspaper would expect now to earn about £50–60,000 if they are any good. The average journalist's salary is £22,500. But one in ten of journalists, almost all in small magazines or local papers, earn less than £12,500. The phenomenal growth in 'free sheets', distributed door to door and funded entirely by advertising, often with a style based on a poor mimicry of the national tabloids, began with the introduction of colour web offset printing, cheaper and easier than the traditional methods. The new business was spearheaded by local printers and small businessmen, rather than by large newspaper groups, who later struggled to catch up, small operations rising up from the high street, with tiny staffs expected to turn their hands to almost everything. This is more or less where we came in, back in the 1700s.

The trade is neither professional, nor a complete meritocracy. Strings are pulled. The children of famous journalists are given a leg-up by their parents' colleagues. But by and large, the rewards do go to the talented and the persistent. Modern journalism is in this respect the same as journalism has been for 300 years. It is a carnival of insecurity where teetotallers are less successful than they expect.

What is different, though, is the sheer variety of people. I have worked alongside the children of immigrants from the Caribbean and Uganda; working-class Marxists; former Army officers; novelists; at least one former Irish terrorist; hopeless alcoholics and serial drug-abusers; vegetarian anarchists; dissipated aristocrats; anger-fuelled men who left school at sixteen; refugees from the law, the City and from factory lines; fastidious professionals who cared about the truth of every phrase they used, and sloppy, cynical liars. But as generalization is also a form of untruth, let us conclude by looking at one of the most feared, admired and also hated journalists in the country, a survivor who is about as controversial in the trade as anyone has ever been, but who also represents one slice of its modern reality.

Mazer, our Sala

Mazer Mahmood has secured 118 criminal convictions, of paedophiles, forgers, con men and others, including vengeful members of the Russian mafia. He was the reporter responsible for exposing David Mellor the Tory Cabinet minister's affair with Antonia de Sancha, which ended his political career. He performed a similar service for another Tory minister, Tim Yeo, and for the then Conservative whip Michael Brown, who is now a journalist himself. He got into deep hot water in a sting operation involving alleged would-be kidnappers of David and Victoria Beckham. He has often been beaten up. He has had contracts taken out on his life. His parents' house in Birmingham has been attacked by a gang wielding machetes, who smashed everything inside it. He has been forced to move house himself and now lives in a heavily protected apartment. When I met him, over cappuccinos in the anonymous back room of a cafe at a London hotel, he was with a very tall, impassive and well-built man he introduced only as 'Jaws'. Qureshi, as he is more formally called, smiled to show a mouth full of gold teeth. He is Mahmood's full-time protection, who has been employed by the *News of the World* for the past seven years to guard their prized investigative reporter.

Born in Birmingham to parents who also had ink in their blood, by the age of sixteen Mahmood was pestering the *Birmingham Evening Mail* to take him on during the school holidays, without success. Then his parents had some family friends round to dinner one evening who were involved in a new scam, video piracy, making illicit copies of new films on VCR tapes and selling them. As the conversation continued, Mahmood crept upstairs to his bedroom, called the *News of the World* and told their famous investigative reporter Ray Chapman, 'I've got a story for you.' His fare to London was paid and he was put up in a hotel. For six weeks, he worked with Chapman on the story, which also got him onto the local TV news, then presented by Anne Robinson. 'My parents were mad,' Mahmood says, 'They threatened to throw me out for exposing family friends, and it did take a long time to get back in with them.' But, aged sixteen, he had got the bug. 'That's the great thing about newspapers. Nobody gives a damn about your age, or what your background is, as long as you have got a story. If you've got the story, then you're in.'

Mahmood started his career proper aged eighteen with the *Sunday People*, working on child labour rackets in London and stories on racism. 'Fortunately for me, the race riots started in the early 1980s. It was absolutely perfect for me because news desks saw this Asian who could report . . . and I had a lot of contacts in Handsworth.' He was taken on by Robin Morgan of the *Sunday Times* to cover the riots, and to go underground to investigate trouble in the Sikh community, before moving on to other stories, notably the then well-known Paedophile Information Exchange. Mahmood is good at disguise, and seems to enjoy the thrill of it. In his *Sunday Times* years he uncovered many scams, including immigration smuggling rackets, and his single most dangerous story, the exposure of a Libyan hit squad training at Abingdon flying school, near Oxford. He moved to television for a while, with *TV-am*, producing Sir David Frost, but found it all a little cumbersome and dull. So he went to the *News of the World* and it seems to have been a match made in heaven.

'For me personally, the best stories are the ones where we are rescuing kids or getting paedophiles banged up . . . I got a lovely letter from a twelve-year-old girl thanking me, saying I was her hero for rescuing her. That's what makes it worthwhile.' The perpetrator, says Mahmood, 'sent people with shotguns trying to get the tapes back off me . . . It's not surprising. You befriend them, you spend a lot of time with them, you have dinner with them – then you betray them. There's very few people who can take it on the chin so, yes, you get a lot of death threats.' In general, he says, the villains who abuse him are the ones who concern him least. It's the silent ones he worries about.

Though his newspaper constantly asks people to call him, 98 per

cent of the calls are useless, he says, merely about a neighbour selling
drugs or an affair. Mostly, his stories come from informers, contacts
he has cultivated for years. He prefers it when people ask for cash,
since 'you know where you are', but not everyone wants money:
'people want revenge, they're disgruntled employees, or rivals, or
sometimes they just hate paedophiles, or whatever'. Mahmood now
works with a team, including 'the technicians' who bug conversations, help him disguise himself and film meetings. The technology
has changed hugely. In his early *Sunday Times* days colleagues were
surprised when he taped conversations. Now the Internet can be used
for following payments; bugging devices are vastly more effective;
mobile phones provide easily accessible records of numbers called. And
his paper is prepared to spend the money: Mahmood says he's spent
£30–40,000 on stories which simply didn't work out 'and nobody's
batted an eyelid. It's a business – you have to make the investment'.
Selling papers is what it's all about: 'the question is, are people talking
about it in the pubs?' That, he says, not journalistic awards (and he's
had a fair few of those), is the measure of success.

Mahmood is a cautious, smart, pleasant-looking man but very open
about what the job has done to him. 'You soon get hardened, you
get inured . . . It makes you cynical. I find it hard to trust people . . .'
Later he adds: 'I have very few friends. People I knew on the *Frost*
programme, and the politicians and celebrities, would be horrified if I
turned up at a party. It's just . . . you become a bit of a pariah.' He
seems sad about this, but not very.

To many he is the epitome of what real investigative journalism is
all about. To others, not only his victims, but some judges, politicians
and broadsheet journalists, he is a bugging, intrusive menace and a
blot on the trade. Mahmood says, 'I think we have a very important
role to play in exposing these characters [by which he means the
politicians and violent villains, but sometimes involving first-time
prostitutes too] . . . There must be at least a dozen or so doctors I
have got struck off. Frankly, it justifies the paper, it's the backbone of
the paper.' As for himself, 'I still get a huge buzz. When you think
of these people who think, "we are untouchable, nobody can get to
us . . ."' So he accepts the danger, the loneliness, the disdain of other
journalists and the strangeness of a life led half undercover and always
watching your back. There are obvious questions, about who has the

right to what quantity of privacy, and the distinction between a powerless young prostitute and a vicious mafia boss; but Mahmood is no more a vicar than he is a policeman. He is a hugely successful, driven, obsessive reporter who works in the scummy gutters of human life and entertains millions every Sunday by doing so. He thinks that if he wasn't an investigative hack, there are only two other possible jobs. One is editor – 'but no one's going to make me that' – and the other is a life as a criminal. Self-made, self-confident and honest about what the job entails, he is as much the emblem of British reporting in our time as Sala was in the nineteenth century.

2

What is News?

'Sex, sensation, pets, heroism.'

Donald Zec

'Good stories flow like honey. Bad stories stick in the craw. What is a bad story? It is a story that cannot be absorbed on the first time of reading. It is a story that leaves questions unanswered.'

Arthur Christiansen (or maybe Lord Beaverbrook)

Hard News and Weak News

The phrase 'hard news' is a good one. Hard news really is hard. It sticks not in the craw, but in the mind. It has an almost physical effect, causing fear, interest, laughter or shock. The death of Diana was hard news. The first atom bomb, the Cuban missile crisis, England's 1966 World Cup victory, the shooting of John Lennon, the fall of Margaret Thatcher are examples of what we all, readers and journalists, editors and viewers, immediately recognize as hard news because it shapes our world, demands an emotional reaction and produces an almost physical thirst for more information.

Brighton, 11 September 2001. I have been lazing in the autumn sun before returning to the artificial fug of the town's conference centre. Tony Blair is here and so is the Trades Union Congress, for its annual conference. Blair's spin doctors have assured us that he is to make a confrontational speech defending his ideas for getting private money into state hospitals and schools. The TUC loathe this; delegates will probably boo and heckle the prime minister, which will produce dramatic pictures for that night's news. I am guaranteed, I think, the

top story on the BBC 10 p.m. news and a chunky 'live' analysing the
argument. Meanwhile I have to do the live commentary on the speech.
That means entering a specially built glass and plywood box in a
balcony overlooking the hall and being interviewed by my wife, Jackie
Ashley, who has been fronting coverage of the TUC. It is an odd,
slightly uncomfortable prospect for both of us. As I am waiting, she is
interviewing a trade union general secretary: he seems to be going on a
bit. My 'turn' involves revealing a slice of what Blair will say, something
briefed to me some twenty minutes earlier by Alastair Campbell. Out
of the corner of one eye I am watching a news channel on a television
monitor, with the sound off, and notice that it has suddenly switched
to a picture of some kind of tower block, burning. I read the strapline.
It's the World Trade Center in New York. Even I know thousands of
people work there and may be in danger. I call the producer in charge
of the TUC programme and say Jackie needs to be told immediately
what is happening, to break in and inform viewers of BBC 2, even if
the result is that they switch channels. There is some resistance. The
actors' union Equity apparently has an interesting motion coming up
about the pay rates for child actors. By now, I am hopping up and
down with frustration. Then, while I am watching the screen and
arguing down my mobile phone line, I see it – the second aircraft, the
second tower. Like so many millions, I have that hot, icy, panting,
scalp-crawling feeling – terrorism; this is *it*, this is the biggest . . . Jackie
can see me gesticulating and is angrily trying to glare me to composure
so I don't put her off. She doesn't know yet . . .

The destruction of the Twin Towers was an event which no sane
person would fail to understand immediately as the hardest of hard
news, a world-changing moment with awesome consequences. Within
a minute or two Jackie Ashley had been given the PA wire copy and I
was in her hardboard and perspex 'bubble' and we were breaking the
news to people whose first instinct would quite rightly have been to
change to a twenty-four-hour news channel. Below us, in the hall, that
year's TUC president Bill Morris was puzzled. He had just received
what he assumed was a spoof note about some attack on the World
Trade Center in New York. All the journalists in the conference hall
were suddenly talking on their mobile phones. From the podium he
asked them to be quiet. The moment when the news dawned on Bill

Morris was when they responded by simply leaving the hall. A few minutes later, Tony Blair arrived, confirmed what had happened, and made a moving short statement, cancelling his speech.

As he was scrambling for his words, those of us in political journalism were scrambling for our bags and racing to the station and, with him, the train back to London and a different world. This news made everyone who could, rush to a television set to look. It threw up instant questions. What? Who? Why? It provoked horror and pity – the flying bodies, the bereaved, the coincidences and the final calls. Its force waves created wars in Afghanistan and Iraq. It changed laws in countries the world over, including Britain, where it rubbed out legal rights people have had for centuries. It flattened villages, sent people into exile, threatened governments, made architects tear up and redraw plans, filled churches and mosques, emptied aircraft, bankrupted companies, changed the diplomatic power game, produced new icons and anti-heroes, added words to common languages, subtracted the lives of innocents. It sent blast waves into underground tunnels, columns of tanks into Iraq and put the fear of God, and Allah, into millions of hearts. And let us be absolutely clear. It excited journalists very much indeed. We were not happy, exactly, but we were thrilled – thrilled and horrified simultaneously.

That is hard news. Here for contrast is ordinary, weak news being gathered.

8 September 2002. The air is stale, almost sticky with dirt. In the half-light there are sleeping bodies tied tightly in white quilting or sprawled under dark rugs. Naked feet stick out; there is a youngish man, out for the count, sitting fully dressed, pages of squiggles on his lap. The Westminster lobby journalists, London's finest, are flying home over the Atlantic after a summit meeting between the prime minister and President George W. Bush. We left yesterday at noon and flew to Andrews Air Force Base outside Washington. An hour or so into the flight, Tony Blair had come back to brief us about what we all thought would be an important moment, a 'council of war', however much Number Ten disliked the term. Blair and Bush were in trouble. President Bush seemed determined to destroy Saddam, and expected to have to do so by declaring war on him. The prime minister was equally determined to stick by Bush but, with any attack only coming after UN

authorization, emphasized instead the need to deal with Iraq's nuclear, chemical and biological weapons. But the world was against them, at least when it came to the threat of war. The other European leaders, the Russians, the Chinese, all the Arab world, were sounding notes of caution and alarm. Mr Blair faced an impressive array of sceptics and critics at home. It seemed clear that he would have to persuade Mr Bush to go again to the United Nations, and to internationalize the struggle against Saddam as much as possible; while privately and simultaneously discussing the details of a military attack. So when he strolled along the chartered BA plane and stood for twenty minutes with his back to a partition, surrounded by microphones and reporters, we expected him to say something fresh, something newsworthy.

He didn't. He repeated the same warnings about Iraq's potential nuclear capability, its threat to peace, the joint determination he shared with Bush, the importance of winning people round but the danger of the UN becoming an excuse for inaction rather than a solution. I'd listened to him four days earlier in his Sedgefield constituency and spoken to him semi-privately then as well; and for the life of me I could hear not a syllable or semi-colon I hadn't heard before. He was asked about the nuclear threat, yet again. And again he was general about it. Saddam was trying to acquire nuclear weapons and would get them some time. But as he'd said before, for four long years there had been no inspections. Here was the root of world scepticism: why now? Was Britain really threatened by him? Blair answered that we were: if Saddam began a new war in the Middle East, we'd be drawn in as we were in the Gulf War. 'British interests' would be threatened. So much, so obvious. He wouldn't talk about timetables. There was nothing really newsy. It was frankly disappointing. As the journalists milled around afterwards, the Sunday reporters were under immediate pressure to deliver. Several thought 'Saddam's Nuclear Threat to Britain' was the headline. He hadn't said it that way, of course . . . and then came the fatal phrase I've heard a hundred times: 'But he didn't knock it down.' Nor had he.

By the time some of the Sundays had done their work, you would have thought a nuclear strike on Birmingham was only weeks away. This distortion did not annoy Blair's team. Far from it. It helped them in their first task of trying to move public opinion towards war; yet it did so in a way that could never be blamed on Blair. He had chosen his words carefully. Journalists had hyped them up in a way that was hugely helpful. Number Ten benefited. The reporters benefited: they had justified their expensive airline tickets and salaries for another week. The newspapers benefited; they had strong-looking, dramatic front-page stories that might help win casual sales in shops and petrol stations. Only the public had been short-changed. They had been given a story which happened to be a scare story. Some of them would remember and mistrust the news a little more next time. A handful might even stop buying the paper. But most would forget the distortion. Nuance doesn't make for good headlines. When we landed at the airforce base, Blair and a small party of officials, defence specialists and political aides were taken by helicopter to George W. Bush's retreat at Camp David for four hours of talks about Iraq. We journalists were left behind, kicking our heels in a departure lounge. The BBC and Sky struggled with technical problems. Soon, photocopies of the Sunday front pages were faxed to the Downing Street staffers with us, who passed them around. There were hoots of laughter and wry grins at the spine-chilling headlines and shameless overwriting. The officials were good humoured about it too, as well they might be. For my part, I had a mixed record. I did tell viewers of that night's late news bulletin that the tactic was to scare the flying pants off the public, which was a useful warning of the hype all around. But later, when Blair returned and gave an anodyne press conference followed by a couple of short interviews, I elicited only lacklustre responses while my rival, Adam Boulton of Sky, managed to get some colourful quotes. I think it was because Blair had relaxed by then, and Adam was lucky. But I felt a failure, and that I'd let the BBC down. We flew back overnight and the truth was we had learned absolutely nothing about what Bush and Blair had really agreed. We had traversed the Atlantic twice in twenty-four hours in the search for the inside dope, and told the world nothing useful.

This is no good. Those TV and radio bulletins still have to be filled. After Alastair Campbell came back for a second briefing, we at least had details like the cast list of the meeting, its structure, even the food served at dinner. He confirmed that the UN push was important and that military matters had been on the agenda. We were able to patch together enough to fill the air and front pages. The story kept going. The truth was that no editor, either of a paper or a bulletin, wanted to lead with anything other than Iraq and the possibility of a war. Our lack of hard facts, real news, was inconvenient . . . but we coped.

When there is less news, the newsreaders don't take the day off and the headlines don't become smaller, or less black. Journalism mimics urgency, screws up the semblance of excitement. I'm not saying we make it up, though some people do, some of the time – and more of that later. Rather, unlike September 11, most news is weak. More days are days of poised decisions, complicated arguments, well-kept official secrets and hesitation, than are days of vivid drama and sharp endings. We skate over our very thin knowledge, talking desperately, and fooling fewer than we used to.

The Mystery of News

Over the years, I have had my share of scoops, though I was never a good investigative reporter – too interested in the general, too impatient about the detail, too butterfly-minded. I learned that scoops come from luck as much as judgement. Writing a political diary during the party conference season for the *Independent*, I angered a much younger Peter Mandelson, who had just been appointed by the Labour Party to shake up its image, by mocking a memo he had sent to shadow Cabinet members ordering them to check their speeches with him first. Very early the next morning, an envelope was pushed under my hotel bedroom door. It contained a handwritten note from Peter, informing me that after what I'd written, he never wished to speak to me again: would I please not try to call him by phone, or contact him in any way? The note was signed, with a flourish, 'Labour Party director of communications' – which made a second diary paragraph. Thanks to this, we fell out rather badly for a year. As a result of this estrangement, the Trotskyist Militant Tendency decided that I could be trusted by them. As a result, I was slipped numerous stories from the party's national executive committee, including the entire contents of Neil Kinnock's secret policy review, the first detailed evidence of the planned shift away from the left and towards the electorate. I picked up Ministry of Defence leaks from Alan Clark – engagingly, while journalists are supposed never to reveal their sources, he 'outed' me in the first volume of his diaries. I missed stories, too: one excellent tale about South African diamond smuggling, money and drugs, which involved hedge-hopping plane trips to the Isle of Man and a serious-sounding 'warning off' never saw the light of day because . . . well, it just never quite stood up; there were just too many unanswered questions. I have suppressed stories – at least one involving the family life of someone I regarded as a good colleague if not friend. As an editor, I have broken stories of government wrong-doing, MPs' greed and al-Qaeda; and I've splashed 'scoops of interpretation', such as the first hard evidence of the disappearance of North Sea fish species, which struck me as more important for the British people than nine-tenths of what passes for news.

All my working life I've been surrounded by 'the story' – some-where out there, day after day, waiting to be discovered. But there is a mystery here. What *is* a news story? This confronts most hacks most days of their working life. Of course, there are human events which interest almost everyone. We are perpetually intrigued by the extreme, the gruesome, the outlandish. But there is not a reliable supply of these events. The news industry requires constant raw material to fuel it, enough stories to fill perhaps twenty large pages of paper every day, and broadcast bulletins every hour. Because the news should be new, and must come in a regular stream, hour by hour, day by day, there is no way that journalists can limit themselves to the genuinely extraordinary event. There just aren't enough of them to go round. And sometimes, a 'good news day', too much comes at once.

So journalists learn to take less extraordinary things and fashion them into words that will make them seem like news instead. We learn to look for anything even slightly curious. It is a dingy alchemy – the dross of a local court, or a mundane political speech, turned into a story which catches the attention of readers and listeners, however briefly. To work the alchemy, journalists reshape real life, cutting away details, simplifying events, 'improving' ordinary speech, sometimes inventing quotes, to create a narrative which will work. It isn't only journalists. Everyone does it, all the time, mostly unconsciously. We hear a piece of gossip and as we retell it, we improve it, smoothing away irrelevance and sharpening the point; we turn experiences of friends and relatives into bolder, more heroic or tragic episodes than they really were. Above all, we turn our own daily lives into a chain of 'stories', always looking for shape and meaning in the cascade of experience. As scientists begin to properly map the brain, they will find pathways and areas particularly concerned with story telling and story making. These will be closely connected to speech and grammar: the impulse to tell stories is hard-wired and fundamental to being human. Journalism is the industrialization of gossip.

Yet, because of its power, the events that journalism turns into stories achieve an impetus of their own. How do we choose which things end up on the front page, or halfway down a news bulletin; and how do we rewrite them to get them there? Is this remark by the Foreign Secretary really 'a story'? Is that blurred photograph of two moderately well-known people hugging worth a front page – or a page lead – or nothing at all? If a journalist says to you that he or she can always answer such questions, and has never experienced doubt about a news story then that person is not necessarily a liar, but singularly unreflective.

Journalists are not taught what news is. We learn by copying. We look at what news *was*, in yesterday's paper, and the week before. This is why one striking story, perhaps about a dog attacking a child in a park, or about a mysterious virus, tends to be followed by a rash of other dog-attack or killer-bug stories. Journalists become more alert to snippets of information about dogs and viruses, and continue to look for them and sell them until news editors, like readers, get bored by the repetition. Different kinds of journalists are attuned to different kinds of stories, and different newspapers or broadcasters have different varieties of favourite story, which are then learned and passed on by their reporters. *Hull Daily Mail* journalists learn about their kind of news, BBC World Service journalists learn about their news, *France-Soir* journalists learn about their news. Most of us prefer not to analyse news. We have the 'nose' for it, we say. 'You know when you've got a story; it's a prickling feeling.' News 'just is'. A thousand news editors have told us: if you need to probe deeper, you shouldn't be in the job to start with. Asking a proper reporter to define a story is like asking a teenager what lust is.

That's the theory. But journalists often fail to spot stories. They argue amongst themselves about whether something is a story or not. Gregarious as Trafalgar Square pigeons, suggestible as toddlers, we huddle together after some event, a press conference or a royal walkabout and create a storm. 'OK, what's the story?' someone will say after a princess has shaken hands with people in a crowd. 'Well, didn't seem anything new to me,' responds a miserable-looking man from the *Mirror*. 'Hold on, what was that thing she said to the li'l girl, it wasn't "Don't push those flowers at me" was it?' says a doggedly optimistic woman from the *Star*. 'No, she didn't say that, I was nearby . . . but I couldn't quite get it,' murmurs *The Times*. 'She looked upset, I thought,' replies the *Star*. 'Where is the girl, anyhow?' asks the *Mail*. It turns out she's vanished. By the time the huddle is over, and it concludes with a brisk 'all agreed?', the princess has rudely snubbed a tearful girl who had to be led quickly away by her mother; gossip columnists will speculate on her foul temper; leader writers will have dubbed her Princess Prune, and a story will have been manufactured.

The journalists will have done the job they are paid for, which is not, repeat *not*, to give a blandly accurate account of an unremarkable moment, but to have found 'the story' or failing that 'a story'. There is no more influential phrase to come out of a rival reporter's mouth than, 'Well, I'm writing it, anyway.' It's right up there with 'he didn't knock it down'. Stories are 'improved', buffed up, spun out of spindly strands of everyday dullness. 'What's the intro?' we say as we leave a Tony Blair press conference. 'What did you make of that?' asks the colleague after a police statement. Often I have come away feeling that the story or 'the line' has emerged only because one colleague had the loudest voice that morning or the most aggressive opinion. Had there been another group of journalists there, the story of the same event would have been different. One can test this by reading accounts of a speech or press conference by journalists who haven't collaborated: they often describe different planets.

News is a relatively recent, made-up human commodity. It is designed, copied and passed on in a tradition that goes back only a few hundred years. Almost all reporters are imprinted after a while with the sense of how news stories read, but they didn't get this from their DNA. There may be inquisitive and persistent people, but there are no 'born reporters'. Charles Reiss, former political editor of the London *Evening Standard*, told me he was struck how, sitting at the back of some interminable, tedious committee of MPs he and rival hacks suddenly found their pens moving across their notepads, all at the same time. Barely conscious of why they were doing so, they had restarted a shorthand note of what someone was saying. Why? Years of listening to political language and being able to spot the unexpected nuance, he thought. Political journalists have a particular knowledge, but most hacks have similar experiences.

Most journalists, certainly when I was trained, were taught how to structure a story. It is the 'inverted triangle', with all the essential information squat at the top, and the less relevant stuff dribbling down towards the end-point. It may have the 'delayed drop' – a chatty, descriptive or intriguing first paragraph, which leads the reader in, until the real story is revealed a little later but it always answers the questions: Who? What? When? Where? Why? Sometimes it asks How? (Because of the decay in English grammar it no longer asks Whom? since nobody any longer remembers what this word means.) Beyond that, generations of news reporters and the training schools have little to add. News is spoken of as a kind of self-regenerating yet timid natural resource – virtual haddock or mental fruit which must be gathered and collected by highly trained people, using telephones, tape recorders, pens and cameras instead of nets to catch it, and notebooks or videotapes instead of wheelbarrows to cart it home.

The vital spirit of urban mankind, it stays miraculously fresh . . . until the moment when it is printed or broadcast. Then it dies. For the most important thing is the newness of news. Back in the far-distant past, say about 4 p.m. yesterday, the latest news was incredibly valuable. Editors were shouting for it, writing cheques and begging reporters to bust a gut, lie, break a leg to get it. Organizations with hundreds of highly paid, sometimes even trained, people were scampering after it, elbowing one another aside. High in orbit over the earth, satellites were being used to pick it up and beam it on. Videophones, camera teams, surveillance vehicles, were bleeping, cursing, changing gear. Witnesses and experts were being called at work, or doorstepped at home. They were being bribed, bullied, flattered. This news, whatever it was – just a few words, perhaps ('the most shameful moment of my life' or 'we will resist with full force'), or an unexpected denial, or the first sight of a face presumed to be dead – was very valuable. Given the manpower expended and the technology, it was far more costly, ounce for ounce, than caviar or plutonium. But that was yesterday afternoon. Now has passed a whole day, and that news is old. Go away, old news. Don't bother me, yesterday's story. You're manky and dull.

One moment news is verbal diamonds, the next it is dust. It seems in this respect like a drug, such as heroin or nicotine – worth a fortune so long as it is being collected, prepared and passed on to the end-user, but then used up and worth nothing at all. A drug becomes a brief chemical flurry in the brain, then just a dirty smudge. News is a little like this. It is a mental effect, which becomes habitual, and requires constant hits. And by repetition, like a drug, it changes minds. Scientists such as Susan Greenfield argue that the shut-down effect of opiates on the brain can, over time, become permanent – connections are shaken loose so regularly that they don't close and the intricate architecture of consciousness is changed. Similarly – this is a simile not a parallel – your world view is altered by the news you get. One story saying that killer French bees are coming to get you might make you laugh. A dozen, over a few days, might make you scared. If you hear that people have indeed died, and this is repeated, and similar stories recur the next spring, and the next, then you may come to believe in killer French bees. Multiply that a thousand-fold to account for all the running stories in different papers and one begins to understand the power of news. It takes a heroic, or insane, mind to stand outside it.

Similarities between drugs and news don't stop there. There's the addiction. People 'consume news', but they eat it with their eyes and ears. It has an emotional effect. As they eat, news can brighten their faces, or strike them with grief. It certainly becomes a habit. Nobody has to turn to crime to feed their news habit: the same news that is so fantastically expensive to produce, is very cheap to buy, costing a few coins or a few seconds flicking a radio dial. Yet like more carefully controlled substances, it can have unexpected effects. It can create an immediate sense of well being – the team has won, or the hated politician is in trouble or bank holiday weather is going to be great. It can infuriate you and cause spontaneous fights, just like some drugs. It can waste fantastic amounts of time. I spend far more time poring through badly written paragraphs of nonsense by people I don't trust than the average cannabis enthusiast spends in his haze. And yet, chances are, you will be back at the newsagent, your friendly neighbourhood dealer, next morning, ready for more.

The raw material of news, as it appears in old papers, broadcasts and books, doesn't change very much, though it does a bit, as we shall see. Kennedy Jones, one of the first Northcliffe editors, said his perfect newspaper recipe could be contained in four words: 'Crime, love, money and food.' So it has been throughout most of the papers I have scanned. We must add 'disaster' and 'power' to the list but that is about the lot. There are jewellery thieves mugging passing pedestrians. A famous woman has given birth to twins. A famous man has run off with a young girl. A boy has been bitten by a dog. Eight people are ill after eating local fish. That toffee-nosed family have lost their fortune in speculations. All this is old. All this is new. The same things happened in Kentucky in 1928 and Parma in 1707 and Bombay last year – the endless repeated wheel of deaths and sex and births and coincidences, the crimes and technical failures, the accidents and risks of nerve or mathematics, the old love scorned and the young loves triumphant. And all these things are happening still, just differently coloured, with names changed and switched details. And if they happen today, they are somebody's news. And if they happen today and near you, they are your news.

For news has its own geography and its own speed. People say news travels fast. But that is not the whole story. It slows, and decays, as it travels. For every mile most news speeds towards you, it loses a little of its force and its weight. If news happens a long way away, it can lose so much of itself that it is merely a shadow by the time it arrives. It does not grip you. The bigger the news, the more of it will still be there by the time it reaches you. A dam breaks in China, and a million people lose their homes. *A million!* That is big enough to get right into your front room, and your front brain, and stay there, at least for an hour. But if the news is that there has been a coach crash in Armenia, killing six passengers, it makes less impact. By the time that news has travelled to a British home it is almost transparent, a short paragraph on page twenty-six which hardly anyone stops to read – unless of course they come from a British-Armenian family. But suppose there has been a coach crash in Armenia, which only *injures* six passengers . . . well that loses so much of its bodyweight in travelling that it never gets here at all. That story might have made it to Istanbul, but there it would have stopped. News lives on a weird globe, distorted so that the local is magnified, and the distant compressed. There was said to be a headline in a paper published in the north-east of Scotland: 'Aberdeen Man Feared Lost at Sea. 200 Also Drowned.' Then there was Claude Cockburn's famous spoof headline, 'Small Earthquake in Chile: Not Many Dead.' Which most people now believe was for real.

Through this chapter, we will look at news, what the different kinds of news do, and where they come from. But the key to all this is to understand that 'news' is not 'facts'. News is based on fact. We have to believe, at least for a while, that what is said to have happened, did happen – that the American oil company really has gone bankrupt, or that when the TV presenter says someone has been arrested, they actually have been. But our interest comes from how effectively we can use these facts to make sense of the world and our place in it. News is a source of emotion, belonging and even morality.

Yes: scratch the surface of most news stories and you find a moral agenda. Journalists are taught inconsistent things. We are taught to 'play it straight' or 'tell both sides' or 'refrain from comment' – all good enough mottoes. But we are also taught to 'make it human' and 'engage the reader'. And that really means playing it bent – taking a viewpoint and telling one side more vividly than the other; in other words, commenting. And that 'engage the reader' form of bias changes the real world too.

Take the great British paedophilia panic. The number of child sex murders in Britain carried out by a stranger is roughly static, about five to seven a year. The number of convictions or cautions for sex crimes involving children has fallen in recent years. An exhaustive study of the statistics on the abuse of children reveals only that we have no knowledge at all of how widespread it is: 'the number of children sexually abused each year in England and Wales lies somewhere between 3,500 and 72,600. In other words, a detailed analysis of the statistics produces such a wide margin of possible error that no published figures can provide the basis for reliable assumptions, let alone sensible policy-making.'[1] Yet the number of stories about paedophiles has rocketed since the mid-1990s, particularly in the tabloid press. The effect has been enormous, not only on the government legislation on sex crimes, and on the treatment (or lack of it) for paedophiles, but on the way families live their lives – how much children are allowed out by themselves, how worried parents are about the Internet, how suspicious society in general has become about men who work as Scout leaders, in youth groups, for swimming clubs and so on. Is this good or bad? It is possible that the 'paedophile panic' is our way of setting limits on sexuality in an increasingly sexual age; perhaps the papers who whipped up enough hysteria to produce mobs on the streets are in the long term helping society by warning it of a real and underestimated danger to children. On the other hand, much innocent voluntary work has been curtailed and many innocent men have been made miserable, while many children have been unnecessarily frightened. For good or ill, it is a classic example of the effect of news values on society. A British press that was less interested in paedophiles would have produced a different Britain. News is the nervous system of urban humanity.

Because of its problems, one could simply try to opt out of the news culture. I know people who barely read a paper and who think most broadcast news is mindless nonsense. I think, however, they are wrong. They might go through their weekly round, taking kids to school, shopping, praying, doing some voluntary work, phoning elderly relatives, and do more good than harm as they go. But they have disconnected themselves from the wider world; rather like secular monks, they have cloistered themselves in the local. And this is not good enough. We are either players in open, democratic societies, all playing a tiny part in their ultimate direction, or we are deserters.

These are questions for all of us. What do we think about a news agenda whose overarching story about public life is that everyone in it is a lying hypocrite who deserves ridicule; which downgrades any thought that public life can include genuine idealism, some self-sacrifice, hard work and interesting thinking? Or how about a news media that shies away from major financial scandals until it is too late, and the pensions or jobs of tens of thousands of people are blown away? What about when the effort, money and space that could have gone into investigating them was spent instead on spurious opinion polls, or buying some B-grade TV personality's kiss-and-tell memoirs? Is a newspaper devoured by gossip and voyeurism, which fails to report the looming political or military crises affecting its readers, 'professional' in understanding what people want, or 'unprofessional' in failing to report the stories that its journalists know matter more? Suppose in an average week you are aware of a dozen news stories. It is probably many more than that, but take twelve as the

number you think about, even briefly. Those stories, 600 in a year –
though since stories intermingle and repeat themselves, let's cut it to
300 – affect you. They colour your attitude to the world, and often
condition how you take specific decisions, from holiday plans, to
saving or spending, to how you look at a possible mugger. An
accumulation of 'good' stories, by which I only mean ones which are
as truthful as possible, and which give a reasonably accurate account
of the world, will have a powerful effect for good on any society.
Brave, intelligent, probing journalism is so important that it is now
impossible to imagine a decent society surviving without it. Bad
journalism – cowardly, corruptly involved with the powerful or rich,
ready to smear the weak and to whip up irrational fears – is a fast
route to social perdition.

So the bland-seeming question What is news? turns out to be
complicated, political and important. In the lives of most journalists, it
is the elephant in the corner, huge and mildly embarrassing, but rarely
openly discussed. This chapter looks not at journalists, but at their
work. What is the history of British news, and how does today's news
measure up? I have read a reasonable cross-section of newspapers
going back to the 1680s and tried to draw general conclusions. This is
only an impressionistic view, of course, since it would take a lifetime
to read everything that has been kept. But the trends are clear enough.

Early News Stories

They were not respectable. The earliest papers I have burrowed
through, from the 1680s to the 1740s, are often frankly bemusing.
They are typically quite small, about eleven inches by eight, and either
just two sides, or four, or – rarely – six. Take the *Observator* for 4 July
1682, a relatively well-known paper of the day. It is entirely taken up
with a fictitious conversation between a Whig and a Tory about
London civic politics, and now completely unintelligible to anyone
except a specialist historian. There is not a word or jot of what we
would call news. In Isaac Bickerstaff's *Tatler* of 31 October 1709,
another single sheet of two columns, produced from 'White's Chocolate House', most of the paper is taken up with an essay comparing
political writers with different kinds of gunners. In these and other

papers of the day, one has the sense of a tiny, disputatious and intensely political group of Londoners, a specialist readership conducting obscure quarrels.

But there was a growing appetite for real news. Addison wrote as early as 1712 that 'There is no Humour in my Countrymen, which I am more inclined to wonder at than their general Thirst after News.' The *Weekly Packet* for 30 August 1718 opens with a court report from Dublin, about the conviction of a mob who attacked an informer against 'Popish Priests' (and who were fined, imprisoned and whipped for their pains). Then we get a good overseas story, though it starts in a roundabout way, and only gets going in the third or fourth paragraph. The Spanish fleet has, it seems, been attacked by Admiral Byng off Syracuse, where he has sunk nine ships, burned two and taken four prisoner, with thirteen fleeing. Next follows a letter to the Spanish ambassador, written by an anonymous British 'minister of state' explaining why his ships were attacked; it was apparently to 'preserve the Peace and Neutrality of Italy'. But the Spanish ambassador is having none of it: the paper then repeats, without comment, a very long and outraged letter back. The story is then left, and the *Weekly Packet* moves on to a stream of other news, none of it with headlines or separated at all: there has been a row in a church in Chiselhurst, Kent, about charity money; the Duke of Marlborough returns from Tonbridge; then, in a single, throwaway line, something that every tabloid would lead on today: 'We hear that Her Royal Highness, the Princess of Wales, is with child.' Then thirteen warships are being sent to the West Indies; oh, yes, and a seditious clergyman has been convicted in Wells. Next, a sporting accident, reported with commendable brevity: 'On the 19th Instant, Sir Edward Longueville, Bart., fell off his Horse at a Horse-Race near Bristol and dy'd immediately.' Then, a Spanish flotilla has arrived at Cadiz with 18 million crowns aboard; and 108 felons have been sent from Newgate prison to be transported to the West Indies; and Lady Dixwell, sister of the Countess of Portland, has 'dy'd at her Seat in Kent'; and a yacht has been ordered to fetch the Earl Cadogan from Holland; and the air in Urbino doesn't suit the Pretender, the Chevalier de St George, so he's off to Tivoli; and the Spanish have taken Fort St Salvador, with the loss of a thousand men, two galleys and a frigate; and the peace treaty between the Czar and the King of Sweden has arrived at Rostock; and finally, a last piece of domestic news which reads, in full: 'Casualties. Drown'd accidentally in the River Thames, 4. Found dead in the Street, 1. Overlaid, 1. Broken Legg, 1.'

It is a breathless tumble. Military and diplomatic news is clearly most important to readers of the *Packet*, but it acknowledges social gossip and, briefly, local news. A much more interesting paper is the six-page *Original Weekly Journal* printed in London 'by John Applebee, over-against Bridewell bridge, in Black-Fryers'. At last we get something that sounds like a modern news story. There has been, the previous Saturday, 'a very Remarkable, tho' uncommon, Accident . . . in Albermarle-street, near Piccadilly'. It turns out that 'a certain old Usurer' was counting his money when he

> by Chance, let fall out of his Window, 3 Stories high, a seal'd Bagg, containing 500 Guineas, which gave a person like a Carpenter or Joyner then passing by, a Violent Blow on the Head; who never stood to demand Satisfaction for the Assault or to enquire from whence it came, but immediately brushed off [sic] with the Booty, well knowing that would make sufficient Reparation for his Damages. The Usurer continued bawling after him for some time, but to no purpose, it being so Early that scarce any People were abroad, neither do we learn that he has since been heard of.

This is vividly done, with a real sense of reporting – and a whiff of anti-Semitism too – but we are given suspiciously few details and the tale is perhaps a little neat. Why no names? How did the victim guess what was in the 'Bagg'? It has the feel of a tale that has passed through a few coffee shops and taverns on the way to Mr Applebee beside the Bridewell Bridge. Other stories in the same paper are downright infuriating in their lack of further detail. One, for instance, tells us that a kidnapper has been seized at the Royal Exchange, 'it being sworn that he had trepann'd and sold several young People to the Plantations against their wills'. *What?* But no more follows. On 6 July 1717 the *Journal* begins rather like the *Packet* with a long piece of foreign and military news, followed by more diplomatic gossip from Vienna, Paris, Rostock and the Hague.

The rest of the paper is taken up with an account of the Earl of Oxford's trial in parliament; news of 'the Pretender in Rome' (clearly a source of news-making anxiety in London), social titbits about the movements of aristocrats and more bloodthirsty crime snippets, such as the whipping of foot soldiers in Hyde Park. There are frank admissions about what the paper doesn't know and even, finally, a correction: 'What we mentioned in our last in relation to Mr Bowen of the Custom-House being suspended, proves a Mistake . . .' What can we make of all this? There is a growing sense of an audience. Here is a young and nervous empire looking out agog at the dangerous world around it, with only a brief time to cast around close at hand for local or 'human interest' stories. But what is important to the British elite is being slowly challenged by what may be interesting to the general reader.

As the century progresses, the papers grow larger in size and start containing more local news, though there is still the same jumble of material, without headlines or any obvious organizing principle, and with a heavy bias towards diplomacy and politics, however abstruse. The provincial papers were simply rehashing foreign and political news from London, though the Jacobite rebellion of 1745–6 produced a rash of local eyewitness reports. But papers from Kendal to Exeter are curiously full of who preached at which church in London, and London fires, and London muggings. Generally, it is all in a bit of a jumble. Local papers tended to fill up from the front, with the earliest reports from London, adding later news until it was time to print and distribute the papers; so the most important and latest news could simply be a final line or two. Papers unable to supply it pleaded with their readers to forgive them: in the 1720s the *Gloucester Journal* was apologizing for 'the present scarcity of News' and offering poems instead.

By contrast, when real local news is available, such as a riot in Leeds in 1753 or the opening of new assembly rooms in York in 1731, eighteenth-century papers are able to give fairly full and vivid accounts. As the market for news grows, so does blunt, eyewitness reporting. Sometimes it is so strong it is hard to imagine it appearing in print today. Dreadful and detailed accounts of cruelty to children, or of servants being forced to eat their own excrement by their employers, or of sadistic sex crimes, abound. One gets a vivid sense of how much more violent and disordered, not to say downright dangerous, Britain was in the eighteenth and early nineteenth century. In 1772 a Mr Johnson published a long pamphlet from St Paul's Churchyard.

A typical newspaper, he complained, 'without murders and robberies, and rapes and incest, and bestiality and sodomy, and sacrilege, and incendiary letters and forgeries, and executions and duels, and suicides, is said to be void of news: – for such are the melancholy themes that a corrupted and forsaken people are gaping after'.[2] We haven't changed much.

It is worth spending some time and space to get a flavour of the news stories as they develop towards the Victorian age, because so much of what we now think of as news seems to have hardened and clarified then. Most histories of newspapers claim the great revolution in news comes after the final removal of stamp duties in the 1850s. That is true in the numbers of papers sold but not in terms of the news. With a really big and dramatic story, and with eyewitness accounts, you can find excellent reporting from the beginning of the 1800s. In the course of researching this book, I found myself holding an original copy of *The Times* for 7 November 1805, published in the immediate aftermath of Trafalgar: the news of the great victory and the death of Nelson sprawls across the front page, where you generally find advertisements in those days, and continues inside. It is grippingly written, a narrative stitched together from the eyewitness accounts of naval officers whose letters have made it back to London; and with further accounts from more captains and lieutenants inside. Waterloo is done as well, a decade later. The first news comes on 21 June 1815 thanks to a 'Mr Sutton of Colchester' who owned ships sailing between the Essex town and Ostend, and minus his cargo jumped into one to take the good news to England. On that day the battle is still nameless. But the story is told very well:

> Presently Wellington himself came into the field. Buonaparte, too, was said to be present with the rebels. This was the first time those two celebrated Generals were ever personally opposed . . . A most sanguinary combat now ensued. The Cuirassiers of the Imperial Guard charged on the British infantry, who received them in solid squares. The shock was tremendous. The British did their duty. The noble 42nd regiment was almost literally cut to pieces, most of its officers being wounded and only eighty privates surviving the battle; but its losses were amply avenged. The Cuirassiers who made the charge were annihilated on the spot.

And so on. This is strong, staccato writing in the best reporting style. Its story is the one which has passed down through history.

But a history of news stories should focus on the ordinary days. One finds a slow decade-by-decade advance to a more modern presentation of what is fresh and interesting. The *Morning Post* in the first couple of decades of the nineteenth century is a grey wash of columns, five to a page, and starting with adverts before it moves to political leaders and letters of news from abroad, sometimes almost humorously uninformative – 'Last night we received the French papers to the 20th inst. They were barren as usual.' Scraps of poetry, court news and social gossip give the impression of a still-small upper-class readership: 'We accidentally omitted in yesterday's paper, to state that Lady Astley's Quadrille Ball will take place tomorrow evening.' Much of the rest of the news is commercial and imperial – the arrival of ships or news from Jamaica and India. Then one suddenly comes across a poignant, vivid bulletin, like this couple of inches from a *Post* of June 1818:

> Yesterday morning, J. Dennett, the miserable and decrepit old man, who was convicted on Friday of the wilful murder of Jane Rogers, was executed ... He seemed much agitated when he came upon the scaffold: and continued to tremble violently until he was turned off, when his hands clasped together and he seemed to die without the least struggle. After hanging the usual time, his body was delivered over to the surgeons for dissection.

The local papers were still getting most of their material from London – that hanging was reported in many of them, along with the latest general election news. In the *Alfred, or West of England Journal* of 1818, there are many local adverts but there is almost no Exeter or West Country news. *Courdroy's Manchester Gazette* is full of the 'London Mails', news from Hamburg and Paris and parliamentary news, but manages only rare local stories. The same goes for a dozen or so other 'local' papers I looked through: they performed something of the function of a modern TV news bulletin, bringing national and international events to remote corners.

Meanwhile, the national press was organizing its material better. By 1824, the *Morning Post* has headlines such as 'Police Intelligence' for the crime stories, 'Fashionable World' for the reports of dinners, parties and the arrivals or departures from London of grandees, and specific ones too, such as 'The Late Events at Paris'. Readers were learning to look quickly for what they wanted. Life was speeding up. And good reporting was easy to find. Here is one example, from the *Observer* of 18 January 1829, which can stand for many. It could have been a novel, yet it takes up just a column and a half on that paper's front page, entitled 'Extraordinary Investigation: or the Female Husband'. It concerns a 'person known as James Allen, 42' who had been working for a Mr Crisp, a shipwright, sawing wood in his sawpit, when he was hit and killed by a piece of falling timber. He was rushed to St Thomas' Hospital where, the report continues,

> an examination took place, when, to the astonishment of all present, it was discovered that the deceased was of the female sex ... Mary Allen, who had been married to the deceased for 21 years, on hearing of the accident, flew to the hospital and was present when the sex of the deceased was discovered, and was evidently not less astonished than any of the others, positively declaring that she had never before known that her husband was a woman ... Both the coroner and the Jury expressed their astonishment at so extraordinary a circumstance as two females living together as man and wife ...

We then learn that 'James' Allen had been a groom, working for various noblemen in London before his job at the shipwright's. She apparently wore sailor's clothes, including thick flannel waistcoats which hid her 'extremely well-developed breasts'. She never seems to have had sex with Mary but was generally considered 'of rather an ill temper' and would beat her wife 'if she noticed a man particularly'.

It is a sensational story, which would make the front page of the *Sun* today, and the editor of the paper clearly recognizes this, because it is the only domestic news on his advertisement-crowded front page. We don't get all the information we want. We want an interview with Mary, but this is just before the age of shorthand and interviewing journalists. The word 'lesbian' does not appear. We would like to know more about how 'James' survived in a male working world, though it is said she was teased by her workmates for her lack of facial hair and high voice. Above all, we would like to hear something of her early history. Nor is the story quite structured as it would be now. It begins at the beginning, not with the crucial facts. It starts with the accident in the sawpit, the rush to the hospital and the arrival of the shocked wife, before revealing its main point. Generally, in newspapers of the time, there is little editing. Information is printed in the order it arrived, so that one paragraph contradicts an earlier one, printed just a few inches higher. It is like reading a bundle of freshly delivered letters, hurried off as events are still unfolding. This, of course, is much closer to how we experience life than the artificial 'beginning, middle and end' of a modern news story.

The news comes out like tiny flashes of picked-up conversation, half-heard stories, terse reports without analysis and repeated tales from other papers. There is a charm to this, though considerable frustration too: the formal business of finding out what happened next, and cross-checking facts, is still in its infancy. In the story of 'James' Allen, a reporter has discovered the names, ages and some of the history of the couple involved. Neighbours have been interviewed. Not everything can be reported in that issue; but there is no promise of more next week, and so far as I can tell, the story was simply dropped in subsequent papers. Other stories are shorter, leaving one panting for more. On 25 January 1829 we learn that James Pearce, convicted of stealing a coat, turns out to be the son of a Liverpool doctor who was adopted by a Russian count, served in the campaign against Napoleon, became a tutor in the Russian Imperial Gymnasium and fell upon hard times. He then borrowed enough money to come to England where he wanted to beg a living from expatriate Russians. But they turned him out and he was reduced to stealing . . . A great story, again. But is it true? Was it just a wonderful yarn spun to the London magistrates who heard his case? Has anyone checked with Russians living in London? In our professionalized, news-machine world, where raw facts are overinterpreted, it seems extraordinary to leave the story there, surrounded by mystery and question marks. But that is what happened.

Other stories, less mysterious, are nevertheless almost heartbreaking in their terseness. On 30 August of the same year, the *Observer* tells us – and this is the full story – 'On Thursday, at Twerton, Somerset, a boy named Joseph Skrine, having been detected in pelting down walnuts, the property of a tradesman, ran to hide himself in an oat-house, and died immediately, it is supposed from excessive alarm.' Or this: 'Mr Thomas Williams, a respectable farmer at Nass, Gloucester, swallowed a wasp in some beer on Monday last and within three hours was a corpse.' On the stories go, of robberies, frauds, shipping news, murders, still jumbled, and frequently frustrating to the modern eye. Amid the adverts for cosmetic dentistry, balsamic vinegar and pasta (the *Observer* readers of north London haven't changed that much in 175 years) there are almost off-hand stories of riots, and even the sale of murdered corpses to the medical trade. 'A 14-year-old boy, fresh killed' is taken in a hamper to be sold to the surgical department of King's College. When the doctors seem suspicious, the motley crew cut their price of twelve guineas and have no explanation of the gash on the boy's head. They are arrested . . . Here we have a paper which knows a story when it sees one, but is still unscientific in following the story up, haphazard in its selection and disorganized in its presentation.

Sensational, and Dull, Victorian News

Jumble and charm give way to professionalism. If we leaf on a decade and turn to another Sunday paper, the recently launched *News of the World*, we immediately see better organization, and a closer concentration on sensationalism. Victorian Sundays were set aside for churchgoing and genteel family amusements. But they were also, for the working classes and the poorer middle classes, a day of leisure. And on that day, the people wanted a little titillation and shock to help them relax. Papers like *Reynolds's* and the *News of the World* gave them just that; but they were proper papers, not simply scandal-sheets. Each edition of the latter has the foreign, home and crime stories in roughly the same places. There is a populist, tub-thumping leader on the front page, plus a column of execrable jokes, openly stolen from comic papers such as *Punch*. The diplomatic news from abroad gets its place, as does 'country news' which consists of murders by poachers in Cornwall, sheep-stealing in Kent and burglaries, highway robberies and the like. A drunk man, returning from a christening to a tavern in Wells, Somerset, falls asleep by the fire, catching his clothes in a hook meant for the spit, and hangs himself. In Almondsby, Yorkshire, another drunk burns himself to death in his 'hovel'. The news from

Ireland is bloodier. There has been a threat by an armed gang to a landowner in Tipperary. 'A wretched poor creature' has been found starved to death, 'frightfully emaciated and presenting the appearance of a real skeleton'. There has been 'the frightful death of a notorious character' who tried to rob a mill, slipped and was decapitated by the mill wheel.

The paper is a general one, clearly trying to cover the waterfront of politics, overseas news and essential information. Though a populist paper, it is lengthy, literate and vivid. The political news jostling against the murders and scandals tells of a society becoming slowly democratized – it is all about mass meetings to protest about 'Papal aggression' or taxes on windows and paper. There are yet more terrible jokes, collected under the name 'varieties' of which one example had better suffice: 'It is decidedly in bad taste to attend the funeral of a black friend, and then inform your friends that you have been black-berrying.' (Decidedly.) There is even a weather report, which suggests that weird weather may not be entirely attributable to global warming: 'There is no indication of the frost and snow which usually accompany the season of the year. One day we have deep gloom and falling showers, bursts of sunshine, brilliant rainbows, and at nightfall, vivid flashes of lightning; the next, perhaps, a series of tornadoes . . .' There are poems, moralizing mottoes, lists of the whereabouts of the various British armies of the day, and the naval squadrons too, lists of insolvent debtors, adverts for the treatment of venereal diseases, reports of fires in the new parliament buildings and of a planned street nearby, which will rip through the 'lowest and most densely populated parts of Westminster' and will be called Victoria Street.

But what the *News of the World* was really selling is sensation – shock, horror. Sex and violence! The violence was greater than today and the sex more reticent. On the printed page, the violence is everywhere. An eight-year-old boy dies 'in great agony' after being gored in the eye by an enraged bullock at Ludgate. Unpleasant details are given. A young man kills himself with poison in Bird's Coffee House, Lambeth, after the failure of his beer shop. There is a warning about poisoned sugarplums and almonds being sold on the streets in poor neighbourhoods – several have died. Another story is headlined 'Perverse and Mischievous Attempt at Suicide by a Girl'. She is called

Caroline Townsend, aged eleven, who attempts to drown herself in
Regent's Canal, but is taken out and revived at the nearby Duke of
Sussex pub. She says that her grandmother had 'blewed her up' and
hit her for burning a hole in a slipper, and told her 'she might if she
liked go and make a hole in the water'. The grandmother, who
impresses local police as a decent woman, explains that Caroline is
'rather perverse and mischievous': the paper seems to agree. On it
goes – pickpockets, 'a mysterious nocturnal murder of a very diabolical
character', yet another suicide.

Sex, by contrast, is dealt with in a muttering way. It is the era of
servants spying on ladies in a state of undress through keyholes. But
news consists of what can be reported and thanks to the divorce laws
of the time, there were sadistically public cross-examinations. Verbatim
reports from courts of adulteries and attempted rapes become the
standby sex story of mid-Victorian times. As shorthand becomes
efficient and general, almost full accounts of the juiciest parts of cross-
examinations of witnesses start to fill page after page. There is an
added element of voyeurism in these stories, since they are dragged
out of mortified women in public, goggled at by witty judges and rapt
juries.

Victorian critics complained that their news was 'human sewage'.
But it was profitable. The first editor-owner of the *Daily Telegraph*,
Joseph Moses Levy, insisted in the 1850s on what he called 'the human
note', running headlines such as 'Horrible Atrocity. A Child Devoured
by Pigs' and, as a result, put on a big sales increase. People wanted
details. Nasty details. In a study of sensational Victorian crime reports,
the splendidly titled *Black Swine in the Sewers of Hampstead*, Thomas
Boyle cites a London newspaper, the *Leader*, reporting the exhuming
of bodies in a poisoning case of 1856. When the lead lid of the coffin
of one Walter Palmer was removed:

> The cheeks were so terribly distended as to extend to either side
> of the coffin; one eye was opened, and the mouth partially so,
> presenting the appearance of a horrible grin and grimace. Each
> limb was also swollen to prodigious proportions, and the sight
> was revolting in the extreme. Nearly all the jurors were afflicted
> with vomiting and fainting . . . even a week afterwards the close
> room in which the bodies were opened smelt of the disgusting
> odour . . .

Later the same paper reports on the hanging of the poisoner: 'And now the hangman grasps the rope – Palmer bends his head – the noose is slipped over – his face grows yet more ghastly – his throat throbs spasmodically – he moves his neck round, as a man with a tight collar.' The reporter notes how the white cap placed over his head blows out from his chin as the man's breathing speeds up, and then, at the moment of death 'the body whirls round – the hangman from below seizes the legs – one escapes from his grasp, and by a mighty spasm is once drawn up – the chest thrice heaves convulsively – the hangman loosens his hold – the body again whirls round, then becomes steady, and hangs a dull, grey, shapeless mass, facing the newly risen sun'. We have become accustomed to describing horrific depictions of crime as 'Dickensian' but this out-Dickens Dickens – as indeed, critics of the paper noted at the time. The pieces were written by one Edward Whitty, a journalist who also produced a novel before drinking himself to death on a temperance ship bound for Australia.[3]

So by modern standards, early-Victorian journalism did not spare the reader. William Russell's despatches on the Crimean War for *The Times* are famous as war reportage which had a major political impact at home. But when one actually goes back and reads them, they are shockingly graphic. Here, for instance, is his account of walking into the Russian army hospital at Sebastopol:

> In a long, low room, supported by square pillars arched at the top, and dimly lighted through shattered and unglazed window-frames, lay the wounded Russians. The wounded, did I say? No, but the dead – the rotten and festering corpses of the soldiers, who were left to die in their extreme agony, untended, uncared for, packed as close as they could be stowed, some on the floor, others on wretched trestles and bedsteads or pallets of straw, sopped and saturated with blood which oozed and trickled through upon the floor, mingling with the droppings of corruption . . . Many lay, yet alive, with maggots crawling about in their wounds.

In another copy of the paper, Russell, still identified only as 'our special correspondent' returns to the issue of vermin, though this time describing daily life for the British army:

> Every nook and cranny is infested by flies in millions, which give no rest by day, and little by night. Within the last week, the thing

> has almost assumed the dimensions of a plague ... [they] settle
> on the most irritable parts of the face ... a morsel in its passage
> to the mouth is generally settled upon by two or more of the
> insects, which require to be vigorously shaken before they will let
> go their hold. To remove them from a glass of any liquid before
> tasting it, it is necessary to introduce three fingers and draw them
> from the vessel.

This writing too is as strong as Dickens's journalism. No wonder it eventually helped bring down a government.

The strong impression from reading Victorian newspapers of this period is of a middle class hungrily interested in the world around them, and determined to understand it. Details of medical autopsies, chemical experiments, engines, wars, diplomatic arguments – all these are piled in. Away from the public arena, mid-Victorian papers are still reporting the miseries and dilemmas of domestic life in clear language. One random example comes from *The Times* of 23 July 1855, in the midst of the dramas of the Crimea, and has eerie echoes of the James Bulger case. Headlined 'Extraordinary Murder of a Boy by Two of His Companions', it relates that John Fitzpatrick and Alfred Breen, both ten, killed a seven-year-old called James Fleeson at Saltney near the Leeds and Liverpool Canal. Fitzpatrick,

> taking up a piece of brick, struck the deceased on the temple with
> it, and kicked him down. He then struck Fleeson again while the
> lad was on the ground. Fleeson's hands and feet moved convul-
> sively, but he did not resist or cry out ... Both the prisoners then
> seized the deceased, dragged him to the canal and threw him in.
> The poor lad had struggled for a few minutes, then sank.

This ghastly story takes up only about five inches of text downpage on page ten of the paper.

Over the next few decades, at least in the broadsheets, the quantity of directly reported hard news sharply decreases, and the prose becomes heavier, more abstract and more ornate. As we saw in the last chapter, editors were becoming posher and papers were becoming bigger. A vast quantity of *The Times* in particular is taken up with letters from correspondents around the world, often moralizing, almost always long-winded. As Victorian prosperity booms, the sheer quantity of adverts makes filling the rest of the paper with interesting news harder and harder. Interminable reports of parliamentary debates are part of the editors' response. In *The Times* for 1 July 1880 I found some 18,000 words of parliamentary reporting, none of it of any consequence. In the same paper for 4 August there was 40,500 words or so from the Commons and Lords, again minus the slightest hint of any drama. Much of the rest is made up of overseas reports and correspondence – long-winded, moralistic, preachy and biased. It is the self-important, omniscient murmur of a lost imperial Britain; no doubt in the dim recesses of St James's clubs, ex-ambassadors waded their way through it. But all the vivid immediacy of popular papers from the mid-Victorian era has been bleached out.

It wasn't only *The Times*. Take for example the *Manchester Guardian* for 2 June 1886. Pass over the fact that the paper begins with pages of adverts, commercial information, 'ecclesiastical intelligence' and other dry stuff which was no doubt of use or amusement to the Manchester middle classes of the day. What is more striking is that when we do get news, it is appallingly badly presented and written. One story, which appears prominently, is simply headed 'From our London Correspondent' and begins: 'The meeting of Lord Hartington, and his friends, today attracted little attention, because there could be no doubt as to the result. The situation is unchanged . . .' It does not get much more interesting. Or what about a gripper entitled blandly 'The Present Position of the Chemical Industries' which opens thus: 'The last meeting of the series of the Manchester Section of the Society of Chemical Industry was held last night in the Chemical Theatre of the Owen's College, when a paper on the present position of the chemical industries of Great Britain was read by Mr Ivan Levinstein, vice-president of the society . . .' Again, that's the interesting bit.

Later Victorian papers are often like this. Great events, such as wars, sinkings and earthquakes happen and are reported. But the default attitude to news is bureaucratic, a relentless, passionless noting down of names, speeches, events and social information. It rouses no emotion or interest now and it is hard to imagine that it roused much then: it is 'news' for people who expect to see their names in print, as if the newspaper industry was simply a giant, obsessive social diarist. The reasons for this pulling back from the more vivid and direct news of mid-Victorian Britain seem clear. Journalists, in London at least, had become respectable members of society, with a perhaps exaggerated

respect for their betters. There had been a decades-long struggle for
respectability, a thrusting down of the turbulent, violent and threatening urban life of the 1840s and 50s. By now, there were plenty of
fringe socialist newspapers, but mainstream journalism, like a caricature Victorian lady, had become keen to look the other way when
confronted with the nasty or challenging. These papers attempted
what is impossible – highmindedness in news. Kennedy Jones, of the
early *Daily Mail*, found newspapers of the 1880s to be 'lifeless and
mechanical'. There were huge quantities of parliamentary news but
the rest amounted only to 'a little foreign news, also legal intelligence,
the money market, general markets, shipping, movements of the
nobility and landed gentry . . .' plus 'a sparse amount of sports'. The
more go-ahead journals, he joked, would once a week bestow a
paragraph on the prices in Bond Street shops of salmon, ducklings,
asparagus, strawberries, grouse and other game in due season. It could
not go on. It did not.

The Old New Journalism

Some universally accepted truths are true. One of them is that modern
journalism was reborn in 1896 when Alfred Harmsworth started the
Daily Mail. Things were a little more complicated than that – some of
his ideas came from the livelier papers of New York and Chicago, and
he learned a lot from a man who is today less well known, Alfred
Newnes, whose popular paper *Tit-Bits* was made up of little gobbets of
news and interesting facts, often in response to correspondents, rather
like the *Guardian*'s 'Notes & Queries' of a century later. But it was the
young, audacious, driven and mercurial Harmsworth who remade
journalism. In the history of British journalism, no single act has been
quite as successful or as influential as the launching of the *Mail*.

Alfred's principles were simple. The news should be interesting,
short and always told from a human angle. In a series of careful pre-
publication dummies he tested the new story-writing style that would
within months give him an extraordinary got-rich-quick story. On 17
February 1896 the main story (which nevertheless appears inside the
paper: all respectable papers covered the front page with adverts then)
is headed 'Appalling Fire' and tells of eight people being burned to

death in Soho, in Frith Street. People talk of 'sensationalism' in journalistic writing, and here it is:

> One of the most thrilling scenes in this story of human suffering and destruction was when a bootmaker named Moore, aged twenty-nine, was seen to appear at the front window of the second floor, with his clothes all alight. The room was at the time one dense mass of flame, and escape was impossible. In the fierce light spectators plainly perceived the awful look of despair written on the poor fellow's face. Only one moment did he stand at the window, and then he threw himself into the street below. A sickening feeling passed through the crowd when it was seen that Moore had miscalculated his distance, and that his body was literally impaled on the metal spear-heads of the railings in front of the house. He was heard to murmur, I tried to save them and then I jumped.

Moore dies, as do his wife and children. The reporter then goes to the morgue to look at the charred remains of the victims. It is a chilling story. The same fire was reported in *The Times* of the same day. Its story begins: 'A calamitous fire, which resulted in the loss of eight lives and in serious injury to a ninth person, broke out shortly before 3 o'clock yesterday morning in a lodging-house at 7, Church-street Soho. The premises consisted of a very old-fashioned house of 14 rooms, which was tenanted by several families of lodgers . . .' See?

Another good example of the *Mail* style comes from the same year, the paper of 13 September, with report of 'Murder by a Maniac'. An Essex farm steward has had his head cut off by a farmer, his employer, called Samuel Collins. The report suggests the motive was sexual jealousy and continues: 'Collins first shot Cockerill, then beat him with the butt end of his rifle. He then, with a large knife, ruthlessly severed Cockerill's head from his body and placed it in a large bowl . . . the head was clean severed from the trunk and part of the victim's beard was cut off as though by a keen-edged razor.' Enter, shortly afterwards, Police Constable Cook:

> The officer met Collins, his hands and clothes stained with blood, walking calmly out through the farm gateway, carrying in one hand the BOWL CONTAINING A HUMAN HEAD [the capitals are in the original *Daily Mail* story] and in the other the double-

barrelled gun and some dead chickens. Cook asked him what he
had been doing, to which Collins replied that he had been killing
a sheep . . . and handed the constable the bowl with its ghastly
contents. Cook cried out, 'Why, you have committed murder!'
Collins, in a dazed style, replied: 'Have I? I am sorry. Let me kiss
you' and suiting the action to the word, the murderer stooped
down to embrace the policeman . . .

Intrepid reporters were another key part of the *Mail* style. In the paper
for 24 October 1896 – by which time it was established as one of the
greatest successes in the history of Fleet Street, already selling more
than 220,000 a day – there is a stream of short, vivid, well-written
news gobbets, at a fraction of the length of broadsheet articles. The
general news style of the day was for the reporter to be an opaque
presence, as little visible to the reader as possible. Almost all reporting,
including in the *Mail*, was anonymous and would stay so for decades
to come, but Harmsworth wanted the human to shine from his papers,
and one way of achieving this is for the reporter to make clear that he
was there, on the spot, at the time – a living and active extension of
the reader's own interest. So when the Hon. C. S. Rolls became the
first Englishman to die in a plane crash, the paper's 'special correspondent' was on hand to record what happened: 'There was the sound of
the rending of woodwork . . . The biplane reeled in the air and then,
pitching forward, crashed to earth . . . Mr Rolls lay doubled up in his
driving-seat with blood upon his lips . . .' The reporter emphasizes
his presence all the time: he had been standing only 260 feet from the
crash. Earlier 'I could see him leaning forward in his driving-seat, eager
to make a correct estimate of the distance . . . As I stood near the
palisade . . . At that very instant, while watching the rudders do their
work, I saw them break adrift . . . About a dozen of us, all breathless,
came up to the wreck . . . Mr Rolls's face was ashen grey and a large
blue bruise marked his forehead . . .' Equally breathless, personal
pronoun journalism had arrived.

The style quickly becomes characteristic of the paper. The correspondents are everywhere, making personal comments on MPs as they
speak, or interviewing firemen striking for higher wages, running with
soldiers on army manoeuvres. Wherever possible, direct speech is
used. The paper is filled with awful murders, rapes of small girls, gangs

of 200 to 300 rowdy youths out rampaging and tragic suicides. There are marauding elephants, American transvestites uncovered and long-lost relatives surprisingly reunited. Everywhere the intention seems to be to produce an emotional reaction of some kind – horror, amusement, surprise. Conventional political and military news is covered too, but with a brutal brevity – the *Daily Mail* constantly advertises itself as being 'essentially the busy man's paper' without 'bigoted politics' (shurly shome mishtake?) and boasts of 'the condensation of news, the absence of long political speeches'.

The *Mail* was a runaway success for other reasons too, which remain influential well over a century later. It sold at a low price. It tried to lure readers with part-works about the Royal family, competitions, hype and big financial prizes – none of them new in British journalism, but never before applied so relentlessly and professionally. In its comment pieces it specialized in deliberately provocative and often silly questions ('Should the Clergy Dance?') designed to stimulate debate. Any controversial writer would be used, whether or not the *Mail* approved of him. Max Beerbohm, the cartoonist and satirist, for instance, was used with the disclaimer that 'we do not accept the very wide responsibility of identifying ourselves with Mr Beerbohm's opinions' – just like the paper's use today of the formula, 'the *Mail* does not agree with X but prints his views in the interests of debate'. It realized early that gloom and panic sell papers, and campaigned relentlessly against Germany in the decade before the First World War, running fictional series about invasions and losing no chance to bash the beastly Hun.

But the real secret of success was its reading of what news meant, as against the high-minded rival broadsheets of the era. 'It is hard news that catches them, features that hold them' said Harmsworth; and again, 'Explain, simplify, clarify!'[4] It is impossible to read the young *Daily Mail* without being reminded of the rawer papers of early Victorian England, the *Observer* of the 1840s or the *News of the World*, or *The Times* of the 1850s. It represents a revolution in the proper sense of a return to forgotten earlier ways of doing. There is a self-consciousness and sometimes a salaciousness about its reporting which is absent from the blunter, more innocent-seeming papers of half a century earlier, but its notion of news is remarkably similar. Today, lacking the torrent of mundane horror available in the 1890s, tabloid editors use sexual excitement and one-sided politics to stir their readers. But stories told through real people, intended to arouse anger, laughter or fear, remains the best definition of tabloid 'news' – not what is most important to policy makers, but what makes the reader's heart beat just a little faster.

Often wars shake up journalism, but for a variety of reasons the First World War did not have a revolutionary impact on the reporting of news in Britain. Unlike the Napoleonic Wars, the Crimea or Vietnam, it is remembered through poetry, not prose. All British papers carried reams of facts – each move and countermove in the trenches was faithfully recorded, and maps supplied to help – but of the reality of this most terrible of wars, the horror and the stink, the blood and the misery, very little appeared. Official censorship was part of the reason. The most famous despatches printed were early on, during the British army's pull-back from Mons in August 1914 when the *Daily Mail*'s Hamilton Fyfe and two *Times* reporters were caught up in the draggle and slither of the retreat. The latter's story has much of the drama of earlier war reporting:

> It was a retreating and a broken army, but it was not an army of hunted men . . . since Monday morning last, the German advance has been of almost incredible rapidity . . . They advance in deep sections, so slightly extended as to be almost in close order, with little regard for cover, rushing forward as soon as their own artillery has opened fire . . . Our artillery mows long lanes down the centres of the sections, so that frequently there is nothing left of it but its outsides. But no sooner is this done than more men double up, rushing over heaps of the dead . . . They could no more be stopped than the waves of the sea.

Other acts of real war reporting occurred, notably in the Gallipoli campaign, an appalling disaster, during which British and Australian correspondents including Rupert Murdoch's father managed to get close to the action. There were some 200 British reporters at the Western Front and many proved ingenious at avoiding the censors, slipping through lines in ambulances or on bicycles, disguising themselves and so on. Men like Fyfe, George Curnock and Ferdinand Tuohy took great risks: for a while the *Daily Mail* used ordinary soldiers' letters home and their photographs to give the coverage greater vividness. But the ruthless censorship imposed by Lord Kitchener began to bite by the end of 1914. Fyfe was exiled to Russia to report from there and when Northcliffe's papers defied Kitchener's ban on reporters on the battlefield, Kitchener threatened to shoot journalists who remained.[5]

So journalism declined. It turned to ferocious political campaigns on the home front – one about the shortage of high-explosive shells led to the *Mail* being publicly burned outside the Stock Exchange. Papers ran patriotic German atrocity stories, many of them cynically invented. There was gung-ho propaganda, and much printing of official reports. Even the official history of *The Times* admitted: 'The atmosphere of the trenches in France and Flanders, as it was sensed and smelt and remembered by the men who were there, hardly got into the despatches of any war correspondent.'[6] And there was more to this than censorship. This was a huge slaughter very close to home which debouched its mutilated victims by train into London every day of the week. The future of the empire was at stake, and so was the stability of British society. Again, the history of *The Times* is frank: 'A principal aim of the war policy of Printing House Square was to increase the flow of recruits: it was an aim that would get little help from accounts of what happened to recruits once they had become front-line soldiers.' It was a bad war, badly reported.

The 1920s and 1930s were a hugely important time for our sense of what news could be; but you would pick little of that up from the Establishment broadsheets of the inter-war years. *The Times* was not very different from the paper as it had been in the 1880s. It began with pages, perhaps four, of small advertisements, for parlourmaids and grooms, business opportunities and properties for rent, followed by verbatim court reports, generally unsensational, sporting news and lists of results. Recognizable stories did not start until six, seven or eight pages into the paper, and even then most of them were horribly dull. The edition of 16 February 1927, taken at random, gives a flavour of this. There is a long report of an inquiry into unfair competition in the pottery industry, which had now concluded; an account of an argument between the Food Council and bakers' organizations about the pricing of bread; a report of a lunch where representatives of the chemical industry heard a talk about imperial markets; lists of army promotions, the meetings of various clubs and societies, from Labour

Party factions to the Vintners Company and committees of the London County Council, committees for Prayer Book revision, and so on.

Here and there you find flashes of human life – a boy is bitten by an Alsatian and dies of tetanus. There is a serialization of Winston Churchill's new book on the war, and some good letters. The foreign news is extensive and excellent. But the general impression is that this is, indeed, less a real newspaper than the notice board of the Establishment. 'Lady Redesdale will give a small dance for her daughters on February 28 at 26, Rutland-gate . . . Sir Guy Grant is suffering from an attack of influenza . . . Sir Henry Lunn was prevented by the fog from leaving London on Saturday for New York, to address the Sulgrave Institute on George Washington's birthday . . .' Turn to the same day's paper ten years later, in 1937, and little has changed. Grooms are still in demand and dogs are still a problem – a boy has been bitten by an Airedale, this time, rather than an Alsatian. Military appointments, naval news and extensive foreign coverage, by now of the Spanish Civil War, is still fundamental to the paper, along with the parliamentary debates and law reports. Home news, which we don't get to until page thirteen, is sparse.

It was the middle market papers which led the news business – Beaverbrook's *Daily Express*, the drifting but still formidable *Daily Mail*, and later the first great daily paper of the working classes, the *Mirror*. Reading these papers now, you get a vivid sense of the arrival of forms of modern newspapers – lots of celebrity gossip, lots of disaster, mixed with endless competitions, the new-fangled crosswords and 'what is the world coming to?' complaints. It is the age of speed – faster aircraft, faster cars, trains, women. Yet the aircraft and cars, at least, are still new enough to be ferociously dangerous, so the papers are crammed with disasters and deaths, often of the rich and famous who could afford to buy tickets and open-topped sports cars. 'Yacht race ends in tragedy . . . Tragedy of Sweater that came off when seized', says the *Mirror* on 4 May 1931; 'Opera Star Dead . . . Car Crash Sequel' it reports five days later. Dancing girls have terrible accidents, heiresses die in plane crashes, airships go down in flames. The great editors of the day are the ones who can get the most details, quickest, into the most comprehensively rewritten story, true or not. As now, the papers realize that readers need to recognize and follow a limited cast of characters. Some, like the political stars, Oswald Mosley or Jimmy

Maxton, are self-selecting. By modern standards, there is still an unfeasible quantity of aristocracy on the pages, with duchesses still losing their pearls ... though at least the younger ones are now behaving badly, rather than simply attending dances or getting married.

Increasingly, though, the newspaper celebrities are from show business. 'Miss Beatrix Gwendoline Edna Renwick, the missing 17-year-old actress, was arrested yesterday outside the Gretna Green smithy while she and her lover, Mr Jack Ellison, of Brighton, were asking whether they could get married,' reports the *Mail* on 6 October 1930. Ellison tells its reporter: 'She is a charming girl and a good sport. I fell in love with her. We had some parties at her diggings and we ... decided to elope.' Television has not properly arrived, so the gossip is still about theatre and cinema stars, even radio stars. But, as now, they mostly arrive from America. People complain today about the US-dominated global culture. But because Britain imported so many Hollywood films, and had no indigenous television industry then, British papers of the inter-war period actually seem more American-ized. It is the world of P. G. Wodehouse and Noel Coward, when money and glamour are arriving from New York on every sailing.

But America offered a fresh dose of sensationalism too. There is a stream of jaw-dropping stories from the age of Prohibition and Al Capone, and of Hollywood in her golden years. 'Girl Holds Bank for 2 Hours at Gun Point' reveals the *Mirror*'s New York correspondent on 1 November 1938: 'It was 8.30 in the morning when the girl swung through the doors of the bank, stepped up to the counter and, as the cashier leant forward, drew a gun from under her jacket. "It's a hold-up, kid," she said . . .' On Saturday 5 June 1937 the *Mail*'s special Hollywood correspondent reports on a wild party

> at which Wallace Beery, broad-shouldered he-man of the films, is said to have knocked out three men who were paying unwhole-some attentions to girls ... The party is alleged to have been an orgy staged by one of the leading companies for the entertainment of visiting film salesmen ... The girls complain they were transported to a house decorated like an old-time mining camp with champagne and whisky bottles on the tables ...

There were hundreds of such stories: America offered sex, violence and a glimpse of the world that was coming.

The American stories also helped British readers to muse on progress, just as they would worry about designer babies, superbugs and Botox treatments seventy years later. 'The United States, usually regarded as the land of exuberant youthfulness, is rapidly becoming a nation of older people . . . both men and women are spending yearly a greater proportion of their resources in imparting to their figures and faces an appearance of youthfulness. The nation is now spending more than £20,000,000 a year on cosmetics,' reported the *Mail* in October 1930. It is reassuring to know that the 'experts' were no more accurate then than today, predicting that by the 1940s American men 'beardless since the beginning of this century, would again blossom out in "clouds of beard" and that women will return to pompadours and long tresses . . . the sun-tan craze is on the wane'. Still, the papers were full of arguments, often got up by editors, about society's direction: should married women work, are you glad you married?

The 'survey' and the 'scientists warn' story also dates from this period. Authorities of any kind are used to raise something the editor thinks of general concern. The *Mirror* of 4 May 1931 reports a Father Woodlock warning of the 'temptations involved in the new craze for young unmarried couples taking hiking holidays together'. Increasingly, divine warnings were replaced by medical ones. The *Mail* for 6 October 1930 reports the peril of the 'must-get-slim' craze which, according to a 'distinguished' London surgeon, involved female lunchers dining off only milk and buns, amounting to 'an unwitting attempt at suicide'. It has all the hallmarks of a *Mail* scare today – the physician of the utmost fame goes on: 'It is heartbreaking to discover the number of cases of young women who have come into my hands in a wickedly under-nourished condition, which they have admitted was due to their determination to achieve boyish figures.' The doctor is not named, nor is his hospital.

Were the young people of today better, or worse, than their parents? In May 1931 the *Mirror*, for instance, reports a row between an actor, Ernest Thesiger, and younger theatre people. Thesiger had described

two awful things that happened this week. One was the case of a
young man at a party who was dared to cut his throat, and did it:
the other was of a young girl who declared that she had just

married a millionaire and 'hated him like hell!' Mr Thesiger added:
'The reason our young people do these mad and terrible things
is, I believe, because they have nothing to do and are bored.'

His younger opponents, interviewed by the *Mirror*, were reassuring:
'The Hon. Miss Gladys Jessel, daughter of Lord Jessel, who runs a
Mayfair shop, said: "Most young people are too busy working to spend
their time doing 'mad and terrible things'."'

Away from the great events, life is almost familiar. Domestic
stories are written, in the popular papers, much as they are today.
Short sentences, short paragraphs, simple headlines, with the facts
compressed into the intro; plenty of direct quotations, and much use
of the personal pronoun by reporters, even if they are still mostly
anonymous ... the world they describe may look and sound different, with its bobbed women gazing out through heavy eye make-up,
and its pride in empire and its jazz music, but the journalism is
modern. The news story must connect. Increasingly it does so by
stunts cooked up in the newspaper office – the memoirs of journalists
from the *Daily Mirror, Daily Express* and *Mail* in this period are full of
self-congratulation about how working-class readers were given a night
out at the Savoy, or involved in some publicity-driven wheeze which
brought a little colour into their lives. In retrospect, this may be the
beginning of a slippery slope which led to far too much power accru-
ing to the office-bound editors and too little to reporters, and thus,
eventually, to a dangerous lack of awareness of the outside world. But
it didn't seem so then. Intense competition meant that news must
have an emotional content. It must shock, depress or delight. News
was not what *The Times* of that era still thought it to be, a progressive
accumulation of facts about major world events: it was becoming an
addictive emotional food to be manufactured in conditions of ruthless
competition.

This competition was producing another now-familiar aspect of
news gathering: lying. In the struggle to feed the news machine, many
stories were made up, either through embellishment so ornate that the
original event disappears, or through simple invention. By the thirties,
the public was cottoning on too. A song published in 1932 asked:

> What shall we put in the daily paper?
> Suicide of linen draper,

Duchess poisoned by noxious vapour,
  Early in the morning.
Awful international crisis;
Idiot reader wins three prizes . . .

Some of it's truth and some is lying
What's the odds if the public's buying?
Journalists never leave off trying,
  Early in the morning.[7]

It is rare for journalists to admit making stories up, but some brave souls have done. Henry Williamson, who went on to write *Tarka the Otter* and other novels, started in Fleet Street and left a short memoir he called *The Confessions of a Fake Merchant*[8] in which he described the humiliations of having accurate stories spiked because they were inconvenient or being forced to distort the facts. But it went further. He faked stories, innocent ones mostly. One day, he was being attacked by his editor for falling down on a story and replied that he had a better one:

'Well, what have ye got?'
'The pigeons of St Paul's have been raided by a very fierce and rare hawk, called the peregrine falcon,' I replied, inventing the story as I went on; 'I saw it myself as I came from the Communists' Meeting in Cannon Street Hotel . . . Crowds were watching.'
'It's a good story!' cried the editor, one crease unfolding on his brow. 'Here, Newell, put it on page one. Make it a Top.'

Williamson continued:

These harmless stories were easy to do. I invented a dog under the girders of Ludgate Circus bridge, and its rescue by a man on another man's shoulders standing on the top of a bus. A porpoise also came up the Thames while I was a space-reporter [i.e. paid by the amount of space he filled up in the paper] on *The Weekly*; it came in again the next Saturday too, its adventures being chronicled in other Sunday papers. The falcon must have reappeared too, for I saw accounts of its raids . . . and I hadn't written them.

One of his friends, he said, had invented an entire honeymoon colony of tents in Sussex, where young couples were living because of London's housing shortage.

And once a story is printed other reporters who don't wish to be caught out or seem slow, simply repeat it. In the inter-war period a staple of 'human interest' reporting was the dockside story. As the great liners docked or prepared to sail, reporters would be sent to interview passengers to gather gossip or sentimental stories. One eminent reporter admitted being sent to Liverpool by his paper to do this 'shipside' work but finding nothing interesting at all. In despair, he went drinking at the local press club and, egged on by local colleagues, decided to make up a story about a Shropshire man and woman who were lovers. The man went off to Canada to make his fortune, sent home optimistic letters but then stopped writing. His lover gave him up and eventually emigrated to Canada herself, ending up as a prosperous woman who did voluntary work in a hospital. There she found her fiancé. He was a broken man who had failed in business and, shamed, had been lying in his letters all along. After being reunited, he recovered, made money in property, and they married. The reporter claimed to have met them on a nostalgic return visit to Shropshire, via the SS *Urania*. To his horror, the news desk in London liked it so much that they cabled their Montreal reporter to meet the pair off the boat when they returned to Canada, to find out more. The Liverpool journalist was shaking: 'I would be fired! My God! I shall never forget those days of agonised waiting for the *Urania* to arrive and the blow to fall. My prematurely grey head dates from that time.' In fact, when the day came, he found the interview there, on the main news page, at great length and in great detail: 'Of course, you see at once what had happened. The Montreal man, too, had to hold down his job. I wiped the sweat off my brow.'[9]

The story contains an important psychological essence which explains how lies can continue undetected in journalism. People want to believe them. In particular, other reporters, desperate for copy, hate finding out that there is no story, particularly if they are freelance and paid by results. Phillip Knightley, who we met earlier, recalls making up a story after the war when he was working for the inaptly named Sydney newspaper *Truth*. He was racing to find a front-page lead because another story had collapsed. His news editor told him to use his 'fucking imagination'. Knightley spotted a story about an indecent assault conviction in a suburb of the city after a youth had pressed his groin against a girl in a train corridor. 'To my everlasting shame – I can only plead that I was just twenty-four and very ambitious – I obeyed Finch and used my imagination. I invented a story about a pervert known only to his victims and the police as "The Hook". The Hook, who was unemployed, spent his days travelling the Sydney train network armed with a length of wire cunningly contrived from an old coat hanger.' He used it to hoist up girls' skirts, wrote Knightley, making up horrified quotes from police officers and victims. It made the front page and rival papers struggled to catch up: 'Some rival journalists may well have guessed that it was an invented story but knew better than to try to tell that to their news editors.' More strikingly, when a call finally came from the police, it was to tell Knightley that they had caught the Hook: either he had stumbled upon a true crime, or it was a copycat attempt, or the police were massaging their reputation by arresting some pathetic character and framing him. 'I decided that the last explanation was the most likely and, filled with guilt, swore that would be the first and last time I would ever make up a story.'[10]

While British hacks were creating a lighter, less trustworthy journalism for the consumer age, most of their papers were controlled by appeasers, like *The Times*, or were so blithely anti-communist and optimistic, like the *Daily Express*, that they did not see the international conflagration coming. The Second World War was difficult for the British press in all the obvious ways – there was paper rationing, many of the brightest journalistic stars went off to fight (Cudlipp was among them, though he started the British forces' newspaper, *Union Jack*), Fleet Street was bombed, distribution was difficult and advertising shrank dramatically. Unlike the First World War, with its almost static front line, access to this war was hard for field marshals to control. Newspapers, though uniformly patriotic, did not easily accept the censorship rules that applied in 1914–18. Society was less deferential, and in a 'people's war' the reporters often felt they were working for the ordinary troops as well as their families at home. Famous reporters were bylined; there was more dramatic use of front-page pictures and maps; there was very little pure propaganda make-believe, by compari-son with 1914–18. Yet when it comes to the question of this chapter –

what is news? – wars are almost dull. A war of national survival is the hardest of hard news, affecting every reader emotionally, and full of unexpected twists, terrible defeats, rousing victories. In the years of Dunkirk, the fall of Singapore, Alamein and Berlin, the question 'what is news?' is a stupid one.

Even reading through *The Times* during 1939–45, what is striking is how little it tries to spare its readers the reality of the fighting and the fact of defeats. The first phase of the war, with the defeat of France and the retreat of the British Expeditionary Force from Dunkirk, is dominated by official communiqués, but the momentous events are reported, with photographs, very much as they might be now. The propaganda view from Germany is reported, as is a surprising amount of political news from the enemy side. For once, political speeches are worth every inch they get, though it is interesting that when Churchill's most famous speech is given, verbatim, on 5 June 1940, the headline writer ignores the phrases about fighting on the beaches, and never surrendering, and goes instead for the rather bland 'We Shall Not Flag or Fail'. As the war goes on, the reporting prose, virtually all of it anonymous, can be as tough as anything written by Russell during the Crimea. In the paper for 2 June 1941, for instance, the report of Britain's retreat from Crete, 'from an Australian correspondent', begins like this: 'For the last three days I have been watching tired, bearded men march down the gangways of the warships in which they have been evacuated from Crete – men so tired that they staggered when they walked, men whose tough army boots were in tatters on their feet.' He reports the relentless bombing and machine-gunning they suffered, their extreme thirst and the fact that they were forced to kill and eat their donkeys, and devour raw songbirds, to survive. He speaks of them smoking tea-leaves for want of tobacco and of men 'who had had their arms blown off staggering along towards the coasts in the hope of being evacuated'. It is a far cry from the official voice of *The Times* in 1916: the demands of a people's war have helped provoke better journalism.

From Austerity to Shopping: News and the Modern World

After the war, the news values of most British papers were more serious and comprehensive than at any time before or since. The communist threat, the withdrawal from empire, and the building of the welfare state provided a stream of hugely important stories that touched, potentially, every reader of a newspaper. Paper might have been in short supply, and the country a little bleak, but it was an era when foreign news seemed a matter of life and death, when millions of families were directly affected by Britain's decision to leave India and much of Africa, and when Westminster politics was both more practical and more controversial than ever. People did think of themselves as Conservative or Socialist voters, and did follow political arguments more closely. So for a paper like *The Times*, it was a relatively straightforward business to fill its columns with political and diplomatic news, though the paper retained remarkably few general reporters in Britain – around a dozen in London, at the end of the 1950s, against forty at the *Daily Telegraph*, which had another twenty in the provinces.

In news terms, the *Telegraph* was the go-ahead paper among the broadsheets. It had taken the gamble of front page news as early as 1939. Its general news values were close to those of the mid-market papers and it had a well-deserved reputation for covering dirty court stories in the filthiest possible detail. By the post-war period it had cut out the remaining signs of political bias from its news pages. Its sub-editors were told to keep paragraphs to an average of six lines, and no more than ten. Sentences had to be kept short, with no more than three in a paragraph. Foreign correspondents were told: 'No story should exceed *300 words* unless it is of paramount importance . . . The limit for average-value stories is *150 words*. Many excellent front-page stories are no longer than *50 words*.'[11] Its reporters from around the country were adept at finding humorous or harrowing local stories and its crime reporting was second to none. The *Telegraph* of the fifties and sixties might have been staffed by fine upstanding men with impeccable war records, and might have been entirely out of sympathy with the social revolution beginning to sweep the country . . . but it knew a good news story when it saw one.

The same could not in all honesty be said of the *Manchester Guardian*, as it then was, still very much the pride of north-west England, but a paper which mingled its regional news with a vigorous and acute reporting of overseas events, leaving little in between. It had some wonderful writers even then – Alastair Cooke was its New York correspondent, for instance – but it proudly emphasized its comment and editorial columns and its liberal world view over its home news reporting. This probably had something to do with the overwhelming influence of its greatest editor, C. P. Scott, who dominated it long after his death at the age of eighty-four in 1929. Scott believed the new reading public was 'half-educated, credulous, excitable, and ready to lend itself to neurotic joint movements, like those dangerous bodily swayings, which can so easily be started in standing crowds'.[12] Putting it another way, one of his employees, Howard Spring, said that Scott 'lacked more completely than any man I have ever known the human touch'. Whether you think this a good thing or a bad thing, Scott's creation was a paper which for decades after his death was superbly high-minded and intelligent, without being noticeably good at the ordinary news of the plain people of Britain.

A writer who visited its offices in Cross Street, Manchester – a plain, Victorian pile, stained with soot, now demolished – in the mid-fifties, was struck by the sepulchral calm of its editorial offices ('quiet as a library') and the brilliance of its library, which sums things up. Its financial editor required all the business staff to study Gibbon's *Autobiography* and Rudyard Kipling's *Kim* to hone their style. A good half of the paper's editorial coverage was used for reviews, nature notes and commentaries, and much of the rest was sent from the frantically busy London office. The same writer who visited it in Manchester asked: 'If a newspaper is to be judged solely on the promptness, completeness and accuracy with which it reports the news, can the *Guardian* even be considered a good newspaper?'[13] It was known then as 'a wonderful paper about the day before yesterday'. It sold about the same number of copies as the Communist Party's *Daily Worker*.

Yet it became one of the great successes of post-war journalism, and in doing so it extended the idea of what news is, and can be. If *The Times* slowly caved in to the mid-market news agenda and the *Daily Telegraph* made itself the master of hard news, the *Guardian* created a whole class of people who saw the world through its prism and who needed it as much as a Christian needs the prayer book. What saved the *Guardian* wasn't dropping the word Manchester from its title in 1959 or the move to London in 1964 or the brilliant redesigns of modern times. In the decades ahead the *Guardian* would publish

some of the best journalists of the age, from Ian Aitken, Peter Jenkins
and Michael White at Westminster to the women's page team, some
of the best foreign writers in the business, cartoonists such as Posy
Simmonds and Steve Bell and the likes of John Arlott on cricket and
wine. But its core achievement was to have found a purpose and an
audience which allowed it to seem to speak for a generation. There is
an almost total overlap in the public mind between the 'Guardian-
reading classes', 'the sixties generation' and 'the chattering classes'.
Meant nicely or nastily, it gave the paper a broadsheet agenda which
in turn created its distinctive style of news – the passionate reporting
of overseas revolutions and uprisings, the Whitehall-shaking investigations of 'diggers' like Richard Norton-Taylor and David Hencke, the
wry and balloon-pricking front-page sketches. If it did not develop
immediately into a first-rate newspaper, in the sense of completeness
and a drive to be first, it did develop the curiosity and intellect of a
good popular sociologist. It reported the doings of the tabloid press
not simply because it wanted an excuse to repeat titillating copy, but
because it was genuinely interested in what the other half read, as well
as how they lived.

So what were they reading? Going through issues of the Daily
Express, Daily Mail, News of the World and Daily Sketch from the fifties
and sixties, the first striking thing is the sheer quantity of news stories.
Crime is a heavy seller, written by daredevil correspondents who mixed
with the villains of the day and whose stories have a certain extra drama
because the death penalty was still used. Indeed one of the crime men
of the period, Victor Davis, admitted recently: 'When hanging was
abolished in 1969, much of the buzz went out of crime reporting. The
swinging Sixties swung a little less.'[14] The popular press might lead on
sensational divorces and murders, but it finds space for parliamentary
questions, odd local stories and minor diplomatic news (Nehru wel-
comed in Belgrade) that would struggle to find a place in a broadsheet
today. The News of the World in 1953 has a long and rather dewy-eyed
report of Stalin's funeral, right down to the diplomatic protocol of where
national representatives stood. In 1961 its diplomatic correspondent, no
less, reports, on the front page, about German naval hopes for new
warships, while in 1967 it carries another front-page report on a deal
between finance ministers for better withdrawal facilities for the International Monetary Fund. Like other 'populars', the News of the World

continued to run a near-comprehensive service of other news and features alongside its special fare of defrocked bigamist vicars, dirty old men photographing young girls, and lesbian orgies on foreigners' yachts. It ran excellent crime investigations, not simply of the 'I made my excuses and left' variety, and included sharp political coverage, some excellent features and even classic novels rewritten for a mass audience. For five years at the beginning of the fifties, its circulation stayed above eight million – an astonishing sale. It was a classic paper trying to cover everything a literate working-class audience wanted to know about, but also ought to know about too.

The *Daily Express* was providing a similar, somewhat more upmarket mix of politics, crime, foreign affairs and home stories. But the daily paper that really dominated the 1950s and early 1960s was undoubtedly the *Daily Mirror*. In 1964 it achieved a daily sale of five million. It had found its voice properly during the 1936 abdication crisis, when it took on the Establishment with aggressive front-page headline attacks that would not be out of place on a campaigning issue of the paper today ('Tell Us The Facts, Mr Baldwin!') and became the favoured paper of the British forces during the Second World War. This was partly because it created a fresh style of writing – short sentences, with lots of rhetorical questions and a kind of chirpy sarcasm. It learned from the aggression of New York and Chicago popular journalism and turned it to socialist purposes. During the war it first backed Churchill, then fell out with him, impatient with his elderly Cabinet and quick to criticize his military strategy. Its savage attacks on him in peacetime infuriated the wartime leader, probably helping to swing Labour's 1945 victory, and its 'shock issues' of later decades – on 'Divided Britain' for instance – set the pace for later popular political journalism. Perhaps the best tribute paid to its power came during the 1959 election when Julian Ridsdale, the Tory candidate in north-east Essex, was sufficiently worried by it that he went round the constituency with helpers early in the morning of polling day buying up every single spare copy, until he had some 500 piled up in his office by mid-morning. Something of the *Mirror*'s characteristic voice is caught from an editorial that same year:

People who denounce the Mirror say it is no respecter of persons. That allegation is absolutely true. Read on ... Does the Mirror think NYE BEVAN still has fire in his belly? YES. And silver in his hair. But if Labour wins, he will be our best Foreign Secretary for years and years and years. Does the Mirror think PRESIDENT EISENHOWER plays too much golf? NO. The hobbies of dead men are not the concern of the living . . .

So what did it consider news? Silvester Bolam, editor from 1948 to 1953, was perfectly happy to describe its news style as sensationalist:

Sensationalism does not mean distorting the truth . . . It means the vivid and dramatic presentation of events so as to give them a forceful impact on the mind of the reader. It means big headlines, vigorous writing, simplification into familiar everyday language, and the wide use of illustration by cartoons and photographs. Every great problem facing us . . . will only be understood by the ordinary man busy with his daily tasks if he is hit hard and hit often with the facts. Sensational treatment is the answer, whatever the sober and 'superior' readers of other journals may prefer. No doubt we shall make mistakes, but we are at least alive.

He did make mistakes, and was briefly jailed for one, but Bolam's defence of sensational news has never been bettered. His boss Hugh Cudlipp, distinguishing himself from Arthur Christiansen, the best *Express* editor, who believed above all in scoops and being first, said:

I felt that 'first with the news' was a drug. What newspapers were about, to me, was controversy. Stimulating thought. Destroying the taboos. Taking on the complicated subjects like economics, national health and production, and explaining them in language all could understand . . . presenting the news and views in a sensational manner in the new days of mass readership and democratic responsibility.

All this fairly describes part of what the *Mirror* was about. But no paper sells on the basis of political education. So what were the news stories that filled the rest of the *Mirror* in its glory days? Much of the news is obvious and familiar: there are plenty of royal stories, homing in on the wicked doings of Princess Margaret. They are just as fatuous as any similar ones today, if more sober and accurate – the paper is happy to lead on the eight-year-old Prince Charles having his tonsils removed

('Stimulating thought'? 'Destroying the taboos'?). It is almost as fashion-obsessed as modern papers, full of lacy ball gowns and stories about Christian Dior promising to do away with corsets. It likes death and disaster – babies in houses of death, people burned to death in their seats and plenty of the telling, if grisly, detail you can read in good early Victorian newspapers, and which was revived in the *Daily Mail* of the 1890s. It is visibly and relentlessly a paper of active reporters, tearing round the country from court cases to accidents, expected to file eyewitness stories with plenty of quotes and detail. The headline writers and office-bound rewrite men are vital to the paper's style, but they are working with fresh raw material, provided hourly. The paper doesn't exactly sing, but it roars and it cackles.

Two other kinds of *Mirror* story were becoming popular. One kind is now rare in British national papers. The other has almost taken them over. The former is the local, often mildly humorous story. On 5 January 1959, for instance, the *Mirror* has the story of a council inspector who solved the problem of cockerels on an allotment whose crowing was waking local people up by stretching wire mesh across their pens so they couldn't stretch and so would not crow. The story is detailed, written as a piece of extended comedy, and as much of its time as bicycling bobbies and Humber cars. There are locally provided stories about how the women of north Devon villages have taken up skittles, leaving their men at home while they go off to the pub; about leek saboteurs in Middlesbrough; about eccentric councillors, unfeas-ibly vast families, strange Heath Robinson inventions, musical evenings going horribly wrong, and much else. One has the sensation of local news being 'written up' by freelance journalists – exaggerated and improved with the help of jokes and 'colour'. The style can be patronizing, but in papers of this era one gets a much more vivid sense of Britain as a varied patchwork of localities than you find by reading national papers today.

This is a general trend in British news, not limited to the *Mirror*. Similarly in the *Daily Telegraph*, considered best for sheer quantity of news, coverage of the local news story has diminished. I looked at two randomly, one for 7 February 1979 and the other for 25 February 2003. Both were average-to-quiet news days during busy periods. The earlier paper was full of tales of industrial dispute; the later one was looking ahead to the Iraq War. In numbers of news pages and space available for news they were similar. In home and foreign news, the 1979 paper found space for ninety news stories, big and small. In the later one, there were only fifty-two. What kinds of news story disappeared? Politics survived relatively unscathed. So, contrary to many assumptions about news, had foreign coverage. The biggest change was the lack of local British stories. The 1979 paper has stories about boys from Hampshire getting into scrapes, about councillors from Plymouth and so on; in the later one, every story was London-based. The 1979 paper carried sex and divorce stories, including the revenge of a builder whose girlfriend left him and found he had introduced twenty rats into her home. There was also a nude skateboarding soldier caught on Brighton seafront and fined £15 for being drunk and disorderly. The later paper had stories about media celebrities. This is a trend: stories about ordinary people living in provincial Britain have almost disappeared. On 21 March 2003 *Private Eye* aptly noted that 150 column inches in the national press had been devoted to the renaming of the *Telegraph*'s diary column 'Peterborough' which reappeared as 'London Spy'; while just 100 column inches was devoted to 'news from Peterborough, or indeed anywhere in the UK outside London, in the national press last week'.

Why should this be? Britain still has a thriving local and provincial press scene, with plenty of reporters eager to earn a little extra by tipping off the London papers. There is no shortage of local news agencies, either. Could it be because London dominates modern Britain, with its concentration of money and media? But London has been dominant in news since the beginning of journalism; and the newsrooms of the capital are still filled with Mancunian, Scottish and West Country voices. The answer is that stories about ordinary life in Britain are being pushed aside by stories that are easier to write in the office – stories about new products, new consumer trends – and about brief celebrities. A deadly idleness has gripped journalism. London-based PR companies provide stories about and for their clients; television is easy to write about without leaving the newsroom – and TV people are ready to be interviewed within a short taxi ride of a Docklands office. The effect is to put an anonymous metropolitan sheen over the news, hiding the real variety, smell and vigour of the country. The reality of Britain is glossed over with the virtual reality of product launches and spurious surveys.

This is the second kind of story that is already apparent in the *Mirror* and other papers of the 1950s. The war had introduced a mania for social surveys, to help design rations, allocate scarce resources and, later, plan social policy. But the 'shock survey' and the 'scientists warn' story are developments of the moral panic story we saw examples of from the 1930s, with warnings about slimming, Americans with beards and mixed hiking holidays. After the war, experts, academics, scientists and bureaucrats started to pop up all through the press, warning, exhorting and predicting. On 6 January 1950 the *Mirror* has on its front page a story about 'The Girls Men *Don't* Marry'. It begins: 'Why is it that "again and again well-grown girls, strong, beautiful, intelligent, vital, self-reliant and potential mothers of the choicest citizens fail to marry?" a doctor asked a conference yesterday.' Dr Lindsey W. Batten of Hampstead turns out to be urging a new approach to sex education at a conference in Southport, where he says that 'Sex education should not simply be a grim statement of the facts of life. Its aim should not be merely to protect the child or the young adult from the horrible dangers of sex: it should be to give people a happy and successful sexual life.' Other expert advice has lasted less well: on 8 July 1953 the *Mirror* reports 'There's no proof that smoking is to blame – they say . . . Smokers, warned by research experts that tobacco may be killing them by causing lung cancer, can now take a reflective puff over the latest verdict. It is impossible for anyone to say "with certainty" that lung cancer can, or cannot, be caused by smoking, was the decision of another group of experts yesterday.' Instead, it suggests, coal fires may be to blame.

The trend story is meant to provoke a personal and emotional response. If you don't have the sex or violence to hook readers, then challenging their lifestyles, taste and attitudes works too – remember Cudlipp's maxim that newspapers are about controversy and stirring thought. But today, the trend or survey story has become the single most corrupted area of modern news. Some of it is harmless. When a paper conducts a street survey on the size of people's legs, or claims that a new children's toy has produced an epidemic of sore thumbs, most readers have enough media literacy to shrug or laugh. The back-of-an-envelope 'trend' invented by the feature editor's office – 'I've seen a lot of people using those new skates on the way to work, shall we do something?' – is easy to spot. But what has changed from the 1930s, or indeed the 1950s, is the authority of science and sub-scientific 'research' to direct our fears and guide our habits. We know we live in an accelerating world. Our climate, our manufactured foods, urban air quality, drinking and drug-taking habits, family cultures and holiday-ing are all potential sources of danger and risk. At the same time, we have grown to believe that anything wrong or disappointing can be fixed – cosmetic surgery, a change in diet, new medication, new surveillance techniques to stop terrorists. So we are highly suggestible. We may not be as open to moral panic stories launched by church leaders. But we are open to warnings of all medical, financial, scientific and pseudo-scientific kinds.

The trouble is that most journalists and most readers or viewers are utterly unable to measure risk; and journalism is notoriously reluctant to translate the tentative and balanced assessments of a medical research team or a scientific paper. To sell papers, news must move. Often that means provoking fear. It needs novelty and is far removed from, for instance, real public health priorities. Research carried out by the BBC journalist Roger Harrabin for the King's Fund found that, looking at BBC news programmes, it took 8,571 deaths from smoking for each story on the subject compared with 0.33 deaths from vCJD to produce a story about that disease.[15] The Oxford professor who proved that smoking causes cancer, Sir Richard Doll, told Harrabin that journalism's hunger for novelty often simply resulted in scaring the public: 'You like things that are new, but unfortunately things that are new are often wrong. By the time clear evidence is available, it may no longer be interesting to the media.' The BBC, like other organizations, has guidelines now to help pres-sured news editors grapple with the prominence that might be given to something frightening sounding (such as Asian avian flu) but small-scale, and how to balance risks (such as using the triple vaccine MMR on your child, as against risking measles). But most of us are barely numerate when it comes to risk, and highly suggestible. Harrabin has pointed out that if the cancer-causing risk of a useful drug is estimated at 0.01 per cent and then upgraded to 0.02 per cent, you are still only talking about two patients in 10,000 being affected; yet the emotive headline 'Cancer risk doubles' would be factually accurate.

To this can be added the failure of much journalism to revisit the embarrassing sites of past scare stories and report what then happened, or did not. At one point it seemed that 'mad cow disease', in its vCJD form, was going to be a killer of huge numbers of hamburger-eating British children. The minister John Gummer was savagely attacked for implying that burgers were safe, and indeed feeding his daughter one in front of the cameras. This is still a matter of controversy. Yet in the end, Gummer may have been far nearer the truth than the editors whipping up a frenzy of fear. Similarly, though no one can ever be quite sure, the vast alarm caused by the so-called Y2K millennium bug, which was going to have aircraft falling from the air, public transport systems grinding to a halt and banks simply seizing up as the new year dawned, was probably grossly, and expensively, overstated as a threat. Survey stories, trend stories and moral panic stories are old in journalism. But in a time when science is so powerful and people are less reluctant to accept life's risks, the need for better and clearer reporting of what risks are real, and of the need to balance different risks, is fairly obvious. Conscientious science and consumer reporters are trying: they are an honourable minority.

Sex Stories: A Very Short History

Another major complaint made about today's news values is that British journalism is unhealthily fixated on sex: in a long-lost, better world, news was about matters public, not pubic. But to read a wide range of papers is quickly to understand that 'dirty stories' have been enthusiastically used throughout the history of British journalism. The appetite for them seems constant and sharp, even if the surrounding laws and conventions about taste keep changing. Victorian, Edwardian or mid-twentieth-century public life turned up more than enough 'gay love shame' and 'seedy three-in-a-bed' romps to content the most manic of modern editors. The revelations about the entertainer Michael Barrymore may have shocked British readers in the early 2000s; but they were given fewer details about his gay sex life than readers who followed the Oscar Wilde trial more than a century earlier. Nor was Victorian journalism as universally innocent or homophobic as later historians sometimes pretend: W. T. Stead, discussed earlier, said at the time that if everyone guilty of Wilde's offences was to be jailed, 'there would be a very surprising exodus from Eton and Harrow, Rugby and Winchester, to Pentonville . . .'[16]

Victorian papers were increasingly bound by the new respectability of the age, but continued to report the juiciest details of divorce cases and sexual attacks for as long as they could, as fully as they could. After the adultery court was set up in 1858, the sexual details of famous adulteries, revealed during humiliating public cross-examinations, at which hundreds of people would spend hours standing to hear the evidence, were published in papers like *Reynolds's*, the *Pall Mall Gazette*, the *Daily Telegraph* and the *Illustrated Police Budget*. *Reynolds's Newspaper*, for instance, in the 1870 case of two transvestite men (Ernest Boulton and William Park who dressed up with padded chests and went round music halls leering at men and inviting them outside), published details of the condition of Boulton's anus. And the public humiliation of David Mellor was certainly no worse than that of Sir Charles Dilke's three-in-a-bed romps, exposed in 1886. The Commons had ignored the sex stories pouring into the Sunday papers in Edwardian times, but when, by the twenties, the divorce courts seemed to be filling with too many members of the social and political Establishment, parliament passed an act banning the reporting of 'indecent medical, surgical and physiological details calculated to injure public morals'.

It was censorship, rather than a lack of interest in sex stories, that kept the British press relatively 'clean' during the middle of the twentieth century – the vast interest in 'pornographic' books by Radcliffe Hall, D. H. Lawrence and even Joyce showed the appetite was there, while Sunday papers constantly probed the limits of acceptability, and made rich profits doing so. British hypocrisy ruled: sex was acceptable when accompanied by a thick dousing of outrage. There is a well-known story about a *News of the World* editor after the Second World War who commissioned a readership survey, noted from it how few readers admitted to liking sexy stories, so took them at their word and removed the stories . . . and was promptly fired for terminal stupidity. But you can take things too far the other way. When the *Daily Star* merged with the soft-porn *Sunday Sport* in 1987 under the editorship of Mike Grabbert and tried to take the tits-and-sex-stories agenda to its illogical extreme, with endless stories about kinky sex, pictures of a topless fifteen-year-old schoolgirl and more nipples than a field of breeding sows, it was a famous disaster. Readers did not want to be seen with the paper, which could not be explained away as a bit of harmless fun; advertisers and staff fled, and the deal had to be unwound again. Readers, it seems, like a bit of sex and titillation, but only in the context of something they could defend to friends as a newspaper. Anything more they can buy in cellophane wrapping from the newsagent separately.

Though there was plenty of sex in the Sunday papers and even some sex in the *Daily Mirror* – saucy cartoons, suggestive stories and the odd out-of-focus glimpse of female flesh – it was undeniably the arrival of Murdoch's *Sun* that produced the modern sex revolution in British news. The story of the *Mirror*'s decline and its defeat by the upstart *Sun* is well known. It is a story of one newspaper group, IPC under Cudlipp, losing its hunger and becoming preachy and complacent, while the young Rupert Murdoch and his first *Sun* editor Larry Lamb attacked from below, appealing to the more consumerist working-class Britain the *Mirror* had only tipped its hat to. The simple, propaganda, version of the story has Murdoch introducing naked breasts and raging right-wing politics and the innocents of proletarian England falling for both. In fact, looking purely at the news values of the *Sun*, the story is much more interesting than that.

The *Sun* hired many subs and reporters directly from the *Mirror* but introduced more sex, and franker language. It was no coincidence that Murdoch by then also owned the *News of the World*. Its exposés had helped educate a new and more sexually open generation. To start with the *Sun* style was to use bought-in books, advice columns and readers' letters for exactly the same purpose. The first page three topless model, Stephanie Rahn, who appeared in December 1970, was offering men nothing that they couldn't buy already: indeed, early *Suns* already seem as dated and innocuous as saucy postcards from the thirties or the early version of the *News of the World*. But the stream of thinly disguised 'how to do it' sex features and book extracts followed.

Within a few years this had run out of steam, simply because most people had learned the basics of sexual technique, or realized they could get more detail and raunchier reading in men's and women's weekly magazines. The topless models, sniggering and the atrocious puns continued, and still do; but they were never terribly shocking and now seem as relevant to modern life as the Bayeux Tapestry. When the *Sun* launched an angry save-our-topless models campaign directed at Clare Short in 2004, with page after page of gamely grinning models, it seemed merely limp and embarrassing. Both Lamb and his more famous successor Kelvin MacKenzie were – like Murdoch himself – personally slightly puritanical about sex. They knew it drove up sales but they wanted it to be sanitized and safe. They didn't want homosexuality discussed in the paper. Their favoured euphemism 'bonk' sums up the *Sun*'s actually rather unerotic world view. It is a Donald Gill, or Beryl Cook word.

What really marked out the *Sun* was the fusion of sexually explicit coverage and celebrity coverage. It was a logical development. Part of the problem for popular papers had been where to find the sex stories: there are never quite enough naughty vicars and evil sex cults to go around, certainly for daily journalism. No better excuse had been found by editors than the punishment of famous people, from Oscar Wilde through to the Profumo scandal of 1963. Then salaciousness and high moral outrage could be expertly mingled – oil and vinegar – for the perfect undressing. The ingredients for classic *Sun* style came from the warp and weft of the eighties – from the long-running royal marriage saga, climaxing with the revelation that Prince Charles and Diana had both been having affairs; from a new generation of TV soaps, notably the BBC's *EastEnders*, with its sensational subject matter and its real-life romances and scandals; from the exposure of sixties-generation politicians for activities ranging from gay spanking to multiple affairs; and not least, from the emergence of PR 'gurus' like Max Clifford who milked the market for celebrity sex revelations, acting for the sneaks and sneaked-upon alike. Suddenly it seemed everyone was at it – Major Ronald 'massage parlour' Ferguson; the store boss Ralph 'five-times-a-night' Halpern; the cricket captain Mike 'rough' Gatting; the TV presenter Frank 'stockings and suspenders' Bough; the Tory MP Harvey 'spanking' Proctor . . . and on and on and on. Bishops, much-loved television celebrities, Paddy Ashdown, then Liberal Democrat leader, quiz-show hosts, pop stars, footballers – even Kelvin MacKenzie himself, caught with his girlfriend in Barbados – there was, and is, a never-ending stream of stories of sexual mis-behaviour.

Some of the reasons are humdrum. Mobile phones, electronic listening devices, better and faster telephoto lenses, text messages, emails and the services of corrupt telecommunications engineers have all made it far easier for investigative journalists to catch their prey. As newspapers began to pay higher and higher fees to mistresses, rent boys, prostitutes, the word spread and a market developed. This was the origin of MacKenzie's worst libel at the *Sun*, when he accused Elton John of bondage games with vice boys on the basis of the uncorroborated word of a male prostitute, 'American Barry', who later told the *Mirror*: 'It's all a pack of lies, I made it all up. I only did it for the money and the *Sun* was easy to con.' Of course, most of the stories printed did have at least a germ of truth, or the newspaper industry would have been bankrupted long before. The most damning evidence was often electronic, such as the excruciating taped mobile phone conversation between Charles and Camilla. But quite often the memorable details, such as David Mellor, the Tory minister, wearing his Chelsea football shirt while sucking the toes of the actress Antonia de Sancha, were merely made up to improve the tale.

The pursuit of politicians has lessened somewhat now. Tabloid editors say this is because 'life has moved on' or because Tony Blair never made personal morality an issue. A more compelling reason is that tabloids have found other ways to get sex stories into their pages without risking political or legal retribution. An impressive proportion of the 'snatched' photos of film or TV stars snogging one another on Caribbean beaches, or in London parks, are arranged by agents as part of a carefully targeted publicity strategy. 'TV stunners' or 'anguished former Corrie stunners' or radio DJs have plenty of friends who seem happy to fill the papers in about the state of their sex lives. TV shows like *Pop Idol* manufacture instant, use-and-throw-away celebrities who are anxious enough for fame and money to cooperate with the papers' need for a constant narrative of sex and rejection, splits and clinches. Digital television has proved to be another source of excuses for sex stories: 'Raunchy telly babe Jodie Marsh's wild romp with Westlife singer Kian Egan took her all the way to heaven – and yell! The *Essex Wives* star confessed yesterday: "We were so great together physically that I just couldn't help screaming out loud." ' When papers find it so easy to get sex stories, the impulse to mount expensive and legally risky investigations into people who might bite back recedes. The *Sun* has become almost an Establishment newspaper and it certainly does not spill every secret it knows.

The MacKenzie *Sun*'s most dangerous gift to British journalism, though, is in the pervasive lack of trust felt by most people in popular papers. There were always scams and stunts, but the eighties saw a

kind of madness, in which the truth ceased to matter for too many
powerful journalists. It was all a bit of a laugh at the time. But the
fabricated story which resulted in 'Freddie Starr Ate My Hamster' (he
didn't), and the report that London's Brent Council had banned black
bin bags because they were racist (they didn't) and the *Sun*'s claim
that it had interviewed the widow of the Falklands hero Ian McKay
(it hadn't) and hundreds more such scams filtered into the national
consciousness. Comedians and satirists picked up the mad disdain for
facts that was pouring out of the paper. For a long time it simply
didn't seem to matter. The *Sun* was a good read, and a bit of fun, and
sales kept rising, and the profits rolled in. But all this was bought at
the price of a general disbelief in anything that tabloid papers now say.
Good reporters continue to check their facts. Conscientious editors
decline to take exhilarating 'fliers'. But it is too late. The bond of trust
that editors of papers like the *Daily Express* and *Mirror* took for granted
in the fifties and sixties – that general assumption among their readers
that they were trying to tell the truth – had been broken. And
scrabbling for sales, around this time the broadsheets began to dabble
in the tabloid agenda.

Not Shagging but Shopping – New News Values?

Today perhaps the biggest new area of mass reporting is simply
shopping – 'news' as thinly disguised advertising. With fewer murders
and sex crimes to lavish attention on – paedophilia being the glaring
and controversial exception – editors believe that the British today are
most interested in their number-one leisure activity: buying stuff. So
shopping mad have we become as a society that the adverts, prominent
alongside the news in newspapers for 300 years, are now becoming
the news. If that sounds like hyperbole, take the London *Evening
Standard* on Monday 17 March 2003, the momentous day when
diplomacy to avert a second Iraq War finally collapsed and Robin
Cook resigned from the Cabinet. This is professionally, if briefly,
reported on the front page, and well reported later in the paper. But
page three was devoted entirely to new bikinis and tops being sold by
Marks & Spencer. The 'story' was as thin as the see-through top used
to illustrate it – simply that M&S had bought space in the fashion

magazine *Vogue* to illustrate the new line. And the newspaper's story was written in a breathless style indistinguishable from straight advertising copy: 'First it was underwear and then black polo-neck jumpers. Now it is raw sex appeal. After years spent basing its appeal on practicality, Marks & Spencer has decided earthy sensuality is the key to its new collections . . .' The point is not that the story is odd or exceptional. It is entirely typical. Any day, almost any paper, and you can find stories that are essentially puffs.

Earlier, I looked at papers typical of their era – the *Observer* of early-Victorian England, *The Times* in imperial days, the breakthrough *Daily Mail*, the *Mirror* when it sold five million. But if any paper expresses perfectly the shopping culture of the moment it is that vast, sprawling and hugely successful monster, the *Sunday Times*. Many journalists are privately appalled by it. They regard it as slack and bloated and view its commercial achievement with disdain. They miss the point: it is popular because it is so big, and so crammed with advertisements. I took this giant, twelve-section leader in the Sunday markets on a random day, 21 July 2002, and simply tried to read it in a different way, ignoring the news and columns I normally head for and concentrating instead on its advertising. It was not a prosperous time of year. The stock markets were nose-diving, the summer lull was fast approaching. Yet it was obvious that John Witherow, the editor, was also the general manager of a huge department store, a rambling emporium or virtual bazaar that dwarfs anything in Oxford Street, a place where you can buy luxury cars, scents, bracelets, cruise liner holidays, breaks in Bali, castles in Scotland, farmhouses in Dorset, Greek island hotels, offshore bank accounts, bridging loans, massage tables, wine storage cabinets, anti-ageing patches and theatre tickets. Here you can find – perhaps – your ideal partner, or become a part owner of a French vineyard, or get a job as a bursar in a private school, or become a senior mandarin at the Treasury. You can invest unimaginable sums of money in a bewildering number of schemes and companies. Like other papers – but more so – part of the allure of the *Sunday Times* is that all your fantasies and dreams are on sale inside it.

The first, news, section was dominated by car ads, with swathes of space bought by Mercedes-Benz, Vauxhall, Jeep, Nissan, Ford, Peugeot, Seat and Mitsubishi. Banks, airlines and mortgage companies were also busy selling. Then came 'Sport', very light on ads, but followed by the motoring section, which was crammed. The 'Business' section was filled with ads; the 'News Review' had few of them, until we hit a section of job ads for teachers. By the fifth section, 'Travel', the distinction between journalism and selling had disappeared almost entirely. There were 'stories' by journalists which had obviously been produced in close cooperation with travel companies, hotels or national tourism agencies. It may have been called 'Travel' but there was little here about air or road congestion, the horror of package holiday flying, or the depression of a third-rate hotel on a gritty beach when the rain never stops. 'Travel' was selling dreams. In the sixth section, 'Money', there were more dreams for sale. Ads from investment companies jostled with editorial, rather than sprawling next to it. Much of the journalism was, however, a basic information service of the kind that made *Which?* such a success, trying honestly to rank funds, mortgage deals and shares.

Almost all national papers now carry consumer 'charts' each week, trying to advise readers on the best small car, the ten best health spas, the twenty best pop CDs of the year, the latest electronic gadgets. Essentially the paper, and the journalists concerned, are selling their own standing with the reader: 'I am your paper, on your side' or 'I am the famous motoring journalist and therefore my judgements about reliability or coolness are worth trusting'. This is a difficult area for journalism. Shopping has become the national pastime; yet we are also increasingly mistrustful of authority of all kinds. A sense that a newspaper is actually in bed with the companies whose products are being marketed, or the news that journalists have been taking bribes to write about them, would be instantly damaging. Fortunately, most consumer journalists I've spoken to come across as serious, committed to their public and – if they work for national papers – are well enough paid to avoid direct bribes.

But there is corruption here too and everyone knows it. The 'freebie', a paid-for holiday so long as you write about it, or a parcel full of make-up, or free tickets to the show, is almost ubiquitous. That so much modern journalism works through baksheesh and back-handers is an open secret which only the most simple-minded readers don't spot. When I started at the *Scotsman* freebies almost always meant short trips away to see some new product launch abroad – I well remember the bitter anger and disappointment of a colleague who, after being passed over for golfing weekends in Portugal or visits to new hotels in North Africa, was finally presented with an overnight visit to a new cold store in Belgium. No great damage was done to the paper's integrity, however, partly because it was considered extremely bad form to write a laudatory piece when you returned – which may, come to think of it, explain why freebies were relatively rare in Edinburgh. But the larger use of the freebie, the flash cars loaned for a weekend or longer and the family holidays worth many thousands of pounds showered on editors purely to build up 'goodwill' are a bigger issue. Andreas Whittam Smith was worried enough about the damage being done to the trade that, when he launched the *Independent* in 1986, all freebies were banned as a point of policy . . . one that became harder to sustain as the paper struggled commercially and managers cast around for little baubles to persuade journalists to stay.

There is a scale of greasiness. If an item is a frivolous luxury, bought only by the few in a mood of self-indulgence, no one seems so bothered. Fashion journalism is notorious for the designers who hand over tens of thousands of pounds' worth of clothes, bags, shoes or trips to the powerful writers . . . but everyone sees high fashion as a kind of weird fantasy land anyway where, if you pay hundreds of pounds for a pair of shoes, you deserve what you get (sore feet). Fashion journalists work so closely with the PRs of the big houses that they are constantly in danger of becoming virtually their employees. The good ones fight this every day of their working lives. Some persuade themselves that, really, they are untouched. Toby Young, the journalist who worked for Condé Nast's *Vanity Fair* in New York in the 1990s, caught the self-delusion of a whole mini-industry well: the 'Condé Nasties' as he called them, weren't cynical: 'Admittedly, they occasionally say what advertisers want to hear, they even accept bribes in the form of luxury goods, but they still think of themselves as spotting trends rather than creating them. They're a little like a corrupt priesthood: the fact that they abuse their authority doesn't mean they've lost their faith.' Similarly with holidays or luxury cars, journalists can convince themselves that they can enjoy the trappings and benefits and yet somehow stand outside all that and deliver a completely unbiased verdict. I don't believe it. If you take the money, in the form of plane tickets or swanky clothes, you have entered a bargain and you feel awkward about not delivering, at least a little – a paragraph here, a commercially useful little gush or adjective there. Really powerful arbiters of taste, the top motoring journalists or fashion queens, with the car manufacturers and designers fawning over them, may be able to snap at some of the fingers feeding them, but most journalists will quietly, and a little shame-facedly, complete the transaction.

Returning to the *Sunday Times*, the eighth section, 'The Funday Times' was fascinating. It is the children's part of the paper, full of cartoons and quiz questions. But it was also intensely commercial. On its first page was a cartoon featuring Scooby-Doo. Was this related to the general release of the summer blockbuster film? No mention of it there. But halfway into the section was an advertisement feature which said: 'Everybody's going Scooby crazy and to celebrate the movie release, we've put together this dog-a-logue [that's Scooby's answer to a catalogue!] so you can see some of the grooviest Scooby stuff that's out on the streets!' This included Scooby Nutella spread which, like the HP Scooby-Doo pasta shapes, was available at ASDA; Scooby fudge-flavoured cookies, a Scooby-Doo Gameboy Advance game, a Scooby-Doo lampshade and other unmissable objects of desire. A page further on and we seemed to have returned to the editorial part of the pull-out, with a Scooby-Doo mystery photostory. But this was set at Chessington World of Adventures, the popular theme park just south of London. It featured a band called 3SL, whose new single, we read, ' "Touch Me, Tease Me", is released on August 12'. Film, band, theme park . . . all on one brief tabloid-sized page of product placement. Other parts of the children's pull-out were pushing books, rival bands, computer games and goalkeepers' gloves.

The next *Sunday Times* section was in some ways the toughest to analyse in this regard, because 'Culture' is high-minded: Bryan Appleyard writing on why the British Museum needs an injection of funds was about as traditionalist a piece of high-culture journalism as one could imagine, while the film reviews, interviews, art show criticism and so on that followed was serious, intelligently written stuff. But what of the week's 'essential new releases' of CDs, or the lists of top films and concerts that this paper, like its rivals, runs? These are no more than bite-sized versions of reviews, one might say, and yet they are of serious commercial significance. After the book section, 'Culture' offered a newspaper guide to the best websites for buying, well, in this case, summer barbecue gear. Most of the rest of the paper is a riot of selling – kitchens, floors, knickers, knockers, Chardonnay and conservatories, lipgloss and Toyotas, mossy brickwork, slate and pebble-dash, long shadows on green lawns, weatherboard and wisteria, Norman manor homes and Norfolk hideaways – along with the ads for 'S Ken fan 2 db bd 2 bth flt . . .'

For those who believe that newspapers hold a mirror up to society, then the message of the *Sunday Times* and its competitors is that Britain has gone shopping. On this issue, the 'puff panel' just below the main paper's front-page masthead carried three items, no doubt intended by the editor to appeal to the broadest possible cross-section of readers. One of them was simply about Tiger Woods's awful day at the British Open Golf Championship. What of the other two? One was puffing an article on British surfing, which turned out also to be about selling – in this case the boom in surfing clothes, which is helping finance the sport down in Cornwall. The second was pointing us to an interview with Sadie Frost, the ex-wife of Jude Law. Did she have something to sell too? Why yes: a new sci-fi movie she is investing in, and 'Frost French, the cheeky pret-a-porter fashion label she runs with her pal'. Both these got a mention, alongside carefully risqué facts about Frost's liking for pole dancing and as near to a sexy come-on photo as a seven-month-pregnant woman can manage.

All of the examples I've given from just one paper on one day are taken for granted by most people in the newspaper business. It is also what journalists, thousands of them, actually do. In this paper, after the first hard-news section, I counted almost as many main bylines which were essentially about selling something, fifty-seven of them, as on traditional journalistic stories – sixty-two. And editors who allow their reporters to attack the bigger commercial interests that sustain them are taking big risks. They will be reminded of it, first by their advertising executives, and then at a board meeting or by the proprietor. Being a department store is a wonderful thing, but it rather limits your opportunities to be an urban guerrilla too. This doesn't mean editors are generally supine or that proprietors are craven with their advertisers. Lord Thomson, who once, jokingly (half jokingly), defined journalism as the stuff between the ads, and who built his newspaper empire in Britain on the basis of an aggressive new way of selling ads, nevertheless stood up for his editors when they ran campaigns, as Harry Evans did in an earlier version of the *Sunday Times*, which offended major advertisers. When the Evans Thalidomide campaign began running hard in 1974 its immediate British target, Distillers, was the highest-spending advertiser on the paper and cancelled its £600,000 per annum contract at once. Thomson took it on the chin: he knew that the advertisers need the papers as well as the other way around. The biggest protection for journalistic independence has therefore been commercial muscle – a high-selling newspaper can tell an advertiser to get lost rather more easily than a struggling one.

But the biggest question is whether advertising limits and reshapes the news agenda. It does, of course. It's hard to make the sums add up when you are kicking the people who write the cheques. On the day I chose to analyse the *Sunday Times* its main story was about government proposals to track all 24 million British-registered cars by satellite and then charge them for the road use they incurred, a form of road pricing discussed by the new transport secretary, Alistair Darling. By any standards, it was a good story, a cut above many Sunday political splashes in that it actually had quotes from the minister to back it up. The paper, again quite legitimately, had taken a hostile line: 'The spy-in-the-car plan was attacked yesterday . . . as an unprecedented invasion of privacy as well as "anti-motorist",' said the front-page story. A leader inside agreed, beginning: 'The car is a wonderful invention. Cocooned in your steel capsule you can enjoy creature comforts that rival those in the living room – a well-cushioned chair, warmth, music and protection from the elements . . .' Again, a popular point of view. But that's lucky: this is a paper almost toppling over with the adverts of the big car companies.

As ever, we should beware of thinking the rampant materialism of British journalism is new. In many ways Britain in the 2000s seems like Britain in the 1920s, a hedonistic, somewhat shrill and pleasure-fixated nation. The first time round, of course, the country was like that in reaction to the horrors of the First World War, whereas now it is the result of a half-century of relative European peace and prosperity. But then, as now, papers were selling aspiration, the possibility of sudden wealth and life-changing prizes. Alfred Harmsworth is said to have met a tramp on London's Embankment, who told him his dream was to have £1 a week for the rest of his life. Harmsworth promptly launched a £1-a-week competition, a kind of lottery, in his first paper *Answers to Correspondents* in 1889, calling it 'the Most Gigantic and Simplest Competition the World has seen', thus laying the foundations for his fortune. This is exactly the sort of 'win your mortgage back' competition the *Mail* still brilliantly exploits today. In the later battle between the *Express* and the *Daily Herald* in the 1930s, the papers were flogging free insurance and gifts of all kinds, their canvassers careering round the country offering cutlery, underwear, mangles and tea sets as incentives for new readers who signed up. According to Charles Wintour, an editor of the London *Evening Standard*, 'It was claimed that an entire family could be clothed by subscribing to the *Express* for eight weeks.' This goes a bit further than the free CDs and cinema tickets doled out by desperate newspaper sales departments today.

News Now: Has it Changed?

Most news values have not changed. At the top of the pyramid there is, and always will be, the hardest of hard news. That means the events which change our world, appal us, amaze us, directly affect our lives. Since the development of clear modern prose English, and of cheaply printed news, the way these events have been reported has not changed much either. When it matters, we want the facts, shortly, without rhetoric. We like eyewitness reporting, with the most important facts given to us early, and with vivid detail. There is no essential difference to the way *The Times* reported the Battle of Trafalgar in 1805, patching together eyewitness accounts, and trying to shape an overall narrative to describe and explain the event, and the way it reported the drive of US forces towards Baghdad in 2003. The eyewitnesses were British naval officers in the first case and professional journalists in the second, but the principles of reporting were the same. Over the centuries, newspapers change shape, order the news differently and target different groups of people. Some slant even hard news for political effect. But the hard news agenda itself seems an unalterable part of modern urban life.

This includes, below the level of world-shaking events, the stories which touch the extreme edges of human experience. Appalling murders, child suicides, brutal separations and people who survive against all odds interest us and always will, because they make us think about what could happen to us, or to our family. Looking at news coverage of a murder in Essex in the 1790s, or in Paris in the 1850s, or in Richmond in the 1960s, one can see different styles of reporting, from the blunt, almost matter-of-fact notes of a world where murder was very common, to today's agonized coverage of urban shootings. But journalism which did not find murder interesting would represent a fantastically violent society. Murder is extreme behaviour; and all extreme behaviour is interesting to those who live in the tepid middle of things. Close by that are the stories of abnormal behaviour which help define and police the limits of the acceptable. Whether they are revelations from Victorian divorce courts, or rows between neighbours over their garden fences, these stories are interesting because they make us ask: would I do that? Or: what if that happened to me?

Then there are the news stories which come and go, reflecting the economics and interests of different generations. The empire made British journalism more outward-looking than it would otherwise be. Looking back, the daily journalism of the 1930s through to the 1980s is probably more political than journalism ever was before, and probably ever will be again. In the 1970s, strikes and industrial trouble were big stories; they aren't now. We no longer pore over shipping lists to discover whether relatives are safe, or if our investment in coffee has arrived safely. Later generations will look back with amusement on our current fascination with television stories, which will one day perhaps seem as quaint as the reprinted sermons and clerical appointments that interested Victorians. In the future, it is hard to imagine that a journalism obsessed by climate change will not develop further.

Though it is true that modern news has been heavily affected by celebrity stories and by sex stories, it would be wrong to get too steamed up about either. From my reading of old papers, the interest in sex comes and goes depending on the surrounding censorship only. It may be that we are becoming sated with our sexualized culture, a little bored by all the bonking. And today's celebrity journalism is no more fatuous than the days of Hollywood starlets or plucky fox-hunting debutantes; indeed celebrity has been democratized. Papers are showing success and glamour to their unsuccessful and unglamorous readers. As they have always done. But now part of the message is that this could be you. A celebrity culture based on manufactured pop bands, quiz-show winners and TV weather girls may be shallow – and what celebrity culture is deep? – but it is open to anyone with the looks and the luck to join it. Celebrity journalism only requires that there is a story, with constant twists and turns: no television 'stunner' who gets happily married and settles down is going to win free publicity for that. The splits and tearful reunions are part of the deal. The strongest criticism one can make of today's celeb culture is that it is cynically manufactured on an almost industrial scale ... but we all know *that*.

The more worrying trends in British news values are related instead to the growth of an office-based, editorial culture, rather than a reporters' journalism. Rupert Murdoch's Wapping revolution may have saved the economics of the national press, but it has come at a price: physical isolation in compounds, converted warehouses and gleaming new towers has undermined reporting. Once the editor thought he knew who their readers were. Kelvin MacKenzie famously described the *Sun*'s target reader as 'the bloke you see in the pub – a right old fascist, wants to send the wogs back, buy his poxy council house, he's afraid of the unions, afraid of the Russians, hates the queers and weirdos and drug-dealers'.[17] David English at the *Daily Mail* had a similarly sharp-edged view of the ideal Middle-English housewife he was aiming for. These days the marketing teams at all major newspapers have constructed complex pictures of the ideal readership profile – and journalists are trained to narrow their field of vision to find stories which flatter and intrigue only those people.

The trouble is office-bound journalists from modern newspapers become dependent on fixers: the PR men manipulating celebrity careers; the media-trained university experts; the polling companies with a story to sell. The survey is used to create health fears or moral panic, or both. 'Syndromes', from the obsessional worship of celebrities to a fear of fresh fruit, are discovered every other day. Behind a bland torrent of 'shock discovery' stories can lie deeper and darker currents. Some drug companies commission and plant research to persuade readers that there is a problem or 'syndrome' which needs to be dealt with – and, hey presto! – six months later, along comes the miracle cure. Desk-bound journalists desperate to fill their newspapers rarely have the motive, still less the expert knowledge, to question the carefully packaged story delivered on behalf of experts with a little fan of letters after their names.

With more journalists office-bound, with reporting seen as expensive, and with the massive global PR industry available through every national hack's laptop, pumping out suggestions, it is perhaps not surprising that we are also seeing signs of a closing of the gap between posh papers, or broadsheets, and the popular or tabloid papers. Apart from the *Financial Times* at one end and perhaps the *Star* at the other, all of them report the same stories about film openings, scientific discoveries, medical breakthroughs, crime, TV celebrity scandals and marriage break-ups. It is not uncommon to leaf through four tabloids and four broadsheets and find almost exactly the same stories in every one. This leads to dullness, if not childishness. Against this the media commentator Stephen Glover announced in February 2004 that, having been involved in launching the *Independent*, he wanted to try again with a rigorously upmarket paper, provisionally called the *World*. His motives included deep frustration at the convergence of news agendas: 'there are many serious voices in the broadsheets, but they exist alongside ever more lavish coverage of celebrities and daft pieces about animals . . . All this has happened over the last few years. If you study *The Times* of 1990 you will find almost no stories about celebrities or furry animals . . . It is difficult to believe we are all getting much more stupid at such an alarming rate.'[18]

Whatever becomes of his dream, he is absolutely right. Celebrity is fine, in its place. So are furry animals in theirs. But there is an idle, office-bound, marketing-directed copycat culture in modern news which is turning off readers and viewers. The biggest problems are not caused by lying or intrusion. They are caused by conformity and dullness. Remember the early Victorians. Remember the early *Daily Mail*. Remember Cudlipp's *Mirror*. The best slogan for a more vigorous and useful news agenda today would be: get out more often.

3

The Dirty Art of Political Journalism

Coming Home

Coming home to London by plane, I sometimes stare down through gaps in the clouds at the buildings I have worked in. First, coming low from east to west, the Chicagoan glinting towers of Canary Wharf, where the *Independent* was based for a few years, and which is still home to the *Daily Telegraph* and *Mirror*. A short time later towards central London, the old heart of the city, there's the wobbling smudge of buildings which is Fleet Street, now empty of journalists, except during memorial services. To the north, if there is a splash of sun on Camden, I might glimpse my first paper, the *Scotsman*'s, old London office, a white gleam. Mind you, no one seemed to spend much time actually in the office; a nearby Greek restaurant called the New Zorba was where Scotland's finest could be found, draining retsina bottles. Squinting down, I can make out a small square of soft green, which is Bunhill Fields, where Bunyan and Daniel Defoe lie buried, and where the *Independent* spent its exciting first few years. I can see a dark waving line of buildings running north to south, which is probably Farringdon Road, containing the monstrous seventies-style building where the *Guardian* lives slightly crossly with the *Observer*, its lodger in the attic.

The geography of London journalism is infinitely complicated these days, after the disintegration of Fleet Street. On the south bank of the river, there's the steel-coloured former home of the *Express* where I slowly recovered my self-respect after being fired as an editor, and taught myself how to write a tabloid column. Looking north again, there is St James's Park and a squat, award-winning 1960s tower where I earned my first good salary, at *The Economist*. A little further north still is Broadcasting House, where I learned to do radio programmes and near it, the old ITN headquarters. I never went in, but I loitered outside while waiting for my wife, who spent her evenings with the rest of the *News at Ten* team drinking expensive Chablis in the wine bar over the road. Out west, coming up soon, are the grey-white buildings of the BBC, my current employer.

But the buildings that matter most to me are the famous butter-coloured rectangles of carved stone squeezed onto the north side of the Thames, squatting on a reclaimed mudbank. The Palace of West-minster prints no newspapers and broadcasts no news. But it is the great story factory, pumping out the power struggles, scandals and sometimes the breakthrough changes in British public life that affect us all. Here, the most impressive single building in London, was where I reported for duty as a rather fat, nervous new parliamentary correspondent in 1985. I had needed to get to London somehow. I was chasing a woman working for a glossy magazine. Besides that, I had promised myself not to spend all my life in Scotland – too comfortable, too easy. I would go to London just to see what it was like. A City firm had offered me a London job as an investment analyst, paying about three times what I was earning as a journalist. There was a languid approach from the *Financial Times* too. But I thought that if I had to introduce myself to girls as a mere stockbroker I would have no chance (how naïve can you be?) and the *FT* approach frankly terrified me. I was a fraudulent financial journalist. I was scared of numbers and instantly bored by spreadsheets and quarterly reports. If I joined a rigorous City paper I would quickly be found out. But the Gods of Ink were with me: when the *Scotsman* realized I was determined to try my luck in London, they offered me the job of parliamentary correspondent. The girl I'd followed seemed, at first, delighted. I arrived at her flat with bundles of political biographies to mug up on and an Italian double-breasted suit I'd found in a sale. I had a new life. A few weeks later she chucked me out.

Nor was the job of parliamentary correspondent as glamorous as it had seemed from the outside. These were the last days of the 'paper of record', something the *Scotsman* considered itself to be, along with *The Times*, the *Guardian* and the *Daily Telegraph*. It carried at least a full broadsheet page, and often more, of parliamentary stories, sometimes little more than strings of quotes from MPs connected by the briefest of explanations. My job was to take the quotes down and stick them in. High literature this was not. And as I quickly learned, political journalism was as stratified as the cliffs of the English south coast. There was an elite, the lobby. Its older and more experienced figures were regarded with respect, if not awe. They seemed to be mostly large, florid men with a 1950s sartorial twist who yet walked lightly on their feet, like dukes' butlers. They murmured only to one another. If a junior boy, like myself, happened to pass by in a corridor they would sometimes fall silent and stare at the nearest notice board or bookcase until one had passed, when the mysterious conversation would resume. They were discussing, I later learned, lobby matters, obeying one of the rules first set down in the 1940s: 'Don't talk about lobby meetings . . . If outsiders appear to know that a lobby meeting is to be, or has been held, do not confirm their conjectures . . .'

Of course, later they turned out to be idiosyncratic, often lovable human beings who had worked their own way up. Below the grandees of the lobby were the newer, cheerier lobby hacks, including correspondents of the Scottish, Irish and English provincial papers. They took the whole thing less seriously. They bought newcomers drinks and explained the mysteries of which plastic photo pass could get you where, and how the sprawling architecture of Westminster could be negotiated. Finally, below decks entirely, were the parliamentary correspondents, or 'the gallery men', which made us sound a little like condemned oarsmen, heaving in a hulk. It was our job to produce those verbatim quotes. This meant, first of all, good shorthand. Mine was adequate. It also meant concentration – dogged concentration. Too often my concentration was merely doggy: tail-waving and eager to please, but also inclined to roll over at short notice and fall asleep during the crucial speech.

I would start work most days at 10 a.m. and attend the parliamentary committees, either examining bills or carrying out some investigation. The committees carried out their business off the long 'committee corridor', an oak-panelled thoroughfare filled with MPs smoking as they signed letters, and self-important clerks and policemen shooing witnesses and reporters in and out of the rooms. After a hard morning of note-taking, we returned to our room, which I shared with reporters from the *Financial Times*, Aberdeen *Press & Journal* and *Glasgow* (as it then was) *Herald*, the oldest national English-language daily in the world. Our stories were hammered out on typewriters and taken along to be wired to our respective head offices before lunch. This would be gobbled down in the press gallery canteen or taken in liquid form at the bar. Nuts make a good lunch.

Then we hurried to take our seats in the gallery shortly after 2.30 p.m., when following prayers, which journalists cannot attend, the real day's work began. Scottish MPs expected at least one fat paragraph in the next day's copy of the *Scotsman* and the paper was happy then to oblige them. But I would also be expected to produce quotation-based stories on any other parliamentary debates running, and go through the press releases and written ministerial answers piling up on a long table; so the word-shovelling would be constant until the main edition of the paper was away, just before 9 p.m. Then everyone who was not already in the press bar would rush to the press gallery restaurant, which stopped taking orders at the same hour. It had a special table, strictly reserved for lobby correspondents, where the great figures of the day would sit and challenge each other on obscure points of political information – James Naughtie, later of the *Today* programme, and Peter Riddell, later of *The Times*, and Gordon Greig, the handsome roguish political editor of the *Daily Mail*, and Geoffrey Parkhouse, the aristo-cratic-seeming horse-riding political editor of the *Glasgow Herald*, would engage in banter about who had the lowest majority in Wales, or how many sitting MPs had moved party, or who lost the by-election to old Stubbs in '72. Most of us learn from the generation just above, and I was lucky to learn from experienced reporters who had mostly joined the press gallery in the heyday of Fleet Street, during the 1960s and 1970s. I learned first that political journalism was a proud trade based on deep and constantly accumulated knowledge. You were expected to study the election statistics, to meet and know the MPs in your area, to read all the new political biographies and memoirs as they came out, and to have enough of a grounding in political history not to make an idiot of yourself by confusing Bevan and Bevin, or Crosland and Cross-man. Maybe some of the journalists were self-important about their knowledge, but it is a bad thing that the habit of reading and remem-bering, of following politics in detail, is unravelling today.

After a dinner of some tasteless soup largely composed of corn-flour, and dry cutlets with cabbage, or kedgeree and apple pie, washed down with a cheap wine, we gallery staff would often have to return to the chamber for the 10 p.m. vote, which in those days sometimes mattered. If it was close, we would be scrabbling for the voting lists when the papers arrived upstairs, to check for rebels or suspicious absentees. If there was an adjournment debate involving some topical issue, or anything Scottish, we had to stay for that too. I often returned to my flat long after midnight, buzzing with gossip and adrenalin. I taught myself the geography of central London by pounding the night streets for hours, until I was tired enough to sleep.

What I know now and did not then was that I was also watching the end of an era in political journalism. Parliament during the Thatcher years was still an unreformed, clubbish institution, which managed to be hierarchical and anarchic at the same time. It kept very late hours. Journalists were allowed during the summer to drink with MPs on the Commons terrace overlooking the Thames, where gossip swirled and wild misbehaviour was decently overlooked. The newspapers still carried great slabs of old-style political reporting every day. The lobby still operated in its old secretive fashion. Things were much as they had been throughout the post-war era, and indeed not dissimilar from the pre-Luftwaffe Westminster world of the 1930s. It was not a puritanical world. The amount of drinking and fornication indulged in by some Westminster journalists, in the days before dogs devoured dogs, was formidable.

In her book about Hugh Cudlipp and Cecil King, the twin genii of the old *Daily Mirror*, Ruth Dudley Edwards describes the fantastic drinking and sexual enthusiasms of old Fleet Street. She notes: 'The mystery of 1950s' journalism is how papers ever came out.'[1] The same could be said of political journalism thirty years later. High above the busy Westminster corridors were beds set aside for exhausted, all-night palace officials. They were much used by senior political editors and a range of parliamentary secretaries, energetic MPs and lobby reporters. One revered political correspondent was famous for returning covered in rainwater after sessions on nearby park benches. Another, Walter Terry, set up in a flat with the then prime minister Harold Wilson's private secretary, Marcia Falkender, siring two sons and receiving his mistress's official red boxes from government despatch-riders in his dressing gown. When *Private Eye* broke the story of a liaison between Marcia Williams, as she then was, and an unnamed political correspondent, Terry's then editor at the *Daily Mail* called him in and asked him to investigate the cracking story, having no idea it featured the man standing with a lop-sided smile in front of him.

The drinking was if anything more enthusiastic – certainly more widespread. There were then thirteen bars in the Palace, each with its own rules and ritual purposes, from the grand, gloomy Pugin Room, where MPs bought drinks for impressionable journalists, and indeed research assistants; to the burly squalor of the Sports & Social Bar, frequented by policemen and the more desperate tabloid hacks, or the Lords bar, much favoured for illicit trysts. The most-used were, and are, the press gallery bar, a cosy hell-hole where the desperate started the day and, once upon a time, where everyone finished it, and Strangers' Bar, which has now moved from its old quarters, but is still the easiest place for MPs and journalists to mingle and gossip. Ian Aitken, then political editor of the *Guardian*, was famous for his ability to pick up the phone in the old Annie's Bar and, without notes or hesitation, dictate the paper's front page splash off the top of his head. Drinks were relatively cheap and the games were endless. Two reporters were known for a particularly violent form of head-butting contest late at night, when scalps would be split and blood would be spilt. The bars have partly emptied but on a recent visit to the press bar the author was reassured to find half a dozen colleagues debating the important, complicated and delicate question of which MP they would most like to physically beat up: 'Yes, but if he was held tightly so he *couldn't* hit you back?'

The wives of some senior male editors would wait on windy rail platforms deep in the Home Counties in the small hours, knowing that if their husbands were not woken and scooped up, they would spend the night slumped on a carriage floor at the end of the line. Journalism and alcohol, as attentive readers will have noticed, go together like betting and racehorses. It is easy, indeed irresistible, to be nostalgic about this. But I should record that some excellent political journalists became hopeless alcoholics, dying early from cirrhosis or heart failure, if lung cancer didn't get them first. The mortality rate from the press gallery was relatively high. I started in the gallery alongside a fine rival reporter about my age, a handsome, hard-working, optimistic Scot with a wicked sense of humour who loved the trade and was a delight to talk to in the press gallery bar. He died, still in his thirties, in horrible circumstances, having lost his marriage, job and self-respect entirely because of the drink that was always 'part of the fun'.

The Daily Life of the Gallery Slaves

The work of a parliamentary correspondent, work which has almost disappeared over the last fifteen years, was not easy. Samuel Taylor Coleridge found it made his head ache and was too tiring. Charles Dickens was by all accounts a good parliamentary reporter in the 1830s but complained about the hard graft and discomfort: 'I have worn my knees by writing on them on the old back row of the old gallery of the House of Commons and I have worn my feet by standing to write in a preposterous pen in the old House of Lords, where we used to be huddled together like so many sheep.'[2] The work needed then, and needs now, some intelligence, more stamina, and excellent short-hand. Dickens's David Copperfield, like the author, had to buy a teach-yourself-shorthand manual and learn the dots and dashes, 'the wonderful vagaries that were played by circles; the unaccountable consequences that resulted from marks like flies' legs; the tremendous effects of a curve in the wrong place . . .' Shorthand goes back a long way – as we saw earlier, Daniel Defoe used it to report on the Scottish parliament of the early 1700s. But it developed a special place in parliamentary reporting; today Pitman's and Teeline are the favoured systems. If you have one of them you don't have to rely on tape recorders and slow transcribing afterwards.

But reporting was for a long time hampered by the sheer difficulty of hearing what was being said. The work was made easier when the old buildings Dickens worked in burned down and were replaced by the current Palace. This had specially built facilities for journalists though at first the grand new Commons chamber was so high that MPs words' were virtually inaudible to reporters. The ceiling was duly lowered but much of what was said was still very hard to hear. Reporters would work in shifts, transferring their notes from shorthand to longhand in a room behind the shelved seats of the gallery, working together to make sense of scrappy fragments. When Philip Webster joined *The Times* team in the 1970s he reckoned he needed a good 160 words a minute to get by. On really busy days, when there was a

Budget being delivered – and when it had to be reported as heard, without paper copies of the speech – reporters would send their copy in 'takes' of a few paragraphs, dashing from the chamber across a small anteroom ('the lower press gallery') to wooden telephone boxes to dictate the latest. They would light a cigarette, have a deep, fast drag, and leave it smoking for the next reporter to pick up.

Team reporting went back to the 1850s at least. In those days there was more creative work, as reporters used their own longhand notes and education to polish and reshape the speeches they heard into things of greater beauty. But then people started to want accuracy. The acres of parliamentary coverage that the young British democracy required to function exhausted hundreds of reporters. The gallery was a refuge for fast-writing, desperate drunks as well as grimly serious reporters, for the job is only intermittently interesting. When there is a great parliamentary occasion the drama is wonderful. But how many people would enjoy a play if they were required to note down every word said and then rush to the back of the auditorium to phone over the most recent soliloquy to a bored typist? One gallery man in the 1950s and 1960s for the *Daily Telegraph* complained that theatre critics had much easier lives: 'They do not have to sit, night after night, watching the entire Hamlet, or the full cycle of the Ring, put on by some local Women's Institute, with anyone's guess who may be playing or singing the lead parts.'³

Anyway, most of the time most reporters were listening not to drama but to prose of the dullest quality – social security questions, arguments over planning in Walsall, a private member's bill on hill-farming regulations. It is hard to stay attentive during long speeches and irrelevant interventions, just waiting for the moment when something significant might be said, then caught and noted down for the reading public. To change the metaphor, it sometimes reminded me of fly-fishing on a poor river – though the scenery was worse and the catch uglier. The boredom turned some people's heads and explains the wild drinking that went on simultaneously. A recent history of the press gallery quotes a pen portrait of gallery reporters made in 1890, describing reporters then as people such as ' "General" O'Hennessy, a typical fine old Irish gentleman, the pink of politeness and suavity' whose work nevertheless had to be done for him by colleagues; and others prone 'to over-indulge in beverage' plus Kerr, who became 'a dangerous lunatic, who ought to have been removed from the gallery . . .'[4]

Nearly a century later, the gallery was much the same. I sat for a while beside a cheery, fairly extreme gallery man for the *Daily Express*, much given to loudly boasting about the size of his manhood who, as the night went on, found it impossible to keep his contempt for the Labour MPs below us within bounds. He would start to make strange clucking sounds, then literally whistle with anger, then mutter, ever more loudly, 'Stupid wee man. You stuuupid wee fool.' As astonished MPs swivelled and squinted upwards, he would occasionally flick a pen or pencil over at them. (His other mild foible when he'd had a few was ringing up the *Express* night news desk to say a Soviet submarine had been spotted on the Thames. The first time, they took him seriously; but it went on for years.)

The gallery I knew dates from 1950, when the rebuilt Commons chamber was reopened after the Luftwaffe raid of 1941 and was considered spacious in its day. In practice, 'the press gallery' is not simply the tiers of oak and leather benches raked above the Commons chamber at the Speaker's end of the room. It also means the offices and corridors arranged – no, arranged is too strong – scattered haphazardly – in the same quarter of the Palace of Westminster, a little to the west of Big Ben. You can immediately tell when you leave the MPs' area and enter the journalists' quarters, because the oak gives way to grubby paintwork and the thick, vividly coloured carpets disappear in favour of mould-coloured stuff you might find in a condemned mental asylum. At least the smell was then the same everywhere in the building – a curious compound of cabbage, polish, stale smoke and tired bodies, the collective halitosis of a story factory that never slept.

Over time the space given to journalists had slowly increased, from none in the Georgian parliaments, to the small boxes and couple of writing rooms of the early Victorian period, to the semi-respectable offices of the post-1850s Palace, where hacks could find tea, musty bread and a vile ham, to the twentieth-century gallery, with restaurant, bar, library, television room and even showers. Most of the time, though, the expanding demands of the media – the increasing competition among newspapers, the requirements of provincial papers, magazines and weeklies, then the arrival of radio and television reporters, and now online too – meant that the space was never enough. Victorian reporters complained about their smoky, low-ceilinged rooms. A reporter in the mid-1960s described working in his room with at least twelve and sometimes fifteen people: 'The noise is deafening, the ventilation grimly Gothic in character and the heat often insupportable. Similar, and worse, Black Holes of Calcutta are dotted all over the Press Gallery premises.' Today journalists still work in offices that branch out down obscure stairwells and round unlikely corners. Our *Independent* room in 1986 was little bigger than a couple of lavatory cubicles; it had one tiny window looking out onto a drainage pipe, and so little space for the six people regularly working in it that the phones had to be mounted on the walls, with sagging yards of bookshelving winding above them.

The placing of the offices can affect the flow of information – ITN shared quarters with the *Sun*, for instance, which worked to the advantage of both, while the BBC and *The Times*, glorying in their own offices, sometimes missed out on the buzz for vital minutes. Most of us lived and worked off a single corridor, known as the Burma Road – presumably named by ex-servicemen for its singularly bleak appearance. Half-way down it, on the right, was a smaller corridor still, with banks of telephones and a mysterious door. This was the lobby cupboard, where secret lobby notices were posted: 'Blue Mantle 4 p.m.' meant there would be a Number Ten briefing; 'Red Mantle' meant the Labour leader Neil Kinnock would be briefing, while 'Celestial Blue' meant Margaret Thatcher herself. The Burma Road was entered through a small landing, off which are the press canteen, the restaurant, the bar and the library. In all of these places the rule was that MPs were only allowed at the invitation of journalists.

From these rooms, journalists fan out to the famous lobby and the corridors and bars of Westminster. There is a larger lobby, the Central lobby, which has something of the atmosphere of an elderly railway terminus, where members of the public can gather to wait for their MPs. But the marble and stone Members' Lobby was always the key place, barred to everyone except Commons staff, MPs, a few researchers and the lobby journalists. It is a crossroads through which MPs pass between the chamber and their offices, or the tearoom, library, committee rooms and so on. In it there are 'badge-messengers' with their tailcoats and brass badges, and a small cubicle where government and parliamentary documents are handed out. There is an alphabetically marked system of wooden cubbyholes for MPs' messages, a few recessed benches and numerous statues of former Prime Ministers – Churchill with a reverently worn foot, and Lloyd George looking like he wants an argument, and Attlee looking bored. To one side is a tiny corridor leading to the government whips' office and to another one leading to the Opposition whips.

MPs don't have to come through here. They can go 'behind the Speaker's chair', exiting from the other end of the Commons chamber, and so avoiding journalists. But during the Thatcher and Major years few deigned to do so. Lobby journalists could stand in the lobby and watch Cabinet ministers come and go, observe a harassed-looking whip leading some recalcitrant Member by the elbow into the office for abuse or punishment, and generally pick up a good feel for what was happening. On busy days almost everyone important in parliament would come through at some time. The long-established ritual was that you would make eye contact with someone you wanted to speak to, and the target would slow down and have a chat, or briefly shake his head and stride on. If you'd lunched someone, and built up a relationship, you could almost guarantee them stopping. Often, the mere fact of who was 'around' in the lobby available to be talked to would give you a clue to what was going on. At key moments in the anti-Thatcher coup, Michael Heseltine would suddenly saunter through, strangely free for a quick chat. Or the chief whip would be storming in and out, with a face like thunder, ahead of a vote that might be lost. When a vote is on, the journalists are cleared out, but can stand in the adjacent corridor and grab passing MPs.

In the 1980s, and through most of the 1990s, when I was first working there, the lobby was a wonderful place for journalists. It was possible on good days to speak to a dozen senior members of the government in half an hour; to pick up and cross-check rumours; to get the very latest from Cabinet in a way that could never be traced by Number Ten. It was sore on the feet, standing there for hours, and could be mildly demeaning when one's hopeful glances were ignored – like being a wallflower at a gay disco. But the rewards were many and unpredictable. Any spare time could be spent there, meeting MPs with a story to tell, and often taking them to the nearest bar for a pint while they told it.

When New Labour came in, the lobby died. New ministers were warned against randomly walking in the vicinity of journalists. They learned to turn left to the speaker's chair when they left the front bench, rather than right; loitering in the lobby became evidence of disloyalty. But it was also that the huge majorities of 1997 and 2001 meant few votes counted. The Tory factions that had leaked against one another during the Maastricht debates and in the endless leadership agonies of John Major were now a depressed and penitent rump, while New Labour backbenchers were still full of the glories of the new morning and not disposed to gossip against 'Tony'. The lobby emptied. Only Chris Moncrieff, the veteran of the Press Association, could be reliably found propping up a sandstone pillar and waiting for some old mucker to amble past. More recently, with the return of dissent inside Labour, and rebel votes over NHS reform and Iraq, the lobby has started to revive a little and a new generation of journalists are discovering the profitable pleasures of purposeful stasis.

Let us go back upstairs. Physically, the press gallery is among those parts of central London least touched by the past half century. Typewriters have given way to computer keyboards. The food is better. But the accumulated filth, the indescribable smells and the general air of comfortable dilapidation are all the same. Fewer people work late into the night. Fewer get seriously drunk. There is less scholarship around but a late Victorian journalist would recognize much of what goes on there – the sharing of quotes, the pressure from news editors, the camaraderie and the intense competition, the prickly and convivial characters. The greatest change is less easy to spot with the naked eye. It is the vast indifference of journalists, and their public, to almost everything said in the chamber of the Commons; the raw material of parliamentary journalism has fallen as far out of fashion as the antimacassar or spats. This would shock most journalists who covered parliament from the glory days of the British empire right through to the sixties, when Henry Fairlie and many others argued vociferously that it remained the unchallenged cornerstone of national life. It would depress or anger those even earlier journalists who fought and risked so much for the right to report the words MPs said. So why has it happened? Why did straight reporting of the Commons become so important, and why did that importance later shrivel away again?

The Rise and Fall of the Straight Reporter

In the beginning, those words were gold. Apart from a brief period during the Civil War, when parliament found it convenient to be reported for anti-monarchist propaganda reasons, the Commons had hated publicity. Parliament was in no sense a democratic institution. It was the instrument of aristocratic rule, relying on a tiny number of electors, and heavily tilted towards the interests of the great land-owners. The fathers and older brothers might be in the Lords, which retained great power; but the Commons had the younger brothers, the cousins and the friends. Who needed tradesmen, and worse, nosing in? And so, who needed the press, either? Classic expressions of MPs' feelings about the fast-spreading newspaper culture came in a debate in 1738, outlawing the printing of Commons speeches.[5] One MP protested that if reporting was allowed 'you will have every word that is spoken here by gentlemen misrepresented by fellows who thrust themselves into our gallery'. Another, the Tory leader William Pulte-ney argued that it was wrong to report speeches, even accurately, partly because it would mean MPs being careful of what they said, and partly because it 'looks very like making them accountable without doors for what they say within'. The man generally credited as Britain's first prime minister, Sir Robert Walpole, complained that he had read accounts of speeches where all the wit and brilliance was on one side 'and on the other nothing but what was low, mean and ridiculous' – and yet the arguments which lost on paper won in the subsequent vote, making the Commons look stupid. He himself had 'been made to speak the very reverse of what I meant'.

So the Commons passed a motion complaining about the 'high indignity' the House suffered when 'any news writer, in letters or other papers . . . or for any printer or publisher' presumed to report what MPs were saying in parliament, and warning of 'the utmost severity' in pursuing them. The problem the aristocratic politicians faced was the arrival of public opinion and real party conflict. As Britain grew a young empire, and developed an urban, then industrial, middle class, the circle had to be extended. People who read news-papers also paid taxes, sent their sons to fight in America or with the Royal Navy, and cheered for, or rioted against, different factions in parliament. Quite quickly it became necessary for London politicians to be understood and supported by thousands of other people beyond the ranks of peers and MPs – the moneyed men, the East India nabobs, the City speculators, the rabble-rousing lawyers and the influential preachers. It was no longer quite enough to rely on a small group of MPs and the cautious approval of a Germanic monarch and his court. First, the political leaders found they needed their broad arguments to be heard and understood. Then they began to want the words themselves to be recorded and repeated. That meant newspaper reporting.

The shift is neatly seen in the transition from William Pitt to William Pitt. Pitt the Elder came into parliament when there was no real party system. He was an enemy of Walpole, a brilliant, relatively impoverished orator who spoke for the new commercial interests and the colonists, becoming known as 'the voice of England'. Though raised towards power on the coat-tails of the aristocracy, he understood that new thing, public opinion. He was 'the great commoner'. As the prime minister of Britain's great imperial expansion and global war against France, culminating in the 'year of victories', 1759, he had to galvanize the whole nation – the traders, the militia, the financiers, the taxable middle classes and the urban mob. He needed their money, muscle and enthusiasm to prosecute wars from India to Canada, Africa to Prussia. You could not do that with a charmed circle of landowners. Pitt needed the news. And the people he moved with included journalists, like the novelist Henry Fielding, as well as the inevitable Whig aristocrats.

This did not mean, yet, that the Commons, his main platform, had to be reported verbatim. Indeed, there was not yet really an agreed political language. As we saw earlier, the abusive and scurrilous language of the pamphlets was what most literate people came across in the early days of party and factional politics. It was raw, rude stuff, full of similes about arses, farts, tarts and turds, enjoyed by the same robust public which devoured Fielding and Smollett. For the illiterate majority, satirical cartoons taught people the vices and faces of their rulers; popular eighteenth-century satire is full of gluttony, unsavoury sex and malice. The political elite, by contrast, were aristocrats educated to think in a different language. Using ancient models of rhetoric they learned how to express themselves by translating English into Latin, Latin into Greek, and Greek back into English again. As it happens, Pitt's voice was so loud it could be clearly heard, quite literally, outside the Commons chamber. But like many of his rivals he was a life-long admirer of Cicero, reading and rereading his speeches. It followed that for him, the shape of his arguments mattered more than the actual reported words. This was lucky because Pitt, earlier on, in his thirties, had been one of the MPs whose speeches were rewritten and polished for history by Samuel Johnson.

Johnson never set foot in the Commons. He used scraps of information gathered by a critic and part-time doorkeeper William Guthrie, and his publisher, Edward Cave, and turned them into mighty oratory for the *Gentleman's Magazine*. He sometimes had nothing more than the names of the speakers and the topics they were discussing to work from. In later life, Johnson and his friends were discussing a famous speech of Pitt's, and Johnson shocked them by abruptly admitting he had written it himself:

> Sir, I wrote it in Exeter Street. I never was in the gallery of the House of Commons but once. Cave [his editor] had an interest with the doorkeeper. He and the persons under him got admittance. They brought away the subject of discussion, the names of the speakers, the side they took, and the order in which they rose, together with notes of the various arguments . . . I composed the speeches in the form they now have . . .[6]

Johnson, like many other literary people, made money from newspapers and also professed to despise them. He came to regret his time making up other people's speeches, however well they read.

The gap between the raw language of the street pamphlets and the classical prose of aristocratic parliament could not continue, however, as the epic struggle for American independence, and then the long wars against Revolutionary France, turned politics into a matter of national survival. A fresh generation of politicians rose, whose words were nearer the common language of the English streets, and who could sway ordinary electors with their speaking and writing. They included Edmund Burke, who reached out to public opinion in books and pamphlets as well as speeches; his enemy Thomas Paine, whose revolutionary *Rights of Man* was in plain, clear prose everyone could understand; and aristocratic rebels like Charles James Fox; and radical

critics of the Crown such as that master of the mob, and first real hero
of the press, John Wilkes.

Wilkes was a Whig MP, the son of a distiller, famous for his
hideous ill-looks and his acid wit. His first great enemy was Lord Bute,
prime minister and foe of Whigs. Bute was constantly being abused by
the London press. He fought back by hiring the Scottish novelist
Tobias Smollett to bring out a pro-government newspaper, the *Briton*.
There are many fine journalists who turn out to be rotten novelists,
but Smollett was a fine novelist who was a rotten journalist. Wilkes's
counterblast was called the *North Briton*. He didn't mince his words. In
its first issue, he declared a war between the press and the political
elite:

> The liberty of the press is the birthright of a Briton, and is justly
> esteemed the firmest bulwark of this country. It has been the
> terror of all bad ministers; for their dark and dangerous designs,
> or their weakness, inability and duplicity, have thus been detected
> and shewn to the public, generally in too strong and just colours
> for them long to bear up against the odium of mankind . . .

This 'birthright', this bulwark, had pretty much been invented by
Wilkes: as we have seen the British press had been anything but free.
For the previous fifty years or so, it had been getting bolder; but far
from terrorizing bad ministers, it had been fairly effectively under their
control. Inventing convenient 'ancient' traditions is itself a rank and
haggard British tradition.

Wilkes may have been a cynic and hypocrite. He was happy to use
a little bribery. But his is the language of press defiance which has
sustained political journalism, perhaps with an excessive self-importance,
ever since. It is the original journalists' gauntlet. It was put into irresis-
tibly elegant form in 1810 by the playwright and MP Richard Brinsley
Sheridan:

> Give me but liberty of the press, and I will give the minister a
> venal House of peers, I will give him a corrupt and servile House
> of Commons, I will give him the full swing of the patronage of
> office, I will give him the whole host of ministerial influence . . .
> And yet, armed with the liberty of the press, I will go forth to
> meet him undismayed, I will attack the mighty fabric he has
> reared with that mightier engine, I will shake down from its

height corruption, and bury it beneath the ruins of abuses it was meant to shelter.

Sheridan was going it a bit; without a decent Commons and relatively uncorrupt state, no free press would long survive. But he poses a fundamental question about free journalism in politics. What are political journalists really for – to terrorize bad ministers and expose corruption, or simply tell people what politicians say?

The problem for politicians is that once they let the journalists in, and came to realize they needed them, they could not defend the boundary between reportage and pursuit, and could not avoid the press becoming powerful and haughty too. In practice, political journalists responded by dividing the trade into reporters, either in the gallery or the lobby, and commentators or columnists, who in modern times became the ranters, the finger-stabbers, the tellers of truth to power. Later on, in the twentieth century, they were the columnists and sketch writers. Today, many lobby journalists claim to show the public the 'weakness, inability and duplicity' of ministers. Journalists like to smudge the distinction: 'I'm only reporting the facts' says the lobby hack who is in fact moulding a barbed, skin-tearing story intended to damage the quarry. He, or she, is the child of John Wilkes.

Wilkes's famous forty-fifth edition of the *North Briton* was a particularly vituperative attack on the ministry. It was ordered to be burned by the public hangman but was saved by the mob. Because the government grossly and illegally overreacted in trying to crush him, and because he had the support of London, and then Middlesex voters, Wilkes eventually won his titanic battle, though the path to victory took him through arrest, imprisonment, riots and scandal. Press rights to report the Commons were something of a side issue, but the wake of his turbulent revolt helped establish those, too. Charles James Fox, the Whig leader, reckoned that the only way to stop MPs being misreported was by 'throwing open the gallery and making the debates and decisions of the House as public as possible'. It was bitterly fought. One reactionary MP, George Onslow, had printers summoned to the Commons repeatedly to answer for descriptions of him in print as 'little cocking George' and the 'paltry insect' (one of his descendants in the parliaments of the 1980s, Sir Cranley Onslow, suffered the similar indignity of being known almost universally in the press gallery as Sir

Craply Arsehole). But he could not prevail against the new need to be heard. If the radicals and pro-French Revolutionaries could appeal to wider opinion and the mob, then every politician who wanted to shape the country must try to do so, too.

So although the first heroes of parliamentary reporting date from this time, and deserve their place in any history of journalism, it was not all about hacks pushing forward. The politicians needed them. A recent historian of the press gallery, Andrew Sparrow, identifies John Almon, an admirer of Wilkes, and a man called Wall, who supplied newspapers with gossip and bits of speeches, as the original parliamentary reporters. Dodges and wheezes of all sorts were used to tell the reading public what was going on; clerks and MPs in coffee houses passed on their imperfect memories and jottings. William Woodfall, of the *Morning Chronicle*, would stand for hours in the public gallery memorizing the talk below. He was said to be able to sit for sixteen hours at a time – according to one account, with his eyes closed, and his hands on his stick – before returning to the office to write up remarkably accurate accounts of what he had heard. Within a few years rivals such as James Perry, who offered his readers speeches reported by a team, working in relays, had emerged. Reporters were crowding in as the competitive London newspaper market developed; brief comments and descriptions were creeping into the accounts of speeches. 'Memory Woodfall' like other early reporters, and their printers, faced harassment and even imprisonment for their depictions. But this could not last, and the break came with William Pitt – the other William Pitt.

Like his father, Pitt the Younger was a great parliamentary debater, and a great war leader. The struggle against the French monarchy in the 1750s had been expensive enough, and had widened the circle of British political life. The struggles against first Revolutionary and then Napoleonic France from the 1790s were of an even greater scale, forcing the introduction of income tax, the arrival of a large standing army and systems of espionage, censorship and repression. Pitt the Son was a chillier and less liberal character than Pitt the Father, who in old age had become a defender of the press and of Wilkes too. But the younger man needed public opinion even more. A dozen years after Pitt had imposed income tax, the MP and playwright Richard Sheridan argued that he had only got away with it thanks to the influence of newspapers with public opinion: 'the publicity given to . . . great measures of finance in modern times, had been the principal, if not the sole means of reconciling the nation to a weight of taxes which . . . would neither have been thought of, nor supposed likely to be borne or endured by the country'. Pitt did not depend entirely on the patriotism of journalists, of course. He bribed people to back him, too – including an early editor of *The Times*.

Throughout his glory years, Pitt relied on being reported by the men who squeezed themselves into the cramped public gallery of the Commons, sometimes after many hours of queuing. In May 1803 he had just been summoned back to power after the renewed outbreak of war with Napoleon. The Battle of Trafalgar was still ahead; the danger of a French invasion was real and present; and on 23 May, as a two-day debate on the war began, the country was agog to hear its leader speak. Members of the public, newspaper reporters among them, stood waiting around the doors of the Commons and surrounding lanes from 8 a.m. until the chamber finally opened at 3.30 p.m. But by then the galleries were already crammed, filled up with friends of MPs who had been smuggled in. As a result, Pitt's historic speech was reported not at all. The Speaker realized the absurdity of this and ordered that in future the Commons housekeeper should let in news reporters to allotted seats. This formal acceptance of journalists' right to be there was what the present press gallery used to mark its two hundredth anniversary celebrations in May 2003.

The story of parliamentary reporting in the next 150 years is fairly simple. There was more and more verbatim coverage of speeches by more and more reporters, now using shorthand and working in teams, more pages of more newspapers being read by more people, more of whom, over the decades, were allowed to vote. Print democracy turned the old era of eccentric or heroic individual reporters into a scribbling industry. Accurate, exact reporting of what MPs actually said, widely regarded as offensive in the eighteenth century, and still relatively uncommon in the 1820s, became a shibboleth by the middle of the nineteenth century. Again, this was not because journalists heroically fought for the right to report every word, so much as that the politicians, now trying to control mass parties, suddenly needed to be reported. The journalism was being driven by the politics, not the politics by the journalism.

Not everyone understood what was happening. There were plenty of MPs who resented the pushy, socially inferior hacks. There were plenty of hacks who deluded themselves they were great figures in the system of government, not least after Macaulay grandiloquently called their gallery 'a fourth estate of the realm' in 1828. His point was that reporting had moved from being seen as dangerous, to being regarded as a great safeguard of liberty. The technical expertise required to safeguard liberty then hardly changed for generations. There are many different systems of shorthand, from its Elizabethan origins, through Dickens's struggling spiders and wild swoops, to the modern squiggles and dashes of Teeline . . . but they are more or less equally hard to master and can be kept accurate and fast only by constant practice. The transmission of stories from the Commons to newspapers has moved from street runners, sprinting up Whitehall towards Fleet Street, through telegraph wires and phones to computers. Political pages can be designed and sub-edited from the Commons, but they mostly are not.

The real difference is how few words are now sent by parliamentary reporters to the media outlets. As we have seen, Victorian papers required vast screeds of verbatim text from the Commons; they overdid it. Shrewd editors knew perfectly well how boring tens of thousands of words of parliamentary reporting actually were. Shortly after the *Daily Telegraph* was launched, in the 1850s, it made much of how compressed and selected its Commons reporting was – not, it implied, the interminable wastes you found in *The Times*. And, as we have seen, when the *Daily Mail* launched nearly half a century later, it advertised its shortened version of parliamentary coverage 'for the busy man' too. So although Simon Jenkins, the then editor of *The Times*, took some stick as a barbarian for scrapping that paper's historic parliamentary page in 1990, he was following the instinct of many earlier editors. *The Times*, however, had been the gold standard of the old ways, and its decision was fairly rapidly followed by the other broadsheets, until by the late 1990s parliamentary coverage had almost dried up, except when there were big days, such as Budgets or ministerial resignations, or following prime minister's questions, which itself was increasingly treated as a sporting bout, with an appointed winner and loser. Otherwise the press gallery is almost empty almost all of the time.

Today *The Times*, which once needed a full-time team of a dozen reporters each day, and still had a large team when I arrived, has nobody on full-time gallery duty. Even the Press Association, the last organization attempting to provide a pretty full parliamentary service, is down to four gallery reporters – as compared with perhaps eight to ten for a broadsheet newspaper in the Edwardian heyday of verbatim coverage. Enoch Powell once joked that the best way of keeping a state secret in Britain was to announce it on the floor of the Commons at 8 p.m. – when MPs and journalists were often at dinner. Now, it's hardly a joke and you could say what you liked at almost any time of the day, secure in the knowledge that hardly anyone would be watching. The gallery quarters are a sad relict these days, often half empty, with a shabby and desolate air. The old phone boxes are still there, useless, but with preservation orders on them. The library has had many of its best books stolen and has become mainly a place where tired officials and a few hacks sleep. The offices which teemed with life are dead by the mid-evening and even the bar is now the preserve of a small gathering of determined nostalgics, like white settlers refusing to give up their land long after the empire has left. This does not mean that words have lost their power in politics, far from it. But the kind of words that are reported, and why – *that* is a revolutionary change. 'Straight' reporting of MPs' words, once dangerous and radical, then essential to mainstream journalism, has collapsed. It is the biggest single change in how politics is brought to voters since the origin of British democracy and deserves to be thought about. The single greatest loser is, quite clearly, the House of Commons itself.

Real power quit the chamber a long time ago and partly because of the need for privacy in policy discussion. We have been brought up for so many generations on the public's right to know that the arguments against reporting can now seem absurd, the remnants of another age. Yet they have some substance and they have not disappeared, merely migrated. If serious, difficult arguments are misrepresented by the media, then the whole point of political debate – which is that bad arguments are answered, and driven out by better ones, and so good governance advances – is destroyed. The twisting of politicians' views by hostile newspapers infuriates them but, more to the point, persuades them to keep their real thoughts to themselves and so robs the rest of us of thoughts we may need to read about.

The most profound argument remains Pulteney's. Instant publicity can
kill honest argument. Government requires full frankness; and frankness can look bad in print.

This is so everywhere. If you are in charge of a business, or part of
government, or even if you are talking to a partner about your future
plans, you need to be able to think and talk a little wildly, to test
extreme positions and unlikely ideas, to speculate and joke, before you
settle on a course of action. Almost all of us say things in private
which we would be aghast to hear loudly quoted among our friends
and neighbours. When the curtains are drawn and the lights turned
low, the freedom of not having to watch every word, and to talk in a
fully relaxed way, is a human need. Even if you decide not to close
your traditional head office, or invade a country, or move your family
to the Hebrides, you may need to consider doing so, and to talk about
what would happen if you did. Without speculation there can be no
good decision-taking: yet such is the authority and importance of
government that its speculation, if revealed, can cause people to riot,
foreign governments to protest, and ministers to seem very foolish
indeed. The ill-considered private joke becomes a deadly headline. The
wild surmise becomes a plan. The nose-tapping warning becomes a
public libel. If we were all publicly judged on our private, intimate
conversations we would dry into inner silence, and the same is true of
governments.

They know it. This explains the surviving code of civil service
confidentiality today. It is why the advice given to Cabinet ministers
about different ways they might act, and the debates in their private
offices, and the negotiations inside Cabinet committees, all stay private. There are many journalists and others who would like to thrust
themselves, like the early Commons reporters, into those private
places, and report on what is said. We have a natural curiosity about
what people in power say to one another when we are not around,
and what their 'blue skies' thinking amounts to. But, so far, the need
for honest, open and therefore private discussion before decisions are
taken has survived. All that has changed from Walpole's day is that
the chambers of the Lords and the Commons are no longer places
where any meaningful discussions happen. Walpole's 'cabinet' or
private, wood-lined ministerial rooms, replaced parliament as the
cockpit of frankness. The Commons became the place where decisions

were merely announced, then voted on, rather than made. Walpole's successors receded ever more privately. Revelations about private discussions, from Richard Crossman's frank diaries about the Cabinet meetings of the Wilson era, to the publication of internal Number Ten emails during the Hutton inquiry, have driven truly frank discussion further underground. Like badgers, the real arguments recoil from human light and bustle.

So Pulteney's argument is not bogus or ridiculous at all, if you make the mental leap of trying to imagine a parliament which really thought and argued. But parliament would not be taken so seriously as once it was, even if it did enjoy fuller reporting. The trouble is that the quality of what is said in the Commons is mostly so banal that the average Briton, with today's choice of enticing media, shopping opportunities and so on, would rather have a nail driven slowly through the forebrain than be forced to read or watch it. The sad but unsurprising stories of unfortunate constituents; the repetition of stale views about every subject under the sun; detailed party point-scoring as legislation slithers through . . . I defy any member of the public to sit through a day of ordinary parliamentary business and enjoy it. The great Victorian journalist Walter Bagehot once said that the best antidote to a reverence for the House of Lords was to go and listen to it; the same is now true of the Commons.

A loser from the collapse in straight parliamentary reporting, as well as a proximate cause, is the disappearance of 'oratory'. Outside a few black evangelical churches, formal rhetoric is almost dead in Britain; there are as few people left in the country who can hold an audience spellbound for an hour by the sheer power of their language as there are sword-swallowers. MPs often respond that it is entirely because of the modern media that the Commons has declined. The arrival of radio broadcasting of the Commons in 1978, then television broadcasting in 1989, meant that newspapers were no longer the only place (apart from public libraries carrying copies of *Hansard*) where people could go to find out what MPs had said. So the general, if untrue, assumption that 'it was all on the record somewhere' meant that newspapers could relax and give their readers more of what they wanted. They had no duty to report any more. Sensing this, MPs tried less hard. Some listened to debates not in the chamber, but on radios or TVs in their offices. The struggle to get reported meant that some politicians gave up and looked for more effective outlets. They cultivated the different, matey techniques of the broadcast discussion, which are a million miles away from the techniques of the Commons chamber.

An argument that might have been made over ten minutes, or longer, had to be contracted to a minute. Interruptions, which in the Commons might have added up to a lengthy paragraph of this book, must in a studio be snipped back to a sentence. The really ambitious MPs learned to master the even terser requirements of 'clips' for TV news packages, first delivered outside the Commons on a patch of muddy grass, and later honed for prime minister's questions in the chamber itself. A clip is most effective at about fifteen seconds, which means fewer than fifty words. Tony Blair knows this: he delivers clips of just the appropriate length for news programmes. Sometimes I think he pauses briefly just before and afterwards, to give the videotape editors the moment they need to cut; but this is perhaps over-suspicious. In the US, where TV audiences have even shorter attention spans – perhaps because of the frequency of commercial breaks – political soundbites are often around half the length of typical British ones, perhaps twenty words or so.

Terse can be good. Any well-written tabloid argument uses clear, direct English, in short sentences, to make strong points. Politicians, if they want to catch the attention of busy people, have to be able to do exactly the same. But what is lost is the lengthy, detailed building-up of an argument which, boiled down, might seem nonsensical. And so fresh thinking is rarely heard. It can take time to marshal the facts, explain unfamiliar thoughts and lead the listener towards unexpected conclusions. A soundbite culture leads to bland, familiar thoughts – triggers rather than arguments. Are soundbites removing the mental openness a healthy society needs in order to think its way forward?

Despite the victory of televisual brevity the later twentieth century did hear a few great parliamentary orators, the last survivors of a tradition going back hundreds of years. When the monitors around Westminster signalled that Michael Foot had risen to speak, or Enoch Powell, or John Biffen, or Tony Benn, then people would carefully put down their pint glasses, or drain a wine, or finish a conversation, and hurry into the chamber to listen, for the sheer thrill of hearing people who could speak in perfect sentences and full, satisfying paragraphs, using images which stayed in the head and statistics which really shocked. It is no coincidence that each of these men was outside the mainstream of consensus politics, at least when they were at their best as speakers. The driving of party manifestos towards a narrow managerial middle meant political language itself became cautious. To stir the blood became a sign of unsoundness, as inappropriate as bankers reciting love poetry in shareholders' meetings. When Neil Kinnock became Labour leader and drove his party towards the safer centre, his tongue turned from silver to wood, and his expression stiffened into a rictus of misery: his facial muscles became buttons and clamps.

Yet there still are good speeches made in the old way. The remorseless dissection of the Conservative case over the arms-to-Iraq saga by Robin Cook, when he was a Labour Opposition spokesman; or the full force of Geoffrey Howe's resignation speech when he assaulted Margaret Thatcher's handling of European affairs, had to be heard in complete form to be understood and appreciated. If there were more speakers like that in the Commons, the galleries would be packed, the parliamentary pages of the broadsheet newspapers would never have been cut, and the BBC parliamentary channel would have very substantial viewer figures. But there are not, and the few technically excellent speakers left are at the margins of Westminster life, like exotic birds on the verge of extinction – George Galloway, the left-wing MP exiled from New Labour, or Alex Salmond, parliamentary leader of the insignificant platoon of Scottish Nationalists.

In the past few years, there have probably been twenty to thirty occasions when as a BBC political reporter I wanted to be able to devote ten minutes to a speech, not the two minutes or less allocated. We sometimes run much longer clips of very fine speaking, but it is hard for viewers used to a constantly changing film to concentrate on one person, and some empty green benches, for long. Complexity and detail are, undoubtedly, victims of the television age – though good radio political programming, such as *The Week at Westminster* or *Any Questions?*, can encourage proper argument.

When Neil Kinnock made his Llandudno speech before the 1987 general election, and asked why he had been the first of a thousand generations of Kinnocks to go to university, commentators had a field day with his mathematics, pointing out that in the Stone Age tertiary education was pretty hard to come by anyway. And the US presidential hopeful Joe Biden got into trouble for plagiarizing the thought later. But at the time, in that hall, it was a hugely effective act. Mr Kinnock's police protection officer, who had shown no sign of enthusiasm at all for the Labour leader up until then, was standing on duty at the front of the hall with tears streaming down his face. Listening, one had a glimpse of what it must have been like to hear Nye Bevan on form, or Lloyd George thrilling with impudence and outrage.

That we no longer hear great oratory is less the fault of reporting than of the tendency of modern politics to avoid the vivid for fear of frightening floating voters. Class war produced war music. So did real war. But the Age of Shopping produces politicians who sound, most of the time, about as exciting as the recorded safety instructions in passenger jets. And does it really matter? There are other human skills which have mostly gone – fresco painting; the composing of traditional Gaelic songs; the sculpting, by hand, of cascades of marble; the art of tracking wild bears by their smell . . . why should the system of running a modern democracy be anything to do with the preservation of archaic mouth-music? My answer is that to hear a really good orator take an audience through a complicated argument, mingling intellect and emotion to win you, almost as a lover, to a point of view, is a thrilling, deluging experience everyone should have once, if only to teach them what politics can be.

In the parliaments of several decades ago, MPs were generally trained either in the Oxbridge Union school of self-conscious but polished speech making and debating, or they came up through the trade union mass meeting; the chapel and the party conference platform – rougher schools which produced fine speakers. Today the ranks of teachers, lecturers and even lawyers produce, inevitably, a staider, lecturing, self-satisfied style of speech. Given how many MPs are unable to speak grippingly at all, they have clearly never been forced to hold their own in front of an angry audience. Rare are those, like Jack Straw, who make a point of putting up a soapbox in the street and taking on constituents as they pass.

And has the public been the loser? I for one regret that in the Commons it is almost never possible to hear one great speaker take on another, as in the titanic clashes of Disraeli and Gladstone, or Churchill and Bevan. But it is not a strong argument, really: it is only like saying I'd rather like to see a chariot race. Oratory did not make for calmly scientific decision making, nor have great speakers ever been necessarily good departmental administrators. The flow of policy ideas into Whitehall from the think tanks and lobby groups is at least as vigorous as it was in the days of parliamentary supremacy, and the newspapers are more informative about the wider world, if not about Westminster. A numerate public, able to distinguish billions from trillions, and aware of the tricks played with percentages, would be better able to hold politicians to account than a public sobbing its eyes out after a great political speech. Politics has not stopped because the Commons chamber has been nudged, a little, aside. So long as a parliamentary majority is needed to sustain a government in power, MPs will still matter. They increasingly exercise their power through parliamentary committee investigations, and by denouncing their masters on the *Today* programme poking them with carefully sharpened soundbites. The press gallery, with much of its life sucked out of it, is a little like a minor industrial unit in the West Midlands, neither bankrupt nor prosperous, its machines lying all round, its old order books left in piles. The shadow of indifference hangs over the chamber, and the physical, oaken gallery is sepulchral. But some MPs are learning to be quite effective in the open air.

Bent and Twisted Journalism?

Meanwhile, the decline of old-fashioned verbatim reporting of the Commons has been accompanied by an inflationary surge in every other form of political journalism. There are more satirical sketches, more opinionated columns, more non-stories dredged from the subconscious of ministerial aides. Alastair Campbell, Tony Blair's former spin doctor, argued in 2001 that because London was one of the world's most competitive media marketplaces, in which 'there's frankly not that much massive news around most days', the commentators were taking over: 'The separation of news and comment has effectively gone in most newspapers. News *is* now largely comment and agenda in the press. And on TV and radio, far more time is now given to mediated "commentary by experts" and far less to politicians . . .'[7] Though many journalists are reluctant to listen to any analysis from Mr Campbell, this is only a mild exaggeration of the situation. News and comment are separated, but loaded descriptions and aggressive campaigning-style prose infects many news stories; commentators are invited to write alongside news reports; sketches take precedence over most ordinary acts of political reporting. The line is still just about visible, but it is trampled, dusty and has disappeared in places. Campbell argues that the opinionating of news began in the tabloids and migrated to the broadsheets; and he is absolutely right about that.

The effect, according to the prosecution, has been to rob the British people of hard facts about the policies under which they live, and the real condition of their government and country. Instead, say numerous ministers, the voters are buried under a frothy, multi-coloured gloop of hysteria and nonsense – the unverified allegations that companies have bought favours from the party in power, or that vicious, ancient personal feuds have dictated policy over the currency, or that the prime minister has been rebuked by the queen (who, constitutionally, never says anything and therefore can safely have words put in her pursed mouth by journalists). The people responsible for this sad decay of democratic debate are variously 'the lobby', or 'tabloid hacks', or 'the spinners of Fleet Street'. A good example of this type of criticism comes from Charles Clarke, a thoughtful and combative Labour Cabinet minister who also served as Neil Kinnock's chief of staff:

> The political lobby has a job that is, perhaps, more important than that of any other group of journalists in interpreting politics for the people of the country . . . And I would claim that there is a minority of people in the lobby who don't understand politics at all and are more interested in using the lobby pass to get a story around the scandal of some personality that will help to sell their newspaper . . . The fact is that personality and the theatre of politics mean much more in terms of selling the paper than substance . . . [8]

There is a lot of truth in this, but several defences need to be entered early on. The creeping of commentary, jokes, gossip and satire into 'straight' reporting certainly goes back to Victorian times, with the arrival of the first sketch writers like Sir Henry Lucy in the *Daily News*. Gallery reporters in particular have looked down on lobby reporting as a shabby, gossip-riddled trade, nearer to fiction than journalism, for over a century. So it isn't new. Second, the questions of what a political story is, and should be, cannot be left to a simple 'serious stories about policy' versus 'froth' formula. This flatters politicians and civil servants far too lavishly and fails to account for what interests most of the people, most of the time. Until we understand what a political story is, and what it isn't, it is impossible to assess honestly how good or bad political journalism is today.

What is a Political Story?

Across Whitehall, in the great stone ministries and innumerable glass-fronted offshoots, tremendous work gets done every day. Taxpayers' money is being allocated to, or withdrawn from, struggling northern businesses, local primary schools and the makers of electronic parts for naval destroyers. Regulations are being argued over that may criminalize your neighbour, or protect a child in care. Prickly, painstaking negotiations continue with Brussels about exactly what fish may be caught in which corners of the ocean, and whether a particular subsidy, supporting hundreds of desperately needed jobs, is still legal. Plans are being laid for changes to the way magistrates' courts handle young witnesses. Someone is drawing up a highly confidential paper on the implications of charging for the use of all urban A roads in Britain. Keen people in their thirties from four departments are holding yet another meeting on how to coordinate an action plan for disruptive teenagers in such a way that both the Downing Street policy unit and the Treasury will give it their blessing . . .

But none of this is likely to make the political pages of tomorrow's newspapers. Most of what happens in Whitehall is not quite news. It is a rolling, endless conversation, during which proposals are recycled, brewed, mulched and spat out, so that hardly anything is entirely unexpected and almost everything is provisional . . . until it suddenly becomes a determined government plan, with time allocated to turn it into law. Even then, in the law making of the country there is a rhythm to the cycles of centralization and devolution; regulation, and then bonfires of regulation; technological optimism, and its failure in practice, that lulls the greatest enthusiast.

Good Whitehall stories are, therefore, hard to get hold of. They must be fresh, which is rare. They must be possible to explain clearly. They must have real effects. Ideally, they will provoke a reaction – anger, embarrassment, excitement. All this must be drawn out of a culture which is institutionally secretive and dislikes revealing even humdrum information. More fundamentally, because Whitehall is mostly about detail and slow change, its stories only make sense to people who pay close attention to the evolution of policy – people who can remember what the minister of state said about the tax treatment of forestry two years ago, and how the select committee replied, and the pledge given in the spring. Most people frankly don't give a damn, and that goes for most political journalists, too. When I have had a leak of a document, or a secret briefing about some policy issue, I've had to spend more time trying to persuade an editor about why it might matter than I ever did getting the story in the first place. Whitehall correspondents, those specialists periodically tasked to 'get the real stories', of whom the first was Anthony Howard in 1965 and the most successful has been David Hencke, working for the *Guardian*, have had a hard time of it. Every so often Hencke breaks a story everyone understands, and breaks a minister too; but many of his stories are published because his paper knows they keep civil servants on their toes, even if they can be difficult for ordinary readers.

The Whitehall stories which are given prominence tend to have 'secret and confidential' plastered over them, or concern easily under-stood human arguments. I have heard ministers suggest that they may leave announcements that journalists would otherwise ignore lying next to a photocopier with 'secret' stamped on the cover. Certainly these ministers would have a better chance of getting their pet schemes reported that way than by depositing the same papers with the scores of official press releases left each afternoon in the press gallery. The working assumption of every post-Watergate hack is that a leaked document must by definition be worth reporting. If someone was worked up enough to defy the Official Secrets Act and slip it to a journalist then there must be a reason, even if the report or memo looks boring. Also, getting a 'leak' shows to your editor that you not only have 'contacts' but that you 'work' them, all of which is a good thing.

The tepid drama of surreptitious meetings and brown envelopes –

chaps in trench coats, that echo of secret agents' heroics – can give stories which would normally be spiked a front page appeal. Sometimes the leak *is* significant because it shows that two departments are fighting: the Treasury is trying to warn the Health Department off an expensive proposal, or Transport and Environment have come to radically different estimates of the real cost of a motorway extension. These arguments are the very life of Whitehall and are normally resolved in Cabinet committees. But if things are hot enough for civil servants to leak against their rivals, then it is likely that their bosses are fighting too. So a single leak can, if read right, produce a story about (relatively) well-known politicians being locked in a ferocious struggle, threatening resignation, and the rest of it.

But very few political stories are leaks from Whitehall. And leaks rarely make waves, except when there is a titanic struggle going on, such as the Westland affair which ripped apart Margaret Thatcher's Cabinet in 1985, or Labour's struggles over the euro. When a good journalist gets a tip-off from a civil servant, or receives a smuggled piece of paper, the first instinct is to ask: who benefits from publishing this? Who is damaged? Is it up to date, or an earlier draft intended to sabotage a later draft? Is it a double bluff, which allows the minister, feigning embarrassment on the *Today* programme, to acknowledge a plan he otherwise thought would have been blocked by Number Ten? Reading the real meaning of leaked documents is difficult and beyond all but real insiders. The truth is that although a journalist who gets a leak always preens himself, or herself, on it, in most cases they are simply being used by someone pursuing an internal Whitehall vendetta.

When the Cold War was still in progress, and political passions were raised by the modernization of nuclear weapons, and many leftish civil servants felt real dislike for Margaret Thatcher, there were more politically motivated leaks – Sarah Tisdall and Clive Ponting were both uncovered and prosecuted for leaks from the Ministry of Defence. In the case of the Andrew Gilligan and David Kelly story, one of the reasons for anger in the security services was that they believed the failure to turn up weapons of mass destruction in Iraq would be blamed on them. Aside from his argument with the BBC Tony Blair took the point and, through a press spokesman, immedi-

ately offered a fulsome bouquet of praise to the spooks. They are not
people politicians lightly cross, because their authority and credibility
with the public remain high.

If Whitehall stories make up only a small percentage of political
coverage, the same is true of parliamentary stories. As we have seen,
little of the daily work of parliament is much noticed these days. It is
slow, methodical, underwhelming. There are moments of real drama
– an unexpected government defeat (these days, mostly in the Lords),
or the spilling-out of an extraordinary admission by some witness to a
select committee, or a sudden U-turn on fox-hunting. But for most of
the time, as with Whitehall, you have to be a close observer, day after
day, to really spot where a policy is being changed, or a scandal is
beginning to glint in the undergrowth of public spending. Little that
happens in the Commons chamber is properly news. The repetition of
familiar arguments and lengthy special pleading on behalf of constituents is not news. Ritual denunciations are not news. Arguments, even
passionate ones, about the clauses of bills are not news if it has long
been clear that they will pass into law anyway.

Attentive readers may by now be asking themselves a question: if
political stories are not mostly about Whitehall, where the government
hatches its plans, and they are also not about Westminster, where MPs
pick over those plans, and make them law . . . then what *are* political
stories about? The answer is that political stories, like politics, are
about power. They are about who has it, who is trying to get it, who's
losing it and who is fighting for it. In every human society that has left
a record, power is an obsessive, fixating cultural magnet. The personality of the prince, the plotting of the courtiers, the plumage of the
priests, the errant phallus of the president . . . without stories of human
power, nine-tenths of history and much of art and literature would be
void. Policy interpenetrates this, and is affected by its outcomes – the
decisions, the tax levels, the alliances, the management of public
services. But to ask which is primary, the naked struggle for power, or
the policies that struggle uses to clothe itself, and which are imple-
mented, or not, as a result . . . well, that is as futile as asking whether
opera is mainly music or mainly theatre.

Democratic societies affect a prissiness about this. Tony Benn is
like many MPs in insisting that the media is wrongly obsessed with
'personalities' rather than 'issues'. Yet Benn, with his meticulous,

regularly released volumes of diaries, his trademark pipe, sweater and mug of tea and his superb oratorical style, knows very well that personality matters: all he wants is to be able to control his own trademark. He made himself a national figure and pursued a head-long, perilous struggle for power during the leftist revolt in the Labour Party during the early 1980s. In that struggle, his personality was very important, and his image, or trademark, was the vehicle for those famous 'issues'.

Most leading politicians are acutely aware of their own images. Tony Blair is the best-known current example, with his actor's abilities, carefully chosen wardrobe, crafted 'classless' vowels, infectious school-boy smile and frown of destiny. Image and personality are crucial in politics, just as they are in a school playground or a company boardroom. Power always involves the projection of personality over the heads of other people. In today's media culture, where we are mostly confused about authority and credibility, politicians struggle to prove themselves authentic. They want to be matey, yet somehow inspiring; 'ordinary' and extraordinary at the same time. This must be exhausting. But it is simply fatuous to suggest that the struggle to gain and hold power in the Britain of the 2000s is not about personality and character, image and authority. This is why Shakespeare remains a useful political reference book. To reject journalism about who's up and who's down, or about Cabinet splits, or about personal vendettas, as 'trivia' is to reject an inner truth of any political system, parliamentary or tyrannical. MPs who ask for this are woefully ignorant or are trying to fool the public into thinking that they are really professors or priests, not politicians.

Stories about people gaining, holding and losing power have been central to my reporting career. Most political journalists would say the same. The split in the Thatcher Cabinet over Westland in 1985 was an absolute classic of clashing personalities, boldness and treachery. The cause of the war was the supply of helicopters, and the extent of Britain's European destiny, but the storyline itself was hot from a Jacobean play, which was why so many people kept following it. Michael Heseltine's walkout from Cabinet, and his stalk down Down-ing Street into the wilderness was sheer public theatre. Westland's cast of characters was glorious; the prime minister herself, at the zenith of her power – an overreaching, sometimes frightened, angrily determined Tory Boudicca. Then there was her splenetic, ferret-eyebrowed press spokesman and gravel-voiced Machiavelli, Bernard Ingham; Leon Brittan, like a sly cardinal, and his press officer, the slightly mysterious and glamorously named Colette Bowe ... never mind the lesser figures of Opposition leaders, rival hacks and back-benchers. It felt like a political version of experimental drama, a work in constant progress acted out on morning radio bulletins, at press conferences and in the Commons chamber.

After the opening scenes which took place away from the cameras, the great denouement came on the floor of the Commons, in public, and was reported from the gallery by the same lobby correspondents who had been following it all along. Margaret Thatcher entered the chamber believing that it could be her last day in office; for Neil Kinnock, the then Labour leader, it was his great chance to destroy her. The place was a bear pit, though a cockfight might be a better description, raucous with noise, trembling with tension. She performed magnificently and Kinnock's attack missed her. Weeks of radio interviews, private briefings, newspaper articles, press conferences and angry private conversations had converged to this single hour or so of public argument. The prize was power. Had she lost the argument, and failed to convince the Commons, Michael Heseltine might have become prime minister in her place. Had Kinnock had a great triumph he might have turned round his reputation in the media and with voters generally, and found himself, one day, in Downing Street. These things did not happen. The struggle for power known as 'Westland' was real. I have used the metaphor of theatre but great political stories are better than that: in theatre the ending has been written long before the audience sits down and the actors already know who ends up dead.

Roughly the same pattern can be seen in the other great political crises of the past two decades, though the public action takes different forms. The careful Coal Board and Whitehall planning, and the argumentative politics behind the miners' strike, or the poll tax, led to scenes of riot and bloodshed on the streets of England, Wales and Scotland. Again, these were stories about power – the power of the trade union movement, which Mrs Thatcher decided to destroy for ever, and the power of a democratically elected government to impose a form of taxation seen by a majority of the voters as grossly unfair, which was tested to destruction. As with Westland, we were dealing with large, seemingly unstoppable personalities – Scargill, MacGregor, Tebbit, Ridley. The same goes for the epic confrontation between Thatcher and the IRA, again a power struggle, which involved murder at the Tory conference, acts of bravery and barbarism which still divide people today, and young men deliberately starving themselves to death. The struggle with the Provos was 'about' the history of British involvement in Ireland, the history of Northern Ireland since the 1920s, economics, and discrimination in housing. But it was also a highly personal struggle for dominance between, on the one hand, Margaret Thatcher, with the British state behind her, and, on the other hand, men like Gerry Adams and Bobby Sands.

What of the putsch that finally removed her from office, perhaps the most intense Westminster drama of the past twenty-five years? It was theatrical in every aspect. The struggle over who really had her ear, between two opposite alpha males – the lean, bone-dry economist Sir Alan Walters and the swaggeringly large chancellor Nigel Lawson, a contemptuous Falstaff – was a first act any playwright would have been delighted with. The interlude of the challenge by Sir Anthony Meyer, the little-known Tory MP, always shadowed by his formidable wife, and known derisively as the 'stalking donkey' was a comic sub-plot. The resignation of the put-upon, apparently modest, Geoffrey Howe, mocked as a 'dead sheep', and his transformation into the lethal accuser in his Commons statement, was then followed by the gathering of plotters and counter-plotters, furious arguments throughout the Palace and the breaking of old friendships. Margaret Thatcher's regal determination to leave for a Paris summit at the crucial moment and her 'we fight on' statement on the night-time steps, then the wringingly painful series of interviews with Cabinet ministers, craven and bold-eyed, which led to her surrender; her astonishingly brave resignation statement in the Commons, which had MPs openly weeping behind her, and her own tears as she left Downing Street for the last time . . . at many moments in all this one felt that everyone involved should be wearing doublets, hose and carrying rapiers. *The Reign of Margaret Thatcher*, Parts One, Two and Three, could have kept the groundlings gripped in the original Globe.

John Major's tenure was less spectacular, though, like the Thatcher years, the dramas tended to end publicly in the Commons. The crashing out of sterling from the European exchange rate mechanism introduced Norman Lamont to a wider public as a more comedic version of Lawson, with his raccoon looks and his insouciant *je ne regrette rien* style. 'Black Wednesday', when the government lost both its economic and foreign policies in a single afternoon, marked the real end of Major's hopes of being a major player in the story of modern Britain. It was matched during the mid-1990s by the appallingly personal and vicious Tory war over Europe as Major struggled to get the Maastricht treaty ratified by parliament, and the 'bastards' inside and outside his government struggled just as hard to stop him. Again, this was a story about the destiny of the country, but also one about raw power. It was tragedy of a kind, for the upwardly mobile 'Brixton boy' who seethed about the snobs who were out to get him and whose father sold garden gnomes; but it was a tragedy with many comic interludes, such as the bizarre 'barmy army' group of John Redwood supporters in the leadership contest against John Major, with their striped blazers, kilts, silk dresses and fixed grins – not all, I hasten to add, attached simultaneously to the same person. Much of it was played out publicly, but not all. I remember being with Lamont in the Treasury as he assured me that 'John' would never sack him and had full confidence in him as chancellor, very shortly before John did sack him. I remember too walking down Whitehall after his resignation when a formidable Tory whip crossed the road to warn him that if he pursued a vendetta against the prime minister, 'I'll tear your fucking arms off and I'll tear your fucking legs off and I'll stick them up your . . .'

Throughout the latter Tory years, there was the additional excitement of the possibility of the government losing key votes on the floor of the Commons. It may seem paradoxical that it was during the 1990s that broadsheet newspapers finally shed their traditional parliamentary coverage. But the conspiring of the anti-Major rebels, which was a lobby story, occurring before our eyes on sticky June nights on the booze-scented terrace of the Commons, or against the oak panelling of dimly lit corridors, provided the real clue to what happened night by night in the chamber. It was not surprising that the effective fusing of lobby and gallery work and the collapse of traditional parliamentary coverage was taking place during the John Major years. It was a time of shadow games, and the 'sleaze' era, when the reporting of the private lives and misbehaviour of Tory politicians finally oozed into mainstream political journalism.

Up to this point, the question of what a political story is, at its best, has been hard to dispute. None of the examples I have given would be contested as 'good stories' by any politician. They all touched upon great issues for the future of Britain, including the power of the unions, relations with Europe and America and economic policy, and they were all immediate public theatre too. From now on, however, the story grows murkier.

Let us spool back a bit. Newspapers and broadcast bulletins come out on every day of the year. There has never been a year, even in the most hectic political climate, when great political stories were running constantly to oblige them. Between dramas like the ones listed above come many months of relative dullness. Does the lobby rest? The lobby does not. When the Paris office has little news to file, or things are quiet in the north of England, reporters there simply relax. At Westminster, things are not like that. On days when there are no major overseas stories, or transport disasters, or well-known killers being convicted, news desks tend to ring up their Westminster correspondents with the demand that they 'find something' to fill up the gaps. A century ago, or fifty years ago, this was no problem. Some bore with a beard and a baronetcy was always making a speech somewhere or other.

But today speeches won't do. The public will not read them. One answer is to stretch genuine political stories out for days longer than they really warrant, with accusation and counter-accusation, ministers chased for answers, and relatively small verbal slips being elevated into major scandals. (One of my BBC colleagues, Martha Kearney, jokes that when she writes her autobiography she will call it *Cheap Lead*. This is what she means.) Collective Cabinet responsibility started out as a sensible idea – broadly, that it was a bad idea for members of the same government to disagree fundamentally with one another in public, since then no one would be able to tell what 'the government' really thought. But it has been elevated into a fetish. The smallest divergence from the stated policy thus becomes a mark of disloyalty.

John Major's government marked the moment when this became a raging problem, since on the tortured European question, the Tory Party was on the brink of collapse. Nerves were taut. Every subtle nuance of difference by a minister or 'senior Tory back-bencher' could be read as a further crack and splinter in the ship. Either onscreen, or through the chatter of printers, ministers' texts were minutely compared and contrasted. Remarkably small variations of argument could then be put through the cliché-laden prose of desperate journalism so that poor Mr Major was 'plunged into a new crisis last night' or 'faced with a stunning new challenge to his authority'. Real differences of opinion over Europe were highlighted and rammed at the public, who quickly decided that the Tories were indeed hopelessly split. Watching from opposition, New Labour was learning the lesson that its people must be word-perfect in their mutual agreement. They had to become 'on-message', like chirruping insects, with their chirruping pagers to keep the song as monotonous as possible. In response, journalists followed politicians even more closely, looking for slips of tense or the slightest pause to attack the smallest deviation from 'the line'. For a while this provided a source of second-rate, overwritten stories. But it must have bored readers senseless and it stifled real political debate.

This, though, was not the worst thing that happened to political journalism in the Major years. 'Sleaze' was a useful word for journalists because it was vague. It connected acts of clear political wrongdoing, such as MPs taking bribes to ask questions, or the shenanigans over illicit arms sales to Iraq, with private sexual misbehaviour. Sleaze began with old-fashioned, if aggressive, political digging: in July 1994 the *Sunday Times* revealed that a reporter from its 'Insight' team, posing as a businessman, had persuaded Tory MPs to take £1,000 to ask parliamentary questions. A few months later the *Guardian* said that two more Tory MPs, Neil Hamilton and Tim Smith, both junior ministers, had been paid by the would-be owner of Harrods Mohamed Al Fayed to ask helpful questions in the Commons. Hamilton was also accused of taking lavish hospitality from Fayed while staying with his wife at the Paris Ritz, which Fayed owned. Hamilton sued for libel but the paper stuck to its guns and by its reporters, including David Hencke and David Leigh, and eventually forced the MP to climb down in a dangerous court battle, emerging with the devastating headline 'A Liar and a Cheat' in October 1996. A third minister, Jonathan Aitken, who had been promoted by John Major to the Cabinet, was also accused of taking hospitality at the Paris Ritz from an Arab arms broker. As the allegations mounted, both from the *Guardian* and the

Granada TV programme *World in Action*, Aitken promised to 'start a fight to cut out the cancer of bent and twisted journalism in our country with the simple sword of truth and the trusty shield of British fairplay . . .' He left the Cabinet to fight his libel action, was caught lying thanks to some deft and last-minute journalism, lost his seat and was successfully prosecuted for perjury and perverting the course of justice, for which he was sent to prison.

All of these stories were undoubtedly in the public interest, as well as being interesting. They involved the vertiginous fall from power of self-confident men and they touched upon issues of real public concern – the greed culture, now seeping into Westminster from the City, and the cloyingly close relationship between some businessmen and some politicians. But 'sleaze' was expandable to include sexual misbehaviour, too. Sex as we have seen sells newspapers and always has. After the Profumo affair, involving sex, lies and espionage, in 1963 and then the Jeremy Thorpe affair, which added homosexuality and dog-killing to the mix and ran from 1976 to 1979, Cecil Parkinson was the first leading Tory of the Thatcher years to be caught out over an extra-marital affair. But in the Major years the death of the Tory MP Stephen Milligan after a sex game went wrong; then the exposure of David Mellor, and a stream of other, lesser stories involving Tory ministers such as Tim Yeo and Steve Norris, the latter of whom had five mistresses, and the Liberal Democrat leader Paddy Ashdown, meant there was a dirty stream of revelations.

Few of these ministers helped themselves. They blustered, or posed with their wives and children, or had been caught earlier lecturing the press on its standards. Embarrassing details, often untrue, were leaked to the press to make their lives harder. Yet it is hard to argue that someone's private sexual life, unless very energetic and time consuming, or incredibly dangerous, impacts on their conduct of public business. John Major's 1993 conference slogan 'back to basics' had been meant to herald a return to traditional political values. Major himself, who had had a then-secret affair with the Tory MP and minister Edwina Currie, was uncensorious about people's private lives (as was Margaret Thatcher) and he had never intended the slogan to apply to consenting adult sex. But it was taken as the unchallengeable excuse ('hypocrisy') for the sexual sleaze stories run with memorable élan in the mid-1990s. These tales provided the raw material for the aggressive, wild-eyed tabloid journalism pioneered by Kelvin MacKenzie's *Sun* and described earlier. They catered to a public that was franker about sex, was becoming increasingly derisive about the divided Tory leadership of the country, and enjoyed seeing the toffs brought down. Not only were MPs on the take but they were dirty devils, too.

A very large number of these stories did not originate from the lobby teams, but had been taken on by investigative journalists from newspaper offices who had no need to worry about their political contacts, or any intention of staying on social terms with MPs. But the political backwash of sleaze – the raucous scenes at prime minister's questions, and the pursuit of accused ministers until they resigned – was dealt with by political journalists. So sex and corruption became core themes of political journalism, and this was encouraged by Opposition politicians and spin doctors. Much of the agony that overcame New Labour after 1997 flowed directly from the Major years and had been prepared for by the very same people who were skewered themselves in due course. They helped turn us nasty and then we turned nasty on them. Meanwhile the coda of the sleaze era involved Jeffrey Archer, who had won a bitter libel battle in 1986 over stories that he had had sex with a prostitute. The *Daily Star* was forced to pay £500,000 in damages, and even more in costs, and the premature death of its then editor was widely thought to have been partly caused by the stress of the case. But in 1999, as he was preparing to stand as mayor of London, the *News of the World* revealed that he had persuaded a friend to perjure himself in the original trial and Archer, after being expelled from the Tory party, was sent to jail. Like two of his own fat novels, Archer's story forms the before and after bookends of the story of sleaze.

Throughout this period, as the Tories fell apart, New Labour believed it had finally solved the problem of handling the media. Under Peter Mandelson and then Alastair Campbell, it had imposed ruthless discipline on its main figures. It had a sophisticated, endless media strategy, partly learned from the US Democrats, which involved menaces and isolation for unfriendly journalists, and help and flattery for those prepared to be bought. Most ominously its leader Tony Blair was proving adept at telling people what they wanted to hear. For pro-Europeans at the *Guardian* and *Independent*, he was impeccably Europhile and mustard-keen on the euro. For the sceptics at the *Sun* and *The Times*, he was a powerful critic of European federalism. When he was talking to liberal journalists, he was the civil rights lawyer and when he was with conservative ones, he was hotly populist for law and order. Tough on crime with the *Daily Mail*; tough on the causes of crime with the *Guardian*. During 1995–97 this seemed a brilliant strategy. Blair's star rose ever higher. Papers of different views agreed that he was fresh, exciting, moderate, sensible. Questioning hacks were cowed, or pushed to the margins and ridiculed.

It is a myth that New Labour invented spin, or that New Labour MPs were the first to be kept 'on message' and encouraged to repeat the same carefully honed mantras until voters could finish the phrase themselves. In the early years of Margaret Thatcher's first administration, for example, Sir Angus Maude was, with the title paymaster-general, in effect her minister for information. Like Alastair Campbell, he had been a journalist himself and had a natural talent for party propaganda – 'Labour's Dirty Dozen – Twelve Lies They Hope Will Save Them' in the *Daily Mail* of 26 April 1979 was one of his. Maude's task was to centralize the Tory message and his belief was that 'unless you say something at least 20 times nobody ever hears it, and if one could get every minister to say the same things over and over again, it did begin to work'.[9]

Maude pioneered the placing and timing of bad news to soften its impact and produced soundbites for other ministers – such as 'There's no such thing as a free lunch and no such thing as a bad day's work for a good day's pay.' Though largely forgotten now, he had some success at the time. It was by watching and copying what the Tories were doing in the eighties that New Labour learned its tricks. Campbell and Mandelson merely pushed them further. Alastair Campbell said later that 'we did make a concerted effort to get a better dialogue with some parts of the media where before there had been pretty much none' and pointed out, reasonably, that Blair's inner circle was stuffed with people who had seen, first-hand, the terrible damage wrought on Neil Kinnock by hostile newspapers. He went on to admit that after 'the longest honeymoon in history' Labour then got into increasing trouble with spin: 'We appeared, and perhaps we were, over-controlling, manipulative.'[10]

But, more than that, New Labour had misread the real media mood. This was a media composed of people who were sick of the

Tories, bored witless by the endless arguments over Europe, and desperate for a change of government. That was why Blair got such a long and easy ride. What he failed to recognize sufficiently was that it was also a media trained by the era of sleaze to mistrust all politicians, to ferret out and splash sex stories involving politicians, and to 'follow the money' whenever there was the faintest suspicion that politicians were getting cosy with business. In the early period of New Labour the press was neither bridegroom nor bride. Honeymoon was not the right image. The press was a sleeping dog, enjoying the sunshine, wagging its tail as it luxuriated in being stroked . . . but a dog that had learned to bite, and would quickly grow snappish again. Journalists like David Hencke who had made their names uncovering Tory misbehaviour were keen to keep on going with the new lot. A cadre of new political correspondents without the cosy clubbiness of the traditional lobby, had arrived in the Commons well aware that sex stories sell papers.

In Opposition New Labour had introduced vibrating pagers to help control MPs in the chamber, and began a programme of chilling threats to producers of TV and radio programmes, and a tight circle of insiders and outsiders. In government, with the use of an Order in Council, Campbell, the former tabloid political hack, was given authority over a regiment of civil servants, and a process of reconstruction of the government information service began. The hope and intention was to control the news from Whitehall with a 'grid' of planned stories, which neither clashed nor stopped flowing. Journalists would be given what they needed, which was news, timed carefully for the best effect and updated to account for the news cycle of daily Westminster life. Ministers would always agree with one another. If they were cross-questioned on TV or radio programmes, they would refuse to play ball, and would simply repeat their soundbite. This might irritate people trying to concentrate on Harriet Harman or Gordon Brown first thing in the morning, but the messages would get across. Nothing was left to chance. Every significant journalist was watched, cajoled, reprimanded and rewarded. What could possibly go wrong?

What couldn't? Things started well because New Labour had a few cracking political stories of its own, which it made much of in the first flush of office: Gordon Brown's *coup de théâtre* in making the Bank of

England independent over monetary policy and his subsequent, much messier, determination that Britain would not attempt to join the first wave of euro entrants were obvious examples. Later, the referendums about a Scottish Parliament and a Welsh National Assembly, followed by their establishment; the revived Northern Ireland peace process, with its Good Friday Agreement; and the Kosovo crisis of 1998–99, leading to the toppling of the Serb president Slobodan Milosevic, were major political narratives driven by the determination of Tony Blair. Early on, too, he established a rhetoric which seemed, to most of the people for most of the time, to be attractive – fresh, empathetic, informal. The nation heard it when Princess Diana was killed in a Paris car crash and Blair responded with his 'people's princess' tribute; and when he appealed to British optimism in going ahead with the Millennium Dome project; and in the arrival of rock stars and TV personalities for Downing Street parties. There was goodwill in the country and there was goodwill in the press, an almost visible yearning for things to be better.

But the media habits which had ravaged the Tory years had become ingrained and, from early on, Labour showed that it too was vulnerable. When it emerged in the autumn of 1997 that Bernie Ecclestone, who created Formula 1 racing as a hugely lucrative business, had donated £1 million to the party and was being asked for more, and had personally lobbied Tony Blair against a ban on tobacco advertising being extended to motor racing, there was all hell to pay. Ecclestone insisted he had paid the money on learning that Labour would not put up the top rate of tax, thereby saving him £5–6 million, and it had nothing to do with the decision on advertising. But Labour did change its policy of a blanket tobacco advertising ban and wrote to the EU asking for a Formula 1 exemption. Number Ten then twisted and dodged desperately as the story came out and Blair himself was forced to plead for the benefit of the doubt: 'I think most people who have dealt with me think I'm a pretty straight sort of guy, and I am.' Then came attacks on the business practices of Geoffrey Robinson, a rich businessman who had given the Blairs free holidays in his Tuscan villa and been made a Treasury minister; and after that the revelation that Robinson had, before the election, given Peter Mandelson, who became trade and industry secretary, a £373,000 loan to buy a house in 1996. This affair, which led to two ministerial resignations, was followed by other financial headaches for New Labour, from the involvement of the Hinduja brothers in the funding of the crisis-hit Dome to donations from Lakshmi Mittal, whose steel combine was trying to win a Romanian privatization deal, backed by the British government. Later came the involvement of a con man, Peter Foster, in arranging the purchase of two flats for the Blairs in Bristol.

The details of all these do not matter here, except in that they convinced journalists that New Labour's relationship with rich, and sometimes dodgy, characters was no purer than the Tories' had been in the bad old days of 'sleaze'. There was a rich, high-rolling circle around Downing Street once more. In a notorious aside, part of a sting operation by the *Observer*, which mimicked the behaviour of the *Sunday Times* in its cash-for-questions investigation, one lobbyist claimed that in the government 'there are only seventeen people who count'[11] and that he knew all of them. In some ways it was worse than in John Major's time, however, because Blair himself had insisted his lot would be different, 'purer than pure'. So the habits of suspicious cross-examination, sting operations, angrily censorious columns and an ingrained scepticism about Number Ten denials returned. As for money, so for sex. Ron Davies, the Welsh secretary, had his 'moment of madness' on the gay cruising ground of Clapham Common in October 1998. Robin Cook had to end his marriage in a Heathrow departure lounge after the *News of the World* told Alastair Campbell it was about to break the news of his affair with his secretary – and later his second wife – Gaynor Regan.

Even this might not have mattered had trust remained intact between Number Ten and political journalists. But the very techniques for managing the press that had seemed so clever in the mid-1990s quickly became lethal. It was the perceived cynicism that made ordinary journalistic business difficult – the ultimate example being the notorious email from Jo Moore, special adviser at the transport department, on the day of the Twin Towers attack, suggesting that it would be a good day to 'bury' bad news. But this was about more than over-zealous and relatively junior apparatchiks. The clever, lawyerly language used to slide over the unpleasant local difficulties such as the Ecclestone affair, or Cherie Blair's deep involvement with Carole Caplin and, through her, with Foster, convinced a growing number of journalists that this was a government prepared to try to lie its way out of trouble. One commentator asked: what else, in a government (then) headed by a lawyer and a tabloid journalist, could one expect? There were many other incidents. Alastair Campbell tried to take two newspapers to the Press Complaints Commission about allegations that Tony Blair had tried to muscle his way into a bigger role in the Queen Mother's lying-in-state at Westminster, then gave way after a key parliamentary official failed to back him. Stephen Byers had to resign as transport secretary after he was accused of lying about what he said during meetings with survivors of the Paddington rail crash, on the subject of Railtrack's future.

As trust crumbled, so did reporters' willingness to defer to the government. Tales of how New Labour had bullied junior reporters or producers spread through the warren of press gallery offices and between broadcasters' headquarters. The backlash was slow, but it came. By the end of Blair's first two years, it was a badge of honour to be 'bollocked' by Campbell or Mandelson, and to shout back just as loudly. The persistent attempts to dictate what should appear on a front page, or at the top of a running order, became infuriating and hardened journalistic hearts. Even before the 1997 election it was obvious that Labour had spies tipping it off about the running orders, script lines and correspondents being used for news programmes and was attempting to ambush them before they went on air to get more favourable coverage. In lobby meetings, Alastair Campbell and others would single out and ridicule the correspondents of editorially hostile newspapers – George Jones, political editor of the *Daily Telegraph* and a studiously fair reporter of the old school was a favourite target. Favoured reporters were given special treatment, just as their editors were made much of in Downing Street and invited to weekends at Chequers. But the political correspondents have a certain esprit de corps alongside their professional rivalry, and the cynical way in which some were favoured because they worked for Rupert Murdoch, while others were sneered at because they worked for Conrad Black, disgusted many who worked for neither.

The greatest difference in political stories during the Major years and the early Blair years, meanwhile, was the absence of parliamentary uncertainty. The knife-edge votes, and the leadership plots, simply had no relevance to a prime minister who enjoyed a majority of 179 and unrivalled personal authority in his party. Cartoonists and sketch writers quickly started to mock the bovine obedience and predictability of hundreds of Labour MPs who seemed to say the same thing, think the same thing and who were controlled by their pagers. Relentlessly repeated mantra messages – 'the fairness agenda' – 'beyond left and right' – were dazing the most conscientious of reporters.

But the devastating effects of a deeply divided party and the stories that flowed from the Tory civil war were not, for many years, to bedevil Labour. Instead another story emerged which replaced this, the psycho-drama of the relationship between Tony Blair and Gordon Brown. This was new; there had been nothing quite like it in anyone's political memory. It was bigger, closer, more difficult and more intense than the rivalries between Attlee and Morrison, Wilson and George Brown, Thatcher and Lawson. The fact that both men had grown up in parliament together, the David and Jonathan of the New Labour project, and that Brown had long been the senior partner, until suddenly scooped for the top job by the more ruthless Blair, gave this a history and timbre that attracted journalists from the start.

Earlier, I argued that the great political stories were about power, with major issues of national destiny wrapped around the personal drama. Blair–Brown measured up to that. It had the theatrical detail – the famous dinner at Islington's Granita restaurant, and the 'Brown gang' of garrulous, Eurosceptical briefers and advisers, the shouting matches in Downing Street and the verbal aggression filtered through the press. It had two very different characters playing out their fates – the light-voiced, socially easy Blair, with his infectious smile and his easy, lawyer's way with words, against the grimmer, lonelier Brown, with his clogged, sometimes impenetrable sentences and his chewed nails and his absolute lack of smoothness or fashion sense. It had an uneasy division of power, with Brown taking a larger territory than previous chancellors of the domestic agenda, and increasingly hemming in the prime minister when it came to the overarching foreign issue, the euro. It had a wonderful cast of extras, including the rival advisers, the mutually suspicious wives and the wilder partisans, such as Brown's sometime spin doctor Charlie Whelan or the devoted Blairite who told me that if he ever thought Brown would become prime minister, 'I'll wrap the explosives around my chest and run at him myself.'

The contest between Blair and Brown was always about who was really politically dominant, and therefore about subtly different variants of the New Labour project; and it was about whether, and when, Brown would finally succeed as prime minister. It has been the biggest and longest-running political story of the New Labour years, overshadowing ministerial resignations, popular revolts over fuel costs or hunting, and even foreign wars. It has been the subject of a book, large chunks of other books, a TV film and perhaps ten thousand newspaper columns. It is not froth, not trivia. Blair and Brown have very different attitudes to key political questions: the New Labour blanket conceals two dissimilar political minds. Because the chancellor has always been more sceptical about British membership of the euro, and more worried about the democratic problems posed by Euro-federalism, he stands apart from Blair's genuine keenness about Europe. Brown also has a more technocratic attitude to the improvement of public services, as well as a more profound sense of Labour history. Blair would never by himself have determined to try to save the 1945 Labour government's NHS by the injection of massive extra funds. By its nature this is not a story that is played out in public. We can observe the body language at press conferences and in the Commons. But there has been no public row, no storming out of a Cabinet meeting, nothing visible to the cameras. That, in turn, has licensed background briefers, Number Ten and Treasury staffers, senior ministers and 'friends' to pour their accounts into journalists' ears and then their columns. It has produced exactly the kind of unattributable, gossipy journalism that Campbell and Blair say they deplore and tried to reform the lobby system to eradicate.

So the political story has become degraded, but for reasons that have as much to do with politics as with journalism. Today's media culture has a shorter attention span. We live in a televisual world, with shorter stories, less tolerance for long policy-related articles and less deference. All that is true, and it makes it harder for political journalism to fully examine the complicated dance of logic, funding and ideology that we call the legislative process. This is a loss to democracy. The automatic assumption that what government says is mostly true has been destroyed. This is also a loss to democracy. Good people both in the media and government have been agonizing about how to turn back those clocks and put the evil, mocking genii back in their bottles. Meanwhile, the essence of the political story has survived intact. It is the struggle for power among people under great pressure, during which their characters become their fates, and as a result of which the country is well run, or badly run. And offered that to read on the way to work, as against a thorough account of the latest stages in the argument about the funding of foundation hospital trusts, who would really prefer the latter? Not, I bet, Tony Benn.

An Incredibly Short History of the Lobby

The lobby has been at the heart of British political journalism for half a century now. It has become an essential drainpipe between the world of politics and the real world. Its importance has made it controversial for much of its history. It has been seen as a virtuous and efficient journalistic device for getting the private thinking and real views of politicians out to the general public; and as a corrupt, closed shop for idle journalists and irresponsible politicians, thanks to which nobody actually has to account for what they say.

So which is it? At first sight, it is odd that a democratic political system operating in an open society should need any 'device' to convey the real views of politicians to voters. Surely if they think something, they should say it, and be openly reported; and if they aren't brave enough to speak openly, they should not expect wider circulation?

But sophisticated social animals are necessarily hypocrites. Try it yourself. Try saying everything you think. Try, for just a day, a policy of absolute honesty. You think the neighbours are dreary or obese? For God's sake, don't hide it. You find your daughter wittering? Tell her – never mind the tears. Your boss has a bad body odour problem? Tell the brute, as frankly as you inhale it. A day of honesty would be enough to finish most of us. We would be pitied, ostracized and perhaps sacked too. For all of us move around one another buffered by genteel evasions and polite euphemism. Those who refuse to deploy them are shunned.

Politicians are no different, except that they really do speak in public, and their private thinking may be more interesting and important than my views about the vicar. They talk about progressive politics, or honesty in taxation, but they are also thinking about whether X can hold her job, and if there's promotion coming, and they fear the party leader is a booby who will lose them their Commons seat. If all these more private thoughts were cut out of journalism, then voters would understand very little about what was really going on – all those manoeuvres in the dark. It would be like trying to understand a battle only through the viewfinder of a handheld camera on the front line – no tactics, no strategy, no overview. It is a fair point that any journalism which exposes the private plots and inner agendas of politicians is bound to lead to a certain public scepticism. But it also reveals, again and again, the real story behind the apparent one. And who really wants to know less?

The origins of the lobby are in the gossip mongers and tipsters of old taverns and Westminster coffee houses. But the actual system began in a thoroughly modern way, with the breakdown of our much-prized open society. Today, the Commons is surrounded by concrete barriers and police toting machine-guns, while Downing Street has long been closed off behind steel gates and mechanical roadblocks. The reason was IRA terrorism. The reason is now Islamic terrorism. But the effect is the same – to keep public and politicians apart. The lobby was also created by terrorism, again Irish, in 1885, when a dynamite attack on Parliament resulted in everyone except MPs, peers and a few officials being banned from the Members' lobby and some other parts of the Palace. Journalists who had been used to mingling with MPs there were outraged and called protest meetings, as a result of which the Speaker drew up a list of hacks allowed back in. The inevitable followed. People who had been given a privilege banded together and even began to think they deserved the privilege. The lobby journalists of the 1870s had been a raffish lot who didn't take themselves too seriously and did not get very much space in the newspapers either. But the lobby of the early twentieth century became a club. And clubs do take themselves seriously. This one got its own rooms. By the First World War, the lobby hacks even had a bath.

But clean and well housed though they were, the real lobby system did not get going until the late 1920s. From then on newspapers were regularly including reports, first anonymous and later far from anonymous, which were in effect the higher political gossip. More and more, official story placing was carried out through the convenient daily group meetings in Downing Street and, more and more, the journalists came to confuse themselves with parliamentary authority itself. The

lobby made life easier, particularly for journalists working for provincial papers who would not otherwise find it simple to persuade
ministers to make time for them. It always included many conscientious and probing reporters, who were nobody's poodles, and at crucial
moments such as before the D-Day landings, the lobby's ability to
keep a secret was genuinely important. But it undoubtedly encouraged
pack journalism and a lazy swapping of stories which covered the
backs of reporters without serving their readers; it felt conformist and
far too comfortably part of the Establishment.

A sense of that is given by the lobby's own rules, which are
thought to have been first set down on paper after the Second World
War, and which mutated slightly over the decades. The maroon-
covered booklet issued under the title *Notes on the Practice of Lobby
Journalism* in 1982 gives an authentic feel of the institution:

> The Lobby journalist . . . owes a duty to the Lobby as a whole, in
> that he should do nothing to prejudice the communal life of the
> Lobby or its relations with the two Houses and the authorities . . .
> The work of a Lobby journalist brings him into close daily touch
> with Ministers and Members of Parliament of all parties and imposes
> on him a very high standard of responsibility and discretion in
> making use of the special facilities given him for writing about
> political affairs. The cardinal rule of the Lobby is never to identify
> its informant without specific permission . . . DON'T TALK ABOUT
> LOBBY MEETINGS BEFORE OR AFTER THEY ARE HELD
> especially in the presence of those not entitled to attend them. If
> outsiders appear to know something of the arrangements made
> by the Lobby do not confirm their conjectures or assume that as
> they appear to know so much they may safely be told the rest.

But this was only the start. There was a web of other unwritten
rules, against running, butting in on conversations, and general inde-
corum that could weigh heavily on new members. Peter Rose, who
joined the lobby for Northcliffe newspapers in 1966, was twice hauled
up before the lobby's disciplinary committee to answer charges they
considered serious. On the first occasion, his crime was to approach
the MP Stephen Swingler in Stranger's Bar, where they had agreed to
meet for a drink. The MP was there but talking to another lobby
journalist, who was more senior. Peter joined the conversation and

was immediately reported to the lobby committee for a breach of etiquette. He was ordered to attend a hearing and explain himself. He said later, 'I was very scared.' On another occasion, when the Blackshirt leader and fascist Sir Oswald Mosley died, Peter Rose, who is Jewish, bought a bottle of champagne in the Press Gallery bar to celebrate. He was told that he had behaved disgracefully: no lobby man should celebrate the death of a former Member of Parliament, which Mosley had been. Whatever you think of either case, it is easy to see how independent-spirited journalists who had arrived in the Commons hoping to hold power to account felt stifled by the lobby and quickly came to resent it.

The push-and-pull rhythm of governments trying to deal with journalists by smothering them with love, and then trying to bypass them, or exile them, shows that the lobby system was never, in practice, quite the comfortable arrangement it looks like in theory. That was because politicians always pushed it a little farther, enticed by their dream of press control; and because journalists, working in competition, never quite played ball. Given their later reputation for being easily led, gullible creatures, it is interesting that lobby correspondents so often believed themselves to be spin-repelling, hard-boiled sceptics. According to the *Guardian*'s Harry Boardman, writing in the mid-sixties, lobby men had a better quality of earwax which allowed them protection against political propaganda. But at the same time they kept the oath of silence. In an essay by Geoffrey Wakeford of the *Daily Mail* in 1966, he spoke of the 'generally pleasant business and social relationship' between the then sixty-odd lobby journalists and MPs, and the 'mutual tolerance' which allowed them to use some places in the Palace but not others. But he never once mentioned what the lobby was really all about.[12]

For the heart of the twentieth-century lobby system was the twice-daily secret briefings by a spokesman authorized to speak on behalf of the prime minister and therefore, in the British system, the whole government. A single private daily channel of communication between the most powerful figure in the country and every significant media outlet is an extraordinarily powerful weapon. It is the media equivalent of the prime minister's powers of patronage and the declaration of war under royal prerogative in other fields – a kind of giant prosthetic extension of Downing Street's already considerable reach. When it started, though, it must have seemed to the journalists involved a useful act of modernization. There was, then, no steel-gate barrier at the entrance of Downing Street. Political journalists could knock on Number Ten's door and, though they might not be admitted, would cluster in the street outside and nobble passing Cabinet ministers. It was chancy, inefficient and undignified. Ministers had, of course, been briefing journalists individually for ages. But during the general strike of 1926, with its late-night emergency meetings, they were allowed to wait in number 12 Downing Street and began to exclude outsiders from their group meetings. The Labour government of 1929 arranged for an MP, the son of the then Foreign Secretary, to brief the lobby, but he seems to have been pretty useless. In the crisis of 1931, by the time Labour fell and was replaced by a National Government, lobby hacks were back to the indignity of hanging around outside the Downing Street door.

The National Government is not remembered with much affection by political historians. So far as one can tell, it is not remembered at all by the general public. But it did begin the lobby system, with regular meetings between the select band of journalists and the well-named George Steward, speaking for Number Ten. Hacks were initially suspicious, fearing that their individual access to ministers would be made harder, but they soon came to enjoy the smoother, less stressful business of political spoon-feeding. Steward was the first in a long succession of Number Ten spokesmen, of greater or lesser controversy. In recent decades, many have been former journalists who crossed the line to work for their political heroes. Most of the time, the personality of the prime minister played a large role in how the system worked – Winston Churchill, for instance, though once a journalist himself, thought it below him to brief political correspondents, or socialize with them. In general, he dealt with proprietors.

Harold Wilson, on the other hand, was a journalist manqué who adored the gossipy world of Fleet Street. He first employed Trevor Lloyd-Hughes, a former political correspondent himself, during his early years when he endlessly flattered and tickled the vanity of the lobby. Like Tony Blair and Campbell, Wilson and Lloyd-Hughes convinced themselves they could tame the beast of journalism. In one famous incident another press secretary under Wilson, Henry James, got a call from the prime minister, who was then on holiday in the

Scilly Isles and wanted a damaging story kept off the front pages. The next day a particularly loathsome sex murder was discovered at Shepherd's Bush in west London. Wilson called his press officer: 'Henry . . . You've gone too far this time.' Edward Heath never had the easy relations with journalists that Wilson had enjoyed and tried to exploit. In his stiff, formal way he had tried to call the lobby's bluff and suggest that both sides dispense with secrecy and go on the record. His suspicion was clearly that the twice-daily private briefings, with nothing attributed, gave too much power to sceptical journalists and stopped him getting his message over. He even tried open press conferences, as Tony Blair did later. But Heath's attempts at openness were rebuffed by the lobby journalists themselves.

By Wilson's second term, relations with the lobby had soured nastily. As with a later Labour government, many journalists felt conned or let down. David Watt, the *Financial Times* lobby man, wrote that: 'The cynicism or contempt with which political correspondents at Westminster are at present apt to regard the Prime Minister derives at least to some extent from the fact that they regard him as having abused the system and themselves. It is partly that they have been steered in the wrong direction too often by the No. 10 machine.' Joe Haines, a pugnacious former political journalist had been appointed spokesman by then. Haines had little time for many of his former colleagues. He eventually stopped the private briefings, trying to work instead through on-the-record statements, though they were quickly reinstated under Jim Callaghan. Like Alastair Campbell, who seems to have been much influenced by him, Haines argued that journalists should never rely on a single source anyway.

Margaret Thatcher had a curious relationship with journalism. She rose in politics thanks partly to the enthusiastic support of key Fleet Street players, including David English at the *Daily Mail* and Larry Lamb at Rupert Murdoch's *Sun*. Her intellectual outriders included journalists at the *Daily Telegraph* and *The Times*. Her prime ministership was boosted by the almost fanatic support of a large swathe of Fleet Street. In her flights around the world she was punctilious in chatting socially with the lobby who accompanied her; she had regular drinks with journalists too. Yet against all that, she found the questioning and access of less supportive journalism infuriating and, through crisis after crisis, fought against journalists' demands for more access to information. In Bernard Ingham, the former Labour-supporting industrial journalist, she found an unlikely soulmate and he was her press spokesman for eleven years, during which time he reckoned he gave some 5,000 formal briefings and 30,000 informal ones. Ingham, speaking also for many lobby conservatives, said later he regarded the freedom of information campaign as 'monumentally hypocritical and its espousal by editors and our so-called liberal media elite as simply a means of putting themselves in a better position to run the country without the inconvenience of being elected'. In general, he felt political journalists in his day 'have been required progressively to personalize, trivialize and sensationalize politics into a good, intrusive gossip'.[13]

Ingham was himself a large and easily personalized character – irascible, quotable, gregarious, with eyebrows the size of unkempt Yorkshire hedgerows. He was accused by the anti-lobby campaign of briefing personally against a series of Cabinet ministers who had incurred the wrath of Margaret Thatcher and who were then anonymously knifed with barbed Ingham quotes behind the cloak of collective anonymity. He defended himself against these charges but his behaviour certainly prompted the lobby revolt of 1986, when three papers, the *Independent*, the *Guardian* and the *Scotsman*, broke away from the system, ultimately forcing the Number Ten press office under John Major to concede that it could be named as the source of the material quoted.

Neither man would like the comparison but there are similarities between Ingham and Alastair Campbell. Both were partisan journalists who never quite settled into the London newspaper world, both served dominant leaders for a similar number of years and both found themselves at least half-despising the trade that had nurtured them. The most obvious difference, and one Ingham makes much of, is that Margaret Thatcher's communications chief came up through the civil service system, and owed allegiance to it, while Tony Blair's man joined as a party political figure and had to be given special powers by Order in Council to oversee professional civil servants. But they both wrestled with the media octopus and both suffered accusations that they misused their powers. Is it a coincidence that two of the largest characters in modern politics were never elected but found themselves as gatekeepers between a prime minister and the media, at a time when 'media democracy' was emerging out of the parliamentary democracy of old?

In any social system, Ingham and Campbell, a pair of alpha males, would have found themselves near the top. In Britain by the end of the twentieth century, a position controlling traffic between the government and the media was that spot. Like Ingham, Campbell found himself suffering from the law of unintended consequences. In his case attacks on 'spin' meant that a natural frontman had to try to recede into the shadows. To answer accusations that Number Ten could not be trusted Campbell ended the seventy-odd-year-old system of secret unattributable briefings. It had been damaged by the earlier rebellion, but it was finally killed off when he opened the lobby up to foreign journalists and non-Westminster reporters, putting it on the record, and moving its morning meeting from Downing Street to the nearby premises of the Foreign Press Association. These meetings have become dull, at times to the point of absurdity. As I write, the lobby is discussing proposals by Number Ten to televise their morning briefings, with a minister mostly speaking for the prime minister. Newspaper journalists are wary, seeing it as a distraction, and a temptation for limelight-hogging TV reporters. But it would give great influence to whoever then became minister for information. Meanwhile, Campbell had put up Tony Blair at monthly press conferences in front of the cameras: Mr Blair proved more than adept at dealing with the hardest questions Fleet Street's finest could think to throw at him, and the experiment showed that news was not something this prime minister, at least, could be tricked into making. Eventually, worn down by his persistent failure to lasso the media or control its prickly hostility, and by the demands of the job, Campbell resigned.

Within days, the prime minister announced that he had accepted wide-ranging changes suggested by an independent committee of academics, journalists and civil servants. The huge powers enjoyed by Campbell were to be dismantled and his job split. A Labour Party man, and old-fashioned press officer David Hill was to be head of communications and do the political job. But a new civil service structure was to be set up alongside him, with a permanent secretary and a chief official spokesman. The idea seemed to be that the prime minister would have rival personalities – a party-political little red devil on one shoulder, and a purer-than-pure civil service angel for official communications on the other. If the lobby wanted facts they would turn to the angel; if they wanted the dirty stuff of political spin they would go to Beelzebub Hill. There would be a fresh start, a new cleaner way of communicating political events. Life is not like this. Personalities count more than structures, and anyway, journalists are more interested in the dirty raw meat of politics than in statistics. They go to the briefer who they think is closest to the prime minister, whatever he is called. Yet Campbell's eventual defeat was an important moment in the story of political journalism. More than anyone else he had taken personal powers over the whole civil service communications machine and tried to control how the government was seen in the media. He was, and is, a hugely able, intelligent, energetic and driven man. Yet he had been unable to win. Central control and manipulation created, within a few years, some of the worst press coverage any government in modern times has suffered.

What Political Journalists Do

We have now looked at the history of straight parliamentary reporting; and the ticklish question of exactly what a political story is; and at that odd, controversial body, the lobby. Onto the heart of the mystery: how is political journalism now actually done? Where do the stories come from that lead so many broadcast bulletins and newspaper front pages, day after day after day? And what do the journalist-players need to know to take part in the news cycle effectively?

No political journalist is any good who does not know the overall story of politics in his or her time. You need to know who the main characters are, what they think of one another, what they hope to achieve, quite a bit about their histories. You need to know which minister is pushing which plan, and what Downing Street and the Treasury think. You need to have a mental map of the alliances, friendships (those bits are short) and entangled vendettas in each party; only thus can you tell why someone's telling you something about someone else. You need to understand the rhetoric, even if you don't believe it, or take it seriously: you need to know where the third way came from, and how it differs from Labour 'modernization'. And, as said before, you must also know your political history, at least well enough to spot deliberate references to, say, Labour's 1945 programme, and to know what Sir Bernard Ingham said about John Biffen. If you don't know these things – and at the risk of being an old bore, a worrying number of younger political reporters don't seem to bother with the histories and biographies – then you will miss messages sent by one politician to others. They all know their own party history, and journalists hunting for stories need to understand their private code too.

Once you have these maps and references in your head, you have a fair chance of knowing a story when you see one. After that, it's up to you to make the contacts which will provide you with gossip or fact about the next moves. There is a rhythm to the political day which every Westminster journalist understands and which drives the 'story cycle'. From 6.30 a.m. many of us will be sleepily turning on the *Today* programme on Radio 4 and picking up a thick bundle of newspapers from the doormat. *Today* makes news when it reveals something surprising or, more often, when a politician or senior public servant is interviewed on it and says something worth recording – another twist in a story, perhaps just a few words which contradict what the government said the previous week; or a particularly violent political attack. The hottest spot on the programme is at ten minutes past eight, when the editor of the day tries to schedule the best potential interview, though ten past seven is also valuable. Political hacks will organize showers and children's breakfasts around those moments. At the same time, we will be reading the papers. Actually, we won't: we will be gutting them, throwing away all the carefully written sports, arts and other sections, ignoring murders, riots, earthquakes, foreign coups and anything to do with science, and focusing on a narrow range of domestic political stories. Most of us know who our colleagues are particularly close to and can guess the source of stories – who has leaked, and where and why? The papers are compared and guesses are made about which stories are reliable. The political columns are quickly scanned: a good column, as we shall see, should sometimes have a news story buried in it, but this is rare.

On the basis of *Today* and the morning papers, the next part of the London political news cycle clicks in: the political team of London's *Evening Standard* will make their early calls to departments, ministers and Number Ten, following up what has broken already, or confirming stories of their own. By the time most morning newspaper journalists have arrived in central London, clutching coffees and having had their first mobile phone conversations with their news desks, the *Standard* version will be on the streets. That then helps set the agenda for the 11 a.m. news conference, the contemporary equivalent of the lobby briefing, which happens in the white stuccoed terrace house on the Mall where Gladstone once lived and where now the Foreign Press Association resides. There, in the first-floor music room, all moulded plaster and mirrors, the Number Ten press officer reads out the prime minister's business for the day – a bowdlerized, meagre version of it, obviously; we don't get warning of private rows, or read-outs of what was really said to the Israeli prime minister – and lists of ministerial announcements, speeches and visits. This is generally routine but allows papers advance warning of where to send reporters, and tells broadcasters where cameras may usefully be positioned. There is then a question-and-answer session which can last for between a quarter of an hour and an hour, as the hacks challenge the spokesman.

'Tom, what are you saying about the *Herald* story? Has the Foreign Secretary protested about what the prime minister said on Angola and is he prepared to resign?'

'We don't recognize that.'

'Sorry, Tom, don't recognize what? Has the Foreign Secretary spoken to the prime minister about Angola?'

'The prime minister and the Foreign Secretary speak constantly about a wide range of issues, as you know.'

'Is he upset, though?'

'You'd better ask the Foreign Office.'

Collective 'ooh!' since this is not the routine flat denial we might have expected. The spokesman retorts: 'Don't overinterpret.'

Another reporter tries: 'What about the firemen? Is it true that the government is prepared to send troops into the fire stations for training in case the strike is called for Monday?'

'Let's not get ahead of ourselves. The government's position was laid out very clearly by the deputy prime minister . . .'

And on it goes. Most of these exchanges are ritual and almost sleepy. The journalists are trying it on, hoping for an opening, testing the rhetorical fences that have been agreed an hour earlier in Downing

Street. Sometimes the government has a clear message it is trying to sell – that a bill being challenged in the Lords will be lost entirely if Tory peers succeed in their amendment, or that the *Daily Mail* report about the prime minister's holiday plans are a gross intrusion and also inaccurate. Sometimes, the journalists are acting as a pack, trying to force an admission out of the spokesman about a patent inconsistency or failure. This can be a surreal experience, because the spokesman is well briefed and has dogged defensive strokes to play ('I don't recognize that . . . Let's not get ahead of ourselves . . . I've nothing to add to what we said last week . . . That seems like process-ology to me . . . What really matters to the general public is . . .'). In response, the journalists will test out every semi-colon or apparent change in phrasing.

It appears dreadfully nit-picking but derives from a well-founded suspicion about how the government subtly changes its ground when in trouble. For instance, when under pressure over the non-appearance of weapons of mass destruction in Iraq, which journalists had been warned might be deployed against British forces within forty-five minutes of Saddam giving the order, Mr Blair and his spokesmen moved from promising 'weapons' would turn up, to saying that 'programmes' and then 'evidence of programmes' would. There is a substantial difference between a missile, loaded with biological agent, and a typed interview with a retired scientist. Yet if the shift in language had not been picked up, the failure to find the former could, months later, be explained: 'We were very clear, back in February, that we were talking about evidence of former programmes . . . This is a very old story.' In response to a subtle, word-sensitive style of political management, journalists become suspicious lexicographers and fussy grammarians. It is neither exciting nor noble but it is necessary.

Stumbling out of the morning briefing, phones glued to their ears, the correspondents brief their news desks. The next edition of the *Evening Standard* which gains its power partly because it gets to all London just as the day's news agenda is being formed, is already being pumped out. Now, it is time for broadcasting to kick in again. The first BBC call from the briefing is to Radio 4's *The World at One*, which specializes in a forensic analysis of a major story, often political, built up through clips of speeches, interviews and correspondents' reports. If there is anything new from the briefing, the chances are that it will turn up on 'Wato' as well as on TV news bulletins. If a minister or spokesman responds to the story on the lunchtime programmes, the Press Association will feed those morsels into the machine, which in turn will fuel the afternoon news hunt.

When New Labour came into power, ridiculous demands were made by Downing Street that ministers should not lunch with or talk to journalists without telling the Number Ten press office first. The idea behind it was not stupid: Alastair Campbell, having worked as a journalist himself through the Tory years, knew very well how many embarrassing stories came from lunches or dinners. He was hopelessly naïve, though, in expecting ambitious politicians to cut off their own private links to the media, and to go through him instead. Although for a few months there was a certain embarrassment and difficulty about setting up lunches, and ministers decided they preferred to avoid the best-known venues, trade quickly picked up. The recent changes to the Commons hours, with sittings straddling the middle of the day, rather than beginning after lunch and meandering on until the small hours, have made lunches harder, though dinners seem easier to arrange. And it is often lamented that less alcohol is consumed than it was twenty years ago.

This is undoubtedly true, though the booze does not always work in the journalist's interests. I vividly remember taking a rising Scottish Labour MP to one of the then-favoured political restaurants, La Poule au Pot in Ebury Street, which served large portions of rich, simple French food and was overseen by an enormous patron, helped by numerous 'boys'. One of its quirks was that the wine was served in French rustic fashion, from huge two-litre bottles, which were placed on each table; at the end of the meal, a mark would be made to calculate how much had been consumed and you would be charged accordingly. My guest looked on the bottle as a personal challenge, consumed almost the entire two litres (I had a glass) and had to be carried out of the taxi by two policemen when we returned to Westminster. The story he had for me, about the Kinnock leadership crisis, dissolved in his head some time into the meal. On another occasion, with my then lunching-partner Alan Travis of the *Guardian*, I took Alan Clark, the great Tory diarist and then a trade minister, to lunch at Christmas time at a restaurant in St James's Street. It was overbooked and we were placed in a chilly, comfortless basement. The food took ages to come. Alan became increasingly grim, so stupidly I offered to let him choose 'some decent wine' to cheer us up. His eyes lit up, his lizard smile returned and, two hours and two bottles later, Mr Travis and I returned through the slush wondering desperately how we were ever going to explain the horrendous cost of our Burgundy to our respective offices. So stricken were we by the cost of the wine that in our panic we completely forgot about the very good story Clark had told us about how he was colluding in breaking trade embargoes to Saddam Hussein's Iraq, a regime he favoured, at least by comparison with its deadly rival, Ayatollah Khomeini's Iran.

So the booze doesn't always help. But lunching is important. It not only allows you to form a personal relationship with a minister, or leading Opposition politician, but it gives them a chance to size you up. More junior political journalists often lunch in a group of two or three, or even in a club of up to twenty. There was a longstanding lunch club for parliamentary reporters who did not have lobby tickets, so they met MPs in a Commons dining room. Female political correspondents currently have their own lunching group, where both Stephen Byers, discussing the euro, and Peter Mandelson, discussing the same subject, have found themselves reported on the record and badly embarrassed. It is frankly impossible to have an 'off the record' conversation with that number of competitive journalists and expect not to be quoted, then to be sourced, as the story passes round the lobby. But groups are not, in general, a good idea. It means that the politician is outnumbered. His account of what he's said can be countered by several witnesses, the hacks. If they cook up a version of the conversation, a little spicier than it really was, the politician has no redress and is scuppered. So experienced MPs tend to refuse group invitations. An entirely malign counter-development is that some ministers are so nervous of lunching, yet so ambitious or curious too, that they arrive with a press officer or spin doctor in tow as chaperone. Thus the journalist is expected to buy lunch for the story-killing censor. It is like the Chinese custom of charging the family of executed prisoners for the bullet used to despatch them. Except in a couple of wholly unusual cases, I refuse to buy lunch for chaperones.

The lunch must be prepared for. The proper reporter will read through old stories about the politician, check all the running questions from the department, and perhaps ask relevant newspaper specialists –

the health correspondent, the economics correspondent – what they think the current controversies are. It is rare to go to a lunch with no idea of what stories you might get from it, and still return with good material. The setting matters too. Many politicians have favourite restaurants and at any one time, there is a popular list. The grandest Tories often insist on the Savoy Grill – or did so before it was modernized to provide decent food – or one of several other places offering conservative, traditional fare at very high prices, but at tables widely spaced apart. The spacing of tables is obviously expensive in high-rent London, but useful for genuine discretion. Then there are the best-known political restaurants, like Shepherd's in Marsham Street, the Tate Gallery restaurant, the Atrium and Quirinale at Millbank and Christopher's in Wellington Street. In each of these you can expect to see other journalists and MPs eating, and you will be seen yourself; but they are handy and near and reliable. Christopher's, owned by the son of the Thatcher-era Tory wet Sir Iain Gilmour, now Lord Gilmour, started as the meeting place of Tory centrists but has now become hugely popular across the political spectrum. Any political journalist who lunches a lot, though, will have a range of less well-known eateries, obscure Italian joints or chi-chi places tucked away in Mayfair mews, which provide genuine obscurity. When, as often happens, you arrive at your table to see some rival journalist or another MP sitting in earshot, a short pantomime of shrugging, apologetic smiles and whispers follows, and another table is found.

Not every lunch produces a story. Some merely develop or cement relations which will be useful later. But the journalist will often start, after some smalltalk, by referring to a mutual acquaintance in trouble, or by disparaging the guest's well-known enemy, to soften things up. After a while, the journalist and the minister, or Opposition MP, will know a little about each other's families, or sporting interests, or whatever. The illusion, dangerous to both sides, of a real friendship is beginning. At a proper story-hunting lunch, the journalist will try to go through a mental list of possible story subjects without being too obvious, or too boring; and it often becomes obvious that the minister is there with a particular subject to raise. In a relaxed atmosphere, with ninety minutes or so together, there is time to press, probe, and go sideways into a subject, and very few politicians are ruthless enough to say nothing at all. Some do: one member at least of the Blair

Cabinet is notorious with journalists for arriving to lunch with a bloodcurdling demand for absolute secrecy and utter discretion; looking around with wild and hunted eyes; and then whispering a lot of innocuous New Labour pap you could have picked up on a party website for free. No one lunches him twice, except the insatiably greedy. In general, the probing and cross-questioning will produce something. It might be informed speculation about a reshuffle – 'the health minister told me he'd asked Tony to let him try the Home Office next time' – or confirmation that the department was planning a bill on some subject; or an inside account of a Cabinet committee argument. On rare occasions, the story is so good, with so much detail or such strong quotes, that a short visit to the loo to jot notes down on a paper napkin is needed. Few pleasures on this little green planet are so glorious as tucking a real story into your breast pocket and returning for some cheese and a final glass of claret.

Special advisers, who are sometimes spin doctors but are also sometimes genuine policy specialists working for ministers, their shadows, the Treasury or Number Ten, are also worth targeting. Often they are younger and less experienced. Often they are deliberately used to say things that a minister would like said, but would not quite risk saying himself. They have to be treated with a certain caution, since a special adviser is deniable, and may be denied, whereas a Cabinet minister is not. Mainstream Whitehall officials are generally less keen to lunch, and more aware of the Official Secrets Act; but there are always exceptions and a good departmental source with a grudge against the minister is a wonderful prize.

Though lunching has been traditional, much the same applies to dinner and even, occasionally, to breakfast meetings. Shorter chats may be had over drinks in Westminster's Pugin Room or, more publicly, Annie's Bar (the only monument left in British politics to Robert Maxwell, rogue, proprietor and sometime Labour MP who as head of the catering committee created this meeting point for hacks and Members) or the various sordid pubs in the Westminster area, notably the Red Lion off Whitehall. Coffees are grabbed in tearooms or the new, expensively forested barn of Portcullis House, or at the broadcasters' HQ, 4 Millbank. Beyond the immediate cycle of the Westminster news day, party conferences and summer or Christmas parties offer other opportunities for social contact which can produce stories. In his day Jeffrey Archer's vintage Krug and shepherd's pie parties in his suite at the annual Tory conference, and his Christmas parties at his grand flat overlooking the Thames, allowed relatively humble hacks to mingle with the likes of Margaret Thatcher, Lord Saatchi, Nigel Lawson, newspaper editors and most members of the then Cabinet; which partly explains why so many journalists were so reluctant to attack him later. I witnessed some extraordinary scenes at these, and other Tory grandee-sponsored parties late at night – bitter rows, and alcohol-fuelled rapprochements. More conventionally, most newspapers arrange a heavy series of lunches and dinners for the senior politicians at each party conference, with the best restaurants at Blackpool, Bournemouth and Brighton heavily booked months in advance.

The curious intimacy fostered by such events is caught by an incident some years ago when Margaret Thatcher was prime minister. Ted Heath hosted a dinner for journalists, a regular Tory conference custom of his. His table was surrounded by smaller ones, with Thatcher Cabinet ministers also being dined by hacks, and the meal was a good one. At the end of it one of the journalists present, Elinor Goodman of *Channel Four News*, presented Heath with a small box as a thank-you present. He opened it and the room fell silent as he picked out a chocolate replica of Margaret Thatcher. With a great harrumph, Heath seized his knife and hacked it to pieces, watched in horrified amusement by her ministers. On another occasion, at one of the Archer parties, a Cabinet minister arrived in the middle of a ferocious row with his wife. In front of a circle of awestruck journalists she announced that she was off, 'so you can pick up some pretty boys – we all know that's what you like'.

Back at Westminster, the political day continues after lunch with Commons statements and the arrival of snowdrifts of government departmental announcements and printed answers to MPs' written questions. According to statistics collated by Nick Harvey, a culture spokesman for the Liberal Democrats, Tony Blair's government produced 32,766 press releases in its first five years – an average of one every four minutes, day and night, week in, week out, weekends included. Each cost an average of £80 to produce, making a total of £2.6 million since 1997. Labour's response to questions about whether all this money was well spent was, with hardly a quiver of a smirk,

'The fact that we produce so much demonstrates how keen we are to keep the public informed.' Good journalism means sifting through the paper. Scandals of overspending or misspending are tucked in the back of blue-covered reports from select committees or the National Audit Office. Departments sneak out embarrassing facts in bland-looking press releases on the final day of a Commons sitting. Jo Moore was only following, more ruthlessly, an old Whitehall precedent, which is to 'get out' the bad news when journalists might miss it.

Routine and good filing systems produce stories, too. For years the political editor of the *Daily Telegraph*, George Jones, would surprise Whitehall with apparent leaks of forthcoming pay deals for public sector workers. He kept a note in his diary of the day they would be announced, worked out the inflation increase, made a few calls and educated guesses, and got a splash story every time. My modest contribution to the same school of journalism was to note that, in the mid-1980s, the Public Accounts Committee reports into various scandals closely followed the earlier report sent to them by the National Audit Office, with a few predictably stronger phrases added. So I simply used the NAO reports to write stories predicting that the MPs were about to blast this, condemn that and recommend the other. MPs on the committee were convinced I had a mole and wasted a lot of time trying to work out who was leaking to me. Also, stories can be stolen. They can be drawn from colleagues by slyness. David Hencke is an excellent political investigator who has many scalps hanging from his belt. But he has, or had, a weakness for telling colleagues what he was working on. I found that a genial conversation, followed by many expressions of admiration for his hard work, occasionally gave me enough of a lead to get to a story myself. I have never actually stolen a story from a rival's computer, but I know people who have. When the *Independent* first launched, some of its staff had recently left *The Times* and still knew the passwords for its system. We had a vigorous internal debate about whether to hack into its stories and steal them before deciding that we had better not. The press gallery is a ferociously competitive place at times, and people do lurk at the doors of others' offices to overhear stories. Secretaries have been plied with drink and any official who is known to have been passed over or offended by a politician's behaviour is likely to be targeted. It is an enjoyably dirty business.

The lobby day continues with a second briefing, this time in a desolate little room at the top of an obscure spiral staircase. The painted boards displaying the names of lobby chairmen show that it is lobby property; the rather fine collection of old political prints has disappeared, presumed stolen, and the collection of chairs is a grubby sight. Here, at 3.45 p.m., the prime minister's spokesman will continue the themes of the day, though custom and practice dictates that he starts by reading through the prime minister's day, yet again. On busy afternoons, with a major story running, these can be combative sessions. On other days, it is about as lively as morning Mass in the mildewed chapel of a depopulated village.

After that, much of the rest of the day is taken up with calls and writing, plus meetings in corridors, MPs' offices, departments and the inevitable bars. But the heart of the job is not really the physical traipsing about the Palace; it is the strength or weakness of your relationships with the politicians and aides who give you stories. That makes it a social job. It always has been. Earlier we saw how in Victorian times the need for mass journalism gave writing editors an 'in' to the homes and views of the statesmen. Not everyone tolerated this: Churchill never bothered with lobby journalists or press conferences. But later, in the Wilson years, there was intense weekending and private dining between Cabinet ministers and sympathetic journalists. During the Thatcher and Major governments, Tory commentators and even neutral correspondents would visit ministers and their families for Sunday lunch in the country, or invite them over. The SDP was formed with the deep and active engagement of journalists, though they were rarely reporters. And today it continues. There are social circles of senior political journalists, newspaper editors and ministers who meet in Cotswold second homes, or on golf courses, or for long walks in the country, when the higher gossip about what exactly is going on between the prime minister and the chancellor, or the real story behind a resignation, can be thrashed out and chewed over. Journalists will invite ministers, who do become friends, to dinner or lunch at their houses and while the dishes are being cleared, and children play on the grass, deep information is passed on.

What does the public get in return? There are journalists who say all such social contact, from the weekends away to the bibulous dinners, is corrupt. It is unavoidable, they argue, that the hack should become friendly with the politician and go soft, so that the MP moves from being a source of information to being specially protected. Some of the most highly respected political journalists, notably broadcast interviewers such as Jeremy Paxman and John Humphrys, have fairly strict rules against socializing with 'the enemy'. At the other end of the spectrum are the partisan commentators and columnists who openly behave as propagandists and supporters of a politician or faction, and who glory in their enthralment. This is a strain of journalism that goes back to the very dawn of political journalism and the factional hacks of Queen Anne's London, who mingled with Whig or Tory grandees as they wrote, for money, on their behalf. There is nothing wrong with commentators being partisan, since the reading public quickly understands what they are getting. So, for instance, a Tory commentator like Simon Heffer was for a time close to, and highly supportive of, Michael Portillo. Then they fell out in the most intemperate terms and the Heffer guns were swivelled against him. So, again, Gordon Brown has had a group of supportive journalists, such as Paul Routledge of the *Mirror* and Paul Dacre, editor of the *Daily Mail*, who are invited to 11 Downing Street for social evenings and lunches.

But the question is a hard one for the majority of political journalists who are neither tough interviewers by trade – so really don't need to avoid their targets – nor fully declared partisans. How close should you get to politicians, and what are the dangers? Robin Oakley, BBC political editor, was criticized for taking a holiday with Jeffrey Archer; he might have chosen better but he might also retort that almost everyone took something, be it a gift-wrapped whole Cheddar cheese, or a glass of champagne, from Archer. Many senior journalists, including me, have jumped at an invitation to dinner, or lunch, with the Blairs at Chequers. Again, it is a rare chance to see the place and to watch the prime minister being relatively relaxed. The anecdotes can be saved and served up in later columns or articles; the other guests appraised. If you want to know about the man, it is an irresistible offer. Yet a Chequers invitation, casually mentioned in passing to colleagues, is like a (very) minor award – the Order of the Blair Cheeseboard – and can make the recipient just that little bit more understanding of the problems facing the prime minister than he or she might otherwise be. Or ought to be.

The crude argument is that a few glasses of booze, or a dead crayfish, buys good copy. It is never like that. If you really talk with a politician about their in tray, and the problems of rival departments, or of dodgy past initiatives, it is hard to avoid seeing things their way. The same perspective that gives you insight, also blunts your hostility. So is it better to stand outside, defiantly ignorant, making judgements that the crowd will applaud? There is no final answer. If you don't form close understandings with senior politicians, so that you can hear them think aloud, honestly, in a relaxed way, then you are unlikely to understand much of what is really going on. Yet if you do, then you drift closer to them emotionally and may very well flinch from putting the boot in when they have failed in some way.

The unsatisfactory solution is that the 'honest' journalist must behave like a shit – must build up close sources and then, quite often, betray them. I had this experience with, for instance, John Patten. As a rising Tory minister he was an excellent and frank source, loyal to the prime minister but also outspoken about the dilemmas ripping through Whitehall. I thoroughly enjoyed his company, and his wife's, and we lunched together regularly. I visited him at home; he was a wonderful host, and generous with stories. Then came the time when, as education secretary, he was visibly struggling and his policies were unravelling. Instead of writing supportively and understandingly, I joined the critical pack. It seemed to me to be the correct objective judgement of his performance, and therefore a kind of journalistic duty. It seemed to him a personal betrayal and he never forgave me, cutting me dead for years. He was right, too. This pattern has repeated itself in my career several times and is common across Westminster. The cynical but professional answer is to have a range of good sources, with more always under cultivation, so that when one is blown, there are others to fall back on. But we all go easy on pals occasionally – the decent among us, at least. In return, we hope, the public gets a better feeling about what's really happening behind closed doors.

Many people outside Westminster, from editors to film-makers to ordinary consumers of journalism, view the lunches, the drinks and the weekends of lobby journalism with extreme suspicion. What should be adversarial and edgy looks too much like a social class – I call them, after the now defunct bookshop, the Politico's People, a single political elite stretching from print to power. In Victorian and Edwardian politics, the political–journalistic complex did not really exist. Editors and proprietors might mingle with party leaders but the ordinary, top-hatted members of the parliamentary press gallery, and the early lobby journalists, were firmly below the salt. These were still the days of aristocratic politics. By the 1930s this was breaking down: in his memoirs Bill Deedes recalled being ticked off for speaking to an MP he had known at school and who happened to be blacklisted by press reporters at the time.

By the second half of the twentieth century, the leading political journalists and the leading politicians were coming, pretty much, from similar social backgrounds. The grammar-school boys who won scholarships to Oxbridge, and were rising through the Labour Party, were not so different from the journalists reporting them. In the sixties and seventies, it was becoming at least as fashionable for bright graduates to go into Fleet Street or the BBC as to go into politics. Today, ministers are if anything likelier to be less flash than the journalists who trail them. Yet even now common experiences in union debating societies, campaigning groups and even as party workers mean that many MPs and hacks are indeed part of the same tight-knit group. This explains something that may seem a mystery to outsiders – why do politicians, knowing that it may get them into trouble, reach out for friendships with journalists in the first place?

An obvious answer is that they need the publicity and are prepared to barter a few innocuous secrets, which will later be written up in extreme terms, for favourable references. But it rarely works like that. Columnists, not reporters, are the people who mark the cards of up and coming ministers. Reporters are the story-getters and far more dangerous company. It is partly that many ministers are lonely and insecure. If they want to talk politics and assess their rivals, they may not be able to do so with a spouse or partner. They will certainly find it tricky doing so with the rivals. So political journalists, sharing their culture and background, understanding instantly the rivalries and issues, make tempting friends. We are all the same kind of people, sharing the same strange interests. Further, a decent journalist will have unchecked, unpublishable gossip to pass on in return. Hacks are like the seed-spreading birds of Westminster, picking up a little something here, excreting it there, and so keeping the weedy garden fecund. We are parasites in the proper sense: without us, the political system would not quite work, and ministers would go mad with boredom and isolation, immured in their departments, desperate to know what the rest of Whitehall is up to.

Political Journalism Now: Are We Too Powerful?

A few years ago, an American political writer was reflecting on the rise of the pundits, and the way their social status was outstripping the politicians they wrote about. Once, he mused, the columnists had waited outside the doors of the politicians' great houses while they dined. Then the journalists started to dine with them. 'Now, we dine on them.' Something like the same unbalancing rise of unelected journalistic power over elected power has happened here. We have seen how the parliamentary reporters, with their frock coats and salaries well above the Fleet Street average, became the praetorian guard of journalism. Later we shall look at the rise of the press barons, to the point where a couple of them were so touched with pride that they dreamed of overthrowing the democracy itself. We are in nothing like that condition today – there is no overt anti-parliamentarian plotting in the offices of Rupert Murdoch's News International, or at Associated Press. But there is a strong sense that the power to set the agenda and initiate the terms of national debate has passed from ministers to journalists. Trevor Kavanagh, political editor of the *Sun*, was first called the most powerful man in British politics by the former Tory Chancellor Kenneth Clarke with whom he has a longstanding disagreement over the euro. It is an exaggeration, but a telling one. In the Commons today the lobby reporters are generally polite and, on the surface, respectful to the MPs they mingle with. But many feel themselves to be greater, or at least more immediately powerful, than the back-benchers desperate for publicity; and even many ministers. Now the politicians call them up, invite them to lunch, or to parties, not the other way around.

The origins of the rise in contemporary press swagger are in the Thatcher years, when papers like the *Sun* and the *Sunday Times* proved far more effective public advocates of her revolution than most Tory politicians. She in turn courted them and used them against nay-sayers and 'wets' in her own government; their guiding figures became accustomed to being invited round for quiet chats and private advice.

Sir David English of the *Daily Mail*, who was, with Andrew Neil, perhaps her most persuasive print advocate, used to visit her frequently at Number Ten. In those years, at the key social events, from lunches at Chequers to Jeffrey Archer's parties, Cabinet ministers, Number Ten advisers, editors and trusted political journalists would mingle, so that it was sometimes hard to know where the government ended and the media began.

This was all blown asunder when Lady Thatcher was ousted from power and John Major took over. Most of her close press admirers were genuinely traumatized – Woodrow Wyatt's diaries are a classic account. While there was a brief reassembling of forces to keep out Michael Heseltine, widely regarded by the press Thatcherites as her assassin, and a brief period of support for her successor John Major, things were never the same between the Tories and the press. The disappointment and rancour left by her demise curdled into outright contempt for Mr Major. Black Wednesday, in September 1991, when sterling fell out of the European exchange rate mechanism, stripping the government of both its economic and foreign strategy, was the turning point. Even the outward forms of respect shown to elected power by print power were crumbling. In a famous vignette, Mr Major himself telephoned Kelvin MacKenzie at the *Sun* to ask nervously how he was going to treat him over the crisis. 'Let me put it this way, prime minister,' the editor is said to have replied, 'I have two buckets of shit on my desk and tomorrow morning I am going to empty both of them over your head.' The queen's first minister giggled nervously, said something about Kelvin being 'a wag' and replaced the handset. That may be a shocking story, but weak prime ministers have had almost as brutal treatment before. In 1956 Anthony Eden, for instance, summoned Captain Basil Liddell Hart, the great military writer and former *Times* correspondent, to help him to draw up plans for an invasion of Suez. Liddell Hart wrote a first draft, then a second, but both were returned as unsatisfactory. In the end Eden returned no fewer than four draft plans. An angry Liddell Hart sent him the 'fifth' which was in fact the first one again. He then admitted to the prime minister what he had done. In one account,

Eden flushes red; he throws a heavy pewter inkwell at Liddell Hart, spattering his natty off-white linen suit with large ink-stains.

Liddell Hart, tall, slim, moustached, looks down at the damage.
He rises swiftly from his seat, catches up a large government-issue
wastepaper basket, jams it upside down on the Prime Minister's
head, and stalks out.

You have to cheer for Liddell Hart. But the truth is that we
political journalists have spent too much time metaphorically jamming
wastebins on politicians' heads. We have become too powerful, too
much the interpreters, using our talents as communicators to crowd
them out. On paper we mock them more than ever before and report
them less than ever before. On television and radio, we commentators
are edging them out ever more carelessly. Democracy made modern
British journalism. Newspapers and then the broadcasting media
derived their authority from parliament and the ballot box. We are
overshadowing the same institutions that made us; we have become
insufficiently serious. Once my father bought a rose bush for our
garden in Scotland. He supported it with some insignificant-looking
sticks. The rose died and the sticks grew. That is what is happening in
Westminster, too.

4

Lord Copper and his Children

'Some of them are temperamental, tiresome ... A number are ignorant, lazy, opinionated, intellectually dishonest and inadequately supervised.'

Lord Black of Crossharbour on journalists

'Black Faces Racketeering Charges'

Journalists on Lord Black of Crossharbour

Becoming an Editor

The year was 1996. I was walking alone through the echoing glass and marble halls of Canary Wharf in London Docklands, squinting against the rays of the evening sun. I was slightly unsteady on my feet. I had just had a large glass of champagne but that was not the reason. It was that I had also just become a newspaper editor. As it would turn out, I would continue to feel a little unsteady for the next two years. I didn't know that at the time. Then, it was pure delight and self-congratulation. It was like winning the lottery, getting married and finding your hair growing thicker again, all on the same day. Ahead of me, coming the other way, I saw a brisk, rather overweight, familiar figure. It was Kelvin MacKenzie, former editor of the *Sun*, impresario of topless darts on Live TV and also a director of Mirror Group Newspapers, one of the owners of the *Independent*, whose new editor I had just become. He had a wolfish grin. ''Allo,' said Kelvin. 'Congratulations, young Marr ... or Number Four, as I shall now call you.' I blinked and smiled. Why number four, I asked; why not Andrew? 'Because,' said Kelvin, 'you're the fourth of 'em. I'm not going to call you by your name because we don't want to get all human and intimate. Then I might be upset when they sack you ... *as they undoubtedly will*. Ta-ra.'

And as they undoubtedly did. The editorship of the *Independent* in 1996 was less a poisoned chalice than a pint glass of lukewarm ricin. My predecessor but one, Ian Hargreaves, had been sacked in the most brutal of circumstances after a short reign. I was taking over from Charles Wilson, a former editor of *The Times* now working for the Mirror Group, who deeply resented stepping aside, and would now, as ex-acting editor, be one of my immediate bosses. The paper was being fought over by two rivals who hated each other. Its circulation was low, by far the weakest of the national broadsheets. Budgets were correspondingly tight and morale was rock-bottom. Rupert Murdoch had launched a murderous price war, slashing the cost to readers of *The Times*: his main target was the *Daily Telegraph* but he looked likely to sink us in his gigantic wake. And my experience as an editor was limited to commissioning pieces two decades earlier for my school magazine. Some months before I had had lunch with Simon Jenkins, a brilliant journalist, who told me that the trade was divided into natural writers and natural editors. He, like me, was a writer; it had been a mistake for him to edit *The Times* and his strong advice was that I should never even think of going in for editing, either. It was excellent advice and instantly forgotten. As I stood there in the evening sunlight, puzzling over MacKenzie's witticism, I was not only the youngest national broadsheet editor. I was by a good margin the most idiotic.

So, why had I done it? There were, looking back, two crucial factors in my mind. The first was vanity. The second was greed. To be a national newspaper editor is a grand thing. Even at the poor-mouse *Independent*, though I didn't have a chauffeur, I was driven to and from work in a taxi-limousine, barking orders down my mobile phone. Even as the poorest-paid of my contemporary national editors, I was soon on £175,000, which was much more than I was worth. Others were paid more still – the highest paid editor at that time was said to be getting around £600,000 – and many editors had share options which made them, on paper at least, very wealthy men. One is not supposed to admit those things matter but they do, of course. In the office, I was the commander. Eyes swivelled when I arrived and people at least pretended to listen when I spoke. The *Indy* might be small, but she was mine. It was a little like one of those naval novels, where the officer gets command of his first ship and doesn't care that it only has two masts, six small cannon, a nasty hole under the port bow, and a mutinous cook. Out on the high seas, it was still a ship and I was still her captain. Outside the office, I could visit the prime minister, archbishops, famous actors and fellow editors. I would be watched and written about in the trade press and the media columns of other papers. Opposition politicians asked for my opinion which, always generous by nature, I freely gave. Revered writers I had admired for many years from a distance now came and asked about salary increases, which I tried to give them, too. Money and power: what else do people do things for?

I am selling myself a little short. Ideals matter too, and did then. For me the *Independent* was a noble cause and a perpetual delight, not simply a newspaper. It gave me the best years of my working life, as well as some of my closest friends, when it was first launched in 1986 and promised to change the face of broadsheet journalism. The first rumours broke surface just after Christmas 1985, when I was on holiday lazing in front of a fire at my parents' house reading the *Financial Times* and came across a mysterious story about a new paper ('a quality national daily newspaper produced on new electronic equipment and printed by contract outside Fleet Street'). It was apparently being created by journalists, to be launched the following autumn.[1] I can still remember the bubble of excitement as the logs crackled. I was then political correspondent of the *Scotsman* and desperate to get my lobby ticket. As recounted already, Tony Bevins fixed it for me to join the new paper. In the months before it finally launched, and for about a year afterwards, it really seemed that we had broken away from the old world of proprietors. Some of the greatest writers in the trade were working there, from grandees like Rees-Mogg and Peter Jenkins, to the poet-correspondent James Fenton, the cartoonist Nicholas Garland, Alexander Chancellor, Rupert Cornwell, Francis Wheen, and many more. Editorial lines were discussed among the staff, lolling on sofas or sitting on the floor of the Old Street office. Photographers like the great Brian Harris broke every rule to get startling, newsworthy images. Ordinary newspapers are full of daily questions such as, what will the proprietor think? Can we afford that? Is it our kind of story? and so on. For a short, glorious while the only question that mattered at the *Indy* was 'why not?' There was an electric can-do atmosphere in the paper that none of us will ever forget, despite the decline that swiftly followed.

I eventually left to take other jobs, and came back in 1992 as chief political columnist, following the unexpected and early death of Peter Jenkins. By then the paper was in deep trouble. It had been nudging both the *Guardian* and *The Times* in circulation, but it had shallow pockets. A ruthless fightback by Rupert Murdoch and an economic downturn were biting savagely. Arguments among the founding fathers, the ill-timed launch of the Sunday paper, and a tougher commercial environment forced a change in the ownership, away from the safely neutral banks to media bidders. The *Independent*, which had once been able to select the pick of Fleet Street's finest, was now losing key staff back to more secure and higher-selling rivals. There were constant rumours of scaly predators and more distant ones of fabled 'white knights' riding to the rescue. The Italian and Spanish media shareholders were getting out. In was coming, instead, the Mirror Group, headed by David Montgomery. I was one of several staff who wrote and faxed long letters to the Italians begging them not to sell shares to Montgomery. But it was him or Tony O'Reilly's Independent Newspapers. By the time I became editor, both of them had a little over 48 per cent of the shareholding, with a sliver of independents, including Andreas Whittam Smith, the founder, holding the balance.

No writer of exuberant fiction could have dreamed up the confrontation between Montgomery and O'Reilly. One was a lean, dry, sarcastic Ulster Protestant; the other was a large, extrovert, passionate Catholic Irish tycoon, who had made his fortune from years of leading Heinz in America. Their mutual dislike was instant and apparently absolute. Both wanted the *Independent* outright. Each was determined to stop the other at all costs. Both had something to prove. Montgomery had relaunched the mid-market *Today* newspaper with catastrophic consequences a few years earlier and had been booted out by Rupert Murdoch as a result. He wanted to prove that his original vision, a Yuppie paper full of stories for and about expensive, ambitious people, preferably being mugged for their Rolex watches in Mayfair, could still work . . . and he wanted that paper to be the high-minded *Independent*. He thought it could be produced at a fraction of the cost of an ordinary paper, with relatively little ordinary newsgathering journalism, but plenty of rewriting, and big-name columnists to fill up the spaces. He had a ruthless management style, much in evidence since he had persuaded the bank to put him in charge of the Mirror Group. One of the excellent editors he sacked said of Montgomery that 'what he did showed a breathtaking disregard for keeping his word and a merciless savagery unheard of even by Fleet Street's bloodsoaked and hypocritical standards'[2] though some of us would put it a little more strongly than that.

The first go at hitching a broadsheet editor to the Mirror Group style had come in 1994 when Ian Hargreaves, a former senior BBC executive and long-time *Financial Times* man, then its deputy editor, was approached by an intermediary on behalf of the minority Italian shareholders of the *Independent*. He was assured that though Montgomery had a place on the board, he had no say in the choosing of editors. Hargreaves realized this was a fiction. The first time he met Montgomery at a dinner with the other shareholders, 'he was like a man sitting in a personal sauna . . . uncomfortable, hot, irritable. He just about accepted that he had, at this stage of the game, to behave himself but he really wanted to bite someone, or wee on the carpet. There was a tension about him.' Hargreaves, offered the editorship, insisted he had to meet Montgomery privately first, who reluctantly came to his flat on London's South Bank – 'he was like an animal released from his cage. He could barely sit down.' Hargreaves was trying to find a way of working with the Ulsterman, who was initially furious when the *FT* man insisted on taking a short family holiday before starting as editor. But, says Hargreaves, 'My attitude to Montgomery was, the man is clearly an asshole but I am not a snob and if he's a Belfast tabloid oik, he'll know a lot of things I don't know and need to know.'

At this stage the paper was still nominally under the control of Sergio Cellini, an executive appointed by the Italian shareholders, *La Repubblica*. Montgomery wanted real control. Six weeks into Hargreaves's editorship, Montgomery arrived in his office, closed the door and announced that he had heard that 'Sergio is causing you a lot of problems'. Hargreaves, baffled, denied it, but Montgomery pressed on: 'He's wasting your time, you're an editor . . . I think we should take Sergio out of it; what you need is freedom to edit and a clear relationship with the Mirror operation. And that's the view of the board.' This was a common Mirror Group tactic: first isolate the editor, insisting on his need for 'freedom', then try to exercise complete control over him. Hargreaves, by now suspicious, asked which members of the board had said Cellini should go: 'And I ran through the names, the Italian directors and the Spanish, and he said yes [to each name] and I said, well I am going to ring them after this meeting. And he turned an even brighter shade of red, and left.' The directors, when called, all denied saying any such thing.

> So the next time he came I said, David, if you ever lie to me again, we will never be able to make a success of this and it will just be impossible. I had barely got my feet under the table before realizing that either I would leave in high drama, or he would; and I didn't think there was a high chance it would be him. But I didn't think there was no chance. So I dug in and tried to carry on. It was like a cowboy film – you knew there was always the next wooded valley or the next ambush. Life was just a succession of ambushes, supplemented by a campaign of psychological warfare – like having Kelvin MacKenzie standing up saluting every time I came into a room; 'everybody be upstanding, intellectuals coming on board'. Any sign of weakness that you happened to show, and they would be onto it.[3]

Hargreaves cut the paper's budget by a third soon after taking over with the understanding that no more would be demanded for a while, as he tried to make a thinner paper work. 'But almost the next day the pressure started for more . . .' Under him, the paper moved from its sprawling old offices beside Bunhill Fields to the gleaming new Canary Wharf; new columnists joined; 'Bridget Jones's Diary' by Helen Fielding was invented (with the help of Charlie Leadbeater, who later went to work for Tony Blair in Number Ten) and the *Independent* staff learned to work harder. There was less fun about. Hargreaves was working a fourteen-hour day. But it was not enough: 'The way they fired me was kind of poetic.' He was on his way to take a train to Middlesbrough to support a reporter, John Arlidge, in a court case involving British Telecom, when he was asked to stop at the *Irish Independent* offices in Charlotte Street on the way. 'I said I can't, but they said it would only take a minute . . . and they said basically, it was all over and had a press release ready.' Hargreaves had a lunch booked for later in the week with the other main shareholder Tony O'Reilly, who said he was keen to keep the appointment. Hargreaves demurred, but it went ahead: 'So we had lunch at Wilton's and Chryss (O'Reilly's wife) arrived half way through, and it was all perfectly civil, and then he said, I want you to know that your contract will be honoured. Montgomery wants you to come out without a penny but I won't allow that to happen.'

But what else did Montgomery want? What was driving him as he tried to impose the alien culture of a tabloid newspaper group on this young broadsheet? In essence, he wanted to get his own back on Rupert Murdoch by proving there was a new way of doing things. Working alongside him was Charlie Wilson, who had also been sacked by Murdoch, in his case as editor of *The Times*. Together they thought they could match and take on News International. Against Murdoch's *Sun* they would have the *Mirror*; against Sky Television they would have Live TV (run by MacKenzie, the third ex-Murdoch man) . . . and against *The Times* would be the *Independent*. That they were, by contrast with the awesome tycoon, small-scale and second-rate, was the only small blemish in the plan. It was a bit like a few cashiered French generals banding together to teach Napoleon a thing or two.

O'Reilly was a different case entirely. A famous Irish rugby player and hero of the British Lions in his day, he went into marketing (he was responsible for Kerrygold butter) and joined the Heinz Corporation in Pittsburgh, becoming the first non-Heinz to run it. His golden touch with ketchup, beans and other homely products made him a very rich man. He used part of that wealth to build up his own portfolio of companies, notably newspapers in Ireland, Australia and Portugal, as well as marketing businesses, radio interests and glassware. With houses in America, Australia, Ireland and France, and on his second marriage, to the Greek shipping heiress and horse-breeder Chryss Goulandris, O'Reilly was everything that Montgomery was not – charismatic, boomingly self-confident and a vigorous proponent of the enjoyment of life. He wanted the *Independent* because to be a national newspaper owner in London (he already owned local papers in Britain) would put him into the big league. And with the *Irish Independent* doing very well, he thought he could work the same magic in Britain. O'Reilly's reputation preceded him like a rebel army. If he didn't have an empire on the Murdoch scale, it was a pretty fair-sized kingdom. O'Reilly was a pretty fair-sized king, even in old age – a broad, large, fresh-faced man with piercing eyes, a billow of white hair and a generous grin – though as with many powerful men, his eyes always seemed just a little colder than his smile. We knew that he was careful with money, an excellent marketing man with a huge business reputation, and broadly liberal in his politics – pro-European, as the Irish tend to be, and at one remove from the British Establishment. As tycoons went, he seemed made to measure for the *Independent*.

In London, at this time, O'Reilly operated through intermediaries, notably a bow-tied, shrewd former Irish diplomat called Ted Smith. Like most of the paper's staff, before actually becoming editor, my knowledge of both Montgomery and O'Reilly had come second-hand, mainly via Ian Hargreaves. Before Ian was fired, he had been over with his family on holiday in Ireland and had been invited to the O'Reilly home in West Cork. Hargreaves is a natural English Cromwellian – high-minded, serious, loyal and derisive about fripperies and vanity. When he returned he told a worried cluster of *Indy* writers about the O'Reilly butler and swimming pool, the paintings and the flaunted wealth, 'as if he thought it would impress us'. Oh, we said, but you did *pretend* to be impressed, a bit, didn't you? Certainly not, said Hargreaves. Oh dear, we all thought. Oh dear.

My first impressions of Montgomery were not all bad. He was dour, but as a Scot I knew dour. He was awkward, and I find nothing wrong with awkward. He had a shy smile and rarely made eye contact. I discovered later that he loathed personal confrontation and would sub-contract any rows, preferably to Wilson, who was the kind of Scot who positively enjoyed rows, preferably conducted nose-tip to nose-tip. He seemed to be mostly alone in his office overlooking the Thames on the twenty-second floor of the tower. There was little decoration, but there was a farewell front-page montage from *Today* where he was portrayed as 'Monty' in a Second World War tank. (He was known more generally to hacks as Rommel, because 'Montgomery had been on our side'.) Apart from a sparsely covered desk and a table with newspapers neatly arranged, he had a music system, on which he listened to Mozart, and a bowl of untouched fruit. On the rare occasions that food or coffees appeared they would be brought by one of the few obvious remnants of the Maxwell years, the old ogre's amiable butler, Joseph. In the early days, Montgomery was confiding and brisk. We were in this together, fellow professionals: O'Reilly and his people were all bluster and knew nothing of the national newspaper market in London. And then his unvarying themes would appear, one after another, day after day. The 'old *Mirror* culture' had pervaded Fleet Street and had to be stamped out. There were idle people downstairs who had to be 'shown the door'. There were 'agitators' and 'Trots' we'd better get rid of. We wanted nothing of the '*Guardian* culture' either. We had to know our market. We wanted young, aspirational readers. They might have a social conscience, Monty conceded, but they enjoyed the good things in life. They wanted to get on. They would be driving Porsches and they would want Rolexes. We didn't want dreary scenes of poverty in the paper, or 'dead black babies'. That would just put people off. Why were we employing all these people abroad? Couldn't they be 'shown the door' too?

To begin with, I was able to deflect most of this. The paper was already understaffed compared with its competitors. What this meant in real life was that people were – mostly – working long hours, coming in on days off and taking modest pay, out of love of the paper. There were union activists, true. One or two people were aggressive about the management – given its power, and our weakness, stupidly so, I thought. But the NUJ office-holders were among the hardest-working and most dedicated journalists in the building and I had no intention of singling them out, whatever Montgomery said. My idea of the paper was also directly contrary to his. I wanted it to go upmarket, not downmarket. I considered consumer journalism a fact of modern media life, but had no doubt that the soul and purpose of the paper was the very same campaigning and foreign journalism he wanted eradicated. Robert Fisk, our award-winning and highly controversial Middle East correspondent; the brilliant economic essays by Hamish Macrae; the political coverage of Bevins . . . that was the *Indy* I loved. But Montgomery was nothing if not relentless. He had a terrier tenacity. He would flush scarlet with anger and contract his mouth into what Mirror Group colleagues called his 'chicken lips look' when he found yet another foreign lead story, or a page three on some great issue of the day, rather than 'fashionable people'. The friendly discussions turned into arguments. The arguments became rows. It became quickly obvious that if he won complete control, the paper as I knew it was finished.

With my deputy editor, Colin Hughes, who in all honesty would probably have made a better editor than I did, I tried to work out what to do. Montgomery's Mirror Group had effective day-to-day control over the running of the paper. They were the landlords and provided everything from electricity and the phone system to the presses we were printed on. I couldn't simply withdraw from them. Monty and Wilson behaved like proprietors, summoning me to increasingly tense meetings in the boardroom to discuss circulation, promotions and so on. Beyond the daily functioning of the paper, they decided on our commercial tactics: fighting a weekly war with price-cutting rivals, my daily sale was heavily dependent on the promotions, price cuts and advertising they agreed to fund. By simply withdrawing a free CD offer, or deciding to cut 5p off the cover price in Scotland, they could make me look like a failing editor, or a successful one. Yet they couldn't push things too far. They also had to answer to O'Reilly's operation. He valued good journalism enormously and, like me, considered people like Fisk to be the whole point of the paper. Yet he was rarely in town to express his views. Instead, his man in London was a former toiletries marketing executive called Brendan Hopkins, who had a fine glossy head of hair, a good collection of expensive suits and a lovely wife, but who had not risen to the top by the force of his personality or opinions. A ritual developed. I would call O'Reilly to complain about the latest Mirror Group depredations. A 'breakfast with Brendan' would be prescribed. We would meet at an expensive hotel, where Hopkins would order an omelette, with two grilled tomatoes on the side, before assuring me that 'Tony is watching things carefully'. Brendan would then happily eat his omelette, promising that he completely disagreed with Montgomery and that the Irish light cavalry was coming. We must just hold on and do the best we could.

So that is what we did. Colin Hughes drew up increasingly complex lists of staffing and management structures, with a maze of jobs that used to exist, jobs that still did, vacancies which had not been filled, yet still existed on paper, and so on. Whole tiers of actually non-existent management were triumphantly deleted. People who had already left the paper were brutally 'sacked'. Reviews into radical job cuts were launched into filing cabinets, where they shrivelled in the dark. Unsurprisingly, the managers counter-attacked. Wilson became strangely obsessed by a new floor plan, and charged about with drawings of 'modules' in different shapes where editors, subs and reporters would sit. The only point of this was that the exciting, ergonomic new floor plan didn't have enough seats for the current staff; the chairless would be made jobless. On a handful of occasions we had to make real redundancies. Thankfully, there were often people who wanted to take a modest pay-off and go, either to start another kind of life, or to move to another newspaper; but there were miserable farewells too. I always tried to tell people face to face: there is nothing more contemptible than an editor who gets someone else to do the dirty work for them. But as this guerrilla war went on, with more floor plans which would never be used, more detailed lists of non-existent journalists being fired and more angry meetings, the soul of the paper, its journalism, was being squeezed.

I was experimenting with bolder front pages, using dramatic photographs and hand-drawn images by a brilliant artist, Chris Priestley, to highlight particular issues, such as the disappearance of fish from the North Sea, or gun crime, or financial scandals, while conceding ground to Montgomery by using page three for consumer-style stories. My notion of the paper was that it must eventually become a non-financial or 'secular' version of the *Financial Times* – a relatively austere, determinedly upmarket paper for people who wanted facts, and excellent writing, and did not care much about lifestyle surveys or Rolex robberies. I believed that the *Independent* was condemned to long-term decline and collapse if it was not distinctively different from the other three mainstream broadsheets. We were nearest to the *Guardian*, but it had a bigger staff, more money, and was simply better at presenting its material than we were. *The Times* was being allowed to sell below its market price, and so long as that continued, was impossible to deal with. But a paper that did not look or feel like the rest might regain some of the cachet and glamour the *Indy* had had in its early days. I thought (and still do) that there was a market of perhaps 200,000 readers in Britain who would like a tough, serious paper and would be prepared to pay to avoid the mush that often surrounds them. There was absolutely no chance of realizing this dream while Montgomery was around. O'Reilly was an unknown quantity. So the only thing to do was to dig in, just like Ian Hargreaves, concede only what I absolutely had to, to avoid being fired, and hope that O'Reilly might buy the paper and agree to the experiment. Like any siege, it was miserable for the defenders.

There was always some new madness. Perhaps the richest was the so-called Mirror Group Academy of Excellence, another Montgomery wheeze. The idea was that since all journalists were lazy and ignorant, particularly on the *Independent*, they would be taught their jobs again, this time by Mirror men. In this way productivity would increase and the number of journalists could be decreased. This involved, according to the plan, Mirror executives distinguished only by their terrified obedience to Monty, summoning in *Indy* writers from around the world, including such award-winning stars as David McKittrick in Northern Ireland, Fisk, Cornwell, Polly Toynbee and Hamish Macrae, and teaching them how to write. It would have been like limpets teaching dolphins how to swim. The 'Academy of Excellence', much championed by Charlie Wilson, closed its doors before the full black humour of the situation could be fully appreciated. But that was only one episode. On a particularly bleak family holiday I remember standing at the bottom of a garden in a French villa, the only place where I could get mobile phone reception, in the pouring rain, making repeated calls to Montgomery in his Italian villa, and union officials at home in London. Monty had decided that, while I was away, he would have letters sent to all the journalists imposing tough new working conditions: anyone who failed to turn up for a meeting where these would be explained, or who failed to sign up on the spot, could then be instantly sacked for . . . well, something or other. Unfortunately, some journalists hadn't fully realized the intention was to provoke 'militancy' from the paper's fantastically polite and decent NUJ branch, thereby allowing mass sackings . . . and the NUJ was indeed intent on calling a strike. This would have killed the already weakened paper dead. Again, the suicidal confrontation was averted, but only at the cost of several years' nervous tension. The demands for cuts went on. Rosie Boycott was appointed editor of the *Independent on Sunday* and soon stories were appearing in rival papers that she would be given my job. Montgomery, to give him credit, was a bad liar: when I asked if he was responsible for the leaks, he would turn brick red, chew his lips and stare out of the window. It was an old Mirror Group strategy to keep one editor on his toes by publicly lining up a successor.

What I had not appreciated was that O'Reilly was prepared to see how tightly Montgomery could squeeze the paper financially, whatever my squeals of pain. This was silly of me. O'Reilly could hardly lose, after all. Either Monty proved it was possible to run a paper at a far lower cost than traditionally, in which case O'Reilly had half of a more valuable property. Or Monty failed, in which case he could move in and take control. So the squeeze went on, and on. In my desperation, I decided to counter-attack by redesigning the paper entirely. My first plan was to go tabloid, or preferably 'qualoid' – the intermediate size favoured by the best-looking continental newspapers, which is for my money the ideal size for a newspaper. But continental-sized presses were not available. We could not remotely afford to tinker with someone else's presses or buy second-hand ones. As to a tabloid, this was quickly vetoed by the management, though six years later, with sales no better, this is just what the next editor Simon Kelner did, cleverly producing a tabloid version for London commuters, sold alongside the broadsheet before going tabloid nationally. This was a shrewd response to the danger of going entirely tabloid. And so far, at least, it has worked very well indeed.

Instead, I plumped for a radical front page which would have had a single, huge, poster-style image, plus a short essay laying out everything essential a busy reader needed to know. Inside, stories would begin with a paragraph not only summarizing them, but trying to set them in context, a tricky new skill. The idea had been to ask what a newspaper might look like now, if newspapers had never existed before. What order would the stories be in? Would it be more sensible to group them by subject, rather than geography, so that all environment-related stories came together, whether they were about dams in China or badgers in Surrey, and so that people interested in Westminster politics would find political news from Washington and Paris alongside? Colin Hughes and I brought in a designer, Vince Frost, who had designed almost everything except a newspaper. The result was certainly different. We tested it in focus groups and discovered that while some people loathed it, others were delighted by it. If it divided opinion very sharply, it would at least get noticed. I bundled up copies we had printed off and took them to Tony O'Reilly's grand home, Castlemartin, in Ireland. After a reassuring and convivial dinner the previous night, at which he promised that he was moving in to oust Montgomery, O'Reilly summoned me to his study. He was wearing a white towelling dressing gown and sat below a picture I had said looked a bit like a Turner ('It *is* a Turner'). I unveiled the papers. He looked long and closely at them, then sat back. 'Well, Andrew,' he said, 'I like them. I think they are very bold and daring. Personally I like them very much.' I sagged with relief and began to smile. 'On the other hand,' said the great man very slowly, 'I thought *exactly* the same about New Coke.' That, of course, had been the most infamous marketing catastrophe in US corporate history. It was a gentle way to let me know I had boobed. My radical redesign never saw the light of day. A far less extreme redesign did. It proved to be my undoing.

Any redesigned paper needs a substantial advertising and marketing push. Otherwise, readers who don't like it go, and new readers have no way of knowing about it, so the sales must fall. My plan was that by redesigning the *Independent*, which badly needed a clean-up, I would force the joint owners to invest in the commercial push it needed even more. That way we would get a lift, and a fresh start; for them to refuse to invest would be suicide. It was a form of editorial blackmail but by then we were desperate. I had underestimated Montgomery. For, before he would release the needed money, he and Wilson insisted on a series of changes I thought completely crazy. The staff would be dramatically cut. Of the forty-three sub-editors, who checked the copy, cut it to length, wrote the headlines and designed the pages, thirty-eight would be made redundant, leaving the paper with a production staff of five. Instead, reporters would headline their own stories and plonk them, at the right length, straight into ready-designed templates, which would be the same every day. The photographers, who had been responsible for the paper's fine and continuing reputation for stunning images, would also be made redundant: instead, the management would generously invest in digital cameras which would be handed to reporters when they went on assignments. There would be no night staff at all: the paper would be handed over at 8 p.m. to the Press Association to update. Oh yes, and my deputy Colin Hughes must be dismissed as well: editors did not need deputies – they 'only got in the way'.

Confronted by this, we had the most extraordinary scenes. Charlie Wilson was, if nothing else, a classic newspaper character, a tough guy who'd forced his way to the top and whose private life had been as tempestuous as his working habits. During his spell as acting editor of the *Independent*, as at *The Times*, he would stride round the floor like a pantomime pirate captain yelling 'if that's a story, my prick's a bloater' and other imprecations. In an earlier editorial incarnation, in Glasgow, he took to calling one sub-editor 'fingers': when the man eventually plucked up the courage to ask him why, he leered: 'Because that's all you're hanging on by, laddie!' It was because he was a professional who knew very well what was needed to run a proper paper that I became so intensely angry with him for going along with Montgomery. At one point, despite the fact he was much older, I came near to hitting him: he had to hiss that his secretary would hear if there was a fight. I told him I thought the ideas were insane, and sabotage. But he either could do nothing, or chose to do nothing. The meetings with Mirror Group executives were poisonous beyond imagining. Eventually, a miserable compromise was reached: I pretended to agree to some of their demands and they pretended to support me. Only a fraction of the promised money for the relaunch was ever spent. We rose in sales, by some 30,000, but then began to slide. The media commentator Brian MacArthur wrote in *The Times* later: 'Marr stands convicted of a gamble that misfired.' He kindly added that the destabilization campaign had sapped morale and that with support from a sympathetic management I might have succeeded. But his basic judgement was fair.

I was told that the board would discuss a further major cut to the editorial budget. Working through the numbers, it seemed to imply losing another twenty-eight writing journalists, the equivalent of two entire departments – all of foreign, plus all of business, for instance. Payments for freelance writers were to be cut by three-quarters. In January 1988 I wrote to the owners saying the cuts would be too dangerous and would make the paper too thin to survive. The Mirror Group replied that if I wouldn't cut, Rosie Boycott would. Either, I thought, they had all taken leave of their senses or this was their way of forcing me out. My office was crammed with books, photographs, old front pages and cuttings of articles I'd written over the years. I began to sort them into boxes and took the most valuable away: the sackings of MGN editors were rarely civilized affairs. Before the axe fell, however, there was one unexpected and delightful scene to be played out. O'Reilly, who had always been a kind and charming boss, had asked the fabled Ben Bradlee of the *Washington Post* to fly over by Concorde to talk me out of quitting. So after addressing a large group of sixth-formers in Westminster, most of whom wanted to know if I was about to be fired (I told them the answer was probably yes), we met at a discreetly expensive Italian restaurant in Notting Hill. I led Ben Bradlee carefully through the proposed numbers, and the recent arguments I'd had. Eventually I asked: would he really stay, in my place? He pursed his lips, then smiled. 'Andrew . . . It's a crock of shit.' We moved on to talk of happier things. I went back to the office and wrote a letter to the chairman explaining that if asked, I would not implement the cuts the board would discuss the following day. I then called in my senior colleagues, and told them I was about to be fired. Then, once the paper was put to bed, I repaired to the nearest wine bar, one of the Café Rouge chain. An ever-growing crowd of *Indy* journalists, some young, some grizzled, some both, began to gather. Just as the party was warming up, my mobile phone went off. It was my wife, sounding slightly wobbly. A car had arrived at our house, and a letter had been handed over. She thought she had better read it to me. I was instructed to go home, not to speak to any member of staff, and not to approach the vicinity of Canary Wharf until I received further instructions. I left. The following day I was duly fired by fax. Unable to return to say goodbye, I was given the traditional 'banging out' in my absence – the hammering of printers' hammers (now usually journalists' fists) to acknowledge a departing editor they respected – the highest accolade I've ever had. And that, I thought, was that. Kelvin MacKenzie as usual had the last word: the day after my defenestration he stopped the lift at the *Independent*'s office on Canary Wharf's eighteenth floor and boomed out: 'Everybody out for the *Titanic* of British journalism! Don't look so bloody miserable – any one of you idiots could be editor by tomorrow morning.'

It wasn't like that, quite. Rosie Boycott's appointment was announced – I got a one-word mention. As the usual messy arguments over a pay-off went on, Jackie and I fled to Barbados for a week of recuperation. It was the first time I'd had a winter sun holiday and the place seemed magical after the grim winter battles in London. Lying prone on the beach, slowly letting the knots in my stomach unravel, I got a strange message. The Irish wanted to get back in touch. What had happened, it seemed, was that there had been a convulsion inside the Mirror Group and Montgomery had been persuaded – apparently by MacKenzie who, by one account 'put him up against a wall' – that he could never make a go of the *Independent*. So O'Reilly was going to bid for the whole thing, and wanted me back on board to help. The oddest part of the whole arrangement was that he wanted Rosie Boycott to stay, too. She would edit the news pages, bringing the élan she had shown in her legalize cannabis campaign, while I would control the editorial pages as 'editor in chief'. It was highly unusual in British papers, though the *Daily Telegraph* had had a similar arrangement in the old days, and it was common in the US. The idea was Ben Bradlee's, but it would depend on Rosie and me being able to work together, despite the traumas of the past year. We were reintroduced at Brendan Hopkins's London house over dinner and disappeared off to a local pub to look each other in the eye. Warily, we agreed we could try to make a go of it.

The deal went through. O'Reilly's Independent Newspapers committed itself to papers which, in my words would be 'signed up to no political party and free from the taint of commercial pressures . . . For its part the board expects the editors to deliver honest, decent, liberal-minded papers which avoid extremism, report accurately and analyse fairly.' They have kept their promise: indeed, the O'Reilly takeover gave the *Independent* and its Sunday sister their best chance by far of vigorous survival. I had the extraordinary experience of being refenestrated, a mere six weeks after I'd been ejected. Rosie talked of us being a 'dream team'. It wasn't easy but we began to work together relatively well, despite the disbelief of our colleagues and the amused scepticism of the rest of Fleet Street. But then Rosie was offered the editorship of the *Daily Express* and took it. The hurried search for a replacement ended with Simon Kelner, another original *Independent* man and former sports editor, who was not my cup of tea. He, not surprisingly, wanted to be in sole charge of all of the paper, though he asked me to stay on. But I felt enough was enough. A week after Rosie had gone, I left too, this time for good. The in-out, in-out, shake it all about story of my editorship must be one of the more bizarre ones in recent journalism. One colleague told the *Guardian* as it ended that it was like the final scene from *Reservoir Dogs*, 'you know, the bit where everyone shoots everyone else'.

Through all this time, John Major's government had come apart,

the Hamiltons had lost their libel case against the *Guardian*, sleaze had
entered the vocabulary of national politics, mad cow disease erupted
across the land, an almost unknown religious extremist called Osama
bin Laden had been interviewed by the *Independent*'s Robert Fisk, Tony
Blair and New Labour had won their first landslide election and
decided to forge ahead with the Millennium Dome, which was going
to be a tremendous success, William Hague became Tory leader,
Princess Diana died, Nelson Mandela visited Brixton . . . and a lurcher
bitch owned by David MacMillan of Newton Poppleford ate a piece of
the *Independent* and swelled to the size of a Staffordshire bull terrier,
causing a major investigation into whether our printing ink had
become poisonous. Those, and a thousand other stories, were what I
spent most of my time thinking about. Editing involves ferocious
battles with managements and lawyers, but the core of the job is the
hunting out, selection and presentation of news. Every day, every
editor picks up every rival paper and asks: did we do better, or worse?
Did we miss that, and if so why? Was our headline sharper, or duller?
In the end, these individual decisions taken day after day, can help
papers grow and thrive, or kill them off, losing hundreds of people
their jobs and millions of readers a daily habit. The truth is, I was
never a top-notch editor. I was too easily distracted, too interested in
writing myself, and too emotional. Given another time, and less of a
struggle for survival, I might have grown in experience and grown the
Independent too. Then again, I might not have done. The content and
tone of the paper today has not changed so very much. Papers have a
culture, passed on from sub to sub, and reporter to reporter, which
matters as much as the editor's personal qualities . . . or nearly so.

How Real Editors Edit

Though there are almost as many styles of editing as there are editors,
the basics of a modern editorial day are fairly common. In Victorian
times it was possible for great editors to spend most of the day away
from the office. The legendary Garvin of the *Observer* worked mostly
from his home in Beaconsfield. The even more legendary C. P. Scott
of the *Manchester Guardian* lived on the city's outskirts. After starting
the day with a cold bath and raw fruit, he would spend virtually all of

it at home writing letters, before bicycling to the office with his supper of bread, cheese and fruit, to arrive after 7 p.m. He worked frantically hard once he got there, but no editor would get away with arriving at that time now. And of course, neither Garvin nor Scott had the *Today* programme to worry about. These days, daily newspaper editing is an office-bound job which demands frantic activity and long days. Even for those who love every minute of it, editing can be physically punishing. In recent years, epilepsy, heart disease and short retirements have been the lot of editors who failed to get out in time.

It is impossible to be an editor without being a hopeless news junkie. That means rising for the 7 a.m. news, at least, and reading every rival newspaper, while listening to the *Today* programme with one ear, and making key early calls with the other one. I would be picked up in a taxi at around 7.30 and driven from west London through the City to Canary Wharf. On the way, I'd read the broadsheets first, since they were my direct competitors, ringing stories we had missed, or that offered good follow-ups, swearing at excellent ideas we'd failed to think of and smiling happily where I thought we had scored. You start with the masthead, looking to see what promotions and scoops or top writers were being offered to passing customers: a good offer might affect the day's sale, for your paper too. Front pages are, strangely, less interesting on the broadsheets than you might expect, simply because most of the time most of the editorial teams do similar things. You often see the same picture, the same lead story and even the same offbeat 'basement' story. There is no getting away from the fact that, on many days, there just is one obvious, overwhelming, main story – a by-election upset, a resignation, a train crash, another disaster in the NHS – which everyone is going to lead with. Ten to one, it will have been the lead story on the previous day's news as well. But the splash stories have to be scanned anyway, just to check the rivals have not got some killer quote, or unexpected angle, that is missing in one's own paper. At this stage, I barely 'read' a story in the usual way of calmly following it down the page. I'd be flicking through headlines, bylines, looking at page designs and the way pictures had been cropped: but above all, at what had been put where.

For editing is like planning an endless banquet for picky eaters. There may be only four basic tastes, but within that there must be rhythm – light, rich, short, long – and constant variety. A page which is dominated by a heavy, policy-based story with lots of figures in it, must be balanced by a facing page which is lighter. Stories about institutions need to be leavened with stories about people. Page three on many papers is a critical one. Many readers will flick off the front page, vaguely aware that 'I know all that'. Page two, because of how you hold a paper, particularly if travelling, has less impact and is often a jumble of stories that have been 'bounced' off the front, and follow-ups to stories from rival papers. It is a curiously dead area. Page three is what confronts anyone opening a paper and helps set the tone of the day. This is the place where its agenda can first be glimpsed. On huge news days, such as after Princess Diana's death, or during the fall of Baghdad, it might be where the paper's finest writing is allowed space to breathe. Or you might put an investigation there, if it was really good. *The Times* had a habit of gathering five or six good-ish stories there; the *Telegraph* has famously used it for salacious court stories, and higher gossip; the *Guardian* uses it to make some firm statement about its values, often a story or presentation that no one else has. We tried to find 'the way we live now' stories – not very elevated stuff, sometimes, looking at the music industry, or the future of British film. And so one would trawl through the papers, assessing the catch. By that time, if you are going to send anyone to somewhere else in the UK, and expect to get material back for the first edition, you had to get cracking. One regular early call would be to the picture editor, to get the photographers out on the road; another would be to the news editor – should we send someone to that case in Devon?

By the time I clambered out of the car at Canary Wharf, I had a list of stories missed, people to complain about, ideas for that day's paper, thoughts about what our columnists might tackle, and the sure knowledge that some kind of confrontation about something, mild or severe, would await me on the Mirror Group floor. No honest editor is interested in everything in the paper. I have a complete blind spot about sport. I gamely took out the sports staff for a drink a few days after I'd started and tried to make conversation about which writers were good, and how the pages looked. They played the game for a while, then there was a long pause while we all stared down into our pints. 'You know bugger all about sport, don't you?' asked the deputy sports editor. I confessed that was so. Similarly I kept having baffling conversations with the highly talented team of fashion writers about what they were up to, and why having grainy pictures of women in unlikely poses needed to cost quite so much of our scarce money. In his memoirs about editing the *Telegraph*, Max Hastings confessed to similar blind spots. But the point is not that the editor knows about everything; it's only necessary to know who is good in every field, and listen to the advice of people you trust, and make sure every department feels it is being watched.

The first pieces of paper I would see were the page plans – a kind of architect's draft of the next day's paper, with the adverts blocked out in grey. This shows how much space we have, page by page. Every paper has an agreement, a deal, between the advertising side and the editorial side, ultimately policed by the editor. It's like one of those animal fables where both depend on each other, and both can kill one another. The ads keep the paper afloat and must have enough space. A month when advertising is weak means a month of thinner papers. But the ads eat into the area for news. The most valuable sites are exactly where you want them least – on the front page, and page three, and the leading, right-hand, news pages. So there is a constant tension. The first argument of the day might very well be with the managing editor who has allowed an extra half-column on page three and blocked out a huge British Airways double spread on the politics page, making it almost impossible to design decently. If the news pages don't 'work', of course, people won't read them, and the advertisers will be unhappy too. But a paper's managers, desperate to balance the books each month, are equally keen to pack in more ads. They do not want to say no. On huge news days, adverts can simply be ditched to make room. But on ordinary days, when the deal has been breached, there might be a row. Editors can claim back space, but not too often and not too much. Once that is agreed, the page plan is allocated – so many pages for home news, so many for foreign.

After that, letters: I had a constant stream of them, demanding thought and answers. Many were from readers but required a response from the editor directly, rather than an anodyne official reply, or a place on the letters' page. They might be complaints about the line we were taking over the Middle East, allegations that they had been misled by a reporter, or expressions of shock that we had changed the positioning of the crossword. Some were very funny and some were wise, though every editor gets a heavy postbag from lunatics. Sometimes it seemed to me that large swathes of rural England were populated by maniacs who thought that the prime minister was electronically controlling them, or believed the paper was run by a Zionist conspiracy – they at least would not get an answer. But there would be many which did, raising interesting questions about our reporting and values. Perhaps because we had such a small circulation, I tried to answer as many as possible personally. Readers want to feel they are part of a community and it is an editor's job to show they are. After a while I realized that each week there would be one or two issues which deserved a general response, and started a column called 'Letter *from* the Editor' – one of my happier ideas, since it got a big response in turn. But there would be requests too, to meet schoolchildren, or ambassadors, or to give speeches, or to chair conferences. Most of them were rejected with a certain sense of guilt.

But every newspaper's day begins properly with a morning news conference. The senior key staff will have talked before that – the features editor, the op-ed editor, the foreign and home editors, and the home desk, for instance, will already have sent reporters off on jobs. Our morning conference began at 10.30 and went on for around forty minutes, which is probably average. Each department head attended, plus those influential columnists whose views and personality helped form the paper – in my time, Polly Toynbee might be there, with Hamish Macrae, David Aaronovitch, Suzanne Moore or Rupert Cornwell – and sometimes a key reporting journalist, such as the political editor. So there were between a dozen and twenty people in the room. Each department has a list of stories for the following day's paper which are circulated, along with lists of features. Most papers begin the morning conference with a dissection of the current day's paper. This can be an angry, confrontational scene, or calm, depending on the character of the editor and how the departmental heads behave. You find the foreign editor under attack from the home editor, and returning fire; or the features editor confessing that he thought we had the wrong front page lead.

Again, what matters is that every part of the paper must feel it is being watched by the rest, and by the editor above all, and will be held to account for mistakes made, as well as being praised for good ideas or scoops that have come through. After that, the section editors read through their lists. Any good deaths from 'obits'? A stinking scandal from Business? Foreign are trying yet again to get that bloody feature on Indian entrepreneurs in – they should never have commissioned it, but they've clearly spent too much money to spike it. The home desk is gloomy: apart from the Boat Show and day three of a murder trial which isn't as exciting as promised, they have nothing but dreary diary stuff. What the *hell* will we put on page three? Features suggests something from their list, but no one looks interested. Sport pointedly yawns and rolls his eyes. Then halfway down the business list, the deputy editor spots the name of a company being declared bankrupt. Wasn't that the company which launched those fantastically expensive and trendy gastro-pubs a year ago? Yes it was. They never worked. Very good: does that not give us a peg for a piece about how the British are resisting the takeover of the traditional pub – the baked potato and ploughman fight back? And wasn't that TV chef involved with the company? Better still! Find him and do an interview. Let's get a feature writer out to one of the gastro-pubs that is trading. Can we get an old codger from a traditional boozer to try it out and see what he thinks. But who do we have to write it? Simon's on holiday and Katie is off doing the English homeowners who are taking over Cork. Sport sports a rheumy eyeball. Jonners is free. No rugby on now. He's a good writer. Good boozer too. Jonners it is . . .

Most editors – not all – see the morning conference as a crucial moment because it is how a paper's character is formed. Yet since they are partly about lists, even good news conferences can be a bit dull. I worked on one paper where they were virtually meaningless, being simply a monotone recital of typed lists, followed by everyone shuffling off again. Another example of this style is described in the mid-fifties at the *Guardian*, then edited by A. P. Wadsworth, who

> never let the performance run longer than 15 minutes. Both eyebrows resignedly raised, and one at times rising impossibly higher, he would run his pencil down the list, murmuring as if to himself, 'Hmm. Zinkin still not in? Hmm. What's this mean? Myxo-. Oh, myxomatosis. What an awful word. Mmm. How long will the Parliamentary report run? Better hold most of the second page, I suppose. Well, well. Mmm. Lisbon earthquake? Surely that was years ago. Eighteenth century? A bit old even for us, isn't

it? . . .' Wadsworth's attitude towards this daily ritual seemed to say that it was mildly amusing, slightly vexatious, unimportant, a brief interruption of the day's work, like a coffee break. He presided over it lightly and obliquely, almost as if he were trying to create the impression that he was helplessly out of touch with these formidable but rather boring realities.[4]

At the far end of this spectrum are the editors whose command over the paper, if it exists, is so obscure and circuitous no one quite knows how it works. My first editor, Eric Mackay at the *Scotsman*, ruled mostly by oracular silence. He said almost nothing and appeared on the editorial floor very rarely. But he was considered a figure of dreadful power and intellect who observed everything, a secular, silent Jehovah, praised by Neal Ascherson for his 'sheer moral obstinacy': nobody doubted the paper was his *Scotsman*. Peter Preston at the *Guardian* in the 1970s and 1980s was considered reclusive and difficult to talk to, working deep in a warren of offices and intrigues; nor did he dominate by argument. Yet he was a spectacularly brave editor when faced with the 'cash for questions' and Jonathan Aitken stories of the Major years, and he was responsible for the biggest single leap in design and 'look' of that paper's history, by the designer David Hillman, in 1988; highly successful it was. He operated obliquely and through talented favourites, but he had control where it mattered. His successor, Alan Rusbridger, one of the most successful editors, learned a similar subtle style.

Bill Deedes, Fleet Street's oldest villager for decades, when he was editor of the *Daily Telegraph*, only had control over the centre of the paper – the very few jobs at his personal disposal were on the old 'Peterborough', its diary column. He chaired a college of conservative thinkers and writers. He fired not, nor did he hire. As he later admitted with his usual disarming frankness, 'It was not the staff, but the musty appearance of most pages in the *Daily Telegraph* that provoked my attention. To change them proved to be an insuperable task.' Instead, he confined himself to struggling with print union demands and trying to maintain journalists' morale: 'Journalists are sensitive birds, the best of them in constant doubt about themselves and in need of encouragement.' In his memoirs he approvingly quoted Malcolm Muggeridge who, when deputy editor of *Punch*, said his most important function was 'loitering on the staircases wearing a friendly face and allowing journalists you encountered time to unburden themselves'.[5] This style of editing helped make Deedes one of Fleet Street's most loved figures; whether it contributed to a tightly run *Telegraph* is less clear. In fiction, Michael Frayn's 1967 Fleet Street novel *Towards the End of the Morning* has an editor of such painful shyness he skulks his way into the building, scurries for his office and sits there hiding from the staff. Among his models was said to be Wadsworth.

At the other end of the scale are editors who conduct their conferences as one-person floor shows, shouting, screaming, provoking laughter and fear, jabbing and demanding. MacKenzie at the *Sun* and Jack Nener at the *Daily Mirror* were editors of this type, and the great Christiansen was said to conduct his morning conference 'as if he was Master of Ceremonies on a glittering Palladium stage'. In modern times one of the most influential control-freak editors was John Junor of the *Sunday Express*. One of his young appointees was Tom Utley, who said that within three seconds of joining the paper 'I knew who he was and his views on men with beards, men who drank white wine, his birthday and everything about him because he was so much talked about. I've met tyrannical editors galore, but not tyrannical and paternal at the same time, as he was.' He read every word of copy, challenged many of them, and ruled by force of personality and unyielding attention to detail. On Sunday papers the morning conference is less important than on dailies, but some sense of the Junor technique is given in an exchange quoted by his daughter in her biography of him. He was flipping through the *Evening Standard* and buzzed his foreign editor Arthur Brittenden to find out if he had read that day's column by its legendary Paris correspondent Sam White. Brittenden confessed that he had not.

'Arthur, what time is it?'
'I'm not with you, John, I don't understand.'
'I asked you a simple question, Arthur.'
'It's half past five, John.'
'Ah good, your watch agrees with mine. And what position do you hold on the *Sunday Express*, Arthur?'
'I don't understand what you're getting at.'
'I asked you a very simple question. What position do you hold?'

'Foreign editor.'

'The foreign editor of the *Sunday Express*, at 5.30 p.m. on a Friday afternoon has not read Sam White's column in the *Evening Standard*,' said JJ stonily. 'May I suggest, Arthur, that you read the work in question and pay particular attention to item three, and, after you've read it, give me a buzz . . .'[6]

It is no coincidence that one of Junor's senior staff was Peter Dacre, whose son Paul later became editor of the *Daily Mail* and applied a style of meticulous and thoughtful barbarity there. Junor had learned his style partly from Christiansen, Lord Beaverbrook's greatest editor. The journalism Junor favoured, with its campaigns against carefully selected hate figures and its passionate identification with the ordinary reader, was the Beaverbrook way. It survives today not at the *Express* titles, which have passed through different owners and lost any sense of their own culture and history, but at Associated, where Dacre rules, and where Junor spent his sunset years as a columnist, and where other Junor hirings, such as Peter Mackay, are now employed: at the *Daily Mail* Beaverbrook and Rothermere DNA are entirely entangled.

Newspaper cultures can survive for a surprisingly long time – from Wadsworth on, the *Guardian* has been known for holding its conferences more as a general staff argument than as editor's theatre; under Alan Rusbridger they are still probably 'light and oblique' compared with most other papers. But cultures can jump boundaries too, mutating in the process. *Mirror* journalists provided the core of Rupert Murdoch's early *Sun* and brought some of their news techniques with them. Later, when the Murdoch press had become dominant, and the Mirror Group was sickly, it was Murdoch journalists, as we have seen, who moved in. The ferociously abusive campaigns run by tabloid editors of rival groups against one another are family quarrels, which is why they are so violent and so puzzling to outsiders. And news conferences are a primary means of passing on the genes. It might seem straightforward – a reading of lists, and a checking process. But it is a repeated event in an endless prodding, jabbing, argument about the purpose and character of the newspaper being produced. While I was at the *Observer*, Will Hutton would set out his view of the world very clearly, as befitted a major liberal thinker and writer, challenging people to challenge him. Then Roger Alton took over, and sat back, trying to provoke the different writers and editors there to argue with one another. 'I don't have a clue, fucking useless, I'm afraid – Rawnsley, do you know anything about this stuff? Hmm? Any fucking clue, anyone?' The pretence of baffled ignorance was a technique to get sparks flying. There are others but as with journalism generally the only absolute disaster for a news conference is dullness, a sense that no one cares. If there isn't electricity in the editor's room every morning, that paper is drifting. The drift in conference is followed by a drift in stories, then a drift in the readers' attention, and a drift in sales.

At the lowest level, the morning conference is the time when the features editor and the home editor realize they have both planned to tackle the same subject in a similar way, and must be parted, like dogs clamped round either end of a stick. But the conferences should also be when the paper's fundamental news values can be questioned. For instance, as I began to edit I became increasingly aware of how we raised huge questions and anxieties about some story – a tanker spilling oil off the Orkneys, allegedly destroying an entire ecosystem; or a winter NHS crisis caused by a flu bug – and then simply dropped it again, as the news agenda moved on. So we started to consciously return to stories the paper had been running a few weeks earlier, to find out what had happened since. It is at this meeting when the editor's quirks (and every editor is bulging with quirks) become obvious. These quirks can range from the banning of certain words in headlines (no 'bids', no 'experts', no 'crisis') to an urgent desire for more stories about muggings, or a general determination to shift the paper's direction to the right or left. But the editor's directions then have to be followed through during the day. Editing is not about ideas. It is about insistence, driving, pushing, harassing.

The tabloid editing style is to drive and focus the whole paper as a single voice, with a single world view and a set of repetitive stories which hammer home the same messages day after day. This style has become dominant, accepted as the acme of professional journalism. And of course, it suits marketing men who want clarity and focus and talk of 'the product'. The two most influential tabloid editors of the later twentieth century were undoubtedly David English, who turned round the *Daily Mail* in the seventies, and Kelvin MacKenzie of the *Sun* in its eighties wildness. Both were famous modern examples of a driving editor, with a fixed notion of what he wanted each story to look like, and read like. English had an absolutely clear picture of the typical reader in his head, and even put up posters to remind his journalists who they were writing for – and he is the other constant influence in the modern *Mail*, alongside the Junor–Beaverbrook influence. Again, like Junor, he achieved this by personal dominance, including bullying. One of English's journalists, Anthea Disney, said later that 'He always had the best idea, in his opinion. He liked to think he listened to other people but he didn't.' She said of him that he could be evil and dreadful, and described the scene on the back bench of the *Mail* when English was sitting with his jacket off, taunting another executive, Gordon MacKenzie:

> One night David was in a dreadful mood. He had had this idea for
> a piece for page six, and it had not been written to his satisfaction
> . . . Gordon read what I had written and said, 'I think you've got
> it, I think it's great.' He took it over to David, who said, 'What
> do you call this? This isn't the story I was talking about in con-
> ference, this is nothing like the story I was talking about in
> conference!' And there was Gordon, standing there miserably,
> crumbling these pieces of paper in his hands.[7]

Compare that with the famously foul-mouthed 'bollockings' adminis-
tered relentlessly by MacKenzie as he tore up pages and rewrote
headlines:

> Picking a page he would run his eye over it, ringing paragraphs
> with his fat green pen. 'That's crap!' he would spit . . . The
> muttering would continue as he dotted about. 'Bollocks . . .
> Fucking useless . . . Yeah, that's OK . . . Yeah, I like that . . . Naah
> . . . That's bollocks.' The criticism would become more detailed:
> 'Put something in here about how his father was a bastard to
> him, or some bollocks like that, will you?' he would say as he
> studied a profile of some celebrity . . .

In news conferences he would be in perpetual manic motion, dismiss-
ing stories with the phrase 'I wouldn't wipe my arse with it' before
'turning round, sticking out his fat backside and miming pulling down
his trousers before simulating the sanitary act with the offending piece
of paper.'[8] Not quite the Wadsworth technique. But the point is not

only the bullying. That is common enough – under pressure of disappointment many editors behave with unforgivable rudeness and public aggression to colleagues. The point is that the story English was 'talking about in conference' was set in the editor's mind and, in his opinion, clearly explained that morning. Because he had failed to communicate it properly, or because the reporter and home editor hadn't delivered, English had lost a portion of control, which is what editors hate. The same went for MacKenzie. He had a clear idea of what he wanted the story to look and read like, down to each adjective and paragraph break, and would simply rewrite and 'bollock' until he got it. This is all a million miles from what people assume to be the normal way of conducting journalism, which is that the reporter goes out and finds a story, which is then brought back and put in the paper.

How different, really, are modern broadsheets? They are meant to be almost the opposite – open, thoughtful and various, qualities bought at the expense of clarity and excitement. And they are certainly more open. An investigative reporter like David Hencke of the *Guardian* or Steve Boggan, formerly of the *Independent* and now of the London *Evening Standard*, can indeed suddenly arrive in the office with a tale no one there knew anything about, and then see it shepherded quickly into print. The broadsheets also have larger foreign staffs, which means that their overseas coverage is less expected and predictable. But the banal truth is that in news terms, the broadsheets are not so different. Most reporters will turn up each morning waiting to be told what to do by the news desk, who will in turn have discussed with the editor where they should be sent, and what they should be told to do. As with the tabloids, the editor and news desk have forward lists of expected speeches, trials scheduled to start, running tribunals, annual events, launches of new products, plus the torrent of bids for publicity from scores of PR firms and publicity scoundrels, the raw material of events that will turn into news. For instance, suppose there is to be a march in support of fox-hunting, which is to be led by some stars from a TV soap. The march is certainly placed well in advance in newspaper diaries. Interviews may be set up with the stars. But whether the march is judged a success or not is heavily down to the paper being pro- or anti-fox-hunting. The stars can be praised as bravely outspoken or derided as ignorant and selfish. The reporter will know very well what his newspaper's line is, and can be additionally told that the

editor is keen on an angle – even London metropolitan luvvies rally to
the cause of rural England, showing just how out of touch MPs are –
or perhaps, 'dig back and find footage of the old bat wearing a mink
coat, then do her for hypocrisy'.

With the broadsheets too, the more the editor moulds and deter-
mines what should be reported, the more focused the newspaper will
be. If the editor knows his audience, this closed, complete world view
will reassure and underpin the reader's sense of how things are. This
is not enough for editorial success. There may be too few people who
think the same way. (Arguably the problem for the *Independent*, and
certainly so for the *Daily Express* by the mid-1980s, when its form of
patriotic, hang 'em and flog 'em rhetoric had become dated: there
were simply not enough retired prison officers in northern England to
keep it thriving.) Knowing your audience is certainly important and if
it is a large minority, it can bring success. But on the other hand, a
dominant editor who moulds the paper very strongly to his views, but
who has misjudged the audience, can come a sudden cropper. When
Piers Morgan decided to make the *Daily Mirror* an anti-war paper at
the time of the Iraq crisis, he did not simply leave it to a few front
pages and the odd editorial – as a hyperactive, controlling editor, he
turned the whole paper into a seamless cry of anger against what Tony
Blair and George Bush were doing. Once the war started, *Mirror*
readers clearly disagreed, at least with the relentlessness of it, and
many deserted. The furore over faked photos apparently showing
British troops abusing Iraqi prisoners was more toxic still. The pictures
supported Morgan's agenda and raised a real issue to the top of the
political agenda. But they appeared in print because the paper *wanted*
them to be true: and endangered British lives.

The romantic myth of editing may be that the great editors are
always the control freaks, dominating every aspect of the paper, from
the morning meeting to the late-night sessions rewriting headlines
on the back bench. But is it really a good thing? Papers which encourage their reporters to go off and find out for themselves, think for
themselves, and which allow for the editor's prejudices to be challenged, are more various, unexpected and interesting. You never quite
know what you will find in *The Times* in recent years, for instance.
Similarly, during the Iraq War, though the *Guardian* was hostile in
its editorial voice, its writers with the army, and analysts at home,

provided a wide range of thinking. And the *Daily Telegraph*, though clearly on the right, entertains an increasing variety of voices on its comment and feature pages. This is partly about tabloids versus broadsheets, the former being traditionally more editor-driven than the latter; but it is also about what a paper is really for. Is it there to fondle the reader's prejudices or to tweak them?

After the news conference there is normally a leader writers' meeting, where the key editorial people can thrash through what the paper should be saying about X or Y. In the old days of Fleet Street the great broadsheets would have a team of leader writers. *The Times* was famous for the erudition and grandness of its team. Describing the *Daily Telegraph* leader team of the seventies Stephen Glover, later a founder of the *Independent*, said he was one of eight leader writers who were expected between them to produce three leaders a day, of around 330 words. Taking into account Sundays and covering for colleagues on holiday, he reckoned this meant each averaged slightly more than two leaders a week:

> One or two leader writers occasionally exceeded this testing average, and so it was possible to write only one or even no editorials in a week. The skill of 'dodging' an unlooked for editorial had been honed to a fine art by some of the leader writers at their conference which had been thoughtfully fixed by Bill Deedes at 3.45 p.m., allowing them to spend the morning at home before enjoying an unhurried lunch with a politician, fellow journalist or girlfriend.[9]

These days have passed, like Nineveh and Tyre, and few papers now employ more than one or two people to write leaders exclusively.

After the morning and leader conferences come a flurry of other meetings. There will be the picture editor worried about our failure to offer enough money to lure the 'snapper' he wants to hire from Scotland. A lugubrious foreign editor might linger to say that the chap in Ismaelia is no good after all, and will have to be replaced. We pull out his recent stories and go through them. They look all right; but they have been rewritten, says the foreign editor, and he's got someone better in mind for the job. The editor makes a note to call. But if we sack Gibbs in Ismaelia, perhaps the management will delete the job completely? There will be a succession of staff issues to deal with. In some papers they are all taken over by a managing editor. But unless the paper is very large and prosperous, no editor can afford to refuse to talk to valued staff, even if they want to whinge about getting expenses paid on time – once I remember whipping out a couple of twenty-pound notes and pressing them on an anguished photographer for his petrol bill. After the day's staff problems, there will be one of a series of management meetings.

Daily sales figures arrive by late morning – estimates, but pretty reliable – and the weekly figures, then the monthly ones, will be debated with the managers of the company, or the proprietor if there is one. These are hugely important. When I was editing, and the *Independent* was suffering badly in the price war launched by Rupert Murdoch's *The Times*, sales figures could produce a knot of anxiety and fear, or (more rarely) a fillip of pleasure. All editors have the real numbers of papers sold, but these are rarely published honestly. Circulations are massaged by dumping tens of thousands of free papers for 'sampling' on trains or planes; by cutting the price for a week, sometimes only in one part of the country; by sending an unlikely quantity of papers abroad, and confidently claiming them as foreign sales. The Audit Bureau of Circulations, or ABC, has now insisted that most of the old scams are explained, but few quoted figures are fully reliable. Then there is the question of 'readership' – an attempt to measure through the National Readership Survey who actually reads the paper, rather than simply who buys it – which can be used to claim success when sales are actually down. The editor, with his circulation team and the managers, will pore over long charts showing the sales of rival papers, trying to work out what is really happening. There are well-known quirks – the *Guardian*, for instance, tends to suffer a greater percentage fall during the summer months, because it has more public service readers, particularly teachers, who have longer breaks. Some papers sell better on some days each week than others, perhaps because their football coverage is particularly good, or they have a popular supplement; and part of the trick of modern editing is to try to persuade the once or twice a week readers to become three or four times a week ones; so 'puffing' – enticing readers for the following day's paper – has become important.

Circulation is critical not only because of the direct effect from cover price sales, but because advertisers buy space through a complicated formula based on circulation bands, as well as the social profile of the readership – richer, younger readers being more lucrative for car companies or banks than older, poorer ones. But this is art as well as science: if advertisers can be persuaded you are working hard for more of 'their' sort of readers, they may take a chance and pay a little above the odds, or at least keep using your paper. So the circulation strategy, and the editor's plans for a new weekly supplement on sports cars, or for younger women, will be discussed with the advertising trade – more meetings. And if, despite all your best efforts, circulation is sliding, then there are always promotions to be tried. Free offers have underpinned newspaper sales for well over a century, as we have seen. And it isn't always mad. A relentless pattern of generous-looking, eye-catching stunts, from 'win your mortgage' to free CDs, can build long-term sales: if the paper is good enough, readers brought in once or twice by the advertising puff at the top of the page, or through a TV ad, may became habitual buyers. This is expensive, though, and poorer papers will use promotions as short-term fixes, like sugar rushes, to keep them in the game. We gave away classic film videos, wine, cheap flights and holidays. There is a whole business working away at unloading excess production, whether of aircraft seats or jazz CDs, through newspapers. But for people who came into journalism to dig out stories, or to write coruscating denunciations of official corruption, it can all be a little dull.

After those sorts of meetings – and there will be more still, with lawyers to discuss writs, with the printing plant managers to talk about the break in production that lost 20,000 copies in Wales, or the newspaper's own advertising company, proposing a series of billboard slogans you don't like for the autumn – the editor might get a chance to have lunch. As with reporting, editing has become a far less alcoholic job than it used to be. In her account of Hugh Cudlipp, the writer Ruth Dudley Edwards says his papers were produced

> on an ocean of alcohol. Visit Cudlipp before 11am and you would be offered a beer (unless it was a day of celebration, when there would be a champagne conference at 10.30); after eleven, he would open a bottle of white wine. While [Cecil] King, Cudlipp, and senior journalists like the Political Editor, Sydney Jacobson, would tend to go to separate lunches with influential people (aperitif, wine, brandy), most feature writers would drift at lunch-time to the Falcon . . .[10]

This behaviour was, no doubt, mildly disgraceful, even if it produced journalism that at its best was rather better than today's. The physical disintegration of the industry from Fleet Street killed off the easy socializing of editors and writers, and made it harder for editors to lunch with people outside. Some editors now pride themselves on never leaving the building, but rolling up their sleeves and joining the queue in the canteen.

They feel that hobnobbing with politicians or other influential people merely weakens them, diluting the purity of their disgust, helping form friendships which will in the end only weaken the paper. Certainly, many writing journalists hate the idea of editors who lunch, since it means they return to the office full of pet theories which they probably don't understand, or bogus stories, which they then want to see in the paper – under somebody else's byline. Against that, I found the idea of not trying to maintain contact with politicians, writers and others outside the world of the newspaper stultifying and deadening. You have to keep your mind open, and you have to keep touching the world outside, or your world view contracts. (Lunching, or not lunching, is partly the difference between the broadsheet world view and the tabloid one.) Most editors revel in the chance to meet a bewildering variety of people – in my case, it might have been the Archbishop of Canterbury, Richard Branson, the chancellor of the exchequer, a poet, the top team at the Victoria and Albert Museum, a rival editor, or some protest or campaigning group. As national newspapers have left the centre of London, lunching has got harder, and takes longer, and for me became less frequent as time went on; but it was one of the moments in the day I looked forward to most. Normally one would come back to the office with something – a good tip for a story, or an idea for a feature. As newspapers have sealed themselves off physically, in remote glass towers or behind spiked railings, breaking out matters more. Like all newspaper groups, we in turn invited politicians or tycoons to come and lunch with us. The Mirror Group in my day kept a rather bleak and alcohol-free board-room for lunching, so these could be awkward affairs. It always surprised me how many senior ministers would happily traipse out to newspapers to be lunched by a large and often hostile gang of journalists. They presumably thought it would get them good cover-age. In many cases, the withering and dismissive chat once they had gone would have burned their ears on the drive back to Westminster. I know of at least one party leader who destroyed his reputation with a friendly paper simply by turning up to lunch there and being himself.

After lunch, there will be more meetings, and the first chance to go round the departments finding out how the day is panning out. The news desk will be getting the first copy in. The subs will be arriving for work, putting down their broken-backed novels and starting to make little squeaks and groans as they read the raw material pouring in from agencies or correspondents. There will be a promised article from a minister which disappoints (they always do) and a possible front-page picture which is, however, not quite right. Can we crop out that telegraph pole so the soldier is more obvious? No. Can we tint the sky a little? Yes. A good picture editor, and I was blessed with one, will come up with endlessly inventive ideas and images. The ideal is an eye-whackingly strong image, which is also of crucial news importance, but this is rare. Often the choice is between something that is beautiful or striking to look at, and a news picture which is visually dull. We almost always went for the former. The most interesting conversations, of course, will be about stories and real journalistic dilemmas. We have a reporter and a snapper on board the plane taking MPs on a freebie to Malta. Should we snatch pictures and do interviews while they are strapped in their seats? Or there may be a major investigation, perhaps into links between the ruling party and a foreign billionaire, which is nearly, but not quite, watertight. To run, or not to run?

At 4 p.m. we had our afternoon conference; most dailies do the same. It will be a shorter, more business-like affair than the morning one. We race down the lists checking what has worked, and what has not; focusing on breaking stories that will make us rethink our paper. The page plan from the morning might suddenly become controversial again: foreign have four good page leads and really want another page. They pour cold derision on a home page story, delivered early and already subbed, which they think is 'pap' and should be ditched to make way. True enough; but we have very little light relief in the paper today. It is relentlessly grim. What to do? The business editor has a late-breaking story, a scoop interview with the chief executive of a French bank about his takeover bid for our second-biggest banking group. He wants 400 words for the front page. I say it'll have to be

250 and he looks grimly disappointed. Drafts of leaders come in, and are rewritten, or approved. The letters page arrives. This morning we called Scotland Yard and suggested they might like to respond to our columnist who said they were racist: the chief superintendent has faxed over an angry reply saying that many of his senior staff are *Independent* readers. Excellent! The first of the columns for today is in. Oh God, she's called the editor of the *Daily Monster* 'a genteel kind of Nazi'. And I'm meant to be having lunch with him next week. The cartoonist has faxed over four rough drafts before coming in to work on the one I'd picked; but I was out and forgot to look at them and he has chosen his favourite which – agh – has John Major peeing on Michael Portillo and is a *leetle* too graphic for my taste. So I go over to see him and suggest, very carefully, that he might think of a touch of white paint, just a touch. He snarls. We have the following day's education supplement to check over – Colin Hughes thinks the main article is gibberish and wants to rewrite it himself, but warns that the author will kick up a stink. But she is a freelance whose work he does not rate, so that's fine.

After this flurry – and further meetings – I discover one of our best feature writers has been offered a job at the *Guardian* for a few thousand more. Features are over budget this month and I've already had a stand-up row about it with the management, since features are now being asked to cover a slew of extra supplements with no more staff. I should really nip upstairs and try to get Wilson or Montgomery to agree before I counter-bid, but what the hell. Feeling decisive and bold and editorly, I grandly promise to top the *Guardian* offer. The features editor goes off to spread the happy news. Two minutes later, he's back with the writer, who seems mildly embarrassed. It isn't the money, she just prefers the *Guardian*. It isn't my editorship, honestly, she knows I am doing my best, but . . . I feel instantly deflated and rejected but smile and offer best wishes. She smiles back and asks if she can leave at the end of the week. Certainly not, I say. It's hard enough getting people already. Later the features editor is back again: apparently she is owed three weeks' holiday which means her month's notice period is virtually cancelled. Damn. I know that the owners will try to cancel her job and ask the department to manage with one fewer writers. But she is not only good, she is highly productive and fluent. Max Hastings has written that trying to hire writers and having them turn you down has something of the pain of sexual rejection about it; it is the same but more so when they walk over to a rival paper. So that's another problem for tomorrow: the features editor wants a general talk about staffing problems anyway. That will be fun!

By this time of day, say six-ish, the early pages should be complete and must be looked over, headlines changed, last-minute rewriting demanded, before they are sent electronically to the printing plants. The press of work means that each page has to have an 'off-stone' time. The 'stone' was originally just that, the large flat level surface, generally of slate, where the metal type was laid out and locked into its page-sized grid, or 'forme', before printing. Its significance is that it was the last moment in the process when the journalists, in the shape of the 'stone-sub', had control, before the page was off on its industrial journey. So the stone, and indeed the stone-sub, survive as the final stage in the page's creation. Off-stone means finished, complete – at least for that edition. (Another example of the survival of old language is 'copy', which referred to the carbon copy of your story sent to the back bench subs. Journalists were told to make between three and five copies or 'blacks' of each story as they hammered them out on the typewriter, to be stored in different parts of the office. All that is as relevant now as handloom weaving, but a story is still always 'copy'.) As the evening speeds up, the limited number of subs means that the pages have to be finished in a regular order, giving a flow of work. Tension rises. The editor strides about, barking, constantly staring at his watch and getting in the way. The front page and back page sport are the last to go.

You have to get the front page right. Broadsheet or tabloid, this is how editors tend to be judged every day. It is where your worst mistakes are most publicly on display, and where creative headlines or pictures can make a difference, at the margin, to sales. Above or below the paper's masthead will be 'puffs', usually three of them on a broadsheet, advertising what is inside. If there is an expensive promotion, the business people will be pleading for the maximum space for that; but any editor will want to sell journalism first. So it might be a top columnist with some provocative thought – Why We Should Join America or My Teenage Sex Shame. (Columnists jealously count their masthead appearances; editors who can't pay them more had better display them instead.) It might be simply reminding readers that today the paper has its education supplement, with all those jobs. It might be advertising a feature on London Fashion Week. At any rate, these puffs need to be eye-catching and varied. Writing them, in just a few words, needs skill and flair and could take up a surprising amount of time – they would certainly be closely analysed by the management the following day. But the 'splash' is the real thing. What should it be, first of all? If there is a disaster or a huge political story, the splash will choose itself, though the headline won't. On weaker news days, the choice will say a lot about the paper. We would look for health and environment stories, and splash more foreign stories, because we thought that was the sort of paper the *Independent* should be. We rarely led on crime. The point on broadsheets, almost as much as tabloids, is to generate a sense of occasion and excitement, not simply to record the most important stories. So the headline should be short, if possible, and arresting at all costs. This is advertising almost as much as it is journalism – and it is no coincidence that so much of the history of modern newspapers has been influenced by advertising people, from the J. Walter Thompson people who helped create the *Daily Mirror*, to the close involvement of Saatchi & Saatchi in the early *Independent*. Great headline writing is a rare and invaluable skill. You need to take risks, to avoid cliché, to summarize the complex in terse verbal jabs.

All tabloid editors would say they have a far harder job than broadsheet editors. They must pick just one story and do it big. They may cheat and slip a second or third story onto the page, perhaps just as a teaser headline. But because of the vast headline size, only one story will register with passing commuters. The *Sun*'s notorious 'Gotcha!' when the *Belgrano* was sunk, or its dead-parrot attack on William Hague, or the *Mirror*'s then-notorious 'Whose Finger on the Trigger?' attack on Churchill, are classic examples of what tabloids are trying to do – to stop you as you are passing the newsvendor, make you double-take, then buy. But this is an unforgiving game and nothing is more pathetic than the joke that doesn't come off (see the *Mirror*'s unfunny attacks on the Germans in the late nineties) or the too-clever pun, or the boldly wrong prediction, of which the choicest is still perhaps the *Daily Express* in 1938: 'There Will Be No War This Year, Or Next Year Either'. There are rules to the game, though, which every journalist quickly recognizes.

You might be able to get four, five or six stories onto a broadsheet front page; though, as the trend for 'compacts' increases, they too are coming down to tabloid choices. But even for full-sized papers, because they are folded for the newsagent, the top half of the front page, the same size as a tabloid, is what really matters. A third to a quarter of it will be taken up with the masthead of the paper and the puffs, leaving only limited choice for the rest. A classic solution is to have a lead story across three columns on the right, then a picture, which obviously has to have its image high enough to be seen, and then a smaller one-column story on the left. Much of the time you are trying to appeal to as many different readers as possible, so if the lead story is about politics, you might want puffs about music, sex and sport, and the second story to be on foreign affairs, or just funny. Down the page, once it unfolds, there might be a 'basement' by a sketch writer, or a star reporter. On huge news days the whole business is remarkably easy: enormous pictures of burning skyscrapers, or the unmissably good picture of US troops in Saddam's palace, or the gaping mouth of the Paris underpass where Diana died. On such days, you can find identical headlines and pictures on rival newspapers, simply because journalists, wherever they work, have been brought up the same way. No one takes much pride in this. Any decent editor is looking for ways to stand out from the herd. The *Independent* has tried almost word-only front pages, with type size far bigger than ordinary text, but smaller than most headlines. One such, in April 2003, had a headline, 'The Face of Corporate Britain' with three mugshots. The text started:

> Adam Singer took cable firm Telewest to the brink of bankruptcy. Under him, shares fell from £5.63 to 2.1p. In 18 months, 1,500 staff lost their jobs. His reward? A pay-off of £1.8m. Sir Philip Watts has presided over a 27 per cent slump in the share price of Shell in the past year. The company plans to lay off 4,000 staff. His reward? A 55 per cent pay rise to £1.8m . . .

That is good, aggressive front-page layout of a kind Cudlipp would have applauded. It is cousin to the 'shock issues' of the old *Mirror* or the current *Daily Mail*. Is it broadsheet or tabloid presentation? Hard to tell, but it works. Other wheezes might include deliberately shocking pictures, used very big; cartoons or drawings; and giving up much of the front to a beautifully written essay just because you think everyone should read it. In my time we tried most of these. During the more absurd stages of the 'beef war' with France, I ran a multi-deck headline designed to look like a First World War newspaper. Another day, before a crucial England football game, we got a striker to have his naked foot photographed, showing the savage battering to which a professional soccer player subjects his toes. There is nothing quite as satisfying as going home, exhausted, thinking 'that'll surprise them tomorrow'.

Having made all these decisions and got the paper off-stone, work starts immediately on the second edition, with pages being redesigned, stories cut or inserted as rival papers come in and later news breaks. Having criticized Charles Wilson earlier, it is fair to say that one of his good traits was to call every morning to find out whether the paper was off-stone on time and to express pain, grief, anger and amazement if we were more than a minute or so late. Newspaper printing and distribution is a nail-bitingly time-sensitive business and editors cannot afford to be blamed for failing to get the paper out to far-flung newsagents. Being off-stone on time every night without fail is a vital discipline. It is a genuine race against time and one of the most satisfying, adrenalin-pumping moments of an editor's day.

At the *Independent*, my day would usually finish at between 9 and 10 p.m., perhaps with a drink in the local winebar before stumbling into the back of the hired car to be taken home. There would be further changes to be discussed with the night desk en route, and almost always a couple of conversations about something else that one hadn't got round to earlier in the day – a chat with a foreign correspondent, or a call to a writer I wanted to poach from another paper, or an apology to the manager of the printing plant for losing my temper with him earlier. Counting the work I would be doing in the back of a car, then, it was at least a fifteen-hour day, and often more. It was a punishing schedule, not least because one would then spend some of the night awake worrying about how to deal with some passing crisis, or agonizing about why we had done a story less well than some rival. The pressure might have been less had the *Independent* been secure, instead of struggling. Like a football team on the edge of relegation, I always knew that our sales were barely enough to keep us in the advertising market we needed for survival. For the newspaper market has its exits as well as entrances: I knew very well that that many papers had been lost at sea – not just the unlamented failures, such as the *Daily Sketch* or the *Graphic*, but good papers too, such as the *News Chronicle*, which closed in 1960, the *London Daily News*, which survived just five months of ferocious newspaper war in 1987, and the estimable *Sunday Correspondent*, which the *Independent on Sunday* had helped kill off after only thirteen months, in 1990. But it wasn't just that. Arthur Christiansen, the *Daily Express* editor, who worked an eighteen-hour day for more than twenty years and whose newspaper sayings are still relevant ('Lead; don't follow. Never be a copy-cat; Fleet Street is full of dead copy-cats.') said after he retired that newspaper editors had to be lonely and driven people: 'Show me a contented newspaper editor and I will show you a bad newspaper. Throughout my years of office I was brooding, carping, despairing, doleful, self-critical, snarling, suspicious, tendentious, wary and so on, right through the dictionary. I praised extravagantly and kicked unmercifully. I was also praised and kicked in the same measure . . .'[11]

Enter Lord Copper, With a Heavy Tread

And in the end, very often, one is fired. Count the firings in this story alone. I was fired, once and arguably twice within a few weeks. Ian Hargreaves was fired. David Montgomery was fired, not only from *Today* but later from the Mirror Group itself. Kelvin was fired. Eventually, Piers Morgan, who sent me a postcard when I was fired ('one minute you're cock of the walk, the next, you're a feather duster'), was fired, because of those faked pictures. Charlie Wilson was fired. It happens to the greatest of editors too: Christiansen was fired, in sad circumstances, and died shortly afterwards. Harry Evans, who would still be at the top of most people's lists as the greatest broadsheet editor of modern times, was fired. His account of the nerve-racking final days of his editorship of *The Times* in March 1982 is a classic of newspaper politics at their nastiest, which can be a great deal nastier than anything happening at Westminster or Whitehall. Evans had been protected by apparently watertight guarantees over his independence given by Rupert Murdoch as part of the political deal that allowed him to buy the paper without a Monopolies Commission reference in 1981. But Murdoch wanted him out, partly to increase his own hold over the paper and partly because he mistrusted Evans's more centrist politics; so he tried to get round the guarantees and the role of the independent directors meant to police them by persuading Evans to resign. He refused. His deputy, Charles Douglas-Home, was conspiring against him. So were some other journalists. So was his secretary. After refusing to resign to Murdoch in the middle of Budget day, Evans walked downstairs and found his deputy waiting:

> . . . he had his thumb held upwards in the air like someone transfixed in the act of pressing a doorbell.
>
> 'Been upstairs, have you?' One ceilingward jab of doorbell thumb. 'Seen him?' Another jab. 'Too bad.'
>
> He followed me into my office and sat at one end of a sofa. I had nothing to say.
>
> 'He had me up before you,' he began. 'He offered me the editorship of The Times and I have accepted.'
>
> 'But I have not resigned the editorship,' I replied.
>
> The features of his face tightened . . .

As the night goes on, Evans's anger deepens and there is a confrontation: 'How could you betray your editor? How could you do it when you think what you do about Murdoch?' His reply had the merit of candour. 'I would do anything to edit The Times,' he said.[12]

Harry Evans went shortly afterwards, angry but having fought Murdoch longer and harder than any editor before or since. Firing is part of the editing life, unless your circulation is going up pretty constantly and you get on with your owner. Firing the editor is the cheapest and easiest way of trying to improve a paper, and often works. Most tabloid editors are fired sooner or later. In the broadsheet world, people hang on longer and can even retire at a time of their choosing if they work for, say, the Guardian or Financial Times. But even there, the axe falls suddenly. The bad firings are the dishonest ones – the moves sideways to work on 'future projects' or the grandiose titles that fail to disguise a basic lack of daily power. But my favourite account of being fired is Sir Peregrine Worsthorne's which he wrote about in the Spectator after he had been sacked as editor of the Sunday Telegraph by Andrew Knight. The event took place, as a good firing should, at Claridge's:

It was when the waiter had just served two perfectly poached eggs on buttered toast – a dish of which I am inordinately and insatiably fond. In my mind I knew that the information just imparted was a paralysingly painful blow: pretty much a professional death sentence. But for some reason this sense of acute shock did not get through . . . and I continued eating the eggs with as much pleasure as usual; and also, a bit later, the rolls and marmalade.

Later, though, he wept. Many of us do, and not just because of the car that will never be waiting again.

So what makes a good editor? Like generals the greatest are only tested in battle, at moments of real choice, demanding judgement, coolness and courage. So while it may be unfair on the peacetime editors, who simply raise circulation and keep a happy, well-run newspaper going, the 'greats' are the ones who fight and win. Evans will always be remembered for his courageous *Sunday Times* campaigns, on compensation for Thalidomide victims above all, when he was betting his reputation and a large part of his paper's commercial security on his own moral instinct. His technical skills were remarkable; but it was the successive campaigns that made him a great editor. Alan Rusbridger of the *Guardian*, tested in the Hamilton and Aitken libel trials, defending true stories against grim-looking odds, again had the cliff-edge courage not to settle. David Astor's bravery during Suez, which could have caused terrible damage to the *Observer*, was another notable moment when principle won out over common sense. But these examples of editorial guts are rare because, most of the time, the battles editors fight are small-scale legal skirmishes and internal fights about resources. The early days of principled editors being clapped in irons or driven out of public life are long gone. Few modern editors fight their proprietors, because they lose their jobs if they do. And if they have proprietors on the same side, then their fights with outside interests are comparatively risk free.

As I hope I have demonstrated, to be an editor, a strong constitution and readiness to work frantically hard are both essential. Only twenty or thirty years ago, it might not have been so, at least for broadsheet and Sunday editors. There was spaciousness. There really were long, alcohol-laced lunches. The great offices were near the centre of London, or whatever city it was, and in easy reach of the outside world. But that world has gone. So stamina and determination are the first things, and even then they don't automatically carry you through. Kelvin MacKenzie developed a minor form of epilepsy, which colleagues believed was brought on by stress. Paul Dacre needed a multiple heart bypass, at a relatively young age. David English, though he worked like a dervish when he needed to, developed strategies to cope with the stress: he took long holidays, made sure there was always some fun and party-going around, gave up alcohol after a bout of hepatitis, kept himself fit and ate sparingly. Even so, he collapsed and died at the relatively young age of sixty-seven. Max Hastings, who edited both the *Daily Telegraph* and London's *Evening Standard*, famously relaxed by shooting and fishing and retreating to his beloved countryside. Andrew Neil partied; so do many others. But whatever you do, coping with pressure is essential. I worked for one editor who simply could not manage it and retreated to his office with packets of strawberry Complan before giving up and resigning.

Assuming, though, that one has the hide and digestion required, what skills are needed? Like so many jobs in journalism there is no course or book to consult – nothing but on-the-job training. You need to be a politician, a diplomat, an accountant, a salesman, a therapist and a barman. But you need more specific skills too. The tabloids have been dominated by technicians. Layout and headline writing are the absolutely key skills; the importance of good prose has fallen over the decades, as ruthless subs have learned to carve everything into similar tabloid-speak; and reporters have slowly followed their lead. But however predictably dead the prose, the papers need to keep readers' eyes darting about; the ability to lay out WOBs (white on black or reverse-effect headlines) alongside carefully chosen and cropped pictures, and to make every square inch of paper excite is a rare skill. So most tabloid editors have risen through subbing, learning the technical tricks of layout and headline writing from their elders late at night. Even so, this is not universal. Piers Morgan, at the *Mirror*, cut his teeth as a showbiz writer; Rebekah Wade at the *Sun* worked for him and is not, first and foremost, a production journalist. Amanda Platell, of the *Sunday Mirror* and *Sunday Express*, had been a sub-editor and manager, rather than a writer, though she became one later. Stuart Higgins, at the *Sun*, had been a much-baited executive working for MacKenzie before he took over.

Again, on the broadsheets, there is no fixed pattern. *Daily Telegraph* editors have tended to be writers, first and foremost, and big figures in the Conservative world as well. That was true of the great Bill Deedes, who was briefly a Cabinet minister and has now returned in old age to excellent reportage. It was true of Hastings, who won his job partly because of the reputation he made as the 'first man into Port Stanley' during the Falklands War, but also because of his writing on, and deep knowledge of, military history – an enthusiasm shared by Lord Black, his proprietor. Black then chose another writer, Charles Moore, who went from being a columnist to gaining the editorship of the *Spectator* and moved from there. He tacked in a different direction when he chose Moore's successor, Martin Newland, a news man. On the *Guardian*, Peter Preston in 1975 had had a wide range of writing and editing jobs, working as an overseas reporter, as a diary editor and as feature editor among other things. Alan Rusbridger too, had been a reporter, columnist, diary editor and features editor on the paper – indeed he had spent virtually his whole career on the *Guardian*, apart from a short interlude with the *Observer* and *London Daily News*. As with Preston, he was chosen in 1995 not just because of his wide experience, but because of his deep, marinated immersion in the paper's culture. At *The Times*, they dotted about. William Rees-Mogg had been a leader writer, City editor, political correspondent and deputy editor before he got the chair there in 1967. Simon Jenkins, though he was editor of the *Evening Standard* for a couple of years earlier on, was as we have seen essentially a writer when he took over in 1990. He was replaced by Wilson, a technician who started as a reporter. Wilson's successor, Peter Stothard, had had a career almost matching Rusbridger's immersion on the *Guardian*, having been a features editor, leader writer, deputy editor and US editor for *The Times* before he became editor. His successor, Robert Thomson, had been a *Financial Times* man, a reporter who had run departments too.

On the Sundays, Andrew Neil was another transplant: he had done a bewildering variety of editing and writing jobs, including political correspondent, American correspondent and UK editor at *The Economist* before he became editor of the *Sunday Times* in 1983, much to the chagrin of long-timers there. Among those who left, considering him a right-wing barbarian, was the columnist Hugo Young. Yet Neil injected an energy into the paper that had been lacking for years. His successor, John Witherow, came up through the paper, though, having been defence and diplomatic correspondent there before doing a variety of editing jobs. Over at the *Observer*, Donald Trelford had been a writer and editor, covering everything from Africa to being managing editor, before his long reign began in 1975. At roughly the time I was editing the *Independent*, it had another writer, Will Hutton, as editor but it switched to its current editor, Roger Alton, who had been a features editor and wizard technician at the *Guardian* beforehand. The *Sunday Telegraph*, from Peregrine Worsthorne to Dominic Lawson, has maintained the preference of its sister daily for stylish writers as editor. What can one make of all this? Papers which are self-confident, and have strong cultures, are likelier to grow their future editors internally. There is a pattern of proprietors picking writers as editors, presumably because they are better known in the outside world, and then giving up on them and turning to the safer hands of technicians, instead. The only golden rule is that an editor has to be master of several trades, not one – he or she has to have some management skill, some idea of running budgets and some feel for the language, as well as being able to lay out pages and write headlines.

But the secret of brilliant editing is psychological. A good editor is a figure of awe, or love, or both. No newspaper is truly great unless it has at its core a group of highly talented, competitive people who enjoy each other's company and stride in each morning determined to disagree. There has to be an inner circle, but it has to be perpetually capable of being gatecrashed by the talented and bold. Nicholas Tomalin once wrote:

> The best Fleet Street papers are not the open-ended institutions they like to appear, but feudal fiefdoms all bound up in intimate friendships and shared values. All good publications are communities essentially cliquish and inward-looking; the best editors are good because they have the most talented friends.[13]

This understates the role of the best editors, but contains an essential truth all editors need to realize. There has to be an atmosphere, a crackle, at the centre, and the person responsible is the editor. Some do this by showing huge energy and courage, like Evans, to make the *Sunday Times* of his era forever special. Others, like his successor Andrew Neil, do it with raw energy and aggression, forcing editorial change by shouting and firing, driving out the dissenters, demanding a new agenda and almost physically reshaping the culture of the paper. Others still – the *Guardian* editors, classically, and both recent editors at *The Economist* – provide the electricity by creative chairmanship, setting raw, contending egos against one another and channelling the friction, as they rub one another up the wrong way, into heat and light for the following day's or week's paper. Many great papers, and not simply on the comment pages, are office arguments spilt into print.

Being fired is only the last phase of the other relationship which defines success or failure for most editors – the one with the proprietor or boss. This is one of the most obscure and little-discussed relationships in journalism but one of the most important too. For the truth is that, except for editors who are highly influential in trusts or companies owning their titles, editors are hirelings. Proprietors regard their editors as talented and interesting servants; Murdoch has a notorious suspicion of editors, like MacKenzie or Neil, who became public figures in their own right, believing they were stealing his sunlight. Editors may feel themselves to be great figures, swanning around in the back of Mercedes and dining at the Savoy Grill with Cabinet ministers. But they are only there so long as the owner allows them to be; their talents are rarely such that they can dictate terms. Tiny Rowland treated Donald Trelford, the editor of the *Observer* in its Lonrho years, with cold brutality whenever his commercial interests were involved, either in Africa, or in London during his fight with the Al Fayed brothers over House of Fraser. Rowland was exceptionally nasty but Trelford's plight was hardly unique. The editor's servitude is both comfy and peculiarly embarrassing, because the deal is a public one. The national newspaper editor gets status and the apparent respect of the rest of the social elite of modern London, but the proprietor gets what he wants. Well, mostly. Evans held out briefly against Murdoch in the early days of his ownership of *The Times*, when there was the fig leaf of independent directors. And the story is told of how Lord Thomson, a decent liberal proprietor, arrived at the editor's office in the *Sunday Times* one day while the editorial conference was in progress and rather tentatively asked: 'Say, boys, would it be possible to squeeze in the Canadian ice hockey results each Sunday?' There was a moment of shocked silence. Then the deputy editor, Hugo Young, said, 'Lord Thomson, this is an editorial conference to which you've not been invited. If you'd like to put your suggestion in writing, I'm sure that the sports editor will be willing to consider it.' And the next morning there was a note from Lord Thomson apologizing for attempting to interfere with the paper's editorial policy.[14]

But this is unusual. Proprietors set the political limits of the papers, and their direction in many other ways. Some are liberal and others are not, but they are not in the business to tax themselves harder or to help support political structures which will limit their reach.

The First Mystery of the Proprietors

It is not an invariable truth that every proprietor of a British newspaper is mad. Nevertheless, it is a striking thought that so many of the people who owned great newspaper empires were very odd folk. Consider, for instance, Julius Salter Elias, later Lord Southwood, who was responsible for the *Daily Herald* through its glory years. Elias was a shy, grapefruit-juice-drinking little man whose wife waited up for him with hot milk each evening. He hated the idea of travelling outside Britain, read almost nothing except the Bible, allied himself with the foulest xenophobic fraud in the history of British newspapers, Horatio Bottomley, and during the ludicrous circulation war of the 1930s with Beaverbrook and Associated was rightly accused of spending money 'like a drunken sailor'. Among his many idiosyncrasies were a blank refusal to take serious decisions on a Friday and a loathing for any designs containing a peacock. According to Wintour, the famous editor of the London *Evening Standard*, Elias also 'disliked green intensely, so that his wife could never wear a green dress, and he would not keep pennies in his pocket'.

Consider the second Lord Rothermere, with his close interest in fascism, his admiration for Mosley's blackshirts and the strange story of how his family came to be offered the Hungarian throne. Consider the third Lord Rothermere, a brilliant man but one with a close interest in spiritualism who oversaw his *Mail* titles, with their strict family values and their insistent English patriotism, from an apartment in Paris where he lived with his Japanese mistress, to the distress of his ex-actress wife.

Consider also the more famous figure of the first Lord Northcliffe in his final days, living in a hut on the roof of a friend's home in the Mall, waving his revolver at the shape of his dressing gown, convinced it was an assassin, and telephoning wild instructions, including mass sackings, to his editors. He really was mad by then, and historians have divided over whether this was a great mind o'erthrown by some blood disease, or even syphilis, or the poetically right ending for a monster who tried on Napoleon's hat and truly believed himself to be a better director of the British empire's affairs than any of the elected statesmen he so despised. Northcliffe, unlike Southwood, was a brilliant journalist, but his hubris in trying to wrench the nation's destiny away from its democratic system was something shared by lesser men – including his nephew Cecil King, who tried to suborn Lord Louis Mountbatten to lead a cabal of businessmen to overthrow Harold Wilson.

Or consider Beaverbrook, the Canadian business adventurer who bought his first tranche of the *Daily Express* on the steps of the Monte Carlo Casino in 1910 and pursued quixotic political campaigns all his life. He was not mad, but he was far from normal – a manipulative control freak who encouraged his editors to pursue vile personal vendettas and whose mental corruption of journalists led him to be called a rare human example of genuine evil. I prefer the description of his early editor Beverley Baxter, which captures the essence of the great press baron at work:

> Secretaries darted in and out like minnows in a torrent. Three telephones sprang to life and never paused a moment for breath. In the centre of it all, creating the energy which he exhausted, was this strange, buoyant, fascinating figure, chuckling, roaring, winking, frowning, talking while he signed letters, issuing instructions, gossiping like a spinster, buying, selling, interviewing his interviewers, wheedling, terrifying and enjoying himself enormously.

Think of Robert Maxwell, the bloated fantasist, friend of dictators, bully, foul-mouthed ogre and proprietor of the allegedly socialist *Daily*

Mirror, flying off on a mercy mission to an African famine with his butler and a plane-load of personal luxuries. Maxwell, like Beaverbrook and Northcliffe, won the devotion of many perfectly intelligent and decent people, yet to outsiders remains a kind of Blofeld-esque monster, with his helicopters and bizarre friends. He was a man of complex lies and multiple lives whose death, toppling off the end of his luxury yacht as creditors circled, remains one of the great mysteries of Fleet Street. Or Conrad Black, who became entangled in the corporate web he had woven himself – the boy obsessed by money and power from an early age, who had been expelled from his boarding school for copying and selling exam papers, and who later recalled:

> As I was walking out the gates a number of students who literally 24 hours before had been begging for assistance – one of them literally on his knees – were now shaking their fists and shouting words of moralistic execration after me. I have never forgotten how cowardly and greedy people can be.[15]

Black's father, the one-time boss of Canadian Breweries, installed a slot machine in his house to teach young Conrad the bad odds of gambling. He later fell to his death through a balustrade. The last words to his son were: 'life is hell, most people are bastards and everything is bullshit'. Conrad grew into one of the most engaging and voluble tycoons of modern times. But he crashed and burned, partly because of greed. Think, finally, of Richard Desmond, owner of the *Express* titles, goose-stepping around meetings, forcing his executives to sing 'Deutchland über Alles' and denouncing all Germans as Nazis.

Where do we get these people from? Newspapers may be hard to make money from but, for much of the past two centuries, they have brought their owners influence and fame far beyond the purchase price. So they have been a private escalator for pushy outsiders. It doesn't always work. The statue of the Duke of Cambridge in Whitehall is a pretty routine work of equestrian pomp and barely noticed by most. But it could be seen as London's secret monument to the vanity of the press in trying to direct public affairs. Colonel Arthur Burroughs Sleigh founded the *Daily Telegraph* in 1855 to try to stop Cambridge, a royal prince, from becoming commander-in-chief of the British army. As the statue demonstrates, it failed ignominiously: Sleigh sold out three months later to his printer Joseph Moses Levy, who already owned the *Sunday Times*. Levy, later Lord Burnham, understood that sales and profits must come before political campaigning. Price cuts, scandal and ruthless commercial stunts such as uniformed street salesmen made the paper a success.

Levy was like many of the founders of press dynasties in that he was an outsider and a gambler who bought into the business cheaply and then broke all the previous rules to win sales. Then he became an influential insider; his descendants were able to hobnob with royalty and invite Cabinet ministers to slaughter grouse. There's a pattern there. Often, the entry cost of buying a full-blown newspaper has been too much to start with, and many great press dynasties began more humbly before making a grab for national influence. Northcliffe started with a magazine for cyclists, and then a copy of a weekly, *Answers to Correspondents*. William and Gomer Berry were the sons of a Merthyr Tydfil estate agent. The two brothers built two press empires, but started with *Advertising World* and then *Boxing*, whose staff they used to revive the ailing *Sunday Times* after buying it for a song in a London club; Beaverbrook bought into the *Daily Express* in stages, when it was ailing and cheap; Thomson began with Canadian local radio stations. His first transmitter was put together with second-hand radio parts, jam jars, electric irons and so on, and featured local choirs who agreed to sing for free and weather forecasts by the radio announcer who did them by glancing out of the window. He then moved on to tiny weekly papers. Rupert Murdoch's father also built up a portfolio of small local papers in Australia; the newest British press magnate, Richard Desmond, started with magazines. Granted, *Asian Babes* or *Big and Bouncy* were not the same genre as *Boxing* or Northcliffe's cycling magazine, but the trajectory from marginal to mainstream is identical. His journalistic sense is meagre compared with Northcliffe's, but at the time of writing he is already sending waves of concern through the industry because of his determination to produce successful newspapers at below the previous cost base. Another pushy, impertinent outsider is butting in.

Levy and Desmond are at least British outsiders. But many proprietors of British papers start abroad, usually in the English-speaking Commonwealth – Beaverbrook, Thomson and Black from Canada, Murdoch from Australia, Maxwell from Czechoslovakia, O'Reilly from Ireland. Either way, the energy of outsiders has been crucial to our high-selling, nervy press. For much of its modern history, Britain had been a cliquish, snobby country and there were relatively few ways to break into the ranks of the powerful. That is less true now in the age of celebrity but was certainly so during the great age of newspapers. Unlike steel companies, great retail chains or banks, newspapers are often family fiefdoms, passed down through two or more generations. This gives them a Shakespearean whiff. Will the sons and daughters be up to the inheritance? Often they are not. Esmond Rothermere was a poor proprietor. So was the second Lord Levy. So was Beaverbrook's son Max Aitken. In other families, such as the O'Reillys and the Murdochs, the competition between siblings as to which has the capacity to inherit control would delight students of the history plays, or indeed the Ottoman empire, where the first to seize an emptied throne had his less fleet-footed brothers strangled with bowstrings. But even when a dynasty manages to produce several generations of talented newspaper owners, the danger of absolute power turning someone absolutely bonkers is always there. If the company is so structured that there is no countervailing force among shareholders or directors, this can lead to wildness, some examples of which have been given. Powerful families of outsiders, with a back-stairs pass to Downing Street *and* the ear of the crowd . . . it is frankly surprising more of them aren't mad.

And they have the money, too. Journalists can make a good income, but we are not rich. Proprietors are rich. Journalists, particularly editors, depend on their whims. They are the creatures of the proprietors and that defines the relationship before everything else. Because these are democratic times, in general both sides, proprietor and journalist, make a pretence of some equality. Any decent editor will stand up to the proprietor at times, for the sake of self-respect if nothing else, and to convince the proprietor that he has chosen wisely in having someone who will speak back. Yet no editor who survives speaks back very often, or ignores the little errands and favours the proprietor requires. It cannot be a wholly sincere relationship. It is too radically unbalanced for that, and the honest editor is conscious, day and night, that his greatness and power in the world is loaned only. This does not mean that proprietors behave badly. Conrad Black made Max Hastings a rich man through share options, and did not have to. Rupert Murdoch has performed acts of great personal generosity, in deep privacy, to some of his editors. The current Lord Rothermere gives huge latitude to the current editor of the *Daily Mail*, to the extent that it is unclear which is the senior partner. Nor does it mean that proprietors can or should ignore the personalities and views of editors. Indeed, the great breakthrough moments in newspaper history have generally happened when a vigorous proprietor and an inspired editor are working very closely together – as when the *Mail* was reinvented as a tabloid by David English and Vere Rothermere, or when Cecil King, a kind of false proprietor, created the modern *Mirror* with Hugh Cudlipp in the 1950s. But the imbalance is general and inevitable. Proprietors are the greatest forces in the rise or fall of newspapers. Like members of some scattered global royal family, they are obsessively interested in one another, avid for gossip about what Rupert, or Conrad, or Vere, is up to next.

My one, O'Reilly, was certainly like that. About the first thing he told me, in a self-mocking way, when I arrived to meet him at Castlemartin, was that he had been to see Vere Rothermere in Paris to ask his advice about how to turn round the *Independent*. 'Well, Tony,' he had said, his languid drawl mimicked by the Irishman, 'the first thing is that you have to have a lot of money. Then you have to *spend* a lot of money – for *year* upon *year* upon *year*. And then . . . (long, weary pause) very occasionally, *sometimes*, it works.' On another occasion he was sitting with me in his study when a call came through from a British millionaire who wanted to buy the Express Group of papers. Gleefully, O'Reilly asked about earnings per share, costs which could be stripped out and with a few squiggles on a pad had come up with a price range he thought realistic. The deal never went through but he was happy to let me glimpse the speed with which proprietors deal in papers regarded as historic national treasures. Increasingly, they are post-national. Later he was recounting anecdotes about Rupert Murdoch. O'Reilly had once asked him where he lived, and the world's greatest tycoon was completely stumped for an answer. Eventually O'Reilly asked where Murdoch kept his dogs. Los Angeles, was the reply, 'So I guess I live in LA.' O'Reilly roared with laughter at this. Like Murdoch, in this respect at least, he too had homes all round the world.

His country house in Kildare, where the Liffey is just a stream, is Castlemartin, a beautiful home, warmer in style and furnishing than one imagines any Protestant ascendancy house would have been, with a constant stream of petitioning Irish politicians at the gate and rolling acres for the expensive horseflesh to frolic in all around. I mention this only because in the history of relations between proprietors and editors, the sheer gloss and glitter of great wealth, and its effect on middle-class British tradesmen, which is what journalists are, should not be underestimated. Lord Beaverbrook seduced many radical minds at his grand house on the French Riviera. John Junor's daughter Penny recalled how Beaverbrook had given his star writer and later editor a rent-free house for the family in the grounds of his estate at Cherkley in Surrey. But the press lord extracted

> his pound of flesh in return . . . When he was in England, my father was on call night and day seven days a week, and spent almost as much time at the big house as he did with us. Every weekend during those periods he would be telephoned and invited to lunch, and because no Beaverbrook employee ever left his company until he had been dismissed, he would often end up staying for dinner too . . . Beaverbrook had no respect for JJ's free time and gave no thought to the effect his demands might have on the family.[16]

This is an unusually intimate but in principle typical example of the deal between the editor and proprietor. Whether it is the seduction of editors and free-spirited columnists in grand houses in the south of France, or the condition of hope, fear and pride that stalks a Murdoch editor invited to Aspen – it all seems entirely understandable to me. Money talks. Understand how proprietors think and how editors are handled by them – and sometimes, if they are lucky, handle them too – and you understand the inner secret of the British press.

What, for the reader, are the consequences of the rule of press barons? Yes, rich men have rich men's politics. But these are not entirely predictable. Murdoch is as staunchly republican as the average Lenin-admiring student (which he once was). But if you start from the assumption that moguls are driven by the desire to remove commercial forces in their way, the politics makes sense. Beaverbrook saw himself as a child of the empire; his first fortune was made in Canada and he saw imperial protection as good business, not simply patriotism. The Rothermere flirtation with fascism had a lot to do with the rich man's terror of communism and socialism. Rupert Murdoch, born into the era of American market dominance, saw European federalism as an outdated idea and a potential regulatory and taxation threat to his increasingly US-based empire. His most consistent hostility is expressed for organizations that are commercial rivals, such as the BBC, rather than for individuals in power: if he has a preference in politicians, it is simply for the ones in office. Rich newspaper proprietors with TV interests are obsessed with regulatory and competition issues; can mostly avoid paying tax, certainly at normal national rates; and are not much worried by most domestic issues, from crime to public transport, that obsess ordinary voters. The campaigns their editors run, to lock up paedophiles or force some minister to resign, are rarely of more than passing interest to the men at the top.

A few proprietors haven't had rich men's politics. C. P. Scott, already discussed, was one example of a breed that is now dead, the editor-proprietor, and the transformation of the controlling interest of the *Guardian* into a trust has given that paper a tone and independence like no other. The last great editor-proprietor was David Astor of the *Observer*, born into the vastly wealthy Anglo-American family who in Edwardian times owned that paper, and who survived to see it sold in the bleak newspaper years of the 1970s to Tiny Rowland of Lonrho. In strict terms, David Astor was not a proprietor since the paper too passed to a trust in 1944 with rather wonderful fence-sitting principles including that it should help 'destroy the social injustices of an ill-balanced society without creating a sluggish conformity and a dull inertia'. But in practical terms, the trustees rarely interfered with him and he functioned as the kind of owner-editor we think of from Victorian times. Indeed, the man he took over from, James Louis Garvin, had functioned independently after persuading David Astor's father, Waldorf, to buy the paper from Northcliffe and let him carry on editing it unfettered. Garvin or 'the Garve', had started in a coal merchant's office in Newcastle and zig-zagged through the political controversies of late Victorian and Edwardian Britain before becoming the grand and conservative-leaning prophet whose weekly sermons in the *Observer* were widely read. By the time the Astors dumped him he was long past his prime and far too right-wing for the idealistic, left-leaning David.

Right-wing proprietors could respond by pointing out that, with the sole exception of the *Guardian* and its public-sector advertising income, few papers based on leftish or idealistic politics have lasted long. High-mindedness is not exciting and has struggled to find a gripping style of journalism beyond the anti-establishment sniper fire of satirical columns and diary paragraphs. The failure of the *News Chronicle* in 1960, which bitterly angered a generation of left-leaning journalists, is still remembered as a signal defeat for high-minded proprietorship. It was owned by the Cadbury family, of chocolate fame, whose strategy had been memorably set out in 1911 by George Cadbury who announced that he wanted to bring 'the ethical teaching of Jesus Christ to bear upon National Questions and in promoting National Righteousness; for example that Arbitration should take the place of War, and the Sermon on the Mount, especially the Beatitudes, should take the place of Imperialism . . .' It is a happy thought, and the *News Chronicle* employed some brilliant journalists, including James Cameron. But it didn't sell. A succession of left-wing papers, from the old *Daily Herald* to the very brief and chaotic *Scottish Daily News* and the *News on Sunday* similarly failed to break into the mass market.

The British news market would feel duller and deader without the tradition of buccaneering, slightly dodgy and generally right-wing proprietors. The proprietors, seeing themselves as independent of party politics, and often as outsiders, are partly responsible for the strange fact that the British press is both impertinent, and yet also profoundly pro-capitalist, populist. Overall, it has the personality of the insecure and self-made insider.

The proprietors' rivalries have tended to be personal and intense, from late Victorian times to the war between the Rothermeres and Desmonds of today, giving the British press its competitive vitality. And yet, despite the eruption of Richard Desmond onto the scene, and O'Reilly's success in buying the *Independent*, the age of the proprietors seems to be fading. The *Mirror* and its sisters are in the hands of corporate bean counters. News International has simply become too big, and too international, for Rupert Murdoch to really function as a hands-on newspaper proprietor any more. He is in London too little, and in Los Angeles or New York too much, to exercise the kind of control over the *Sun* or the *Sunday Times* that he enjoyed in the 1980s. More and more the major British newspapers are in corporate hands, Pearson, or Trinity Mirror or Gannett. The right-wing maverick proprietor has not been replaced by worker-control leftists, but by nominees of pension funds and banks. It may seem an attractive, relatively safe outcome. But the great danger for British journalism is that without the personal interest of owners, proud of their papers and intensely interested in whether they are beating some family rival, investment in reporters and risk-taking will fall away. Would horse racing be a great national sport if most racehorses were owned by corporations whose executives never trod the turf?

How to Read a Newspaper

By now we have met the tribe of journalists, and looked at their raw material, the news, and the editors, politicians and owners who shape the news they bring. The reader has, I hope, won more of a sense of the industry behind the news. But what of newspapers themselves, today? Why are they that shape? And how does that shape, in turn, shape how you understand things around you?

In the headquarters of most great newspaper companies you will find, hanging on some veneer-panelled wall close to the boardroom, framed front pages going back many years. A Martian, scanning them, would conclude that human beings have been becoming quite rapidly stupider. Some broadsheet papers (the *Daily Mail*, *Daily Express* and even the *Independent*) have shrunk. In others, austere columns of closely packed information, containing perhaps ten or twelve stories on a front page, give way over the decades to larger pictures and fewer stories. A modern *Guardian* carries less news on its front page than a *Mirror* from the 1960s. A black and white, sober, information-laden look is replaced by entertaining colour. The very name of the newspaper is encroached on, and overshadowed, by splashy, playground-pastel oblongs, advertising interviews with rock stars, or that day's sex therapist, almost as if apologizing for those dreary news items below. As for tabloids, they have drastically cut the news. 'Pop' papers that used to have six or so stories on the front now have just one, and that cut to perhaps four short paragraphs under a vastly swollen headline and a huge picture. Newspaper executives have ready-made excuses for this. There are more news pages inside; and more longer stories, because people want context, not simply information; and there is better prose, too. Some of this is true. But so is what strikes anyone looking at the development of newspapers in the past half-century: news is being squeezed.

The reasons are interesting. Other media are changing how we expect things to look. Glossy magazines have been a huge influence on newspapers. Their tricks of balloon captions, strip-cartoon-style illustrations, 'Twenty things about . . .', dodgy questionnaires ('Are you a new wave lover?') and the like have been swallowed whole by newspapers. We have already seen how many editors started in magazines. The modern *Daily Mail* is about 40 per cent a woman's magazine in newsprint; in pure design terms, almost all the *Mirror* is as well. Technology is part of the reason; stretched headlines, weird tricks with photos and multicolour layouts used to be slow and difficult – things you could manage on a monthly, not on a daily. Computerized design and Photoshop changed all that. Suddenly newspaper people found they could be more adventurous. Because they could do it, they did do it. The trouble is that, in design terms, 'adventurous' means visual. It means colour and shape. And that in turn means distracting the eye and brain from verbal information. Apart from magazine publishing, the other great design influence has been television. Think of how much modern newspaper design, those oblong blocks and pictures, unconsciously mimics the shape of a television screen. Think of how often you now see sequences of still photos, used big, which is the closest way print can mimic film. Think of the heavy use of picked-out quotes and fact boxes, very like those the TV news bulletins use. Again, an essentially visual culture is devouring a verbal, written one.

Is this why many older readers find modern newspapers so dissatisfying? Watch them in cafes or buses, flicking rather than reading, then flicking back again. Distraction is not a satisfying condition; and yet concentration has to be learned. It is a habit. Newspapers rely on an army of quiet readers who are prepared to spend time closely reading the words of their best writers, dwelling on arguments, contemplating facts. A printed culture is a dignified thing. It needs people with the time and ability to think for themselves, to ponder, to question. British newspapers emerged, as we have seen, from a printed culture and gained their shape and length from it. Edwardian readers of *The Times* in Home Counties rectories, absorbing

3,000 words of a report about a diplomatic incident in the Far East, and readers of the *Police Gazette*, reading with horrified fascination about a murder in the East End, were alike in this: they imagined for themselves. There may have been maps in the posh paper, and drawings in the cheap one, but both were vehicles crammed with words. Today the words seem to hover at the edge of the images.

Traditional newspapers have text in long narrow blocks, less than two inches wide, so the eye bobs down and then up, down and up, like a yo-yo. It isn't particularly pleasant to look at. Longer words often have to be broken in two, there are awkward and ugly spaces to make the lines fit, and long sentences are very difficult to follow. So, you might reasonably ask, why lay text out this way? Why not make newspapers look more like books, which are easier to read and have more white space around the letters? Once, newspaper publishers did just that. A newspaper page from the 1680s is generally only a little bigger than the page of a modern hardback novel. Back then, newspapers were produced in small quantities and very often by printers who also made books, using the same simple presses and lines of lead. There would be two columns of thick, quite large, text, divided by a central line, on each page: books of the time are generally similar; even today many traditional Bibles are laid out this way. Some early newspapers had title pages with engravings, showing a coat of arms, or a crude view of the towns they served, again, rather like the title pages of books of the time. The physical paper that was used is of much better quality than today: I have picked up newspapers from the 1680s which have been loosely kept in cardboard boxes and marvelled at how lustrous and bright the pages are, sometimes clearer and easier to read than modern newspapers three weeks, rather than 300 years, old.

But the mass market meant that expensive paper and small pages disappeared. Papers needed to cram information, adverts, as well as stories, into each edition. And reading habits changed as the urban middle classes grew. The newspapers were for busy people, who would want to scan a page looking for interesting snippets. Skimmers searching for information prefer bigger pages: you cannot scan a booklet. These bigger pages could be economically produced, as we have seen, with ever-faster mechanical presses. But the economics also meant that the paper, the so-called 'newsprint' had to be strong and cheap so that it did not tear under the strain although it did not have to have a long life. Cheaper paper is also muddier, and quite soon yellower, than the more expensive paper used for books. Big pages and muddy paper means that it is harder to have a long, still-readable line of text. And a news-gathering issue emerges, too. If you are constantly updating, adding and cutting to bring in the latest quotes, scores and events, it is far easier to do this with a narrow line of text. Small paragraphs can be quickly snipped out or added. Imagine trying to edit and repeatedly change a novel-sized page of text, cutting the old and inserting the new. It is impossible. In newspaper layout, paragraphs can be rewritten and the text simply shoved down or nipped to fill the available space. It may not look pretty and it can be hard to read, but for a couple of centuries the short newspaper line was immensely practical. Quick, throwaway sentences, jammed into terse paragraphs, for a faster-moving, throwaway age. No one thought it was an ideal way of reading English: the journals, published monthly or quarterly for smaller audiences, often opted for a size and line length halfway between the newspaper and the book, with each page still divided into two columns.

Long thin columns printed on large rectangles of paper may have suited the Victorians but in the age of computer layout and photocomposition, are they still really necessary? It is a good question. Books, after all, seem wonderful acts of evolved design, which have barely changed in shape or size during the past three centuries, and for good reason. Books generally depend on a line of some four or five inches long, a convenient length for the human size of skull, since it means the eye can scan from left to right (or in other cultures, right to left) without the neck moving. Try reading text only a little wider, say eight or nine inches, and you will literally feel the difference. But book design needs clean, white paper of relatively high quality and a relatively small area to be easily readable. Again, if you doubt this, try reading one of those very cheaply produced modern classics editions on greyish paper with an unusually small type size. It is just more tiring. But newspapers, of course, are designed for a different purpose from books; they are not meant to be read from beginning to end, in one direction, page after page, for a long period of time. And they are a great deal more than ordinary-sized text.

They include headlines. The obvious purpose of a headline is to persuade you to read what sits below it. In fact, headlines are probably more useful in warning you what not to bother reading. Watch someone reading a paper and note how quickly they move from story to story, page to page. For most readers, for every headline that says 'read this', there are several more which say 'it's fine to ignore this bit'. Headlines are there for speed and convenience. The first really popular papers, those of Georgian times, did not have headlines. Georgian newspapers were not chaotic: information was often gathered roughly on the same pages each day, with adverts here, and news from the City there. No doubt many of their readers could go straight to where they wanted. But they seem to be designed for less frantic readers who were interested in a wide range of information, and had time to meander down lines of paragraphs about wildly different subjects until something jumped out at them. Eventually, this seemed to irritate readers and the market favoured those papers which made things easier. First, they did this by using larger or blacker type to alert the reader to where similar stories had been bundled together: society news, or 'recent drownings' or 'correspondence from various capitals'. Then they moved on to highlight individual stories of particular merit, a 'horrid drowning' or 'sensational murder'. By the mid-Victorian popular papers, almost every story of more than a paragraph had its own headline, though they were more sparingly used in, say, *The Times*. Corruption has entered Eden: the headline stops being merely a useful way of organizing information and becomes a turn-on, a bit of verbal spin, to hook the casual eye. That is certainly the case with sensational Victorian and Edwardian papers, and they often used several decks of headline in ever-decreasing size, to pack in more facts. This fell out of fashion during the middle years of the twentieth century, which is a pity. It was almost always more effective than today's huge, simple, brick-like headlines.

You can find, even in the earliest papers, engravings but also pictures – generally stylized impressions which owe more to contemporary paintings than to street witnesses. The greatest British graphic artists of the pre-photography era, such as Phil May of *Punch*, did evolve a fast style of ink drawing, without cross-hatching, which does have a real reporterly feel. Picture-based popular publishing expanded hugely from the 1860s, with magazines like the *Illustrated London News*. But you couldn't depend on having an artist with his inkpot scurrying round the country with your conventional reporter. Even when there was time to make line drawings – of a statesman's face during a public speech, or the accused in a trial – daily papers rarely had the skill or ability to use them. The great breakthrough, quickly and clearly reproduced photographs on newsprint, did not come until the 1900s, when the *Daily Mirror* has a good claim to be the first proper illustrated daily paper.

The photos spread slowly through the British press. The First World War meant there was intense curiosity, a yearning, for images. The use of small portable cameras meant that by the 1920s papers were filling up with images. These were generally quite small, and often simple portrait head shots, though great disasters were now being illustrated by larger images. Broadsheets generally avoided them; even during the Second World War it is striking how few good pictures were used in posh papers, though that also had something to do with censorship. The now-iconic images of Spitfire pilots waiting to take off, or smoke-trails in the sky during the Battle of Britain, or tanks charging across the desert, are mostly lacking from papers of the time. And it is really only in the sixties that broadsheet newspapers begin to carry big front-page pictures, again often austere by our standards. Today almost all papers, except specialist titles such as the *Financial Times*, are what readers of a century ago would have dismissively called 'picture papers'.

The order of stories in newspapers is also governed by technology. It is not possible to print all the pages simultaneously; they have to be sent to the printworks in a staggered order. 'Early pages' must therefore be the pages with the least time-sensitive material. In modern papers, that means most of the features material, many of the columns and much of the foreign coverage, leaving the field clear for late-breaking domestic stories. Why is sport so often on the back pages? Because, as with front page news and the domestic news which follows it, last-minute scores and other sports information is at a premium. The same sheets of paper which at one end have the news, at the other end have the sport. These days, of course, it is possible to get good last-minute foreign stories too, and every night news editor on a daily paper must assume that tomorrow's readers have watched the previous evening's TV news. Even so, a brutal assumption rules: foreign news matters less to people than news nearer home, so it is less time sensitive, and comes later in the run of newspaper pages. Almost every broadsheet paper follows the same assumptions. First, there is the front page of the best British and foreign stories, then the home stories, before the foreign pages, perhaps followed by the comment pages and so on. There is a basic rhythm that is remarkably constant across newspaper titles whose size, politics and market may differ a lot. No one fills the front page with adverts. No one puts business news before foreign news. No one runs foreign pages before home ones – not even, these days, the *Financial Times*. It is hard to avoid the thought that this rhythm has something fundamental about it – that news begins at home; that we need a leavening of lighter stories to compensate for the grimmer ones; that we naturally like to get facts first, then comment – which is why front-page hectoring annoys so many readers. A newspaper is not a series of the most important stories of the previous day, arranged in order; it is a human narrative, a reminder of our common interests, arranged to entice, excite and incite. It is a dance; a familiar dance.

So if you really want to know what is going on, how should you read a newspaper now? Here are a few suggestions . . .

Know what you're buying. Reporting is now so contaminated by bias and campaigning, and general mischief, that no reader can hope to get a picture of what is happening without first knowing who owns the paper, and who it is being published for. The *Mirror* defines its politics as the opposite of the *Sun*'s, which in turn is defined by the geo-politics of Rupert Murdoch's News International – hostile to European federalism and the euro and so forth. If it is ferociously against Tony Blair, this is probably because Number Ten has been passing good stories to the *Sun*. Its support for Gordon Brown was, similarly, driven by the need to find a rival when Blair courted Murdoch. It felt jilted. You need to know these things. You need to aim off.

Follow the names. If you find a reporter who seems to know the score, particularly in an area you know about, cherish him or her. In the trade we generally know who is good. If you are interested in social services and the welfare state, Nicholas Timmins, currently writing for the *Financial Times*, is essential. If you are interested in think tank reports and the cerebral end of Whitehall then Peter Riddell of *The Times* is about the only reporter worth bothering with. But if you

want investigative journalism that covers Whitehall, never miss David
Hencke and Richard Norton-Taylor (aka Richard Naughty Trousers),
both of the *Guardian*. Books? Robert McCrum of the *Observer* writes a
weekly column that almost everyone in the media publishing world
will read. The funniest restaurant reviewer in London? Certainly, the
Spectator's Deborah Ross. Best Northern Ireland correspondent? David
McKittrick, also in the *Indy*. In a crowded market, it is becoming
harder to single out individuals since most fields, from sports reporting to the City or food writing, have two or three top acts. And
everyone has their own favourites. But the point is, watch the bylines.
If you find a friendly style, someone you grow to trust, treasure the
name and follow it. My experience as an editor was that many readers
were surprisingly attuned to the work of individual writers they knew
nothing personally about. Bylines are often the only signal that gold,
rather than dross, lies below.

Register bias. Even when you read the same paper every day, be aware
that reporters are now less embarrassed to let the bias show. This is
rarely direct party-political bias, but you may find that a columnist is
favourably inclined towards one politician – say, that Bruce Anderson
of the *Independent* is generally in favour of the Tory leader of the day,
whoever he or she may be; and that Donald Macintyre, of the same
paper, scrupulously fair, is generally more sympathetic to Peter Mandelson than most of his colleagues; and that Paul Routledge has a
powerful partiality for Gordon Brown. This is all completely legitimate,
but worth remembering; it may also point to the source of the story.
That matters too: no political journalist in the early 2000s would read
a story by *The Times*'s Tom Baldwin without wondering whether he'd
been speaking to Alastair Campbell. Baldwin has many sources, but
Campbell, in the days of his glory, was a key one, giving that reporter's
reporting added interest for the Westminster villagers. Again, worth
knowing.

Read the second paragraph; and look for quote marks. Surprisingly often,
the key fact is not in the first paragraph, which is general and designed
to grab attention. Look for the hard fact in the next paragraph. If it
seems soft and contentless, there is probably very little in the story.
Similarly, always look for direct quotation. If a reporter has actually
done the work, and talked to people who know things, the evidence

will usually be there. Who are the sources? Are they speaking them-selves? Are they named? Generic descriptions, such as 'senior back-bencher' or 'one industry analyst' (my mate on the other side of the desk) or 'observers' (nobody at all), should be treated sceptically. They can be figments of the reporter's own prejudices or guesses, rather than real people. If you keep coming across well-written anonymous quotes, be highly suspicious: these are probably crumbling bricks without the straws of supporting fact.

If the headline asks a question, try answering 'no'. Is This the True Face of Britain's Young? (Sensible reader: No.) Have We Found the Cure for AIDS? (No; or you wouldn't have put the question mark in.) Does This Map Provide the Key for Peace? (Probably not.) A headline with a question mark at the end means, in the vast majority of cases, that the story is tendentious or over-sold. It is often a scare story, or an attempt to elevate some run-of-the-mill piece of reporting into a national controversy and, preferably, a national panic. To a busy journalist hunting for real information a question mark means 'don't bother reading this bit'.

And watch out for quotation marks in headlines, too. If you read 'Marr "Stole" Book Idea' then the story says nothing of the kind. If quotation marks are signs of real reporting in the body of a story, in the headline they are often a sign of failed reporting. That story may say someone else thinks Marr has stolen the idea for a book; but if the newspaper was reporting that this was really so, those giveaway squiggles wouldn't be there. As with question marks, headline quotation marks are mostly a warning sign, meaning 'tendentious, overblown story follows . . .' They certainly save my time in the morning.

Read small stories and attend to page two . . . Just because something is reported in a single paragraph does not mean it is insignificant. Busy sub-editors, with their own blind spots and unexamined prejudices, and with limited space, often cut the most interesting or significant piece of news down to a few lines. And for reasons explained above, page two is often one of the richest sources of real, hard news. Here are the painstakingly researched articles and important tales suddenly stripped off the front page by a night editor in the small hours of the morning to make way for something 'brighter' that may sell from the newsagent's counter.

Suspect 'research'. Hundreds of dodgy academic departments put out bogus or trivial pieces of research purely designed to impress busy newspaper people and win themselves some cheap publicity which can in turn be used in their next funding applications. If something is a survey, see if the paper reports how many people were surveyed, and when. If the behaviour of rats, or flies, has been extrapolated to warn about human behaviour, check whether the story gives any indication of how many rats, and how much caffeine they were injected with; and then pause for a reality check. If someone is described as an expert, look to see who they work for – and ask, would a real world expert be doing that? Also ask whether they are a doctor, or professor or simply 'researcher, Jeff Mutt . . .'

Check the calendar. Not simply for April Fool's, but for the predictable round of hardy annuals that bulk up thin news lists. Anniversaries; stories about the wettest/driest/longest/warmest spring/summer/ autumn; the ritual 'row between judges' stories designed to whip up interest before annual book awards, and the equally synthetic 'public disgust' stories about art shows. Every year there is a slew of tooth-sucking stories about the Royal Academy Summer Exhibition being a bit disappointing; about the autumn TV schedules being dominated by bought-in US miniseries or 'reality TV' shows; about the disgusting and inane finalists for the Turner Prize. You have read this stuff before; you will read it again next year. On a busy day, flick on.

Suspect financial superlatives. Even if the underlying rate of inflation is modest, then in the ordinary way of things, prices for many limited goods – Pre-Raphaelite paintings, or seaside huts, or football shirts, are going to be 'the highest ever'. For the same reason it is completely to be expected that teachers will get 'their highest ever pay deals', however excited the minister sounds about this; and that non-executive directors' earnings will be 'the highest recorded', however outraged the minister sounds about that. What is interesting is how these raw increases relate to inflation, and therefore to other prices and to each other. Are the Van Gogh prices increasing faster than Picasso prices? Are the superstore bosses being paid more than before, relative to their staff? An informative story, as against a merely sensationalist one, will tell you that.

Remember that news is cruel. Reading the awful things that people apparently say about each other, or newspapers say about them, can be depressing. Is life really so writhing with distaste, failure and loathing? No – only the newspapers. Acts of kindness, generosity, forgiveness and mere friendliness are hardly ever news; which is why there is a class of readers who turn their backs on newspapers and graze in the sunnier, gentler places of celebrity and women's magazines; or who obsessively trawl favourite internet sites and trusted periodicals to find news sources they feel they can trust, as they cannot trust the press.

Finally, believe nothing you read about newspaper sales – nothing. Newspaper sales have been falling in Britain for a long time, and steadily. Yet every newspaper manages to tell a heartwarming story about how successful its sales are, almost every month. Work it out for yourself.

5

Into the Crowded Air

If the Face Fits . . .

I had never thought much about television. Radio, yes: for many years, like many other newspaper hacks, I had received derisory cheques from the BBC for making weekly radio programmes or appearing as a radio pundit. It was relatively easy work, and increased one's sense of self-importance. But television was impossible. I have always had the wrong shape of head. It sticks out in awkward places, bulges whenever I think, is only sparsely covered with tufts of colourless hair, and collapses somewhere around the chin, scurrying for cover towards the collar. The ears reach out like large red satellite dishes, the cheeks are covered with lines and rashes caused by decades of overwork and overindulgence and if I dare to smile widely, it looks less like a friendly act than a record of bomb damage in the Blitz. Timothy Winters, teeth like splinters? The lad has nothing on me. All these features are kindly tolerated by family and friends, becoming almost acceptable over time. They are accentuated, brutally, by a television camera lens. I had appeared just enough to know this, and still wince if I catch an unexpected glimpse of myself. This is bad enough, but I also have a tendency to grimace and pull strange faces as I speak. No wonder a producer of the BBC *Today* programme many years ago assured me I had a wonderful face for radio.

So a career on the telly had always seemed off the agenda. By the time the BBC approached me I was forty. Every time one turned on the TV there were people who had made-for-television faces, faces that 'worked' – Jeremy Paxman with his long weary streak of disbelief; Huw Edwards, Martha Kearney and Jeremy Vine, polished, handsome and bouncingly self-confident; Michael Brunson, brimming with glossy, full-throated good humour; and then all the rising, made-for-broadcasting stars such as the bespectacled, cheerful Nick Robinson and droll, hand-waving Mark Mardell. All right, there was John Sergeant too. But in general why would anyone ask someone with a face as off-putting as mine to join this company? Television, after all, is part of the entertainment industry as well as a news source.

Indeed, when I did appear on television, the newspaper critics were quick to make unflattering comparisons. 'One of the strangest-looking males on the planet' was the thoughtful verdict of *Radio Times*. Others were powerfully reminded of anorexic elephants, Gobby the House Elf, Plug from the 'Bash Street Kids', Martin Clunes and even the notoriously grim-faced Russian president Vladimir Putin. I do not much like the look of Putin, so it is disconcerting to discover many people think we are indeed dead ringers. Once, in the Kremlin, following Tony Blair during a summit, I had to leave the press conference early to get to a live TV point overlooking Red Square. The Kremlin remains heavily guarded. I lost my way and found myself pounding along a seemingly endless corridor, at the end of which armed soldiers were standing. When they saw me, they looked aghast and backed against the wall. And they were not the only ones. When Mr Putin visited Britain in the spring of 2003 for the first state visit since Queen Victoria's day, he was seen talking to the Queen with great animation, through an interpreter, as their open landau travelled from Westminster to Buckingham Palace. The Queen was asked later what they were talking about and said she couldn't really recall: 'I just had to keep reminding myself I was talking to the Russian president and not to that man from the BBC.' Andrew Marr, asked one of her staff? 'Yes, that's the chappie.' On another occasion, I was shopping in the local supermarket and noticed someone staring at me. Eventually he came over, put his face close to mine and said: 'Here, you look just like that Andrew Marr . . . you poor bugger.'

Still, despite this disability, the BBC approached me about taking over as political editor. This is a sensitive subject, since the incumbent, Robin Oakley, had hoped to have his contract renewed for several more years. He moved to work for CNN but was badly hurt by his treatment; inevitably, and necessarily, the negotiations about my possible arrival took place in deepest secret. After receiving a cold glare from him one day in the Commons, I had assumed he knew exactly what was up. I was wrong; it was a surprise. He took the news with great dignity and grace and more good humour than I could ever have mustered under similar circumstances. Robin, who had worked for many years as political editor of *The Times*, is an old-fashioned reporter of much integrity. But he was judged to be an insufficiently lively presence on the BBC News at a time of ferocious competitive pressure. I come from a different journalistic generation, all too aware that voters do not feel the slightest obligation to keep up with political news merely because it is there. I believe the job now involves persuading easily bored viewers with remote-control zappers on the arm of the sofa that it is worth paying attention to Westminster news, at least once a day, however briefly. I suppose he might say his generation produced better, straighter journalism.

The other problem when I joined the BBC was that a press campaign was immediately launched against me, with very hostile stories appearing in the *Daily Mail*, *Telegraph* and *Sun*. The theme was that I was a New Labour appointee, an old friend of Tony Blair's selected to go poodle-soppy on the government, alongside the appointment of Greg Dyke, a former Labour donor, as the corporation's director-general. In fact, I had been appointed at the end of the outgoing regime, with Tony Hall, who left to run the Royal Opera House in Covent Garden, one of my main interlocutors, and with John Birt still formally in charge. I did speak to Mr Dyke, once, but he did not mention politics. Over breakfast, we talked about the BBC's business news, and his enthusiasm for hiring Jeff Randall, then editor of *Sunday Business*, to ginger things up there. I had given up any active involvement in politics in 1984, before I left Edinburgh for London to start as a parliamentary reporter, and took the puritanical view that journalists should not belong to any campaigning organization at all. I wasn't even a member of the journalists' union, the NUJ, after becoming an editor. I had known Mr Blair when he was a rising Opposition MP and a good source, as had scores of other journalists. As to Mr Campbell, he had already tried to get me sacked from one job and though I rather admired his aggressive style, we hardly ever spoke.

It was true that I had written for some years as a centre-left columnist. But every journalist worth anything knows the difference between reporting and commentary; I took the view that I was returning to straight reporting. The biggest danger, I thought, would be in over-compensating and, as a result of being attacked by right-wing papers, then falling into unfairness the other way. Still, it was a vociferous campaign. Any mildly favourable remark about anything done by the government was seized on as evidence of bias. It became surreal. One media commentator, after weeks trying to find a biased comment, eventually conceded that he had not been able to; but smoothly continued that it did not matter, since he knew what I was secretly thinking. When I made a short film before the 2001 election urging people to vote – for any party, to exercise their democratic rights, rather than sitting at home – it was alleged that I had been given the run of Downing Street by the prime minister, had used a film-star's pantechnicon, parked outside for my changes of clothing, and had worked to a script dictated by Alastair Campbell. None of this was true. Tory officials were worried that a higher turnout might benefit Labour though, and thought this was a way of warning me off. A few days later one of the press officers at Conservative Central Office laughingly admitted to making the story up and passing it to the *Mail on Sunday* who had never checked it. He thought it was hilarious and didn't think I would mind very much; 'you know the game'.

Well, I came to know it. These problems, facial and political, were a good introduction into why broadcasting journalism is different from newspaper journalism. In so many ways, they are similar – the same kind of people, often; the same struggle for 'top lines' and for scoops; similar tensions between journalists and editors. But there are crucial distinctions. One is the technology of broadcasting. Extraneous questions of how you look, and lighting, and the limitations or opportunities offered by pieces of kit, loom very large in TV news. The reporter is only one part of a large team of technicians, producers, videotape editors and camera staff. Television journalism, if not radio journalism, has an uncomfortable proximity to entertainment. The TV news is surrounded, before and afterwards, by material intended purely to entertain and amuse, in a way broadsheet newspaper journalism, for example, is not. The quality of pictures and the need to tell a visual story are an essential, everyday part of the job. The second distinction is that broadcasting is legally bound to be impartial, in a way newspapers are not. Because of the original rationing of wavelengths as a limited, publicly owned resource, parliament has always had a grip on broadcasting it would not dream of exercising over the press barons. Newspaper ownership is a matter of intense interest to politicians, and lobbying, and regulation. But the ownership of TV channels is even more sensitive; and the BBC's licence fee makes it a controversial player. I was joining a world dedicated to the broadcasting of politics; but the politics of broadcasting was always at the back of our minds. And that is fair enough. A reporter for a national newspaper is working for a specific group – *Sun* readers want different things from *Sunday Times* readers. In television, we are reporting for everybody; we have to engage one end of the market without infuriating the other. It was journalism, Jim, but not as I knew it.

The Clutter of Magic: How Broadcasters Do It

New national broadcast journalists must generally make a pilgrimage. You go south out of London and keep on going until you arrive in the main street of the prosperous, picturesque Home Counties town of Reigate. There you make your way to a small shop, not unlike an optician's, where a waxy resin is pressed deep into each ear. Later, enclosed in small plastic cases, you receive two, or four, earpieces, specially made to fit the whorls of your left or right ear. From them dangles a thin hose of plastic tubing, with a metal clip to attach to the back of your collar. It may be simple technology, but the earpiece is your only lifeline. It connects a live reporter to the studio. If it falls out or gets a kink, you are cut off. The viewer sees a calm, well-known presenter ask you a perfectly sensible question, and then sees you staring blankly back, struck dumb. You have no idea what is happening except that you desperately hope you are not on air. You shake your head, or shrug, and point at one ear, helplessly. It is not a pleasant feeling. One of the joys of overseas reporting with crews whose sound equipment does not match the British earpieces is the 'ping' as a small piece of rubber leaves your ear at speed just as Sophie Raworth, Huw Edwards or another presenter has asked about the prime minister's mood. The simple earpiece is a good example of how reliant broadcast journalists are on the tubes, lenses and electronics all around them.

Once I had joined the BBC, I was given a crash course in the two things a modern television reporter has to be able to do (apart from the mere business of finding things out). The first is the 'two-way', the live interview, of which more later. The second is 'packaging', making the short films, which run at between one and four minutes, but average just under two, which are the building blocks of a TV news bulletin. Radio relies on the same two skills, but there is far less to get in the way. A radio two-way, as long as the microphone and head-phones work, and the line doesn't go down, is a simpler business: you do not have to worry about your face, expression, or anything except what you are saying. Generations of radio reporters learned how to mark and cut tape, splicing together interviews and their own words, to make radio packages. These are not as easy as they might seem to do well – for instance, a little natural sound, birdsong or distant shouting voices, can help a radio package come alive. But again, they are much less cumbersome than television ones.

Before I had properly started, I met Terry Wogan at Wimbledon and received the best single piece of advice about working in television. 'Whatever you do, boy,' said Terry, 'just keep looking straight into the camera. It doesn't matter what you say or what else is going wrong . . . just look into that lens.' It is sometimes harder to do than you'd think. So I went to Television Centre to learn. TV Centre is the vast glass and concrete doughnut near Shepherd's Bush in west London which is the heart of the BBC's television effort. On a site bought by the BBC in 1949 which had had a pre-war empire exhibition on it, TV Centre is surrounded by housing estates, motorway overpasses and grimy streets. It has a very specific, late-1950s-cum-Festival-of-Britain feel about it, all high-minded mosaics, sexless winged statues and interminable, impossible corridors through which you could wander for an airless eternity. Here are the huge studios used for *Top of the Pops*, general election programmes, quiz shows and comedies. For decades it has echoed to pop fans, the laughter of Morecambe and Wise, the tread of Dimblebys and the constant agonizing and sweat of daily news broadcasting. It has been extended, then extended again. It has been picketed by union strikers, stormed by lesbian protesters, bombed by Irish republicans and visited by almost every significant figure in British life in the past forty years.

It is also home to the crafts and skills that have sustained the BBC for that time: the lighting technicians, who have done so many complicated dramas they are living encyclopaedias of their rare art; the news cameramen, who are now freelances and worry that their lifetime of skills and experience is not being passed on to younger people; and the film-makers. Among the film-makers is a man called Duncan Herbert. He is a quietly spoken, wry man who is probably not a household name even in his own house. But to colleagues at TV Centre, Herbert is a figure of awe. 'Duncan is the most brilliant VT [videotape] editor of his generation,' I was firmly told. From him I was to learn how to make a film package. So we sat for several days in a remote corner of the building working on news stories that would never see the light of day. (One of the advantages of a circular building is that, while there are no 'remote corners' by definition, almost everywhere *feels* like a remote corner.) We watched badly made news packages, well-made news packages and everything in between. I learned that, so far as the head honchos of BBC news are concerned, there is a very clear hierarchy of talent among reporters, probably one the reporters themselves don't know about. When I joined, it was believed that along with John Simpson, Matt Frei, then the Far East correspondent, later Washington correspondent, was the single best news packager in the Corporation. Mark Mardell was regarded as superb too. So what skills was Herbert describing when he ranked these apparently simple, and always very brief, works?

Every package is a story. It has narrative – a beginning, a middle and an end. Mostly, this is chronological: Tony Blair leaves Downing Street; he arrives in the Commons and says X; the Opposition is seen outside afterwards saying Y, while protesters are being dragged away for shouting Z. That evening Mr Blair is seen arriving at a dinner for the American ambassador and stops briefly to insist that X has been misunderstood; the real point is W. A news package tells one story, not two. It cannot bear the weight of more than one. It works best when the pictures are fresh and gripping, and support, without overwhelming, the news story they are being used to tell. Often you may hear a producer or director saying to a reporter, 'that's a bit Lord Privy Seal-ish' – a reference to the old sketch which described the Lord Privy Seal with pictures of a man in ermine, a toilet and a barking, frolicking seal. In other words, the phrases are too literal. If the pictures are of British tanks rolling across the desert, the script should not say 'today British tanks were rolling across the desert'. We can see that. But at the same time, the words must not work against the pictures, either. If the tanks are rolling, a script line that talks about the foreign affairs select committee simply won't be heard by the average viewer. Or, if the film is of a quiet English village, where perhaps we are about to meet a group of countryside campaigners, then a script line about anger and confrontation simply sounds bizarre. We have to wait to see that for ourselves. Between 'a quiet village in the rolling Cotswolds . . .' (too Lord Privy Seal-ish) and 'an ugly mood is spreading here' (doesn't fit with the sunlit oaks and silent roads) a good TV reporter will come up with something better. 'There's hardly been a voice raised in anger round these parts since the English Civil War. Until now . . .' might be the sort of thing . . . at which point the producer will lean over and say, 'Too long.' Good words should gesture towards the pictures, at a slight angle to them. For those of us at Westminster, fitting words to pictures is a particular problem. No pictures are duller than empty green leather benches. No squares of grubby grass are more familiar. We work hard to find even slightly unfamiliar corners, angles and shadow.

In a BBC or ITN edit suite, where the packages are made, there are usually three people. There is the reporter, with scribbled notes or a screen, where the script is being written, and a microphone. On the left of the room, working with two screens, two video decks, and an array of knobs, rubber toggles and switches which looks like a cross between the mixing equipment in a music studio and the controls for a superannuated jet bomber, is the picture editor, also sometimes known as the VT (videotape) editor. His or her job is to take the raw material, which will consist of material shot specially that day, and perhaps archive film (what the prime minister was saying last week), interviews, Commons footage and so on, and transfer snippets of them onto the master videotape, building up the story in pictures; while also recording the reporter's words in good sound quality. There are many pitfalls to be avoided. You must not 'cross the line' – that is, jump from one shot to another taken from the opposite side, jolting the viewer's sense of continuity. If you are lucky a lively incident – John Prescott being pelted with an egg during the 2001 election, for instance, and retaliating with a punch – may be caught by several cameras and the whole can be spliced together with the best shots.

More often, you have to make do with film caught slightly late or at the wrong angle, or just a little too far away to make the crucial words out. A quiet barter goes on between the broadcasters – if Sky had a camera in the right spot, and ITN caught the better words as a minister left her house, a trade can be done. On a busy day with a lot of movement, ministers charging in and out of their offices, or demonstrations breaking out simultaneously in different parts of the town, there may be camera crews from rival organizations dotted carefully about to gather in the maximum quantity of movement. A closely negotiated 'pooling' arrangement to enable everyone to share the pictures will have been agreed between the rival operations. But it is mostly the other way: if you have great pictures, you will want to keep them for yourself.

A good picture editor cuts and reshapes the raw film incredibly fast – it can be like watching a classical pianist at the keyboard – while watching for little glitches in the sound, lighting problems and so on. This can be a high-pressure job. In general, it takes about an hour to cut a minute's worth of broadcast news, so two and a half hours for an average *BBC News at Ten O'Clock* package. And a news bulletin is timed to the second: if you have been asked to deliver a two minute, fifteen second package, you can't simply send an extra ten or fifteen seconds and say sorry later. Every two seconds is haggled over; so the package must be on time and to time. But all too often, time itself is at a premium, and you are racing desperately to get the piece finished before the programme goes live. It is the worst sin of all to fail to make your slot. To fail to 'make' or 'make the gate' is a hanging offence. I exaggerate only slightly – do it twice and you will probably be on the way out. With that lurking over them, any reporter and producer arriving in the edit suite will feel like a million dollars if a nimble, experienced editor is waiting for them. And will feel queasy if it's someone less talented.

The producer has a wider job. Producers are in charge of the whole process, words apart, and are directly responsible to the editor of the news programme for getting the right length of package, well made and well shot, on air at the right time. The questions that a producer will be dealing with include discussing what the story is really about with the reporter; negotiating and working with the camera crew; setting up any logistics, including where the completed package is going to be fed back to TV Centre from; writing the cue or intro, which will be read out in the studio and is roughly equivalent to the headline for the story; and generally shepherding, cajoling and bullying the vain and easily distracted reporter into doing his or her job. Just as a good picture editor makes all the difference, so does a good producer. There is always a power tussle going on between the reporter and the producer, sometimes subtle, sometimes not. Some reporters, particularly senior ones, will have very strong ideas about the pictures they want, the story they intend to tell, and the time they need. Their scripts are sacrosanct and the producer dares suggest a change of emphasis at peril of violence. Other reporters are putty in the hands of the producer, lamely following suggestions and ending up as little more than the ventriloquist for the producer's message. You might think that since the reporter's voice and face will be in the package, the reporter has all the power. But this is not necessarily so. A frustrated producer can make a reporter look very silly indeed; and the producer will have a closer relationship with the programme editor too. And just to keep things simple, all producers fight with picture editors. That is virtually in the contract.

Yet film packages must be an exercise in teamwork or they are chaotic and unbearably stressful to make. I have been very lucky in my three producers since starting at the BBC: all have been interested in politics, were quite prepared to make radical suggestions about how to tell the story, and would bust a gut to get that particularly good cameraman, or that extra, hard-to-find piece of archive material. Even so, up against a deadline, with the editor straining and cursing, Television Centre constantly phoning with questions, the equipment seizing up and the words failing to flow, the air in the edit suite often turns blue. Small packets of biscuits and crisps disappear, silences you could cut drag on, and still that bloody shot won't work.

All the while you are working with the raw material provided by the real front-line people, the cameramen and (sometimes) women. The difference between a really good cameraman, who wants to talk through a story, to get shots that help, and who is prepared to take risks to get them, and his run-of-the-mill colleagues is astonishing. For a journalist, it is the difference between working in full-colour oil paint and working with a charcoal twig. At Westminster, for instance, if there is a really tough story to show through film, cameramen Paul

Dickie or Simon Monk are among those called for. Simon Monk specializes in unusual angles, strange effects and beautifully framed long shots. In any political scrimmage, Simon will be the man squirming where no one else has dared to go or being chased by worried-looking officials. We call his work MonkVision. But with or without that magic ingredient, the story needs to be told. The worst moments in making packages are often on the road at party conferences or following the prime minister abroad, when the edit suite is just a freezing plywood box of tangled wires in an underground car park, or a vandalized hotel room. Then comes yet another call from the programme editor, just at the end of a conference, when the impromptu newsroom is being loudly dismantled around your ears. This time, it's sorry, but could we please *not* use that crucial shot of Air Force One landing? And can we trim ten seconds off too? This is heart attack country.

Another crucial element of most news packages is the PTC, the piece to camera, which is where the reporter suddenly appears on the screen and speaks meaningfully at you. This is a much-studied and controversial area of its own. There are television correspondents whose value is heavily based on their pieces to camera – Robert Hall is famous in the trade for his complicated 'walk and talk' routines, often live, but also recorded, weaving in and out of machinery, armoured trucks or puddles without faltering as he speaks intently into the camera. Behind him, on cue, tanks belch fumes, soldiers load their kit or wildlife flaps; but Robert Hall never flaps. Abroad, the PTC in a flak jacket is, as we shall see in a later chapter, a necessary rite of passage towards that first Royal Television Society award. The involuntary flinch, miraculously timed two phrases into the first sentence, and backward flick of the eyes as a 'crump' of exploding shell can be distantly heard, has become a glorious PTC cliché – as familiar a sight as that of a health reporter padding down a hospital corridor behind jars of something nasty in formaldehyde . . . out of focus, but not quite out of focus enough.

At Westminster, as I have said, we have the problem of most backdrops being drearily familiar, so we try almost anything to freshen things up – nearby streets, plastic chess sets, handy statues . . . even walking along the pavement, though I am almost certain to stumble, and cannot on any account walk up stairs and talk to a camera without falling over.

The PTC is used as a grammatical device in the middle of a package, a way of turning from one thought to another, particularly when there are no obvious pictures to use. Different programmes have different conventions. On the *BBC News at Ten O'Clock*, packages often end with a PTC . . . 'Andrew Marr. BBC News. Westminster . . .' But on the Six O'clock bulletin this was for a long time banned, partly because it was thought to have become a deadening, 'on the one hand . . .' cliché and partly because the shift from one talking face, the reporter, to another talking face, the presenter who then picks up, is seen as unattractive. But wherever it comes in a package, the PTC is a chance to speak directly to the viewer about the significance, or meaning, of the story just told, or to add in very recent information, or to cast ahead to the next development expected tomorrow. Because they tend to be recorded late in the process of making a package, they are often very short – say ten or fifteen seconds long – and done at speed. But they shouldn't be bland. This is horribly difficult to pull off.

All this I learned with Duncan Herbert. Slowly, I unlearned newspaper writing, in which the most important facts begin the story, and where you can quote unnamed sources, be handily abstract and make use of acronyms. Instead, I learned to 'write to picture', telling the same story that my newspaper colleagues were relating, but radically stripped down and written in a new order. Vin Ray, the guru of these matters at the BBC, quotes the old advice from John Grierson, a pioneer British documentary film-maker, who said that you could write an article about the postal service but you had to make a film about a single letter. Ray went on:

> Your job is to take an often confusing or complicated situation or series of events and make sense of it for the viewer, and in doing so, it's most often what you leave out that really matters . . . If your story needs to be seen more than once before it can be understood (and too many do), then it will have totally failed . . . You are distilling information, not packing it in. Get to the point, stick to it, know when it's finished, then end it.[1]

Brutal advice, but absolutely right. I even learned the value of silence . . . letting the pictures say more than I could, or allowing natural sound to bubble up in place of my voice – we call this SOF (sound on film) or SOT (sound on tape). One reason Matt Frei was so admired

as a packager was his courage in allowing a silence to go on, and on,
when the pictures were really compelling when a lesser reporter might
be tempted to butt in with poetic, carefully thought-through but
redundant verbiage. In television journalism, less can really be more.

Whales and Elephants

Some readers may by now be asking an obvious question: if the
pictures are so important, are they not in fact leading, with the story
struggling along behind? Is this not a fundamentally corrupt art,
underplaying what is important in order to favour what is vivid? This
is an important, serious question and, as it happens, has been agonized
about from the birth of TV news itself. Television is now seen as part
of the Americanized world. In fact, the world's first regular high-
definition TV service started not in the United States but in London,
from the windswept and dingy grandeur of Alexandra Palace, where
on 2 November 1936 the aptly named Major Tryon inaugurated BBC
broadcasts with a range of twenty-five miles. But in Britain or America
early television was seen as a minority entertainment, with pantomime
horses, chorus girls and drama, plus a few cartoons. It was not seen as
a fit medium for news. Indeed, the BBC itself did not regard TV as fit
for news. Under its first director-general, Sir John Reith, it had a high-
minded culture. One of the pioneers of BBC television later wrote that
though the staff then were of 'unquestioned excellence ... their
speciality was the use of words; they had no knowledge of how to
present either entertainment or information in vision. Moreover, most
of them distrusted the visual; they associated vision with the movies
and the music hall and were afraid that the high purposes of the
Corporation would be trivialised . . .'[2]

Before and during the Second World War this hardly mattered.
Only a tiny number of people had television anyway; the editor of the
BBC's Listener magazine told one of his reviewers that 'television won't
matter in your lifetime or mine', while another Corporation executive
opined, 'Television won't last. It's a flash in the pan.' As late as the
early 1950s American newspaper editors were saying just the same to
ambitious young reporters tempted to jump into the embryonic
television industry. Meanwhile, the real battle for good broadcast news

was being fought out on radio, through the exertions of people like the young Richard Dimbleby. As so often it was American reporters who showed how vividly and immediately one could tell the news – Edward Murrow, the radio reporter of the Second World War, being a classic example, before he too jumped over to television, with his famous *See it Now* news show on CBS from 1951. In the opening days of the war, BBC Television suddenly stopped transmitting – in the middle of a Walt Disney cartoon, as it happens – because the government feared its transmissions would be used to help guide German bombers over the capital. As a news source, the loss in communication was then irrelevant.

When, after the war, television was restarted, the strong BBC bias against mixing news and pictures quickly reasserted itself. In June 1946 a Mary Adams suggested illustrated political talks on TV and was slapped down by Sir William Haley, the then director-general. No, no, and no again. Asked that August whether the BBC might perhaps consider making its own news films, rather than buying them in from the newsreel companies that supplied, rather late in the day, British cinemas, Sir William loftily explained that this was not possible because it would subordinate news to 'the needs of visual presentation' which would 'prejudice all sorts of values on which the BBC's great reputation for news has been founded'. Even enthusiasts for television saw the problem. Grace Wyndham Goldie, one of the pioneers of TV news, said of the debate in the 1940s:

> If, in the opinion of an experienced news editor, a news story merited only 20 [seconds] but there was some specifically shot film of it which could not really make its point in less than half a minute, what should he do? Abandon news values and show the film, even if this meant cutting the length of another and more important news story on which there was only meagre film illustration? But that would be an abandonment of BBC news standards.

This was, and is, a real dilemma. It is not an abstract one. Every night of the week, today, BBC News programme editors wrestle with the problem of what do when an important story of the day has no pictures to go with it, while a rather lesser story has vivid, unforgettable images. We can now use computer graphics to help us, and more 'lives': but the images tend to win out. Television is an impure medium, as much cabaret as lecture hall.

The BBC's first answer was to ignore the pictures almost entirely, in the cause of pure news. The newsreels were still being bought in, often out of date and lacking real sound (in those days cameras that could record simultaneous sound were simply too heavy and expensive to be sent anywhere). By the early 1950s the BBC had its own newsreel department, with excellent cameramen hired from the companies that had been making newsreels for cinema, notably Pathé and British Gaumont. But these were really short feature films – not immediate, often with a foreign travelogue feel, and almost always 'soft' – an early version of the 'well I never' form of news that later infected programmes such as BBC *Nationwide*. For the BBC News people, who had grown up in that Reithian culture of words, this was fine. Moving pictures could never be serious. They conceded that news bulletins should be aired on television too. But how to marry the raw visual power of film with the sacred duty of news reporting? No one could figure that out.

This is why, in the short history of television, news comes late. In the years after the war, there were many earlier 'firsts' – the first TV children's programme in 1946, the first major sporting broadcast, the Wembley Olympics in 1948, the first broadcast golf and the first regular TV weather forecast the following year; the first general election results programme in 1950 and the first sound-and-vision broadcast from parliament in the same year (not real politics, but the opening of the rebuilt, post-Blitz Commons chamber). It was not until then, by which time television was available to 91 per cent of the UK audience, that regular news began. And even then it was a terrible, compromised botch. In the memorable image of Wyndham Goldie, 'The long drawn out war between the News Division at Broadcasting House and the Film Department in Television was like a battle between a school of whales and a herd of elephants. There was no common ground upon which they could meet.'[3] In 1954, a fatuous compromise solution was reached. Radio would provide the words, TV the pictures. 'News and Newsreels' began on air with the BBC coat of arms. The news was then dealt with in words alone, with carefully printed captions, like paragraph headings in a newspaper, held up in front of the camera while an unseen announcer read the appropriate item of news. There then might be a series of still pictures or rather elaborately hand-drawn maps. Sometimes a hand would appear from off screen, like a Monty Python graphic, helpfully pointing to something. Having invented the regular television service, the BBC now seemed to be set on using it as an electric newspaper for idiots.

From Stars to Soup: the ITN Revolution

Then came ITN. Much though it pains a BBC man to admit this, Independent Television News's arrival in 1955, and then the launching of its mould-breaking *News at Ten* in 1967, are the two most important moments in the history of British television news. And the greatest influence on them was that of the United States. In the 1930s the state-sanctioned BBC had stolen a television march on the free-enterprise Americans; in 1933 Columbia had abandoned its attempt at commercial television, W2XAB, just as Britain was getting going. But after the war, the Americans had pioneered sharper, illustrated, filmed news. The great breakthroughs had come for them during the 1948 presidential elections, and then the start of the Korean war in 1950 when cameramen like NBC's Eugene Jones pioneered the use of lightweight, handheld cameras to bring vivid, often horrific, images from the front line. They used characterful frontmen in the studio – Edward Murrow, David Brinkley, Chet Huntley – and a chatty, direct style that was a million miles from the bland, anonymous tones of the unseen BBC newsreaders. At ITN, struggling to get on air with a new team, they listened and learned. In 1955 Britain was sick of the austerity years and undergoing the first rumbles of what would become the social revolution of the sixties. It was ready for a new style of news. The sense of excitement, of breaking all the old taboos, comes vividly across from those writing of the early days of ITN. In the final weeks before the new programme went live, its headquarters in London's Kingsway was chaotic. The studio cameras, like much of the equipment, had not been delivered and the presenters had to deliver their lines to an empty wooden picture frame, through which the editor, Aidan Crawley, and his staff would peer to try to guess the effect.

The new style depended on technological tools coming to hand at the right moment. In the case of ITV, the breakthrough technologies were threefold. First, there was the arrival of the 16mm camera. Before this, TV cameras were horribly heavy, difficult to move around, and did not record simultaneous sound. 'Outside broadcasts' or OBs – anything done outside a television studio – could mean days of careful preparation, with vans, cables, special lighting systems and sound recording. Simultaneous sound was recorded outside the camera; often, in practice, it was dubbed on later from BBC archives. (This led to earnest discussions about how authentic the sound had to be: was it acceptable to show Swiss churches and add the sound of bells that had in fact been recorded in Copenhagen?) The 16mm portable camera changed all this. You could carry it into the streets, or onto the battlefield. It brought the immediacy that the era of newsreels lacked. You could even run with it. It was described by Geoffrey Cox, the most famous of ITN's editors, as 'the reporter's note-book in TV journalism'. As Robin Day noted early in the process, it elevated the role of those TV reporters to something more like players: 'A sweating, shivering, shaken reporter and film team would not merely be *covering* the story. They would be *living* the story, and were part of it. You could call it the "Method" in film reporting.'[4]

The second development for television news had arrived in Britain in the mid-1950s with the first 'teleprompters' or 'autocues' – effectively a system of mirrors laid around a camera lens, which allows you to read words while apparently looking directly at the viewer. There had been paper versions before but they were poor and unreliable. The autocue is so simple and unglamorous that its importance is often overlooked. If you have ever seen a newsreader whose autocue has failed, and seen his or her eyes moving haplessly about, downwards towards a paper script, with little glances back at the camera, then the effect of the autocue is obvious. Before it, newsreaders were sometimes dubbed 'the guilty men' because of the way their eyes darted up and down while reading the papers in front of them, making them seem worryingly shifty. The autocue, instead, allows the illusion of intimacy – the news being told personally to the couple on the sofa. It is a dangerous instrument in its way – to rely on it is to look like an idiot if it fails – and it is also a technical lie, requiring smooth actorly qualities. Wyndham Goldie, somewhat puritanically, criticized politicians like Macmillan who were quick to use it.

However well-written the script, it seldom sounded like impromptu talk. The speaker was too glib. His eyes were focused differently from those of a man who was talking impromptu. He was looking at the surface of the camera lens, over which the written script was passing, rather than trying to look through the lens at the individual viewer . . . Somewhere there was pretence. Somewhere there was deception. And the more the talk had the appearance of being frank person-to-person communication, the deeper the sense of deception was bound to be. Politicians who used teleprompters were therefore in danger of seeming devious.[5]

Be that as it may, autocues or 'teleprompters' allowed the arrival of convincing 'newscasters' – another imported American term.

The third and final development came 7,000 miles above those heavily made-up men and the sweating reporters in the street. On 10 July 1962 NASA launched Telstar 1, a communications satellite just three feet in diameter, which had been developed by Bell Telephone Laboratories. The era of satellite broadcasting had begun; no longer would film of events in far-flung places necessarily have to wait for the next aircraft flight to be taken back to London. Suddenly, events in Chicago and Washington could be seen by viewers in Britain on the same day. On its first day of broadcasting, Telstar brought *Panorama* viewers real-time images from across the United States, from New York to California, with choirs, Red Indians and politicians. In the early days, booking time on these satellites was still very expensive and only small parts of the globe were covered but within twenty years the era of CNN had arrived. If the 16mm camera allowed the news to be much more vivid and down-to-earth, Telstar and its successors made it immediate and global. Though satellite technology has advanced hugely since 1962 – we now carry 'sat-phones' and small plastic dishes that allow us to communicate from almost anywhere in broadcast quality – the essential breakthrough is more than forty years old. The quality has risen and the price has fallen, but that's about it.

ITN's genius was to use, as the sixties developed, all three technical breakthroughs, the 16mm camera, autocues and satellites, to fashion a new kind of television news, which is effectively the news we get today. Its first newscasters, even before *News at Ten*, were the famous sprinter Chris Chataway, though he quickly defected to BBC's *Panorama*, and the young Robin Day. A stream of famous names followed –

Reggie Bosanquet, Alastair Burnet, Sandy Gall, Anna Ford, Selina Scott, Fiona Armstrong, Carol Barnes, Martyn Lewis, Alistair Stewart, Trevor McDonald. 'Trust' and recognition became important qualities for executives selling news to the public; a certain sparkle or tension was added to the mix when ITN pioneered the use of male and female newscasters sitting side-by-side.

Independent Television News pioneered news with a human face. But just as important, if not more so, was the ITN approach to news packaging, which up to then had, at the BBC, been rudimentary and often soundless. The upstart organization determined to cover news with some of the humanity and pzazz of Fleet Street, so far as it could within the legal confines of the Television Act of 1954, which demanded 'due accuracy and impartiality'. ITN sent sound-recordists along with their cameramen, used natural sound, conducted interviews in the street and at strike meetings, or the streets of rebelling Cyprus. The cameras were jostled, and ITN got rough-edged, unpredictable footage. Robin Day like other ITN staff realized that television was changing the nature of news priorities. For one thing, the pictures were so vivid that the need to be first was not always paramount: 'The fact of yesterday's air disaster may no longer be top news tonight – but the *first film* of the scene might well merit first place in this evening's television news . . . [or] a filmed interview may contain no newsworthy statement. It may turn out to be first-class television. The way things are said, the reaction of a face to a question, a revealing pause . . .'

For anyone interested above all in news as news, these early epiphanies from ITN, which caused delight among television reviewers bored senseless by the BBC News, should cause a little disquiet. The arrival of the news reporter as actor, which really began in the mid-1950s but took off during the sixties as ITN's influence spread, introduced showing-off to news broadcasting. ITN calls it 'RI', which stands for Reporter Involvement. A little of this is useful television grammar. If you have been at a press conference, it is not a bad idea to show yourself asking a question, or trying to look alert – that way the audience is reassured that you are telling the story having actually been there to report it yourself. As mentioned already, good pieces to camera are vital building blocks. But a little goes a long way: the caricature of RI now has reporters making more of their own questions and their presence, reducing mere prime ministers, army soldiers or bereaved parents to bit-part players. The reporter crowds out the rest, too in love with the camera lens to share it. So you see TV reporters interviewing ministers, with a second camera team beside them, to film them doing the interview ... Method acting was good for the theatre but it is bogus in the news business. Second, note Robin Day's distinction between what is (merely) newsworthy and what is 'first-class television'. Day himself, of course, was also a first-class show-off who took his gifts into the studio with occasionally mesmeric results. He was a performer. But the early worries of BBC purists about the loss of real news values in the flash and theatre of television no longer look so silly.

The next great technical revolution came with electronic news gathering in the late 1970s and the use of electronic equipment, which simply made life much easier and quicker for news teams. Gone were the heavy, cumbersome reels of film which had to be ferried back by plane, taxi or motorbike. ITN's Michael Brunson was one of those who lived through the change. Before, he was dependent on magazines of film that had to be transferred into tin cans – using black 'changing bags' known in the trade as 'Queen Mary's knickers' – before being sent for developing. Once the film was ready for developing, says another reporter of that era, Kate Adie, there was plenty of trouble still to come. In the late 1970s, the developing process was known simply as Soup:

> Blank, Fogged and Buggered were Soup's main achievements with celluloid. If the film survived Soup, it was rushed into the cutting room, where reporter and film editor viewed the results as the film juddered through a table-top editing machine. The reporter then wrote a script, recording it in yet another studio, and the whole lot was chopped and stitched together, usually very much against deadline.

If the package was late, it might have to be voiced live from a corner of the news studio, itself a dangerous place: 'Falling over monitors and shouting "Bugger" used to annoy Angela Rippon, especially if she was in mid-pronunciation.'[6] That is a reporter's view: it should be recorded that some picture editors who have worked with film, and then the various generations of video and digital equipment which followed, believe the business of cutting pictures together at speed is slowing, not speeding; and that the latest equipment gives poorer quality, not better. 'Just nonsense' retorts a more senior figure. But as with newspapers, newer technologies are not always more convenient for journalism. For the BBC, the 1991 Bosnian War was really the moment the new system, from lightweight editing to satellite, became fully operational. Now a relatively small camera, a bagful of video cartridges and a piece of editing equipment that would fit in a suitcase, plus microphone, is all that is needed to produce a TV film. Whatever the impact in studios, the effect on the ground was to speed things up, particularly for foreign stories and when reporters were on the road with politicians. Reporters who had been used to disappearing off for a few days virtually out of contact with advancing troops, or fleeing refugees, now found themselves tied to a routine of hourly reporting.

Not everyone thought the cheap availability of satellite links, which meant stories could be filed at the last minute, actually made for better journalism. A BBC manager points out that once the cost of getting gear to a location has been swallowed, it tends to be used simply because it is there and cheap to deliver when up and running. 'Thus, for example, a relatively unimportant summit gets long hours of coverage because it's virtually free. This is a wretched trap that we seem to find difficult to avoid.' As the technology improved, it meant journalists could send more reports in the same time for the same money. But that meant they were spending more time actually filing and cutting and talking to cameras, and therefore less time on the phone, or meeting people, or simply going and looking for themselves. Just like the newspaper journalists cooped up in offices and expected to write after making a quick phone call and checking Press Association stories on their computer screens, TV journalists have been cramped, as often as they have been liberated, by progress.

633 Squadron: Current Affairs and the Rise of the Reporter

At this point let there be heard, deep in the belly of the BBC, a roar of household gods – and they *are* jealous gods. For I have devoted some time to ITN. Is there not another side to the story of the modern television news industry? There is. Although the news programme that broke the mould was created by commercial television, much of the style and many of the basic techniques of British TV reporting came from the BBC. It is just that they did not come from news, but from current affairs programmes – first *Foreign Correspondent* and later the early-evening *Tonight*, or the forerunner of *Newsnight*, which was called *24 Hours* and, above all others, the BBC's fifty-year-old flagship *Panorama*. In a smaller television world, they dominated in ways no television programme can now. By the autumn of 1958, for instance, within months of going on air to fill the so-called 'toddlers' truce' between 6 and 7 p.m. (when British television had been off air, allegedly to help parents get their children to bed) *Tonight* was getting seven million viewers a night. *Panorama* was being watched each week by up to fourteen million, a quarter of the adult population, and expected to regularly dominate the following day's front pages.

In these programmes, the reporters' pieces-to-camera, and the basic art of fitting together words and pictures, with cutaways, 'noddies' and the rest of the bag of tricks, were first tried out. Here the giants of early television reporting – Robin Day, Woodrow Wyatt, Robert Kee, Cliff Mitchelmore, Kenneth Allsopp, Michael Barratt and Ludovic Kennedy – first strutted, informed and commanded. Here the difficult, never-yet-resolved struggle between the reporter and the producer was first enacted. Who was to dominate – the reporter with the words and the contacts, or the producer, who understood the pictures? Angry memos, resignations and stand-up fights litter the history of early television current affairs. Wyatt loathed being made in any way subservient to a mere producer; Robin Day, whose stock-in-trade was the interview which he controlled, complained that television was 'a crude medium which strikes at the emotions rather than the intellect'; because of its 'insatiable appetite for visual action . . . it tended to distort and to trivialise'. Such early reporters too often regarded the pictures as a barely relevant background flicker which provided the setting for their all-important words. Producers were bag carriers, and because in those days heavy reels of film had to be physically carried back to London to be cut into a narrative, it was easier for the reporters to think of the 'picture side' as secondary, physical labour stuff.

Yet anyone who was really looking knew it couldn't be so. Right at the very start of the history of British television news reporting, during one of the early reports for *Foreign Correspondent* in 1949, Chester Wilmot, who had been a successful radio journalist, and the pioneering cameraman Charles de Jaeger had been sent to Belgrade to report on the economic aftermath of war. They set up a shot of one of the city's main boulevards, down which a single horse-drawn cart was moving, the only traffic of any kind. It was a stunning image, but Wilmot was in some ways appalled: all he actually needed to say was 'look', he reflected. All those beautifully honed words by which he had made his living were suddenly redundant: 'this is the end of descriptive journalism'. It wasn't, of course, because pictures like that are rare and stories are complicated. But the news events remembered as TV milestones were all about pictures, from the pioneering shots by ITN of the first hijacked airliner being blown up on the tarmac in Jordan through to the US army helicopters being toppled from ships as the Americans evacuated Saigon, or Biafran children starving, or firefights in Northern Ireland, or the space shuttle *Discovery* blowing up, or the Berlin Wall falling, or the destruction of the twin towers. Crude? Emotional? Certainly. Distorting? Not really; rather, an essential slice of the modern world.

As editors in London offices began to recognize the power of the image, the role of great producers rose and the power of the reporters was challenged; by the 1960s ambitious, very clever people were joining TV news because they wanted to produce and edit, working with the camera crews and in front of monitors, not because they wanted to be in front of cameras. In many cases, forceful producers and weak reporters reversed the old relationship, so that the reporter became a kind of useful doll for the producer – or, as Jeremy Paxman once balefully put it, 'a gob on a stick'.

This, though, was only a cloud on the horizon of early current affairs programme-making, where many of today's conventions first grew. These programmes were made by and for a different Britain, one in which the upper middle classes informed and commanded in a way that is impossible to imagine now. Television had a high purpose, to educate the masses about the world around them and to raise them up. There was a BBC agenda: the Corporation existed to protect and promote British values and democracy in a paternalistic way. This could result in liberal arguments, for instance about apartheid in South Africa, or the 'colour bar' on British railways, as well as conservative attitudes to state occasions and the Establishment; but looking at old programmes, whatever the argument, there is a hugely self-confident, often condescending tone. The early generations of reporters, producers and editors were often ex-army people, and most of them were Oxbridge too, not much lacking in self-assurance. When Granada's *World in Action* came on the scene in 1961, part of its purpose was a Manchester-grammar-school blast against all that. Sir Denis Foreman, managing director of Granada, said later:

> The approach was anti-Dimbleby. What we were fed up with was the complacent, well-meaning, middle-class programmes, like *Panorama* and *This Week*, always following, on the whole, the middle of the road, comfortable, decent line.

World in Action's grainy, still-startling images of coffins representing deaths from tuberculosis in northern towns, and of half-abandoned senile women in hospitals set a different standard of shock-journalism which also made its way into mainstream news reporting. Interestingly, today's climate is in some ways less open than that of the sixties: we tolerate far greater explicitness about sex, but are more resistant to images of poverty or suffering. The images of old people defecating would be considered unacceptable to modern sensibilities – we hide that away and concentrate on pneumatic, tanned youth instead.

Throughout the evolution of television news, one of the core issues has been how far the individual reporter should let his, or her, personal opinion about a story show. This was a problem for *Panorama* in the late 1950s; it is a daily problem on news bulletins today. There is a simple, purist answer – not at all. Gavin Hewitt, John Simpson, Andrew Marr and the rest are employed to be studiously neutral, expressing little emotion and certainly no opinion; millions of people would say that news is the conveying of fact, and nothing more. Current affairs programmes, during which a reporter may saturate himself in a country or subject for months before the final film, may arguably be different; but news comes only in vanilla. Yet the worm of individuality has been in it from the start – both in the revolutionary ITN bulletins and in the BBC's pioneering current affairs programmes. In his biography of *Panorama* the journalist Richard Lindley recounts early examples of committed, or tilted, or perhaps plain biased, journalism. He cites, for instance, Woodrow Wyatt stories about communist infiltration of the electricians' union in which, as a *Panorama* reporter, he openly urged its members to turn out and vote. In his May 1956 script he told members of the AEU:

> at this very moment your union is just on the verge of coming under the control of the Communists ... Now of course if you want a Communist-dominated AEU, well, that's entirely your affair. This is a democratic country and you've the right to vote in as many Communist officials as you like. But do you really want your union to be run by the Communists?[7]

That caused a complicated storm, both of praise and blame, at the time. It is hard to imagine any current *Panorama* journalist, indeed any BBC news journalist, editorializing to that extent now. Wyatt's excuse would have been that he was only encouraging people to vote; and that in a democratic political system, the prime broadcaster should not be neutral about whether voting is a good idea. As we have seen, voting always has an effect: encouraging people to vote may result in an altered verdict. The bigger question, though, is whether it is possible to remove the character and therefore the character-bias of the reporter. Wyatt was blatant and direct; yet a raised eyebrow, a softening tone of the voice, the use of one adjective rather than another, in short, almost any act of normal human communication, affects the viewer and therefore corrupts the purity of the news.

There are many styles of reporting and some are indeed studiously neutral; radio and television reporters exist who not only avoid almost any value judgement but can keep the emotion out of their voices and faces in any situation, whether they are viewing the effects of a bomb blast, or reporting the death of a famous politician. To look at Soviet-era TV news from Moscow is to watch, even if one cannot understand, a monotone service, with expressionless faces and even, robotic voices. But this style of reporting has collapsed across most of the world not just because it is boring, but because it is repellent. A mask-like face or monotone voice conveys not fairness, or open-mindedness, but coldness. A reporter who shows fear, pity, concern (passive, reactive emotions, appropriate to an observer) is a reporter who will be listened to more attentively – there is a human connection made. But where does this properly stop? What about the reporter who shows anger? An angry reporter is moving from being an observer to being

a participant and would be distrusted by most viewers of news programmes, quite rightly. The more common reaction of boredom is
equally unacceptable; if the reporter is bored, the viewer will be bored.
Political bias is equally easy to describe and relatively easy to strip
out. If all reporters have some political views of their own, they do
not need to let them show. This is not just about using fair language
to represent the views of different sides; it is also about avoiding
expressions of disbelief, or inappropriate surprise, still less disgust.

But the trouble is that television reporting is an exhibitionist's
game. Right from the start it has attracted big characters, with strong
views and few inhibitions; it may be related to newspapers, but it is
half-brother to the theatre too. The first television reporter in Britain
who showed that you could become as big a figure as most politicians
simply by standing and telling was Richard Dimbleby – a genuine
news star, who never felt he was properly appreciated by the BBC.
But after him came bigger and bigger show-offs.

In the early days, political reporting featured lots of former, would-
be or 'resting' politicians – not just Wyatt himself, but John Freeman,
the former Labour minister; Chris Chataway and Geoffrey Johnson
Smith, who later became Tory MPs; Jack Ashley, who became a
famous Labour MP; and others. Robin Day and Ludovic Kennedy both
tried, and both failed, to become Liberal MPs. And of course people
who would like to give their views to the House of Commons, or
large meetings, also like giving their views to cameras. As early as
1959, the *Listener* magazine was observing of TV journalists that

> Quickness and edge are only a short step from aggressiveness and
> even rudeness; a keen mind can lead the interviewer to do more
> of the talking than the man he is interviewing; success and
> popularity can breed pomposity or condescension . . .

Although the big characters started by colonizing current affairs, they
quickly spread into news too. As a young reporter I remember vividly
arriving at the *Panorama* office where I was to make a film about the
Tories and crime and being greeted by a room which seemed full of
men in desert boots and flying jackets (well, leather ones, anyway)
sprawled nonchalantly around like the crew of 633 Squadron. Some of
them migrated to BBC News later; but News grew its own stars as
well.

Charles Wheeler with his lined, laconic, bird-like presence; Sandy Gall, crumpled and somehow the embodiment of agonized British decency; John Cole, a wise guide and a man you wouldn't want to cross; Kate Adie, the nation's plucky Girl Guide leader; then another Irish voice, Orla Guerin, shaking with exhaustion and despair in another bloody Israeli street; John Simpson, the granddaddy and battered panda of BBC journalism today; wry, worldly wise Elinor Goodman at Westminster; and recently Rageh Omaar, the boyishly handsome witness to the fall of Baghdad . . . all these and many more are the human conduits without which television cannot flow. And when the newspapers conspire to make a correspondent into a star, the transformation can be startling. When he first arrived in Baghdad for the start of the war, Simpson having been refused a visa, Omaar was hoping to be appointed the BBC's man in Delhi. By the time he left, the 'Scud Stud' had a huge presence, agents fighting to represent him and a reported £850,000 book deal. Earlier, Kate Adie had enjoyed a similar rocket trip to national fame and it lasted for a long time. In the late 1990s the BBC commissioned research into which reporters the public perceived as having been on television most often in the previous six months. Adie was overwhelmingly declared to have been on the news most; in fact she had not appeared on main bulletins during the relevant period.

Few television correspondents *are* retiring characters. Their form of exhibitionism may be understated, even laconic, but in different ways it is always there. You can have pure information, unadulterated factual news, in a printed list, black ink on white paper – but you cannot have that dry anonymity during a conversation with other people, which is what TV news is. No British television reporter has quite broken through like the global stars of CNN or ABC, though Adie and Michael Buerk came close. But take away the individual reporter and you take away much of the interest too, which seems to be about character and trust, rather than looks. The fashion for bimbo reporters, of either sex, has fallen back because they all look much the same, and though they may be instantly appealing, they fail to forge a longer-term relationship with viewers.

So does one have to accept that television news is partly show-business? The BBC, at different times, tried to simply cancel the reporter from the equation. As we have seen, there was a great muddle in the

1950s and few people have been so mocked in memoirs as the New Zealand-born Tahu Hole, then head of news. Hole, a large man with a lugubrious, bloodhound, Charles de Gaulle face, believed in the verbal sanctity of news. It was hard, public information that must not be sullied by entertaining pictures, or by the distraction of individuals seen presenting it. Under Tahu Hole's regime, television newsreaders were kept out of vision and were preferred to be anonymous bass voices, or at least commanding baritones. As we have seen, captions and stills dominated. Indeed, Hole once said to the producer David Wheeler, 'Don't let anybody tell you, Mr Wheeler, that stills don't make good television.'⁸ When the ITN revolution blew into town, the BBC was forced to respond by putting its anonymous faces, Dougall and Kendall, into vision. It held out against showbusiness by ensuring that they remained entirely grave and unemotional, and by keeping moving pictures at arms' length. But the power of the medium, and the power of filmed news, was irresistible. Tahu Hole's idea of TV news has gone into the garbage disposal of history, gurgling away just like that early belief that the telephone would be essentially an instrument for delivering symphony orchestra concerts to middle-class homes.

Much later, under different *Panorama* and *World in Action* editors, current affairs documentaries were made in which the 'reporter', though perhaps involved in scripting and analysing, was almost unheard. In extreme cases, producers such as Angela Pope and Tom Bower sometimes disposed of the reporter entirely. And, coming at the question of the reporter's individuality from a different angle, John Birt, in his famous series of articles written with Peter Jay, argued that television journalism was biased against understanding. Why? Because it was too emotive and insufficiently analytical: 'making a film about homeless people is not an adequate way of approaching the problems created by our housing shortage . . .' The 'incoherent highlight of societies' sores by television' could lead to a failure to confront fundamental causes. Part of his answer was, much later, the recruitment of brainy specialists (like Peter Jay, the co-author) but this was also a blast against the emotive journalism of the heart-on-sleeve reporter-guide. It was an updated version of the original worries of the BBC radio chiefs about television itself. Trying to deal with this, Birt and his colleagues from ITV's *Weekend World* assembled complicated filmed arguments on paper, building up their reports like essays – independent reporters, with their messy views and messier adjectives, barely featured. Team Birt took these beliefs to the BBC in the 1980s with mixed results.

The trouble is that anonymity does not remove the human element or the potential bias from the film; it simply hides it. A reporter has quirks, biases, a family history, all of which colour the reporting, however subtly. But the same is true of the producer, the editor, or the members of the team sitting in a glass box in some west London office drawing up the plan for a filmed report. No broadcaster films and transmits the unvarnished, unmediated truth: everything is selected, cut and assembled for effect. In his book on *Panorama* Lindley, quoting many other eminent film-makers, argues that having a narrative reporter as your guide is the least-bad option. You get a recognizable face and voice whom you can judge and assess more clearly than the hidden hand of the producer; if there is bias it is visible and can be felt as such by the viewer. He notes that the early fashion for ex-politicians to be those guides, which has had such a long-term impact on television style, also meant they were 'guest stars' who could be disowned by the BBC if they overstepped the mark. That is no longer so; perhaps it should be, with more opinionated reporters being used, balancing each other out, to give viewers the choice of more aggressive arguments. But even then you would not be able to cut out the intervention of the professional correspondent. In a guide for would-be television news journalists, the BBC's Vin Ray, who oversaw my training, writes:

> information alone doesn't necessarily make us wiser. However, great journalists do ... there is now a greater need than ever before for trusted, good journalists to select the most significant stories and explain why they matter in a way our citizens enjoy and understand. Great journalists turn what audiences *need* to know into what they *want* to know.[9]

This is the bold creed born of those current affairs pioneers, the reporter as bringer of interpretation and sense to a befuddled world, striding with necessary questions and clear judgements through the morass of apparently meaningless events. It is challenged by politicians. 'Who elected you?' they ask, increasingly angrily, much like the purists of the early BBC, as the TV reporters sashay in with their carefully honed certainties. News, goes the argument, is about fact not opinion and the more you have human interpreters, taking a larger share of the show, the more 'news' has become something else, a tendentious political argument, however appetizingly packaged and surrounded by images of the immediate. One example of this came during a prolonged attack on the alleged loss of trust in the BBC from the *Financial Times* journalist John Lloyd. He began by quoting an anonymous aide in Tony Blair's Number Ten team who said of political reporters, including those from the BBC, that 'many of them make it up . . . We don't see the BBC as a medium any more. It's a barrier.' He went on to argue that a desperate desire to make news more appealing to younger viewers had overemphasized the role of reporters, particularly in the 'two-ways' described earlier. To make the point, Lloyd then quoted Tim Allen, a former Blair spin doctor:

> This is something of a constitutional coup: senior and other journalists putting themselves in the frame instead of politicians. Political parties are reduced to fighting like ferrets in a sack to influence Andrew Marr or Nick Robinson [political editor of Independent TV News] or Adam Boulton [political editor of Sky News]. They give politicians less and less air time. Spin is largely theirs. The BBC must look again at its two-way culture. It's a usurpation of democratic power.[10]

This is a formidable and serious charge. So let us put to one side the fact that Mr Allen was in his day one of the most abusive arm-twisters our affable prime minister has employed; has never been elected to anything; and subsequently went to work for Rupert Murdoch's Sky News.

What about the 'two-way culture'? The two-way is a formidable weapon and is seen by news programme editors as so effective they regularly overuse it. 'So what's the mood among the prime minister's aides now, Andrew?' (Absolutely no idea. It's two in the morning here and they all went to bed hours ago.) All too often the reporter has just arrived, or has had no access to the subject of the story, or has been left in a field for many hours simply so that the presenter can say, 'Now we go live to the scene of the crash . . .' There then follows a ritual exchange of banalities: 'How are families taking it?' ('Well, this is a tragedy for them. They must be distraught.') It might be interesting if the families were whooping it up and throwing hundred-dollar bills around, but if people are saddened by sad events, even made very sad by very sad events, it barely needs saying. Yet a strong two-way, with a correspondent who knows his subject and has something clear to say, is powerful. It is, after all, just a short conversation. Its joy is that for once you can forget about what filmed pictures you do or don't have and can simply give verbal information about what you know, just like a radio or newspaper reporter. Sandwiched among filmed reports, and if they are conducted live at real news moments, two-ways can have huge impact. And yes, it does put the reporter into a different role than simply telling; he or she is being asked questions, often loaded and sensitive questions.

The point of the two-way in politics should be to cut through spin. Politicians do get a lot of coverage, but they tend to speak in the code of their trade. The job of the two-way is to tell the viewers and listeners, so far as one is able, what is actually going on. And even when there is not a hidden story which politicians refuse to describe openly, they will often speak in such technical and abstruse language that ordinary viewers need translation: the reporter is the translator. When a chancellor talks of the virtue of flexible labour markets and asymmetric inflation targets, the viewer may need to be told that he is attacking early entry of Britain into the euro. Often what reporters say will be reflecting off-the-record conversations: in a newspaper this is as easy as inserting a few quotation marks and mentioning 'senior sources'. In television, when we do not have the pictures, the two-way must take the strain. At least the reporter's face is in vision and to that extent the reporter is always taking responsibility for the accuracy or otherwise of what the anonymous politician has said. And yes, the two-way is also where the reporter's personality comes across to the viewer most clearly.

Pinned up in my Westminster office I have a cutting from the *Express* with the headline: 'Why We Listen to Arm Twirlers Like Clinton, Marr . . . and Hitler.' It says we have one thing in common, animated arm-waving. According to the report, 'BBC bosses have criticised news reporters for excessive hand-waving' yet, according to a paper given to the British Psychological Society's annual conference, 'Our brains have evolved to take into account both gestures and speech. Hand movements can get across size and position better than words.' This is true, but only the start of a good two-way. When I began at the BBC, I would work out exactly what I wanted to say, time it and then learn it, so that when the question came, despite nerves or distractions, I would be able simply to repeat my lines. It looked awful. Television is a great way of gauging authenticity and these performances looked just like what they were – wooden, over-rehearsed performances. I don't believe viewers would have realized that the answers had been learned and pre-scripted; they would just have felt vaguely cheated and uneasy.

So I went to the opposite extreme and took to the air banking on my background knowledge, with only the vaguest idea about what I would say. This was scarier, but not much more effective. One tended to waffle, wasting time before crystallizing the thought. And in television, where every second counts, it was an unacceptable waste. So I now think about the obvious questions I'd ask myself, check them in general terms with the newsreader, and walk about for five minutes, working out what I would really like to say. If a good plain image pops up, which might help make the story vivid, so much the better. Then I put the whole business out of my mind and think about something else while I wait to speak. Often I'm simply listening to the rest of the bulletin. That way, with luck, the answers come out as well formed yet also at least partly spontaneous. Even so, one easily gets into a rut. One happy image or joke provokes you to try again, and again, until you become a metaphor bore. So you stop metaphors for a while, and bore in a different way. I have never, ever, finished a two-way entirely happy about what I've said and how I've said it. One day . . .

And yes, politicians feel bitterly that journalists are simply getting their faces on the television too much while they are not getting on enough. They feel that the news is, or ought to be, their servant and not simply an entertainment-driven tube colonized by professional communicators. So politicians are now actually jealous of the report-ers? They certainly are. Do they have half a point about the messengers crowding out the story? Yes they do – and yet really vivid politicians, who can communicate and who say things which are not so predictable most people simply don't hear them, are valued and chased after by their TV reporter rivals. The answer is not less good communication by journalists: it is better communication by politicians. If they learn how to use the prime medium of the age, people like me will be out of a job.

The common sense answer to the dilemma of the presence of reporters in the middle of news, is simply to distinguish between *character* – the human colour a reporter lays across a story by telling it – and *bias*. Character cannot be conquered. Bias can be. An ordinary emotional response to a story from a reporter merely places that reporter where most viewers stand too. It says: when the plane went down, or when the bereaved mother screamed, I happened to be there; but if you were there, you would have felt this, and witnessed it, just like me. A biased response distances the reporter, immediately and for ever, from a large swathe of those watching. It says to everyone who disagrees: I am *not* you, and I was not here on your behalf. This is why good reporting, even the small fragments of film that make up a TV bulletin, rather than a documentary, can be a moral act. The reporter's emotional response, the pity or sadness or delight, confirms that this is the right or normal, expected common response to some event or act 'out there'. The good reporter is the representative, perhaps the mimic, of the ordinary. This is why so many well-known names in reporting are easy to imagine as family members. In fact, the good reporter is odd, obsessive, egocentric and probably fairly unpleasant to live with; it is perhaps because of the strain of pretending so frantically to be normal.

The Mix

So there is the technology – from the little plastic earpieces, to the satellites and the clutter of the edit suites. There is a brutally short history of television news, and the dilemmas it throws up about pictures, and reporters. But I have not finished the story, for the news as it is actually watched by millions of Britons every day is also a particular selection, carefully blended and chosen from a much wider possible agenda. Each item has been commissioned by a pro-gramme editor, who has sent a reporter, producer and camera crew to somewhere; they have mingled their skills, stamina and hunches to return a few minutes of assertion and pictures; that then takes its place in a jostling queue of possible stories, which is cut down and rearranged by the editor. It is her job – and I'm not being politically correct; in the BBC, at least, programme editors are more often women – to create an engaging narrative which will persuade viewers to settle down for up to half an hour and watch, and listen. They simply will not do that if the news is stodgy, badly told or 'all the same'; television is entertainment and the high, civic purpose of informing the voters struggles constantly against the urge of weary people, slumped down with a beer or a cup of tea, for relaxation and an honest laugh.

Newscasters can be a lot more than simply heads telling you things. In the US in the 1960s television became, in the famous NBC phrase, a kind of 'national church' where people mourned the loss of President Kennedy and celebrated their triumphs in space and sport. But it was also entertaining – the national pastor might be Walter Cronkite, but he was a twinkling, welcoming kind of minister and this was mostly a fun, upbeat religion. By the 1970s, there were already the first signs of what later became known as 'dumbing down', with major news companies like CBS introducing softer, humorous and cultural mini-features to leaven the politics and economics. By 1980 a former Miss America had been hired as a newsreader and some of the creased and battered-looking male reporters were being edged out by younger, more appealing faces. Britain was getting *Nationwide* and was being introduced, thanks to Esther Rantzen, to the idea that investigative journalism could be mixed with jokes and silliness. ITN had long used its '. . . and finally' items to end bulletins on a cheerier and frequently dafter note. The first double act started on American television with David Brinkley and Chet Huntley bringing news from Washington and New York. In 1978 ITN signed up Anna Ford to begin double acts with Reginald Bosanquet and Alastair Burnet. From then on, 'chemistry' has been an ingredient news editors yearn for.

So what? So not a lot, except that the need to lure in viewers with a little sugar coating goes well beyond the outward trappings of set design, tie colours and brief, light items. The real dilemma is what should properly be considered news in the first place. A traditional agenda would have every programme led by politics, either at home or abroad, disaster stories and major economic or City stories. These are crucial elements of most bulletins and are still emblems of a programme's 'seriousness'. Is it just a creaky, twenty-first-century male view of the world? No: since our societies are sustained by politics and the economy – the twin sources of our freedoms, our laws, our prosperity and our poverty – then any news which did not describe them would be a shallow take on everyday life. The same goes for developing scientific stories and for the big events overseas: unless you know about the worst famines and wars, and the most serious international arguments, then it is hard to say you are a fully sentient citizen. Unless you know about GM crops and bombings in Baghdad and the latest outbreak of violence on the streets of urban Britain, the moral and political dilemmas facing society are closed to you. In which case, why bother with the news at all?

Yet bulletins made up only of these things, of the major political, diplomatic and business stories, would be off-putting to the huge audiences of modern news programmes. Yes, they might appeal to the readers of the *Guardian* and *Financial Times*, but TV news audiences are typically ten times more than the circulations of broadsheet newspapers. They vastly outstrip even the most popular tabloids. And because they are still mostly interwoven into channels offering a carefully selected mix of viewing, designed to hold viewers through comedies, dramas, films, sport and chat shows, news programmes are expected to hold, and even increase the audience for those channels. The audience of the BBC's news at six o'clock is supposed to bear some relation to the audience of the major soaps and sporting events around it; they are likely, after all, to be the same people. And if they have been enjoying an Aussie soap, and are looking forward to light entertainment, or a thriller, they are not likely to want unadulterated, wall-to-wall politics and business in the middle of all that. So it is wrong to think of a TV news programme as being essentially like a moving, talking version of a newspaper. It is culturally embedded in the middle of a different kind of entertainment. To use a slightly dangerous analogy, it is more like a few pages of news in the middle of a men's or women's magazine. If you found news in *GQ* or *Cosmopolitan*, or indeed *Good Housekeeping*, you would expect it to reflect, just a little, the mood around it. So it is in television. And this weaving of news with other programmes is generally successful:

audiences often rise, not fall, when the news comes on. People don't find it dull, which is entirely the point.

A dull bulletin would be boring to look at, repetitive and irrelevant. So editors are biased towards news that comes with exciting or unusual pictures; news which is refreshing or odd; and news which bears some direct relation to viewers' lives. It is a standing joke in the BBC that any award-winning news package should have helicopters in it, no matter the story – helicopters just feel good to watch. What else feels good to watch? We would all have our different lists, but attention-holding pictures include film of bombs going off; fighting; beautiful people, particularly if they are not wearing much; people we already feel warm about, or already hate (comedians, villainous politicians, royals, sports stars); and glamorous places. This means that television news is likely to be skewed towards war and violence and celebrity, for this is where the most eye-grabbing images come from. And of course it is. So what is television news likely to be biased against? In picture terms, anything that just looks dull – stories about northern European countries, about buses, about old people, about infrastructure, banking, manufacturing, Whitehall and regeneration. Television news has been good at covering the controversy over whether fox-hunting should be banned. This has something to do with the visual appeal of foxes, hounds, horses, red coats and picturesque lanes, not to mention colourful urban demonstrations. Television news has been less good at covering the struggle over the European constitution, or the fight for better long-term care for the elderly. Television news likes plane crashes and train crashes because of how they look. It is mostly bored rigid by car crashes, which kill many more people, but not all at once. Similarly, television news looks overseas and it likes boy soldiers and tanks rather than peacemaking and reconciliation. Characteristically, it arrives when politics and old wisdom have broken down. It leaves before politics has started to win again, and the slow, hard task of rebuilding has begun. Blessed are the peacemakers? Maybe, but not on my bulletin, thanks.

Vin Ray points out that part of the problem is the news 'peg' – i.e. the moment. Asked by students what his ten top stories would be over the next decade, he talked about water shortages, migration, population issues, malaria – more prevalent than AIDS and intra-Islamic tension. He told me:

> Yet as I drove home I reflected that it's perfectly possible we
> won't cover any of these stories because – fundamentally import-
> ant as they are – they are themes and trends which don't fit easily
> into our idea of news. But with the decline of current affairs it
> has fallen to news to cover these issues, so they fall between the
> gaps, leaving the audience ignorant of some of the most important
> issues facing the planet.

And of course, if there are no cameras there, as is the case for most of the world's conflicts and famines, then in television terms, it simply does not exist. The BBC has an astonishingly wide spread of correspondents and teams, the rival of any other news organization anywhere; but even for the BBC most of the world is necessarily a news blank. When did you last see news from Brazil, China, Canada, Kenya, Sweden, Indonesia, Germany? Martin Bell, one of the longest-serving and most admired BBC correspondents before he went in for politics, put it pithily: 'People tend to suppose journalists are where the news is. This is not so. The news is where journalists are.'

The placing of cameras and journalists implies, inevitably, a political bias too. For instance, the US is comparatively over-covered. It is English-speaking, the global hyperpower, full of glamorous people and places to be filmed, and has time zones that work well for British evening news bulletins. Its own news is closely watched and often copied by British news organizations, and in the near future US media companies are likely to buy into British television in a big way. All this tilts British news, so that we see and think more about America than anywhere else. American politics, which is also sold and explained by Hollywood, is treated almost like British politics – we are assumed to be interested in the US presidential race from an early stage, even though it may make no practical difference to many lives in Britain at all. It makes us feel closer to them. It may be a good thing, or a bad thing. But we don't see the world as Mexicans, Russians or the French see it; television embeds an American bias, and the world according to the BBC or ITV or Sky is closer than ever to the world according to ABC or MSNBC or Fox.

Another limiting factor in the inevitable bias of television news is the preference for glamour and celebrity. These are images which fit smoothly into the surrounding babble and dance of television before, and after, the news. The ideal story is one that both involves the royal family, particularly one of its younger, more telegenic members, and can be claimed to be of high seriousness too. The Diana saga is the greatest example in modern times, doing for television news what the abdication crisis did for popular newspapers sixty years earlier. Anything which allows bulletins to replay chunks of old interviews with the princess, or show the curled wreckage of that Paris car crash, is going to have a special appeal for programme editors even now. And for years Posh and Becks made the news just because people like to look at them; so did and so do a cavalcade of pop stars, sports stars and sometimes even real stars. The American tilt is emphasized again. Their film stars, rockers and daytime television icons are already familiar. Meg Ryan, Arnie, O. J. Simpson, Oprah, Tiger Woods and Springsteen are all examples of faces that news editors would like to see 'brighten up' their bulletins. Television adores interesting faces. Politicians with a certain charisma, or quirks that can be remembered and mimicked, get on more often than those who look plain and talk normally. Swathes of professional life are excluded. When did you last see an engineer on the news? Or a professor, or a quantity surveyor with an interesting point about why the motorway was costing so much? By contrast, even second-order sports stories, if they involve famous footballing names, can now lead news bulletins.

Even the bias towards news that is relevant to ordinary lives can have its downside. Interest rates are covered endlessly because they directly affect mortgages, and Britain is a property-owning, mortgage-addicted country. But there is little coverage of public housing, or rented housing, or other equally important economic stories, such as the collapse in savings and household over-borrowing. The pensions crisis has begun to make it onto bulletins, but quite late in the day – for years the quiet collapse of fund values was simply too dreary and complex to be noticed. And there is a huge category of news that could be called 'irrelevant to us directly but important to know', including stories about the disappearance of species across the world, or the spread of Hindu fundamentalism, or arguments about the future of the House of Lords. None of us may ever directly notice the impact of an all-appointed second chamber, as against an elected one. But the question of whether the historic peers' chamber should be a 'house of cronies' or a 'rival to the Commons' is important in the British constitution and we should be aware of it. Often, the desperate struggle to be 'relevant' degenerates into soft, feature packages telling viewers little or nothing they don't know, but showing them 'ordinary people'. It is the metropolitan TV culture going off into the provinces to say, 'Hello, common people, we know you are there.' You can find puzzled-looking shoppers being asked for their response to Budget details they don't know about – because television news has not yet got around to telling them.

I have painted here a stark, even derisive picture of the temptations inherent in television news, the magnetic pull towards certain kinds of story. And it is true that there are some awful bulletins – programmes beginning with a minor hitch in training among the England football squad, followed by a 'special report' into fat children (which concludes that there are some, and that it's somebody's fault, but not anyone in particular) followed by a story about a new British-made film, which is a dud, but includes a mildly sexy clip, followed by a light aircraft exploding in California and a completely untrue story about Prince Harry, lifted from a tabloid newspaper. But the vast majority of programme editors are very well aware of the temptations, and yield to them only in moderation. Most will genuinely try to tell the serious stories, preferably through people and film rather than abstractly (Grierson's letter, not the postal service), and will go home feeling bad if they think an important story was squeezed out by glamour or pseudo-relevance. And there are answers. If you tell stories in clear, easily understood language, without jargon, and with a little humour, and if you have a good cameraman who manages to make familiar scenes look a little more interesting, then even Westminster intrigues can be turned into popular news items. A little music, some archive material, shots of the restaurant where the confrontation took place (what a colleague calls the 'we name the guilty buildings' school) and a finger-jabbing piece to camera and it's almost watchable.

Editors ration and mingle different textures of news story. If Westminster produces one cracking story in the day, that is very welcome. If it produces two great stories, that is a problem, but one which can be handled. If there are three – forget it. The same goes for the City, or anything else. Two wars in a bulletin is one too many. A bulletin is like a piece of music. It must have variety, pace and rhythm. Some of that can come from a judicious use of live reports, packages and different correspondents, but most of it comes from the selection of stories. If you have just made the viewer sit through a complicated story on the Tory leadership, you might want to lob in a royal story, or a sporting scandal next ... before you go to the struggle to keep order in Basra, which isn't much fun (but does have a helicopter). Every programme editor groans inwardly at the important running stories that never seem to change – the latest breakdown in Northern Ireland, the latest suicide bomb in Jerusalem. And indeed, when these stories are featured in news headlines, viewing figures for the bulletins immediately drop. You can watch it happening. But, in the BBC at least, after a rolled eyeball and a 'tsk' every programme editor will do her best to carry them.

The struggle to reconcile the impact of moving pictures and the more abstract agenda of news values is as old as television itself and finally irresolvable. The battle between whales and elephants never ends. If you accept that television has become a medium of relaxation and entertainment, and news is a serious and urgent matter, then the mere phrase 'television news' starts to look uneasy, if not quite oxymoronic. This is an impure trade, for fallen people. But so long as the argument continues, so long as there is that tension ('great pictures but rubbish story ... great tale, but there's nothing to see') then something worth watching is still being made.

Interlude: from Home Service to Light Programme?

This chapter has so far been mainly about television journalism: radio journalism is much easier to explain. It is closer to print than to television. The words are all. The same skills that produced great newspaper reports during the Second World War – Martha Gellhorn's writing about the US troops in France, say – also produced the great radio reporting. Richard Dimbleby had endless fights with BBC bureaucrats in London as he pushed for more license to give atmosphere and colour during the darker days of the battles in North Africa, or while flying extremely dangerous missions with Bomber Command. Like those who followed him, he learned how to add to the immediacy and

drama of his reports with 'natural sound' – the crump of artillery, the
drone of engines – and the shake and excitement of his own voice,
breaking away from the surreal, emotionless calm favoured before.
But his reports are works of written English, almost as much as those
in any newspaper. On 19 April 1945 his report from Belsen began: 'I
picked my way over corpse after corpse in the gloom, until I heard
one voice raised above the gentle undulating moaning. I found a girl.
She was a living skeleton – impossible to gauge her age for she had
practically no hair left, and her face was only a yellow parchment sheet
with two holes in it for eyes . . .' His report ended with the line: 'I
have never seen British soldiers so moved to cold fury as the men who
opened the Belsen camp this week.' Dimbleby's despatch is about 500
words long, somewhere between the length of a substantial press news
report and a feature. Its English is very slightly looser. He favours
shorter sentences than most newspaper journalists of the 1940s and he
uses a staccato rhythm at times. But these differences are tiny. His
report would have read perfectly on the page.

As radio developed from the thirties to the fifties as the prime
news service, it slowly learned small tricks of pace and informality.
Radio news reporters had their technical breakthroughs, as clumsy old
reel-to-reel tape machines gave way to smaller, lighter ones; as the
quality and range of microphones increased; and as the skills of cutting
interviews with razor blades and marking them with chinagraph pencils
became redundant in the age of digital recorders. They acquired more
efficient radio cars which could get interviewees for studios on air in
good quality, and ISDN mixer kits for home use. But radio had always
been relatively footloose and flexible, fast moving and easy to do,
which is why so many reporters much prefer it to blundering television. Radio news has not changed radically in 'bulletin' terms – in
the end, it has to be a list of news stories read into a microphone by a
man or a woman, and there is not a great deal you can do about that.
But the surrounding atmosphere has changed. The chat-show style of
interaction with audiences, and the breezy informality that arrived
with pirate stations and, more generally, the creation of BBC local
radio stations in the 1960s, has now spread widely. Five Live, chris-
tened 'Radio Bloke' at the BBC, has pioneered a particular mix of
chatty authority that owes something to the Jimmy Young era yet fits
perfectly with public broadcasting in the 2000s. Radio interviews often

break the news which then has to be delivered, gracelessly, by television, over pictures of the radio studio.

But actually, reading the accounts of the post-war atmosphere in the BBC radio newsrooms, it seems anything but serious back then. A BBC spokesman of the time helpfully explained: 'News readers never get drunk, but they are sometimes *very* upset.' In fact, being moderately drunk on air seems to have been commonplace and the famous Jack de Manio himself left a detailed guide to which pubs could be used for the maximum drinking time while programmes were going on, allowing presenters to reach the Portland Place and Oxford Street studio microphones in the nick of time:

> 1. The Feathers, which took 2 and half minutes at a smart trot . . .
> 2. The Ramilles, which took 4 and a half minutes at a smart trot
> . . . 4. The George, Great Portland Street, known at one time as
> The Glue Pot – 6 minutes. This house was not recommended
> except to those in the peak of condition . . .

Alongside the drink there was a lively culture of practical jokes:

> Ordeal by water was very simple and really rather crude. It consisted of emptying a glass or bucket of water over the news reader's head as he was reading. Since the poor wretch couldn't stop reading, the water could either be flung in one swift deluge in the hope of producing a howl of surprise in the middle of the bulletin, or it could be poured slowly and remorselessly, trickle by trickle . . . David Jacobs . . . was subjected to this treatment to such an extent on one occasion that he had to take most of his clothes off as he was reading and ended the broadcast practically naked.[11]

This air of wild and refreshing amateurism pervaded the *Today* programme too in its early years. The programme that is at the heart of the story of modern British radio journalism has become an institution as no single television programme, certainly since the high days of *Panorama*, could be. *Today*, though, has changed so radically over the decades that it is barely the same programme as it was in its early incarnation, going out in two twenty-minute bursts at 7.15 and 8.15 on the Home Service, from October 1957, fusing and extending under the wildly unsteady grip of de Manio, the raffish half-Italian news presenter who had very nearly been sacked for mis-announcing a talk on Nigeria while the queen was visiting there. As de Manio later recalled it, just before 9 p.m. on 29 January 1956 he said: 'And after the news at 9 o'clock you may like to know that there will be a talk by Sir John MacPherson on "The Land of the Nigger".' De Manio continues, speaking of himself: 'He felt a sudden moment of unease. He put down the key which connected him to the control cubicle. His unease was beginning to turn into terror. "Shouldn't that have been 'Niger'?" he asked nervously. "I rather think it should," replied the studio manager.'[12] He came within a whisker of dismissal.

When *Today* was launched as a relatively light melange of stories, de Manio was used to present it largely because the BBC hierarchy was so terrified of letting him loose on the far more serious business of mainstream newsreading. There was a gallery of extraordinary characters, starting with de Manio himself, who was rebuked for littering the studio with champagne corks and oyster shells; Gilbert Harding; and the military expert Colonel A. D. Wintle. Wintle once sent de Manio an appeal for more broadcasting work, taking the form of a Booth's gin bottle sent through the post, bearing a message inside reading simply: 'Help! Signed A. D. Wintle.' Something of his style is caught by his dress code of bowler hat, spectacles with one lens painted red, so he would remember that eye didn't need glasses, and a rolled umbrella which was never unfurled since only 'scoundrels' used umbrellas to keep off the rain. His single unfurling was to protect it from thieves: anyone who did nick it would find the words 'Stolen from A. D. Wintle' written across it in large white letters. Somehow, one cannot imagine Colonel Wintle being regularly employed by the programme now. Among its many early madnesses was a protest against the favouritism shown to other radio and TV programmes allowed abroad to do special reports from exotic foreign capitals. *Today* was not allowed to travel; and responded by broadcasting an entire morning's output from a hole in the road in Langham Place, outside the BBC headquarters. Again, you can't imagine them doing it now.

Jack de Manio was cast out, famous for his imprecise timekeeping, and finally fired from *Today* in 1971, and he died in poverty in a council flat. Slowly, during the 1970s, the programme became more political, more serious and harder for the country's leaders to ignore. There have been two crucial moments in the history of the programme. The first came in 1975 when the bumptious, brilliant, self-regarding former editor of the *Guardian*'s Northern edition and the *Manchester Evening News*, Brian Redhead, joined, quickly forming a partnership with the smoother, calmer John Timpson and giving it the tone it has kept ever since. The second was the relaunch of the programme in 1978 which gave it its current length and structure. Sometimes programmes just gel, and *Today* gelled. Before breakfast television was up and running as a potential rival, it had grabbed the audience of movers and shakers, and all who were interested in them. It was born of the age of the car radio, and of busy professionals who could catch some, at least, of a long programme of news, interviews and – decreasingly – whimsy. For those who did not have the time or inclination to read a broadsheet newspaper from cover to cover, *Today* offered a good summary of the main stories from Westminster, the City and abroad, sports news, weather and astonishingly unsuccessful horse-race tips. Its political interviews, however, were by now its key weapons. Before the late 1970s, the premier radio programme for politics had been *The World at One*, which had begun in 1965, with William Hardcastle, a former editor of the *Daily Mail*, and Robin Day as its presenters. Under editor Andrew Boyle it became the favoured programme for Labour and many Tory politicians during the 1970s and featured some spectacular verbal punch-ups, often involving well-known print journalists such as Alan Watkins and Peregrine Worsthorne. But for the modern news cycle, a lunchtime show was just too late. Politicians realized that if they said something on *Today* it would be picked up by the Press Association, and would go to every morning news conference at every national paper, hopefully running on through the day. The penalty was that they would face tough interviews with Redhead, Timpson, Peter Hobday and, from 1984, Sue MacGregor.

The programme's urgent need to get 'lines', or stories, from interviews, thereby establishing its importance in the national conversation, meant that the team of competing interviewers, particularly the alpha males, like Redhead and John Humphrys, would harass and chide in a way MPs found unsettling and – once they were in government – impertinent and offensive. In a famous exchange with Tebbit, Timpson simply let him bang on, and then when a silence arrived asked with deliberately overstated politeness, 'May I, er, possibly . . . ask a question?'[13] In the Thatcher years, ministers suspected that the stream of hand-wringing clerics, special-interest groups demanding more money and the political instincts of Redhead, showed that the programme, like much of the BBC, was biased against them. Pressure was piled on, with major confrontations in 1985 and 1986. The most famous moment came in March 1987 after the Budget when Nigel Lawson was being interviewed by Redhead, who had been questioning his job clubs, intended to help the unemployed. The chancellor responded: 'Well, you've been a supporter of the Labour Party all your life, Brian, so I expect you to say something like that. But you really shouldn't sneer at these job clubs . . .' An audibly furious Redhead replied: 'Do you think we should have one minute's silence, now, in this interview, one for you to apologise for daring to suggest that you know how I vote; and secondly, perhaps, in memory of monetarism, which you've now discarded?' Incidents such as these led to a sustained government bombardment against the programme, led by Tebbit, Peter Lilley and Jeffrey Archer.

Redhead was a difficult man. I had a short try-out for *Today* in the early 1990s when I was working for *The Economist*. I stumbled in for my first morning at 3 a.m. and was given no indication of what to do beyond being shown a pile of paper and a typewriter and a completely silent, distracted Redhead. Eventually, with my scripts, sweating with fear, I sat down at my side of the studio table. Redhead had not even acknowledged my presence. Then, just before we were about to go on air, he suddenly looked across. 'Thought you *had* a job?' Yes, I said, at *The Economist*. 'Then what the bloody hell are you doing sitting here?' asked Redhead, with perfect timing, just as the little red light came on, telling me I was live (but speechless). He was a huge and compelling personality, whose theatrical presence was essential to *Today*'s break-through, just as Humphrys and Naughtie became essential later. His bravery and professionalism before his death at sixty-four in January 1994 were spectacular. Under Redhead and his successors, the pro-gramme has depended partly on slightly irascible, middle-class, middle-aged men who originated well away from the metropolis and are not easily seduced by its power brokers. Margaret Thatcher's ministers assaulted it for being incorrigibly left wing. Yet Mrs Thatcher, by making it clear that she was a regular listener, even to the extent of once calling it up to get on air herself, set the seal on its reputation as essential morning fare. She may have been against monopolies but the whole point of *Today* is that it has no rivals. The Establishment needs one place to talk and be heard, not two.

From the mid-1990s onwards, New Labour spin doctors started to beat up the programme with equal enthusiasm. By 1996 the party thought enough of its influence to try to rig 'Personality of the Year' for Tony Blair. (They were caught out and he did not get it.) With an election imminent, Peter Mandelson and his staff in Labour's director-ate of communications were calling up and abusing its staff. In that year it seemed that Mandelson actually had access to *Today* running orders before the programme was on air: he called up to try to get the political reporter Nick Robinson removed from a story because 'He's a Tory. He is biased.' He bullied the producer Honor Wilson for a full hour as she doggedly refused to budge. Two years later, with Labour in power and beginning to feel as hostile to *Today* as the Tories had when they were in office, Alastair Campbell was describing the programme during a Downing Street briefing as cynical and sloppy, part of a 'downmarket, dumbed-down, over-staffed, over-bureaucratic, ridiculous organisation'. Norman Tebbit would have been proud.

In 1998 as Jon Barton left as editor – he had followed Roger Mosey, now a key figure in BBC news – there was the usual struggle to succeed him and it was widely thought that Campbell and his colleagues were running a campaign against the appointment of Kevin Marsh, then of *The World at One*. Marsh, a ferociously driven and independent-minded journalist, was not an easy man and had given Labour ministers a rigorously hard time on his programmes – his style is caught by his response to colleagues eager to chew the cud, which was to tape a sign to his door reading 'no, I haven't got a fucking minute'. At any rate, Rod Liddle, the loping, mop-haired, chain-smoking iconoclast, got the job and pursued a strategy of trying to get *Today* better known for its original journalistic scoops. To do this, he momentously hired Andrew Gilligan: so it is a pleasing thought that Alastair Campbell might be held indirectly responsible for Gilligan being hired in the first place. As it happened, Marsh in due course replaced Liddle and was therefore in the hot seat when the Gilligan crisis broke.

Today continues to be a zone of discomfort and anxiety. It always should be. John Humphrys infuriates a segment of the nation and delights a larger segment; he fights with his editor and pushes interviewees to the limit. For BBC journalists *Today* can come across as impossibly high-handed and difficult. Early on in my time as political editor, I was told to be ready to broadcast from home on some story. Then, a few minutes beforehand, with my notes all ready and early morning phone calls made, I was suddenly stood down. I set off for a regular run round the local park. After ten minutes I heard desperate hooting. It was my wife in the car, waving frantically. I had to come back *immediately*. Something had gone off air and *Today* needed me in two minutes. I dashed back, panting and reached the mike just in time. 'Coming to you next, fifteen seconds . . .' said the studio producer. Then there was silence. Then a report from Africa. I asked what was happening. 'Oh, we don't need *you*,' came another voice. So I sloped off for a shower. I was naked and soaping when my wife was back, banging on the shower door. Now! Immediately! At once! Major panic! Stark naked and dripping, I sat down, dialled up and waited . . . 'No, sorry . . .' came the voice. I tell this story because it is not so terribly unusual – many BBC staffers have similar tales. *Today* is a national institution, of course, and has all the arrogance and paranoia of a national institution. It is constantly anxious about its status, rife with internal politics and sends some listeners mad with rage. But it is an adornment to the nation and we love it, really. Most of the time. America has shock-jocks and we have John and Jim. Well, which would you prefer?

The Politics of Television

The technology of modern newspapers developed alongside democracy and the Victorian party system, mostly free of state interference. We have seen the struggle to report parliament, and the passing effects of the Stamp Acts, and Georgian censorship; in times of war there have been serious struggles between the government and the press. But the reliance of the broadcasters on the state has been of an entirely different order. Television and radio depended, when they first arrived, on a limited resource – wavebands – which governments controlled and rationed. And they arrived at a time when the state was at its most powerful and when paranoia about political manipulation was rampant. So the politicians were in there from the start. The original

British Broadcasting Company, before it even became a public corporation, was set up under the Telegraph Acts of 1863 to 1922, and came, like the mail system, under the control of a Cabinet role, now defunct, called the postmaster general. When television was invented it was defined in law as 'the representation by telegraph in transitory visible form, of persons or objects in movement or at rest' and it too came under immediate government control.

But broadcasting quickly threatened to become more powerful than its master. Competition, first inside Britain, and now around the world, has loosened the grip of politicians and hugely expanded the quantity of broadcasting. Just as MPs eventually had to give up the idea of controlling the exploding medium of print, so they are close to having to give up much control over broadcasting. They hate this. So books about the BBC, and indeed ITV journalism too, tend quickly to become books about a struggle between broadcasters and politicians. The battles are often over the coverage of genuine national crises – Suez, the Northern Irish 'troubles', the Falklands, Iraq. Sometimes they are about the status of politicians themselves. In each case, the broadcasters assert the same rights of free expression that John Wilkes and other radical press figures asserted more than two hundred years ago. In each case, governments tend to respond with calls to patriotism and authority that echo the ministers of George III. What has changed is that the ministers do now speak for democratic authority, not royal authority; and that their practical powers over broadcasting are greater, because television depends on active parliamentary permission to transmit. The Commons of the late eighteenth century could not intervene to sell newspapers or change their ownership. The Commons of the 2000s can and does intervene directly in the funding, size and status of the BBC, and the ownership and rules under which commercial broadcasters work. But this is changing again: the digital revolution threatens to do to broadcasting what mechanical presses and cheap paper did for print, putting it further beyond the practical control of politicians. They have begun to face up to the looming possibility of a broadcasting world which is as diverse, openly biased and aggressive as print journalism; and they are right to be frightened because such a force might finally destroy the remnants of parliamentary authority.

Originally, though, it was parliament which allowed Britain its world lead in television. Before the Second World War, the BBC was permitted to use its ten-shilling radio licence fee income to cross-subsidize the early development of 'radio-pictures' (rather as, sixty years later, BBC Online built up a premier position in web journalism, using the cross-subsidy of television licences). But the unique position of British television is about more than funding; it is also the child of parliamentary compromise and moderation. During the years of Nazi Germany and fascist Italy, British MPs looked long and hard at the danger of new media being used to stun whole peoples with propaganda. In a quieter, less focused way, they were as worried as George Orwell about the coming totalitarian age. (Given how poor and mistrusted Soviet television actually was, they were too worried; but it was a mistake on the right side of the line.) At the same time, the British parliament of the mid-century was still a place grounded in notions of public service and concerned about the dangers of 'vulgar commercialism' on the American model. So they devised a compromise of a kind which existed nowhere else, which has been widely attacked as an anomaly, and yet which has survived ever since.

It was this. Parliament would lay down rules of impartiality and fairness, and be the final regulator for television, but it would do this with a very light touch, keeping well away from the day-to-day running of TV. The Ullswater Committee of MPs, which reviewed the first ten years of the BBC, reported in 1936:

> It is obvious that a medium whereby expression of political opinion could be brought into seven or eight million homes needs very careful safeguarding if it is not to be abused. It would be possible for those in control of broadcasting to maintain a steady stream of propaganda on behalf of one political party or one school of thought ... [and] ... influence the whole political thought of the country.

The political parties all understood that if the government of the day was allowed to interfere in the everyday agenda of broadcasting, the party in power could simply manipulate radio and television to help keep itself in office. Since, under the British party system, almost everyone had some hope of belonging to the party in power, but also expected to be out of power too, at other times, this hands-off deal was in every party's longer-term interest. So the BBC was set up under a system of rolling Royal Charters renewed, after political debate, at regular intervals. When commercial television arrived in the early fifties it was given a similar structure under the Independent Television Authority. It might be different – and we have seen that its news certainly was – but it had to observe exactly the same rules of political impartiality and taste that limited the BBC. The culture passed over: David Plowright, editor of Granada's *World in Action* in the late 1960s, exulted that British broadcasting 'was not there to sell goods like the American system, it wasn't there to be the instrument of the state like Russia or Prague'. Parliament had television on a leash, but it was a long leash, and as much to protect the interests of Opposition parties and plurality as of ministers.

Today, at a time when politics is surrounded by an acid tide of cynicism, it is worth underlining that this British compromise – a broadcasting system that was neither controlled by the state nor left to the private sector, and was not quite beyond the reach of the democracy – was an act of political wisdom which has enriched Britain for two generations. For most of the rest of the twentieth century, British television was better than television in France, Germany, Italy or other comparable democracies. Even America, that English-speaking giant achieving global dominance, did not overwhelm British broadcasting as it has the British film industry. Certainly, right from the first, US-made programmes were popular here. The UK fell to Disney like everywhere else. American sitcoms, from *I Love Lucy* to *Friends*, gave the British an appealing window onto a sunnier, richer, more optimistic world; so did dramas like *Dallas* or *The Thornbirds*. And the Americans always made better crime series, and still do.

Yet British broadcasting, in radio and television, moulded a specifically British way of seeing the world, which partly defined Britishness itself in the second half of the twentieth century. The plays of Alan Bennett and Dennis Potter; the long-running soaps, from *Coronation Street* to *EastEnders*, the current affairs exposés of *World in Action*, all the cosy silliness of Esther Rantzen, and *Top of the Pops*, the Daleks and sticky-backed plastic, the edgy grime of *Z-Cars* and Alf Garnett, and the untranslatable British humour of *The Royle Family*, *The League of Gentlemen* or *The Office* . . . without these, we would not be British in the way we are British. The same goes, at least as strongly, for radio. *Start the Week* in its Melvyn Bragg days, and occasionally even now, is a programme that leaves American guests openmouthed with wonder:

'We'd never be able to talk on the same show about Mozart, and Plato, and the Palestinians, and genetic research – not back home,' they say. The fear of totalitarian broadcasting has gone, but there is still so much that British broadcasting does which US broadcasting doesn't do. The *Today* programme, discussed earlier; the long-form classical broadcasting of Radio 3; and many other shows have helped define modern British cultural life. The French have subsidised cinema instead; I think we got the better deal.

Above all, even more important perhaps than Morecambe and Wise or Bruce Forsyth, Britishness was buttressed and developed through the news. In the early days, British broadcast news reflected the post-imperial, royalist, welfare-state society we had become . . . it may have been stuffy and the voices seem to belong to another world, but if you watch news from the fifties and early sixties, there is a wry and immediate feeling of recognition – yes, that's us. Just as the Korean War, then Vietnam, helped define the preoccupations of America, so British news gathering was dominated by Cyprus, the withdrawal from Africa, and Northern Ireland. At home, too, it was mostly the state's news – state openings, speeches by prime ministers, cuts in the army, the launching of submarines, the first flight of Concorde, Charles being invested as Prince of Wales. Through daily news broadcasts, all of Britain was drawn into the great social changes and dilemmas, the awful murders that gripped the nation, or the train crashes, or the strikes, or the bewildering new fashions for short skirts, or fights between rockers and mods. From Robert Dougall to Huw Edwards, Reggie Bosanquet to Trevor McDonald, the faces and voices of the newsreaders provided national continuity. In a smaller world, here was Britain's take. We always had more news from the US than anywhere else because it was vivid, in English, and important; but the globe as it looked from London was not the globe seen in Washington.

Britain has avoided the overwhelming of TV news by political interests that occurred in Italy, and increasingly affects US television too. In America, Fox News openly avows Rupert Murdoch's politics: but its British cousin Sky News, constrained and influenced by British television culture, does not. A relatively young tradition of politically impartial news was established here and has taken root. And this came about, let us remember, not because British journalists were more virtuous than journalists anywhere else, but because parliament decided to set up a system which was in deliberate tension – a licence fee for the BBC which kept the politicians relevant, and other constraints for the commercial companies, but day-to-day freedom for broadcasters. Some people, including politicians on the radical right, and academics on the left, argue that the very idea of broadly impartial broadcast news is naïve and impossible. Surely the news reflects underlying values and they always serve somebody's interests – those of a liberal metropolitan elite, or of big business? Surely fairness is an over-optimistic Enlightenment myth? Maybe; but if so it is the myth most British people seem to prefer.

It is important to underline, three times in red ink, how well the system has worked; because the price has been so high. The political history has been one of almost constant conflict between the BBC – and sometimes other broadcasters – and the government. In setting up a deliberate tension between elected power, through parliament, and the broadcasters, Britain also set up a system of confrontation. This has been the story of rival Establishments – the Establishment of Westminster and Whitehall against the Establishment of White City, Portland Place and the other stately homes of broadcasting. In giving the BBC a tax, backed by the ultimate threat of imprisonment for non-payment, and by regulating the ownership and profitability of commercial television, politicians have loaned some of their authority to the broadcasters. In return, they have expected to be heard, and to be respected. But this is harder to deliver. British society, like others, has become ever more dominated by the pleasures of affluence, including entertainment and shopping, and ever less ideological. The power of the broadcasters, as suppliers of addictive popular culture, has grown. The allure of parliament, struggling to excite voters, and of ministers, locked in the state bureaucracy, struggling to deliver efficient and popular public services, has fallen. The bosses of the big television companies do not have votes to bolster their egos; but they have ratings and money. While there is no parliamentary inquiry into the ownership of commercial television under way, and when the BBC licence or charter is not up for renewal, they have tended to regard political complaints as irksome and ignorant, the petulant mewlings of self-interested amateurs.

On the other side, the politicians, like Frankenstein, have seen with horror their media creation clank off, seemingly out of control.

The first major confrontation between the government and the BBC was also the most serious – yes, even worse than the Hutton affair. It was won by the BBC and much of the subsequent story follows from the consequence of the Suez Crisis of 1956. The background had been a post-war deal between the BBC and parliament, which reflected MPs' deep fear that broadcasting would make them irrelevant. It seems extraordinary now, but the BBC had agreed during talks in 1945–6 that when ordinary political broadcasting started again, it would simply not discuss anything that was being debated in parliament, or anything expected to come up in the next two weeks – in other words, almost anything that would now be regarded as humdrum, mainstream politics. The BBC had accepted this restraint because it feared parties might simply ban the broadcasting of politics altogether. Its agreements with the government were drawn up in a series of aide-memoires. The 1948 one said that: 'the BBC will not have discussions or *ex parte* statements on any issues for a period of a fortnight before they are debated in either House . . . [and] while matters are the subjects of legislation, MPs will not be used in such discussions.' But would the government really be prepared to let broadcasting stay out of politics, after all the patriotic use which BBC radio had been to ministers during the dark years of the war? No, of course not. Ministers wanted the radio to work for them, particularly when they needed to address the nation. So the deal also promised that: '. . . the Government should be able to use the wireless from time to time for ministerial broadcasts which, for example, are purely factual, are explanatory of legislation or administrative proposals approved by Parliament; or in the nature of appeals to the nation to cooperate in national policies such as fuel economy or recruiting, which require the active cooperation of the public'.

This was, of course, a deal between the BBC and the post-war Labour government. The Tories were already highly suspicious of the Corporation. They felt the media had been biased against them generally during the 1945 election, and that the BBC had been biased against them in 1950 and in 1951. Winston Churchill believed it was infiltrated by communists. When the Tories returned to power in 1951, they rejected the Beveridge Committee's suggestion that the BBC should get a new charter and licence deal for a full fifteen years ahead, effectively securing it against political influence until the mid-

1960s. Instead, they gave it a six-month extension and decided in favour of a commercial competitor, setting up the Independent Television Authority. The key initial there is 'T' – we had finally arrived in the television age. After years of suffering mouldering, icy conditions in Alexandra Palace, the semi-deserted suburban pleasure dome in north London, surrounded by dusty statues and rats, BBC Television was also at last getting a home of its own, on the site of the old White City exhibition, and buying the Gaumont-British film studios at nearby Lime Grove.

The 1950 general election did have a television results programme, with Richard Dimbleby and a very young David Butler. A million people watched it. The age of political television had arrived in Britain, a couple of years after it had arrived in the US. The BBC had offered the political parties their own broadcasts – astonishingly, they refused, seeing no point. Soon afterwards, BBC TV tried out political discussions too, with a programme called *In the News*, which featured MPs such as Michael Foot and Bob Boothby, as well as someone we would now call a media don, A. J. P. Taylor, and a journalist from *The Economist*. It was a very similar mix to any current affairs discussion line-up now, and the BBC found right from the start that there was a bias in broadcasting in favour of mavericks, on the left and right. They were franker, fresher and spoke more interestingly than mainstream loyalist MPs. Back in 1950, when the Tories complained to the man in charge, George Barnes, who had been the BBC's grandly titled 'director of the spoken word', he responded by agreeing to put duller, more mainstream MPs on the programme. Viewers turned off, just as they would now.

None of the parties could deny that television was beginning to matter. In the 1951 election, the BBC again offered the main parties their own fifteen-minute broadcast each and this time they agreed. Winston Churchill, still deeply suspicious of the BBC, did not take part himself and, once he was back in Downing Street, stolidly refused to broadcast, mainly because he loathed the idea of the Commons being upstaged by what he called the 'robot organisation' of broadcasting. But television was proving irresistible to everyone else; the 1953 Budget was followed by a broadcast from 11 Downing Street, which required a full day's preparation with the clumsy equipment of the time and half the BBC's total outside broadcast resources. It took place in a mood of near reverence. As a key BBC player of the time explained, if invited to Downing Street, a television interviewer '. . . is seen to be asking questions of a man whose surroundings proclaim he has been entrusted by the nation with power. If he seems brash or discourteous he will lose the sympathy of the viewer.'[14] Even Churchill gave way, just a little: when the BBC made a special programme for his eightieth birthday in 1954, he agreed to be filmed watching it; tears ran down his face at some of the tributes and he gave a brief response.

So that was the situation when, in 1956, Anthony Eden and his Conservative government faced the great crisis of British power known simply as Suez. Everyone knew that television mattered; it had shown that again in the general election just past. The BBC was little liked by the Tory establishment, but it was tied down by its agreements which kept it out of current parliamentary affairs. Ministers too were tied down by the deal which allowed them to broadcast only on factual and national issues, avoiding party politics. It had seemed a reasonable stand-off. But Suez changed everything. Eden was a politician of the 1930s, an anti-appeaser who had stood out early against the rising danger of Hitler. Here, in his view, was another dictator, Nasser, with his hand on the choke-point of the Suez Canal. This was not 1938, still less 1939; but it was a moment of national challenge. In taking on Nasser, despite the hostility of the Americans, Eden was standing up for Britain in a dangerous world. It followed, he believed, that the BBC, as the national broadcaster, would be standing with him, or for him. The BBC saw things rather differently. When Eden demanded the right to broadcast to the nation about Suez he was given two slots. But the Corporation realized that Britain was badly split over the invasion of Egypt and felt it had a duty to reflect that split; it could not simply be the voice of the government. Eventually the Opposition leader, Hugh Gaitskell, got a broadcast in reply. This did not please Downing Street. According to Grace Wyndham Goldie, there on the BBC side throughout the crisis, neither Eden nor Macmillan cared 'to be bothered with the aide-memoire nor, indeed, with any rules which would affect their right to use television to address the nation whenever he thought fit to do so'.

Then an unlikely figure intervened. Sir Robert Menzies, prime minister of Australia, was in London for a conference about the future of the Suez Canal. He was an outspoken supporter of Eden and,

Number Ten felt, would be a splendid figure to help rally support for the government. The BBC was duly called to say that Menzies was 'available' to broadcast. The BBC's answer was a polite, no thanks. Eden erupted. The Number Ten press officer, William Clark, phoned Goldie to warn her that the prime minister 'was extremely angry with the BBC and had found its refusal of the offered broadcast to Mr Menzies quite inexcusable. Mr Clark was afraid that in his anger the Prime Minister might take some drastic action which would be permanently harmful to the BBC.' Was that a threat to destroy the BBC's independence? It was. According to another BBC executive, Lord Kilmuir, the Lord Chancellor, had been instructed to prepare an instrument to take over the BBC 'altogether and subject it to the will of the Government'. Later Clark himself said that Eden had intended to take over direct control of overseas BBC broadcasting and force the Corporation to allow ministerial broadcasts whenever he wished, without the right of Opposition reply. But the BBC held firm and it was Eden, not the Corporation, who was broken by Suez, once the Americans pulled the financial plug and the invaders had to withdraw. After Suez, a direct threat by government to take over the BBC, or subject it to direct ministerial control, became for practical purposes unthinkable; a later agreement formally established an Opposition right of reply to ministerial broadcasts, so that a crisis of that sort could never happen again.

Suez was important because it drew a clear line beyond which politicians did not go. And of course once commercial television got under way, the fantasy of political control of broadcasting was that much more difficult. What happened instead was a constant series of debilitating and poisonous battles between successive governments and broadcasters about what was proper to put out. The most important confrontations came during divisive and emotive political crises; others were about the treatment, satirical or politically aggressive, meted out to individual politicians. Very few director-generals of the BBC escaped their passage of fire. We have seen an example of the controversies surrounding *Panorama* in the fifties. In the sixties, Hugh Carleton Green faced bitter anger from Conservatives about the impudent tone of *That Was the Week That Was*, which saw its audience leap from 3.5 million to 10 million within weeks of its launch in November 1963. Tory MPs complained that its bias was 'so extremely left-wing, Socialist and pacifist' that, in 1963, with the BBC's charter renewal looming the next year, it was taken off air allegedly because of the coming general election.

The Profumo affair of 1963 saw a near-revolt by broadcasters about the refusal of the main parties to allow a broadcast debate about the scandal rocking Westminster and Fleet Street: Robin Day staged a ludicrous interview for *Panorama* in the rain outside the Commons, making the point that television was being kept away from the action. With the departure of Macmillan, an early star of political television, the Tories were protesting about the tough questioning meted out to their new, pre-TV-age prime minister, Alec Douglas-Home. In October 1963 internal memos were winging their way around an anxious BBC, complaining that its interviewers (in the days when John Humphrys was unknown and Jeremy Paxman was a small boy) were 'too much like "dogs snapping at the heels"' of Douglas-Home and other politicians, and that BBC interviewing was 'too uniformly accusatory'. It did not help pacify the Conservatives, though. They thought one of the reasons they narrowly lost the 1964 election to Harold Wilson and Labour was that the BBC had cynically used its lighting skills to make Douglas-Home look like a skull when he was being interviewed. It took a special, secret BBC demonstration after the election was over to get the Corporation out of that one: using different lights from different angles Douglas-Home and his advisers were reluctantly persuaded that, actually, he looked like a skull however he was lit.

The arrival of Wilson, whose fireside-chat style of broadcasting had been highly effective, did not produce a long honeymoon with the BBC. He tried to parachute himself into *Panorama*, arguing for a live, unchallenged broadcast during the programme, quite deliberately blurring the distinction between BBC broadcasting and ministerial broadcasting – effectively trying to hijack the BBC's authority for his own purposes. It did not take long for Labour ministers to decide that the BBC was an arrogant conspiracy aimed against it; left-wingers were meanwhile constantly complaining that the Corporation failed to give them a fair show. Labour in power was trying to cope with the arrival of student protest, filmed dramatically by current affairs programmes such as *World in Action*, whose coverage of the riots in Red Lion Square was an instant classic. It faced increasingly embarrassing footage of strike ballots and strikes. These, plus events in Vietnam and later

Northern Ireland, convinced Labour that television was a dangerous new power in the nation and not simply a trendy weapon to tease fuddy-duddy Tories. The party put more and more effort into its own broadcasts; so too did a new generation of more media-savvy Tories under Edward Heath.

As soon as Wilson left office, that impudent young radical David Dimbleby made a *Panorama* called 'Yesterday's Men' about ex-Labour ministers' financial arrangements out of office. It asked blunt questions about how they got by, and caused Wilson huge offence by challenging him about how much a newspaper serialization of his memoirs was going to make him – he insisted the interview be stopped, and was visibly enraged by Dimbleby. But it was the use of pop music, graphics and clever filming that particularly worried Labour – this seemed to be an assault on the authority and status of politicians just as serious as making Alec Douglas-Home look like a skull. Labour's growing mistrust of the BBC eventually resulted, during Wilson's second period in office, with a party document proposing to abolish both the BBC and the Independent Broadcasting Authority and replace them with a Communications Council of 'elected representatives – trade unions and local authorities as well as MPs'. After phasing out the licence fee and advertising this new body would oversee the making of pro-grammes by 'a wide variety of dispersed programme units reflecting the creative talent of all parts of the UK'. This notion that British television would be improved if it was made by trade union com-mittees and local councillors was so barmy it died a natural death from sheer embarrassment.

Yet if the BBC's problems in the seventies were bad, a constant cycle of licence fee threats, rows in parliament and tetchy meetings with Tory back-benchers, they were nothing like as fierce as the con-frontations with Margaret Thatcher's administrations in the eighties. In those days it was still *Panorama*, and current affairs rivals such as *World in Action*, which caused the ructions, rather than BBC radio's *Today* programme. From a decision to interview the Irish National Liberation Army men who murdered her friend Airey Neave with a car bomb at Westminster, to filming an IRA unit openly stopping cars near the border, to interviews showing extremists such as Martin McGuinness as ordinary family men, it was often the Irish 'troubles' which provided the flashpoint. Margaret Thatcher and her key ministers, such as Norman Tebbit, took the view that they were engaged in a war with terrorism, a black and white struggle in which there was no room for neutrality; almost as with Suez, the BBC and other broadcasters had to be patriotic and unequivocal about where they stood. Television journalists who were covering the conflict at the time testify to the tortuous lengths they went to, in trying to find language that did not terminally offend the people whose conflict they were reporting. British journalists were generally seen as the enemy by Republicans and, later, by Unionists too. They were operating in a dangerous, hostile environment. But in Whitehall they were seen as morally dodgy appeasers. The difference with Suez was that there was no major British party which disagreed with the prime minister – the broadcasters felt more isolated then, not less.

As for Northern Ireland, so for the Falklands War, during which the young *Newsnight* programme infuriated the prime minister by referring to 'the British' rather than 'our troops', and so too for controversial programmes about Britain's secret services, and for Kate Adie's reporting of the US bombing of Libya, carried out from British bases. *Today* began to crop up as a problem too. Time and time again, ministers warned publicly that the BBC was left-wing, unpatriotic, out of control and had to be dealt with. Menacing speeches were made at Tory conferences about the licence fee. Alasdair Milne, the director-general Margaret Thatcher blamed for early confrontations, was sacked by the BBC governors under their Thatcher-supporting new chairman 'Duke' Hussey. Producers thought to be particularly objectionable struggled to find work. But Margaret Thatcher had wider concerns than the BBC's specific output. She was trying to change the country's culture, its way of thinking about profits and individualism. Right in her way she saw the Corporation – a classic case of the over-staffed, complacent, anti-market and elitist public organization, disdainful of profits, snootily convinced of its own liberal world view. She constantly berated it for having too many people doing too little and was mightily displeased when a committee which she had hoped would recommend the abolition of the licence fee in favour of advertising failed to do so, arguing instead that the licence fee should be increased rather less than the BBC wanted. She favoured the commercial rival, ITN, when she could, and was an early and enthusiastic champion of Rupert

Murdoch's plans for satellite television to break the 'BBC monopoly'. Unlike Eden, even in her angriest moods, Margaret Thatcher never actually contemplated taking control of the BBC herself. But in the eighties, the idea of privatizing it, and the threat of break up, began to be held over its head.

It was a dangerous time for the BBC because the political deal that underpinned it seemed to have gone: remember that the reason for governments allowing it a hands-off arrangement was that, in practical terms, governing party MPs expected to be in Opposition themselves, and so had a vested interest in laying off. It was a mutual Westminster understanding – we won't mess with the broadcasters because that would be unfair, and one day we know that that unfairness might be visited on us. Yet in the 1980s Labour looked such a hopeless case that for many Tory ministers, this prospect was ridiculous. If their mission was to transform Britain and if they found the country's main broadcaster standing in the way, then perhaps the only option was to push it aside – to privatize it, or break it down to a smaller core. Not all Tory ministers thought this way, of course: for old-style Conservatives the BBC was part of the national fabric, to be scrutinized, but not torn up.

The man brought in, first as deputy director-general and then director-general, to bring the Corporation into the more dynamic post-Thatcher world was John Birt. He was, and is, a man of high seriousness and moral drive. Many journalists hated him for imposing a systems-driven, highly abstract way of thinking on news and current affairs programmes that had until then been wilder, perhaps less reliable, but also more fun. But he convinced the Tories that the BBC was at last being run in the approved, market-mimicking, Harvard-Business-School style; and in doing that, he helped keep the Tory radicals at arms' length. In the end the Corporation may have been saved by its rivals. In the roller-coaster economics of the period, ITV looked on the prospect of having to share its advertising resources with horror. Most newspaper groups had little hope of becoming major TV players and regarded the only player who could – Rupert Murdoch – with fear and suspicion. So whatever radical Tory think tanks thought, and whatever Margaret Thatcher would have liked to do, there was too little support around for breaking up the BBC.

Meanwhile, the arrival of Channel 4, with its rather more challenging programming, showed Tories that you didn't have to work for the BBC to be part of the pinko conspiracy.

This is the essential background without which you cannot really understand the battle between ministers and the BBC in recent years. Like Harold Wilson, Tony Blair arrived in Downing Street assuming he would get on with the BBC – that it was, in the end, a moderate, liberal organization which would find a moderate, liberal man like himself most congenial. But Mr Blair's immediate, personal atmosphere of good-natured cheerfulness is protected by a darker tradition of New Labour behaviour for which he is also responsible. Already, long before it was in power, the party had been bullying BBC producers and using 'rapid rebuttal' to try to intimidate the organization, just as it was doing to certain newspapers. The same trend was clear: if you were thought to be firmly against Blair, you had to be wooed and if you were vaguely on the same side, you might need to be intimidated, to keep you in line. Otherwise Peter Mandelson might withdraw love – and contacts, and help. For journalists hoping to be 'in with' the new regime, it was a worrying thought.

In the rows that followed, it is possible to see close parallels with the Tory years. If the Conservatives fell out with the BBC over the Falklands War, and revelations about the spy satellite Zircon, New Labour fell out over the Iraq War, and revelations about the role of intelligence in that. The Tories had Kate Adie. Labour had Andrew Gilligan. Margaret Thatcher was skewered by a persistent woman on *Nationwide* about why the *Belgrano* was sunk. Tony Blair was skewered by another equally persistent woman live on the news about her husband's hospital treatment – and then later, by the wives and mothers of the victims of terrorism. The Tories hated Brian Redhead. Labour hates John Humphrys. Under the Tories, Number Ten swore it would 'get even' with the BBC. Under Labour, Number Ten swore it would 'get revenge' on the BBC. Under the Tories, the director-general Alasdair Milne was a particular hate figure. Under New Labour, the director-general Greg Dyke became a particular hate figure, first for his determined pursuit of ratings success against his Sky and ITV rivals, and then for his clenched-jaw defence of BBC journalism in the Hutton Inquiry. In the Tory years, Bernard Ingham was very angry. In the Labour ones, Alastair Campbell was very, very angry.

It was partly because they both served very talented communicators. Margaret Thatcher was the first party leader to fully utilize and exploit the photo opportunity, and the speed with which new electronic news-gathering techniques allowed pictures to be fed back to the evening bulletins. She changed her voice and her hair to work better on telly. Blair was the maestro of the emotion-choked clip, a virtuoso of the apparently informal, carefully crafted soundbite. Each became increasingly to believe that the BBC was getting in her, or his, way. All these parallels lead some observers to believe that nothing serious has changed, and that the angry exchanges mean nothing for the future of broadcasting. Behind the huffing and puffing, they feel, this is still the post-Suez media ecology where the BBC remains the biggest gorilla, protected from its natural predators. However, the differences, both in structure and argument, are profound.

Broadcasting in the 2000s is a different game from broadcasting in the 1980s. What kind of power do the politicians now have? The first thing is that the change in the broadcasting structure means that politically inspired threats against the BBC are more credible. In a world with only a handful of channels, where most of the population enjoys the Corporation's programmes, simply dismantling it – selling it off – is hugely politically risky. But in a world with hundreds of channels, in which the very idea of loyalty to a channel or broadcasting brand is much weaker then cutting away parts of the BBC is less risky. Holding the licence fee below inflation; requiring the BBC to sell off radio stations, or its Internet services, or to close its digital channels . . . these are practical options for an angry government in a way that privatization of the Corporation was not in the 1980s. The second thing is that the BBC knows very well that the Conservatives, debilitated or not, are in no mood to ride to its rescue. Their plans for the corporation are more radical still. Indeed, today, the BBC finds itself under attack from both sides. A good example came during the so-called 'Cheriegate' affair of late 2002, when Mrs Blair was found to have had business dealings with a con man, Peter Foster, through her friend, and his lover, Carole Caplin. Right-of-centre commentators, such as Stephen Glover, writing in the *Spectator*, claimed that the BBC was 'apart from a few independent enclaves . . . a loyal servant of New Labour'. In the same edition of the magazine, Peter Hitchens was writing about 'Vichy Britain' as a one-party state in which 'Civil-service

grandees have failed to oppose constitutional revolutions; BBC apparatchiks have abandoned their duty to question the government's policies
as well as its performance; individual journalists have become mouth-
pieces of the state.'

In fact, cautious of jumping into the 'Cheriegate' story after firm
denials about it from Downing Street, the BBC, like other organizations, found it had been conned – the story was true after all. Hitchens
wrote in the paper which first made the allegations, the *Mail on Sunday*:

> The BBC was silent about it (the story) for days. Its huge political
> department, which occupies a warehouse-size news factory at
> Millbank, apparently could not find a single reporter to follow up
> this story. Their first grudging mention came on Thursday, after
> the *Daily Mail* proved beyond doubt that Mr Foster and Mrs Blair
> did indeed have a business relationship . . . After the emails were
> revealed and Downing Street had climbed down, the BBC and all
> the other papers suddenly discovered that they had a major story
> on their hands and splashed it everywhere, confirming our judge-
> ment that it was important, and tacitly admitting that they had
> been fooled by the state for a full five days. Why were they so
> ready to be fooled? Was it connected with the fact that the BBC
> director-general is the Labour supporter Greg Dyke and that the
> BBC chairman is the Labour supporter and close friend of senior
> Labour figures Gavyn Davies? Both these outrageous and cynical
> appointments were made without shame . . .

Yet at the same time the BBC was under equally severe attack for
having run the story so big: ministers and Blair aides came up to me
complaining bitterly that we were following a Tory and *Daily Mail*
agenda, and being increasingly sucked into personalized vendettas that
were demeaning politics.

There are obvious answers to all this: the story was true; the
Downing Street machine was, at whatever level, misled and misleading; a link between the prime minister's wife and a con man is a valid
story, whoever first discovered it; and the BBC, trying to offer a higher
level of veracity than many newspapers, is duty bound not to jump
onto air with every unsubstantiated allegation as soon as it is made,
fun though that might be. Meanwhile, surrounding all that, the rest of
the broadcasting ecology is not as helpful for the BBC as it once was.

Rupert Murdoch's interest in Sky is reality, not prospect. He may have a minority shareholding, but the links to his powerful and politically well-connected newspapers mean that ministers feel they have another useful friend, and a would-be player in terrestrial broadcasting. During the Iraq War, the prime minister had the prospect of America's Fox Television, with its gung-ho coverage of the fighting, as a constant contrast to the BBC. Would he not have been happier with a British Fox? He did not answer the question himself; but among the people urging Sky journalists to be tougher on the BBC during the row over its reporting of the war was the prime minister's wife. The other main player is, of course, ITV, though it lost much of its political influence when its old *News at Ten* disappeared from the schedules. It has had a miserable time though its news coverage has been improving again. Many in the industry believe that ITV will eventually be taken over by much richer, bigger American media interests. This would not necessarily worry a British government: as global communications groups become more common, they also become shrewder at pandering to local political pressures.

The next big difference between the Thatcher and Blair eras is that the central argument against the BBC has changed. It is no longer that the BBC is left wing. It is that the BBC is 'cynical'. New Labour cannot attack the Corporation for being a Tory conspiracy, though it probably has more Conservative-voting reporters now than ever before. But it experiences exactly the kind of painful, probing questions and unhelpful revelations that earlier governments were jabbed with; and it reacts by accusing the BBC, and the media generally, of simply being above itself. As we have seen, it would like the BBC to step back, to learn to report again in a more neutral, dispassionate way, even if that means many fewer exclusive stories. Labour does not mean 'neutral' in quite the party sense that the BBC's Tory critics mean it; they mean neutral in tone, approach, excitability. What connects the two eras is the feeling that the tone of BBC and other political reporting is biased against the government. In the 1980s the Tories felt that with Labour flat on its back, the BBC had slipped itself in as a new Opposition. In the late 1990s and the early 2000s, with the Tories out for the count, Labour accused the BBC of just the same thing. 'Good thing too,' say some. After all, if the overriding purpose of journalism is to tell truth to power, then good journalism is going to be constitutionally suspicious of governments: an aggressive *Today* or *Newsnight* interviewer is doing God's work, or at least the voter's. It is also often said that it is only the BBC's licence fee that makes media bias against the government an issue at all. If newspapers cut up ministerial reputations, all they can do is shrug. If Sky does a barbed interview with a Tory leader, or ITV News broadcasts an unfairly hostile package, the victims will be privately angry, but they cannot do very much about it. So when they turn to attack the BBC they are really expressing their frustration with the media generally: it is just that the BBC is the only part of it they can realistically get their hands on. Perhaps the BBC should just ignore the criticism and tough it out.

This is not good enough. The BBC has to offer a gold standard for journalistic integrity and fairness or it is doomed: if the Commons does not believe that the licence fee buys Britain a range of broadcast journalism that is better and more reliable than anything the market would provide left to its own devices, then a core reason for the Corporation's existence disappears. We need a culture of public broadcasting to keep the rest honest. Had the allegations against the government which led to the Hutton Inquiry been made by ITV News, or the *Daily Express*, or even the *Financial Times*, they would have been denied, and the caravan would have moved on. No journalist for Sky News, or any newspaper, will ever face the kind of forensic examination of their work that the BBC's Andrew Gilligan endured. But this is right and proper. The government's angry prosecution of BBC journalism in this case was a back-handed compliment: the Corporation has to get it right, because of its huge reputation and international power. In this case, without Gilligan's work, very important issues – issues of genuine national significance about why Britain went to war – would have been hidden in darkness. But his employer lives by its reputation for accuracy. There may be plenty of room for argument about the tone of an interview; there is nowhere to hide if key facts are wrong. This means, sometimes, that the BBC does seem to be holding back, particularly in its news bulletins, waiting for the confirmation that other broadcasters shrug off. In the twenty-four-hour news programmes, being first with breaking news is both exciting and commercially useful. Even in BBC newsrooms, you will often see Sky on a screen for just this reason. But they can be overexcited and get it wrong from time to time, in the interests of being first. The BBC can't.

What the BBC can do is break stories that are accurate and cross-checked, whatever offence they cause. And we do.

And is the BBC institutionally biased? Shock admission: we are. But the BBC is not biased in the way some of its critics think – in a party-political way. I have worked for five newspapers and have a close knowledge of several more. The BBC's obsessive regard for fairness is a different world; press colleagues have no idea about how scrupulously our words and films about the parties are scrutinized, both by the parties and by BBC managers. During election campaigns, the length of coverage is monitored down to the second, and a single inelegant adverb can cause a major row. The rest of the time, we talk amongst ourselves about whether the tone of this piece or that was fair, and we get a blizzard of advice if we cross the invisible line each of us has painted down the inside of our skulls.

Fairness is difficult, though. In the winter of 2003, the Conservative Party was split in several factions, caught between its current leader and would-be rivals. At its Blackpool conference, MPs who wanted Iain Duncan Smith out as Tory leader were patrolling the Winter Gardens Centre and the bars of the larger hotels briefing journalists that a coup was in the offing, that he was useless, was facing a serious investigation into his office expenses and was generally on the slide. The plotters had no intention of coming into the open; they were using journalists, including broadcasters, to try to do their job for them, shaking the Tory tree with gusts of hostile headlines until IDS fell out. That way, they would not have to actually confront him themselves. It did not work, and the plotting had to be resumed later at Westminster. But I took the view that, since Mr Duncan Smith had been elected after a vote of 350,000 people, it was not the job of journalists to turf him out, and I broadcast, pretty robustly, on what was really going on behind the scenes. This had the short-term effect of helping him, and making the plotters look shifty. Now, was that fair? From the point of view of the then Tory leadership, it was. But some of the dissident Tories thought I was objectively biased against the Conservatives because I was not helping them get rid of a useless leader. One of them told me that I was doing Tony Blair's work for him ('typical BBC') because I was making the case for IDS. From his point of view, trying to be fair to the Tory leader meant being unfair to the wider Tory cause. My point is only that we agonize about these things, as few non-BBC journalists do, and it is not always an easy call. We try. I had a single, gently admonitory call during the Hutton Inquiry, perhaps the most sensitive and difficult story we have had to report because the BBC was so much in the firing line: it was a senior manager, himself facing criticism, who thought that perhaps my two-way had not been *quite* harsh enough – on the BBC. I was proud to be working for the Corporation that day.

It isn't party bias: it's cultural bias. 'Where are you coming from?' It is a common question. We all come from somewhere, in the sense of having basic values and instincts. But if people come from some-where, so do institutions. The BBC comes mainly from its own public sector history, and from the sprawling west London site where its main television and radio programmes are based. Its staff are younger, and more often black or Asian, than the population of the UK generally. Being younger, and living in London, they are likely to be more socially liberal in their attitudes to drugs, sexuality and much else.

Above all, if they are journalists or programme-makers they will probably be biased in favour of newness, simply because that is more interesting. This was spotted very early in the BBC's history, before even the first experiments in regular television had begun. A com-mittee of the great and good, looking into the future of broadcasting, said in 1935:

> There is an . . . inevitable tendency in the general programmes of
> the Corporation to devote more time to the expression of new
> ideas and the advocacy of change, in social and other spheres,
> than to the defence of orthodoxy and stability, since the reiteration
> of what exists and is familiar is not so interesting as the exposition
> of what might be.

The sentences might be old-fashioned but the perception is bang up to date. And these younger, more mixed, more urban, more new-worshipping people also imbibe the BBC culture and its folk memories which are constantly distilled and passed around almost without anyone noticing. The BBC culture is, of course, unlike anywhere else, composed of an indescribable mix of Lord Reith, Spike Milligan, numerous Dimblebys, Grace Wyndham Goldie, Jana Bennett – a host of characters, old and new, committed to public service broadcasting –

and vast circular corridors leading nowhere, and thirties statues, and the smell of over-used studios, and the assumptions of *Ariel*, the in-house magazine, and power struggles so complex that no outsider will ever get them. It made a TV series of the Mervyn Peake book *Gormenghast* some years ago, which received only a lukewarm reception from viewers. The point was, of course, that it was really a secret history of the BBC.

So this culture, younger, more liberal and urban and public sector than Britain as a whole, transmits a national broadcasting service which inevitably mimics its origins. This is not the case for everything about the BBC – the Corporation of *Gardeners' World* or *One Man and His Dog* also exists. But it is true that, overall, the BBC's assumptions are more progressive, or trendier, or mildly more radical, than the whiter, older, more conservative, more suburban country it serves. All that can be done about this is for the BBC to be constantly aware of the gap and to 'aim off'. The bias is mostly unconscious and does not mean to offend – I am talking about the presenter's joke that assumes 'we' are all against George Bush, or country vicars are inherently funny. Even in politics, the liberal assumptions sometimes slip in: when BBC correspondents, particularly from London, are reporting the Irish peace process, it could be imagined, occasionally, that the BBC disapproved of people voting for Ian Paisley's Democratic Unionists – though they pay their licence fees like everyone else. What, though, of even harder cases – the racists of the British National Party, and the general unwillingness of the BBC to broadcast the views of people who wish, for instance, to get us out of the EU, or to see an English parliament established?

The cover-all answer is that the BBC is not a neutral ground between parliamentary democracy and any other system, but is the child of the British parliament, even if it would sometimes like to forget its parent. If the BNP, or if English Nationalists, cannot get elected to the Commons, then they do not have the automatic right to be represented on panels for *Question Time* or interviewed on the news, any more than Maoists do. Yet that answer is a get-out too. There are no Greens elected to the Commons. There is no one there elected on a platform for withdrawal from the EU, either. Yet millions upon millions of British people are keen environmentalists, and believe strongly that we should now separate from Brussels. To keep them out of the national conversation as chaired by the BBC would be unfair – metropolitan and elitist. The only answer is for the Corporation to keep catching sight of itself in the mirror, and ask, are you really being fair? A less cohesive, more mixed and disputatious Britain is far harder for a national broadcaster to fairly represent. Yet this is a more interesting Britain than the one Reith set out to educate. And if the fundamental argument for the survival of the BBC is that it articulates and describes Britishness, in a way that bridges the public and private spheres, then the BBC has no choice but to try. When politicians throb with pain after a going-over on the *Today* programme, this is the argument they need to address themselves to. Would a Britain without the BBC have been bound together in the way we have been bound together? And if the BBC goes, won't a whole way of feeling British vanish too?

6

Two Aristocracies

One: Foreign Correspondents, and the Sin of Glamour

> The dining room of the Semiramis was already crowded
> with that international club of foreign correspondents who
> flock to war and crises like nineteenth-century camp follow-
> ers . . . when they meet on the job they greet each other like
> brothers and – in recent times – like sisters. They exchange
> gossip – who's died, who's moved papers, who's new – get
> drunk together and tell the same old stories about stupid
> foreign editors, intransigent censors, lost passports, mangled
> cables, minor triumphs and great scoops. It is a way of life
> they would not exchange for any desk job, however highly
> paid.
>
> Phillip Knightley, describing life in Egypt in 1967,
before the Six-Day War

If domestic journalists have the sin of sloth, the foreign correspondents'
sin is glamour. It is 1935. A lanky, uncertain man stands in a great
London department store. Before him a pile of fascinating objects is
slowly accumulating – huge zinc trunks, bundles of netting, solar topis,
a Mauser sporting rifle, khaki shorts, forked sticks. Ahead, shrouded
in steam at Victoria, smelling of pipe tobacco and oil, is the boat-train
to Paris; followed by a flying boat, bobbing at anchor; or an elderly
steamer amid the clamour and babble of Marseilles; and then, so far
off as to be barely visible in the shimmer of excitement, Abyssinia.
William Boot – or in real life, Evelyn Waugh, George Steer and
William Deedes – is off to cover his first war. They and scores of
other pioneers, by horseback, on camels, fording dangerous rivers and

crawling through paddy fields, lounging in the smoky bars of exotic hotels and sneaking their way into the presence of dictators, were the foreign correspondents who had the best of British journalism. The least complacent, most awkward and eventually often the angriest hacks, they have left these islands for more dangerous and dustier parts of the world, bringing back news without which their fellow citizens would be deaf and blind to the times they lived in. We all have dreams of freedom. Foreign correspondents, more than most people, have lived them.

Many have died doing this. Many have nearly died. It is 1972. In blood-spattered cells in Uganda's notorious Makindye jail, groups of British reporters are cowering. Sandy Gall of ITN, the photojournalist Don McCullin of the *Sunday Times*, John Fairhall of the *Guardian* and Nick Moore of Reuters have been picked up by Idi Amin's secret police, and taken to a place of beatings and murder. Outside, groups of men are being executed not with guns or ropes but with a hammer. The British reporters can hear the sound a hammer makes on a human head. They are pretty sure they are next. These correspondents survived, two of them becoming national icons. They went through the fear and came out the other end. It is 1971, at Glasnevin Cemetery, Dublin, and an IRA funeral is going on. The *Daily Mirror* photographer has just been dragged to the side of the cemetery and is screaming as he is being beaten to a pulp. A young BBC radio reporter called John Simpson, armed only with one of the earliest cassette tape recorders, has just been seized. He protests that he isn't an army spy, but a BBC journalist. 'So show us yer BBC i/d.' He hasn't got it. A red-haired man orders his mates to kill Simpson: 'Give the focker one up the nostril.' It is thirty years later, 2001. Simpson, who had been saved in Glasnevin by the intervention of a *Sunday Times* reporter, is walking into Kabul, which has been liberated from the Taliban, with his cameraman Joe Phua, hobbling in pain from a broken foot, and other BBC colleagues. Around him surges an excited and welcoming crowd. Simpson, who has led a freer life than most men, is witnessing not a dream of freedom, but its waking. It is 2004 in a grim part of Riyadh. The BBC's security correspondent Frank Gardner and one of the most cheerful, hard-working cameramen I have ever come across, Simon Cumbers, are out working. Cars arrive and shots ring out, leaving Simon dead and Frank gravely ill . . .

Why have the foreign correspondents, facing danger and professional uncertainty, amounted to an acknowledged aristocracy in
journalism? Hardly anyone goes off to be a soldier of fortune, and
indeed after the grim African civil wars of the past half century, the
mercenaries are despised figures, not romantic ones. The missionaries
have mostly come home. Jet travel has rather limited the scope for
genuinely adventurous travel writing; the bookshelves are crammed
with guides giving worldly wise advice for holidaying consumers rather
than offering discovery and fresh exploration.

That leaves the foreign correspondents. Though the trade is old,
the real glamour of the job reaches back only about seventy years,
from roughly the time imperial soldiering and missionary exploration
began to decline. Unlike missionaries, foreign correspondents had a
moral message not for the natives out there, but for the folks back
home. Ever since the first wars involving fascism, in Abyssinia and
Spain, the foreign correspondents of the democracies have been
bringers of warnings. They have been adventurers who returned not
with loot but with information. During the Second World War the
mobilization of entire democracies meant that war correspondents
were closer to public opinion than before or since, some of them
gung-ho propagandists, many simply decent patriots recording the
failures as well as the successes. They were alongside the millions of
ordinary citizens, rarely out ahead. But after 1945 as the epic fight with
Communism began around the world, reporter-witnesses were out
there again, bringing fresh news – of the dubious behaviour of Britain's
allies in Korea and Vietnam, or reporting how the H-bomb was posing
questions about the survival of humanity, or returning with urgent
concerns about the behaviour of the Israelis in Gaza, or the South
African army in Namibia. Travel, excitement – and *meaning* as well; a
certain sense of moral superiority, along with the expense accounts.
Life does not get better than this. It is so alluring that the possibility of
facing the Khmer Rouge or Amin's thugs can seem a price worth
paying.

The meaning that foreign correspondents brought back has
changed, of course. Evelyn Waugh was rather in favour of fascist Italy
when he visited Abyssinia. There have been passionate imperialists,
like Winston Churchill, who survived the Boer War, or the great
George Warrington Steevens of the *Daily Mail*, who did not. Very

many have been radicals of different stripes, from Orwell, Martha
Gellhorn and George Steer, whose views were jolted by the Spanish
Civil War, to James Cameron, radicalized by the nuclear bomb, to
John Pilger, radicalized by his reporting of poverty in northern Eng-
land, but then by Vietnam, or Robert Fisk, passionately shaken by
Israel's behaviour in the Lebanon. The majority have been plain vanilla
reporters, whose values were only discernible to their readers and
viewers as a vague, stubborn belief in decency and democracy –
Jonathan Dimbleby, Kate Adie, Murray Sayle, Simpson, Alan Moorehead, Fergal Keane, Ann Leslie. Even in these examples of non-
politically committed journalism, the work has had a political effect.
Since September 11, and the wars that have followed it, the role of
foreign correspondent has grown yet again. The fate of ordinary
commuters, of business people travelling and of western governments
is once again tightly tied to events in Baghdad jails or remote Pakistani
villages.

From Adventurers to Missionaries

The history of British newspapers is the history of foreign news. As a
small, seafaring nation, for three centuries the British hardly distinguished between home and foreign news. Reports from the American
colonies, Jamaica, India, Canada and Australia were stories about kith
and kin. From Bristol to Leith, shipping and trading news was a vital
part of commercial life: Hamburg and Rostock, Lisbon and Genoa,
were as much part of the business world as the Dow-Jones index is
today. And in the centuries of religious and dynastic controversy, the
continental news – the struggles between Turk and Austrian, the
manoeuvres of Bourbon and Swede, were of gripping interest to
educated British readers. This information came in through myriad
human contacts. Anyone who could afford it travelled to the Continent
and many went to university not at Oxford but Leyden or Utrecht.
For generation after generation, husbands and sons would be killed
fighting the Dutch, the French, the Spanish, the Danes – and trading
with them, too. London was from the first an entrepôt of foreign
businessmen and adventurers. Reading old newspapers, one gets a
strong sense of Britain bobbing in the middle of a close-knit world,

connected by weeks of travel on salt water, and long muddy trails. Despite today's European integration and cheap, easy travel, in many ways the British press was more outward-looking and had more of a sense of the nearness and importance of other countries in the 1750s than it does now.

The reporting instinct was there long before professional reporters. The word correspondent, or letter writer, tells the story. Letters from aristocratic travellers home; published books of letters and accounts of travels; the private letters of serving soldiers and commercial travellers – all these are fundamental to British history. There is clear, superb reporting from English merchants in Tartary, from ordinary infantry-men and junior officers in Wellington's Peninsular Campaign, from titled ladies travelling through Turkey or Spain, and from talented literary travellers such as James Boswell, moving through France, Switzerland, Germany and Corsica. Most of this starts as private correspondence or books, published later; but the notion of letters being published in newspapers is as old as newspapers themselves. During the eighteenth century, the emphasis began to shift from correspondence which is merely passed on by the newspaper to correspondence expressly written and designed to be published. The two merged and criss-crossed. Newspaper reporting in *The Times* about Trafalgar and Waterloo was stitched together from the letters home of officers serving Nelson, and eyewitness soldiers' reports, before the official despatches arrived and were printed. Because of the human and commercial need for hard information, many letters were printed from enemy or hostile sources, generally without extra comment – letters from angry foreign ambassadors, or British citizens in Moscow or Paris, reporting what the newspapers in those capitals were saying.

Throughout Victorian times, British papers would be passed letters on every conceivable topic from overseas, and would print them as 'from a correspondent' if they were thought interesting enough. In the age before bylines, readers would have had no clear sense, much of the time, whether they were reading a second-hand private letter, or a work of professional journalism. The title 'from our *special* correspon-dent', famously given to Russell during his war reporting from the Crimea, was like '*own* correspondent', invented to help distinguish the journalist from the amateur letter writer. Because of this, the vig-orous argument about who was the first real foreign correspondent is a pretty spurious one. Professional war correspondents almost all look back to Russell, discussed earlier in this book, though there are arguments for earlier correspondents, such as Henry Crabbe Robinson, who was sent overseas by *The Times*, or Charles Gruneisen of the *Morning Post*. The real difference is that the professionals lose any leisure and must compete to get their material back first. A dragoon captain or a lady adventuress will hope that their accounts will appear in book form, or magazines; a newspaper employee cannot wait. Once the vigorous newspaper culture described earlier in this book had begun to develop then the story of the foreign correspondents is also the story of how one technology overtook another.

Russell in the Crimea was like all previous correspondents in one thing, at least – the frustrating amount of time it took to get his words home and into print. Even using telegraphs for the most important news, his reports would not be published for three weeks or so after he had sent them. Teams of fast horses, pigeons and specially hired boats were all used by pre-steam newspapers to get the stories home, but they would always be long after the event. This meant that the first generation of professional reporters were under a little less pressure than the men and women who followed. They could develop their descriptive prose: Russell's reports would not have been such political dynamite in Victorian London had they not been so detailed, so earthy and long. For the reader, there was often the strange effect of consuming at one sitting a whole bundle of letters sent from abroad on successive days but published in a single edition of the newspaper – a kind of serial news story, in which each letter from the correspondent adds to, or corrects, the one before.

To read the witness accounts by army captains, travelling surgeons, slavers and missionaries is to be disabused of any idea that professional journalists were, or are, necessarily better writers than anyone else. But whoever provided it, a need for global military, diplomatic and financial news is surely the origin of the British media's continuing interest in and investment in world news today, the place from which the BBC World Service and the still impressive British television and press overseas bureaus began. Take Reuters. Founded by a German immigrant who'd started out using pigeons to send news between Aachen and Brussels, the company was founded here in 1851 to transmit stock-market quotations between London and Paris via the new Dover–Calais cable. London's need for hard facts and the new technologies of cable and telegraph meant that, alongside stock prices, Reuters was able to announce President Lincoln's assassination in 1865, before expanding into the Far East in 1872 and South America two years later. Self-interest first, with a wider world view piggybacking in due course.

The era of sail and horses was elbowed aside. The American Civil War was not only the first modern war, with modern levels of slaughter, it was also, famously, the first modern newspaper war, with the fierce rivalry of the Boston, New York and Philadelphia papers spurring the correspondents on to extraordinary feats of daring and cunning in the race to be first with the news of great slaughters. There were no fewer than 500 war correspondents in Washington at the start of the war; considerable numbers were killed and captured in the next few years. The president of the besieged Union, Abraham Lincoln himself, relied for the latest news on front-line reporters from papers such as the *New York Tribune*. As the war went on, steamships and observation balloons, portable photographic studios and Union Army telegraph systems were all used to rush stories back to the head offices of the newspapers; it was the telegraph that really made the difference. At the Crimea, it had been used for very short snaps of information; the American reporters were the first to use it to give full news accounts of the war. Because of the cost and the slight clumsiness involved, the prose was tighter and less meandering than the handwritten despatches of previous correspondents. It was faster, in both senses. These techniques were then brought to London by American journalists in time for the Franco-Prussian war of 1870. The *Tribune* teamed up with the London *Daily News* to use telegraphed reports. It comprehensively and humiliatingly beat *The Times*, which was still relying on Russell and the old methods.[1]

So it has continued. Transatlantic cables, airmail, wired photographs from the front . . . there has always been a new development to exploit. The Second World War was the first radio war, with correspondents sending back vivid sound despatches; Korea saw the arrival of lightweight cameras and television footage from the front line; by Vietnam there was colour. The two Gulf wars were widely described as video-arcade conflicts, because of the eerie green footage of missiles homing in and obliterating targets. The modern impact of satellites, electronic news gathering, sat-phones and digital cameras has been mentioned already. At each stage, technological advances have cut two ways. On the one hand, they have brought speed and vividness. Who could be other than delighted by the freshness that technical change has brought? Now tiny robot cameras can be fixed to infantrymen's helmets, or attached to bombs. We are close to being able to watch battles as they happen, from the viewpoint of soldiers actually fighting, in real time. In Iraqi prisons, US soldiers can take digital images of abuse and email them straight home. All this is, in strict news terms, exhilarating.

But the more time the reporter has to watch, think, listen and compose, the more power that reporter has over the story. Each advance in technology binds the correspondent more closely to the newspaper or broadcasting office, and its deadlines, and its agenda. The same wires or satellite transmissions that bring the news home faster send instructions back just as quickly. For the reporter in the field, initiative and thinking time are cramped. Victoria Brittain, a foreign correspondent and editor for the *Guardian*, put it like this:

> In the 1960s, I remember, we communicated by telex from Vietnam and the only contact we had with London was the monthly cheque and an occasional envelope of clippings. The time difference with London meant that correspondents had time to spend the whole day talking to soldiers, refugees, monks or politicians, and still sober up after dinner before filing their day's story. From 1970s Algiers, Nairobi, Mogadishu, Addis Adaba, Khartoum and Kampala, we painstakingly tapped our words on to the telex, and the one phone call from the foreign editor to me in five years was merely to announce his move to another job and to name the new man who was nominally in charge of my fate. In those days, before satellite communications and the internet, the correspondents had life on their own terms.[2]

They don't now, though the other side of this is put by Robert Fisk, who points out that one of the great problems of the foreign correspondent is misunderstanding – erupting with anger at the tone of a message from London which was meant to be friendly, or finding that your messages have been misinterpreted there. The simplicity and ease of the mobile phone has transformed his life for the better.

Robert Fisk emphasizes the loneliness of being a good foreign correspondent and the consequent need to construct an imagined community of fellow tradesmen. More than any other group of journalists, foreign correspondents have a family tree of heroes and heroines, and a sense that they are a tribe, albeit a scattered and dysfunctional one. They are rarely admirers of head office. For those stationed abroad, there are two classes: the useless and the paranoid. Anyone who is any good is constantly worried about what is happening back home among the ignorant asses who mess with the copy. The normal insecurities of journalists are multiplied by absence and by the mundane problems of filing – the different time zones, the equipment that jams or is dropped, the lack of a working socket. The longer a correspondent spends away from the newspaper or broadcasting head office, the more their view of the world changes, too. For a journalist like Mark Tully, formerly the BBC's man in India, the 'beat' can become home. People go off to report the politics of West Africa, or Paris, or Tokyo, and fall in love with the place.

But their employer does not; nor do the readers. The correspondent quickly comes to realize with renewed force that for most people, most news is local. What bulks large in the foreign capital seems unimportant back home. Time and again, I have met colleagues who are working abroad and who, before the first beer is tasted, will spill out the latest twist of some sex scandal involving a local politician, or a gun battle, full of information about something they bitterly know 'won't make' in London. Every journalist has a compulsion to tell. For them it is often dammed and frustrated. Newspaper people, in particular, file into the unknown, day after day, sending 800 words and hoping for a column of type on the front page, only to discover they've been cut to 150 at the bottom of page eight. They don't know what the priorities really are back home. Why is the paper filled up with dull European politics at the moment when it could have a scoop about Israeli settlers? Why the hell did they take that nonsensical line from Reuters and stick it onto the top of my copy, without even calling? Don't they know I was actually there, and the other guy wasn't? Should I threaten to resign, or is twice in a month asking for it? What did that strange note in the foreign editor's voice mean? Will that half promise to send me to Washington next autumn survive if they're not using this feature about the Russian mafia? What is the point of working for a paper that used to be taken seriously but seems to spike all the real world news for crap about sex and shopping?

Even for those who are based in London, it is remarkably stressful. The BBC's world affairs editor John Simpson, the ultimate fireman, said that the job had not been noticeably good for his private life: 'Like a clumsy waiter, I've left behind me a little trail of smashed relationships . . . Perhaps I should cite Lord Reith as co-respondent.'[3] Many could say the same thing. People with an urge to get out of offices, to keep moving, to put themselves in danger, are unlikely to be settle-downers. The *Guardian*'s Victoria Brittain has written:

> The foreign correspondent is, and always has been, the envy of his or her peers, the despair of his or her family, the model of every aspiring young journalist, the rock or sinking sand, on to or into which a foreign editor will climb or sink. With rare exceptions, successful foreign correspondents are prima donnas and workaholics, selfish loners who are either pushy or cunning . . .

But she proudly adds: 'No job in journalism is harder than the foreign correspondent's. No job in journalism is more important . . .' And that is the crucial point, which helps explain the ambiguity of the foreign correspondent. It is generally hard to get these jobs. People put in years in London offices lobbying for them, though others simply go abroad and file copy randomly until someone starts paying them. They are often relatively high status and in a properly run bureau in a prosperous city they can be decently paid jobs too, with expense accounts, housing allowances and even sometimes help with the children's education. For the war correspondents and danger-zone merchants, the job offers all the excitement and unpredictability anyone could ask. Yet they are characteristically wary, competitive, sharp-elbowed, suspicious, ulcer-nurturing and sometimes miserable people too. Why do they do it?

Because they feel that 'no job in journalism is more important'. Because they regard themselves as the praetorian guard of the trade, to be more respected than editors or political columnists. And though it pains me to say so, never having been one, they are probably right. These are people who have given themselves to the essence of journalism: reporting. They have cut the shackles. The trade-off is the insecurity and paranoia already described; foreign correspondents don't get the stroking and daily chat that other reporters enjoy. Instead they are more likely to be dealing with big news and serious issues. They *know*, or feel they know, that the world is more interesting than London or Edinburgh or Dublin has so far noticed. The importance of the break-up of Yugoslavia and its ethnic wars, or of a famine that threatens millions, or even of a US presidential election, rubs off on the correspondent. Back home, the country may have fallen into a witless obsession with *Big Brother* or the latest dull struggles for the Tory leadership, but they, the foreign corrs, are still in touch with reality.

So it is not surprising that sometimes they become crusaders for causes. With domestic audiences who seem to be dozing through secure, incurious lives, there is a temptation to slap the face, to shout, and to declare media war on behalf of the wretched. In Kosovo, Ethiopia, the occupied territories of Palestine, reporters struggle for a sense of balance. Often the brutalities of one side make it impossible and the reporter decides to become a voice for the voiceless. And the same human types who yearn to be foreign correspondents – the more inquisitive, pushier, perhaps more troubled people – are often also people of passion. It is striking, by the way, that so many great foreign correspondents for British news organizations are either Irish – from Russell to Maggie O'Kane and Orla Guerin – or Australians, such as Pilger, Knightley, Moorehead, Wilfred Burchett and Chester Wilmot. Perhaps it is because they started travelling, reached Fleet Street or the TV Centre, and found they could not keep still. Perhaps it is because the anti-establishment instinct of the outsider is more useful in the foreign correspondent than the sense of security enjoyed by a middle-class Briton.

Alan Moorehead of the *Daily Express*, the brilliant and ultimately tragic writer whose war reporting from the Desert campaign to the final stages of the defeat of Germany turned him into a contemporary star, was an expatriate from 1930s Australia. James Cameron, who also worked for the *Express* for a while, and whom we met earlier, was an exiled Scot. In an age when there were far fewer bylined reporters, Cameron's stature was huge and probably beyond that of any correspondent now. But the family tree of radical correspondents sprawls further than the most famous names. John Pilger, who met James Cameron and greatly admired him, points to the extraordinary career of Wilfred Burchett – again of the *Daily Express* – who slipped away from the official minders after the defeat of Japan in September 1945 and, after taking great risks in a long train ride, brought back the first news of the effects of the Hiroshima bomb. In a world exclusive, his story told *Express* readers that people were still dying mysteriously and horribly from something he called 'the atomic plague'.[4] Though his paper splashed Burchett's report as 'a warning to the world' it managed to get his name wrong, something which would surprise few foreign correspondents. Burchett's story was rubbished by the US military authorities; he later went to report both the Korean and Vietnamese wars from 'the wrong side' – that is, the communist north. One of Pilger's happiest memories is of introducing Burchett to Cameron, who reported on the H-bomb tests, and enjoying a lunch at which, when either of the two veterans was in the loo, the other would remark happily, 'He doesn't seem very well.'

Another pioneer of the politically engaged foreign correspondents of today is Michael Adams, now in his eighties and in retirement in Devon but following the Middle East as closely as ever. He had been a staff correspondent for the *Guardian* in the region and in Italy, but was freelance in 1968 when he visited the occupied Palestinian territories, notably the then-new Gaza Strip. Adams says that visit changed his life: he discovered an Israeli regime of punitive curfews, mass arrests, detentions without trial and the demolition of villages – some of the tinder that helped lead to the fire that burns today. He sent a series of politically explosive reports back to the paper. The first was published on 25 January 1968 and started with the stark statement that 'In the measures it is now taking against the civilian Arab population in the Gaza Strip, the Israeli army of occupation is disregarding the provisions of the 1949 Geneva Convention for the protection of civilians in time of war.' Adams himself had been captured by the Germans in the Second World War – he had been a bomber pilot – and went on: 'I had my ups and downs during four years as a prisoner of war in Germany, but the Germans never treated me as harshly as the Israelis are treating the Arabs of the Gaza Strip, the majority of whom are women and children.'

This, and subsequent pieces, caused uproar. Huge pressure rained down on the *Guardian*. Adams later wrote that the pro-Israel lobby consisted not simply of the openly political groups but came through the British Board of Jewish Deputies and influential Jewish public figures like Lord Janner and Lord Sieff of Marks & Spencer, who wrote directly to Alastair Hetherington, the paper's then editor. There were also of course many Zionist sympathizers among the paper's own journalists, not least reporters based in Israel. Adams wrote that at the time almost all press and BBC reports from the region came from people such as Moshe Brilliant of *The Times*, Walter Gross of the *Guardian*, Michael Elkins of the BBC and Francis Ofner of the *Observer*, who

> were not foreign correspondents in the normal sense of the term, since they were in fact at home in Israel, being themselves Jewish and in most cases actually Israeli citizens, and so subject in either case to the intense pressures of a society which expected the strictest loyalty ... It seems extraordinary that British editors, who would not think of employing in South Africa a South African who was a devotee of apartheid, or in Moscow a dedicated Russian communist, should see no objection to retaining in Israel Jewish correspondents whose sympathy for Zionism must call into question their objectivity.[5]

For Adams the break came when Hetherington spiked a piece he had written about the destruction of the village of Imwas, the Emmaus of the Bible, after the 1967 war. The two had a blazing row and Hetherington told Adams that he would not publish any more of his reporting from the Middle East because 'I no longer feel able completely to trust what you write.' Adams, an intensely courteous and restrained man in person, said that this was 'painful' and the injunction was later partially lifted, though he was never treated as an objective reporter on Israel afterwards.

The most famous of the committed journalists of recent times have been John Pilger and Robert Fisk, both highly controversial figures among the conservative commentators who rarely, themselves, venture out to report in dangerous places. Pilger's name was twisted into a verb meaning, roughly, to exaggerate in a left-wing fashion; Fisk had the honour of being treated in a similar way by the *Spectator* magazine, after warning vigorously of the dangers of the Iraq War and over-estimating the Iraqi defences round Baghdad. Pilger, born in Australia in 1939, arrived in Britain in 1962, and had the great good luck to work for the

Daily Mirror at the zenith of its Cudlipp triumph, when radical journalism was welcome and money was no object. After his tours of the
poorer parts of northern England, which shook and surprised him, Pilger
began to get foreign assignments. He devised an itinerary for himself
that took him 'across every continent, from Rio to Lake Titicaca in the
Andes, from the islands of Polynesia to Papua, Laos, India, the Levant,
Africa . . .'[6] Expecting scorn from Cudlipp, he simply got back a 'Yes!'
scrawled on his proposal and began to explore the world and develop
his left-wing vision. As he later recalled, he once sent a cable asking
what he should do next and received a simple reply: 'YOU WRITE.
WE PUBLISH.' Pilger went on to report from many of the world's
troublespots, from Vietnam and Cambodia to Eritrea and Palestine and
the segregated south of the United States. He wrote coruscating newspaper articles, made hugely controversial personal films and generally
stirred things up with much vigour. Yet Pilger could ignore many of
his British critics because he, unlike them, actually went and saw for
himself. The agonies and wars which other reporters simply described
became for him evidence of a worldwide struggle between ruthless
capitalist powers, notably the US, and the wretched of the earth.

   The career of Fisk, who first became known for his courageous
reporting of Northern Ireland for *The Times* from 1969 and later
became the best-known journalistic advocate of the cause of the dis-
possessed Arabs, has many parallels. Fisk was brought up during the
Second World War to the sound of BBC war correspondents such as
Charles Gardner, Richard Dimbleby and Wynford Vaughan-Thomas –
indeed he can still recite parts of their scripts even now. He started on
the *Sunday Express*, in his words, 'chasing vicars who had run off with
starlets'. But in Northern Ireland, he was shocked by the treatment
being meted out by British soldiers to local protesters, rather as Pilger
had been radicalized by his reporting on the north of England a few
years earlier. Just as Pilger had hands-off editorial treatment from
Cudlipp and the *Mirror*'s Lee Howard, so Fisk was given his head
by the then home editor of *The Times*, Charles Douglas-Home, who
appeared earlier in this book in a less heroic light. Fisk, indeed, also
won the early support of James Cameron when he had a huge run-in
with the British army over a story revealing that soldiers were using
forged accreditation to pass themselves off as journalists. (Which, by
the way, partly explains the John Simpson anecdote earlier.) After a

brief posting in Portugal, he was sent to the Middle East and has been based there – with a second home in Dublin – ever since. His reporting of the hideous massacres of Palestinians by Lebanese militia after the Israeli invasion of southern Lebanon in 1982 at Sabra and Chatila camps was a dark masterpiece of controlled, detailed denunciation. Since then Fisk, from his Beirut flat, has criss-crossed the region, reporting massacres, uprisings and strange disappearances with all the passionate, single-minded engagement of an uncorrupted boy.

His critics call him an anti-American ranter. Though he has had more awards than Marshal Zukhov, they accuse him of exaggeration. His editor, Leonard Doyle, says Fisk is simply the most professional, meticulous and courageous journalist he has ever worked with, generous with his time and scrupulous with his facts. Fisk himself says that his great advantage is simply the number of years he has spent in the Middle East: no one can tell him that the Israelis weren't involved in a massacre, because he was there and saw it happen; or that Saddam did not use gas in the Iran–Iraq War, because he was there and he saw the corpses. Some foreign desks move their correspondents around every three years to stop them 'going native': Fisk argues instead that the correspondent who does not understand the language and history of his area, who fails to know the people whose fates he records, is far more likely to simply tell the story as the great powers would like it told. He quotes an Israeli journalist: 'Our job is to monitor the centres of power.'

So those are a few of the missionaries, telling stories about how things are, not to the natives out there, but to the natives back home. But do we want to listen? At our worst, most introspective moments, we can be so cut off with our material goods and our celebrity culture that we know almost as little about the rest of humanity as South Sea islanders when ships full of cloth-coated men first arrived.

The Natives Back Home: Selfish and Dim?

In some ways the pioneer correspondents of the 1930s had things much easier. Readers were not sated by images of violence and famine. They were easier to shock and to rouse. Now it is harder. The foreign correspondents have to reinvent their stories all the time. More vivid and instant reporting has not engaged audiences more passionately. Far from it. For a while, the arrival of colour television pictures of fighting suggested that wars would become more politically costly for advanced societies to wage. The impact of television during the Vietnam War on American public opinion is the most famous example – it had a broadly 'anti-war' effect. The televised scenes of dead American soldiers being paraded on the streets of Mogadishu was supposed for a while to make the use of US troops abroad virtually impossible. Similarly, for a while, more immediate coverage of famines and disaster suggested that the viewers would be moved to action. Biafra shocked; Ethiopia, with a little help from Bob Geldof, roused; but today's famines get a weaker response.

Image fatigue set in. The scenes of savagery in the Balkan conflicts did lead to belated Western intervention, and angry campaigns in the British, French, Italian, American and other media for that intervention. But if you follow the trail back through the memoirs of the politicians of the time, it becomes quite clear that the West's involvement was always on the edge, a marginal decision. Public opinion did not indicate that people felt immediately threatened, as people had in the Second World War and the Cold War. Viewers who had become accustomed to the constant flicker of images of pain and death found it easy to turn away and soak themselves in the consolations of booming consumer societies. In Africa the sheer savagery of local wars led to a sense of helplessness and even boredom in the West – a quasi-racist assumption that Africa would always be like that. The scale of the continent's challenges, the stupid nastiness of some of its leaders, the corruption of others – well, these were dilemmas that just went round and round. It cannot be said too often that news is a story, a narrative, and if it does not seem to be 'going somewhere', but simply circles, readers and viewers stop wanting to know. That was the Northern Ireland peace process problem; and the Israeli–Palestinian problem; and the modern African problem.

Apart from image fatigue, technology had created another set of problems. The reporter is now dangerously reliant on the computer and email: Fisk was trained in Dublin to take apart, mend and reassemble a telex machine, and could keep himself operating in dirty, obscure terrain. But when his computer moans 'total disk failure' he is lost: 'I can't mend a computer and I don't know of any journalist who can.' The jump in technology has had a far greater impact for broadcasters abroad. As we saw earlier, BBC correspondents like Jeremy Bowen and Martin Bell found that twenty-four-hour news channels demanded their presence in front of the camera so often it was hard to find the time to actually go off and see for themselves. Satellite phones and fast-turnaround electronic news-editing systems meant they had the technical ability to feed more news reports too; and the desk-bound editors in London wanted more reports: they were fighting CNN and Sky. Reporters who had previously been able to tell their editors they were heading off with a group of fighters and then disappear for three days at a time, now found themselves calling in on the hour. As Kate Adie put it,

> Increasingly, hacks were tethered to the satellite dish, always on hand to deliver the 'live spot' in a curious belief that rabbiting on live is a more relevant and informed kind of reporting; in reality, someone stuck next to a dish for hours on end is the last creature on earth to have learned anything new, and probably unaware of a corpse twenty yards away.[7]

Today, argues Victoria Brittain, in similar style, there is a new-style foreign correspondent who is flown in at short notice, clutching their flak jacket and satellite phone:

> These expensive people are now expected to make themselves worthwhile by the sheer volume of work they produce and the competitive speed at which they produce it. There is not much time left for living – or thinking – and certainly not for becoming a specialist on a country or region ... CNN's Christiane Amanpour, for instance, is expected to be able to manage effortlessly not only the flak-jacket work in Bosnia, Iraq or Afghanistan, but also, in the same tone but with a new outfit, a full-scale British Royal funeral. At news organisation headquarters the reign of the desk editors over the foreign correspondents has begun. The former get up early, read papers, magazines and news agencies on the internet, and are then ready to tell the latter where to go and what to write.

This applies to newspaper foreign correspondents as well as to broadcasters, though not quite as violently. Leonard Doyle, the foreign editor of the *Independent*, is a good example on the pros and cons of the new technological age. His paper is a relatively poor one, with just nine overseas correspondents; it now has nobody in Moscow, or Berlin, or Beijing. But he manages: 'What has changed in the past five years is that the online media means that we can now read a far wider range of English-language papers around the world, including in Asia, and are a far better informed desk than ever before.' In the old days, he would have had access to the rather bare Reuters and AP newswire services, Ceefax and the BBC World Service bulletins; now, through Googlenews, he can scan a wide selection of American papers, and English papers from India, Pakistan, Russia, Australia, and even places like Cambodia, too. When I spoke to him he had just confirmed a tip sent in from Pakistan about a diplomatic row, via the Lahore press. The *Independent* then uses other foreign-based journalists, including BBC stringers, to follow up what looks interesting from London. On a bigger story, Doyle can deploy one of his handful of excellent correspondents, such as Phil Reeves in Delhi, Rupert Cornwell in Washington or John Lichfield in Paris. On the one hand, this means Doyle can offer a more comprehensive coverage than a small staff would once have allowed him. But on the other it means that much more of the initiative has to come from him, and from London. The more head office is involved, the less ideas and stories come from the reporters out there, sniffing around for themselves. As with many of the US bureaus of all British news organizations, journalism can be reduced to a glorified and stylish rewrite service.

But there is another side to this, the careers of the 'firemen' sent from London at the drop of a trilby and expected to become instant experts; some of the greatest talents in Fleet Street were just such. Today, this is exemplified by the career of Ann Leslie of the *Daily Mail*. Given that for much of her career she battled against the bone-headed prejudices of men who thought women shouldn't be allowed to do real reporting, it is a pleasing irony that the last of the true 'firemen' is called Ann. A convent girl who won a scholarship to Oxford, she nevertheless came up through newspapers the hard way. Joining the northern office of the *Daily Express* in the early 1960s was no joke for a middle-class young woman: Leslie turned up smartly dressed on her first day and was greeted by her news editor with the words: 'You're not in the fucking Savoy today, Miss – and you're keeping a good man out of a job.' She was given the worst jobs in order to break her. At one point, they sent her to Oldham to interview a dwarf who had been at school with Cary Grant. She arrived in a blizzard, found him when he came home, and was ushered in to be served whisky from his kettle until his furious Amazonian wife arrived and kicked the by-now-pissed Leslie out. Surviving, then thriving, she went on to interview a little-known but opinionated pop combo on 'youth' issues until her editor decided he'd had quite enough of the Beatles in his paper. She was then offered a column in London for the *Express*, where she was advertised on the side of buses as the voice of youth – 'She's Young, She's Provocative and She's only 22'.

At this point Leslie was set fair to be an early example of what are now called 'Polly Filler' columnists, turning out second-hand opinions, fluffed up to sound brash or – worse – 'controversial' to order. But she did something remarkable. She decided 'I didn't like my column – you know the old thing, "someone's boring me, I think it's me" – and I really didn't feel that I knew enough. So I quit.' By most standards giving up a column on a national paper is journalistic suicide; like being offered your first recording contract and turning it down. But it saved Leslie. After feature writing for the *Express*, she was spotted by the young David English, recently back from Washington, who gave her her first foreign jobs and who later hired her when he was asked to edit the *Daily Mail*. Though never a staffer, she has worked for it ever since and worships the memory of English, who was a lifelong enthusiast for foreign stories. She has been virtually everywhere, zig-zagging through Africa, the Middle East, America and the former Soviet bloc. She was in Berlin when the wall came down, doing what she dryly describes as 'my Housewife-Superstar bit'. Ahead of the pack, working her contacts, she realized 'something was in the air'. She is an instinctive reporter, who briefs herself thoroughly, has won endless awards and defends the role of the fireman: 'The advantage is that you carry your readers with you . . . Correspondents based abroad go native. It might seem to them a boring story but the fact is, readers here haven't heard it before.'

At the same time as the consumer societies at home grew richer, the news agenda changed towards gardening, holidays, self-improvement and fashion, stripping budgets from foreign departments and resulting in the closure of bureaus or the cutting adrift of foreign stringers. Don

McCullin, the famous war photographer, whose career took him to most of the wars of the 1960s and 1970s, reflected before he was fired from his paper in 1984:

> I still work for the *Sunday Times*, but they don't use me. I stand around in the office, and don't know why I'm there. The paper has completely changed: it's not a newspaper, it's a consumer magazine, really no different from a mail-order catalogue. And what do I do, model safari suits? . . . People are starting to reject, or at least turn their backs on, my sort. They seem happy with the way the press is developing. They certainly don't need me to show them nasty pictures. I should wise up: what is the point of killing yourself for a newspaper proprietor who wouldn't bat an eyelid on hearing you'd died?

In his book he decided that there was a shock wave going through Fleet Street and the whole magazine world:

> It was the unofficial announcement of the end of photo-journalism. These were the monetarist-sharp Eighties and they didn't want any more shocking pictures of war, horror and famine. They wanted style. They wanted to go for consumer images. No marketing operation wanted its products advertised alongside a dying child in Ethiopia or Beirut. Now they didn't have to worry any more. The newspapers were on their side.[8]

Perhaps the most coherent example of the new pessimism about foreign news came from Godfrey Hodgson, another former foreign editor of the *Independent*, who went to work for the Reuters foundation. Writing in 2000 he analysed the fall in interest in foreign news and concluded:

> Viewers and readers who are less interested in international news than they were before the collapse of the Soviet Union are not stupid . . . They are behaving in a perfectly rational way. From 1914 to 1991, international news was frightening. It could kill you. Now, rightly or wrongly, people are not afraid that a new war is going to affect them. Its consequences will be borne by foreigners with ragged clothes and the pinched faces of hunger or by a handful of professional soldiers who have volunteered to accept a relatively small chance of coming to harm . . . Western readers

and viewers have no motive beyond idle curiosity to concern themselves with events abroad except for a small minority who take real personal responsibility for understanding and intervening in the world's conflicts.

He expressed something close to personal disgust at the inward-turned consumer societies, rather like Don McCullin, noting that people in the West were no longer afraid of war, but of other things, like genital herpes, incompetent surgeons, the consequences of eating too much butter, or having a poor sex life, or the dangers of litigation. Foreign news was suffering from 'the end of the grand narrative'.

And then came September 11. But Hodgson was not just another prophet caught out by events. Quite the reverse. Writing some eighteen months before al-Qaeda struck, he argued that if the Western news agenda did not embrace the breakdown of civil society in parts of the former Soviet Union, or the failed states of Africa, or the Middle East, 'we will be in the position, not of privileged post-moderns, sure that we are beyond the power of the angry billions of the South to hurt us, but of the heedless Edwardians who could not see that they were playing croquet on the edge of a volcano.'⁹ And so it happened. Had the foreign correspondents been more numerous and highly valued before the attacks on the Twin Towers then the West would perhaps have been rather better informed about the nature of the fundamentalist agenda, and its lack of sympathy with the Ba'athist regime of Saddam Hussein.

Yet the journalists working in Afghanistan, Turkey, Indonesia, Pakistan and the Arabian peninsula who became so urgently sought out afterwards – the problem of finding Arabic-speaking correspondents is now frequently mentioned by London foreign editors – were based in exactly the sorts of places where bureaus had been closed and it was assumed would never reopen. Speaking at the London conference of World Press Freedom Day in May 2002, Phillip Knightley asked: 'What happened to all the foreign correspondents who could have explained what was happening? They were sacked to make way for lifestyle, showbiz and all the other trivia. Budget cuts mean foreign correspondents run from one conflict to another.' There is a lot of truth in this. As a newspaper editor in the late 1990s, I remember Robert Fisk arriving in my office to relay his latest scoop interview with a little-known figure called Osama bin Laden who was then holed up in Africa. Bob had been following him and al-Qaeda very closely and believed his warnings of a wider war against America were to be taken entirely seriously. We published Fisk's work, and gave it plenty of space, but I cringe to remember my faint boredom at the time – not *more* on Osama bin Whatnot? This is a morality tale about the importance of good foreign correspondents: they are there not to provide words about what the editor and home office think they know is happening, but to tell them what they don't know. The only duty of the people at home is to listen.

Good News Shock

And, once more, they are listening. Partly because of September 11, the market for foreign news is healthy again. Although, unlike celebrity and consumer news, where the gap between broadsheet and tabloid journalism has closed in Britain, there is now a yawning gulf in expertise. The papers which were once a byword for great foreign coverage, the *Daily Express*, the *Mail* and the *Daily Mirror*, now have hardly any foreign correspondents of their own. Stories with an immediate shock impact on readers are taken off the wire services, Internet or TV and rewritten in the office. But at the other end of the market, there has been a revival of interest in foreign news. We have already seen how the *Independent* honourably struggles to cope with nine correspondents. The *Daily Telegraph* has cut back both its numbers and its foreign pages in recent years but is nevertheless by historic standards well covered. The *Guardian* has sixteen full-time correspondents plus another ten freelance writers abroad contracted to work for the paper full-time, and four London-based foreign correspondents, or 'firemen'. Apart from the obvious places, it staffs Nairobi, Sydney, Zagreb and Iraq full-time. Its part-time stringers include reporters in Tehran, Mexico and Athens. Its foreign editor Harriet Sherwood says that 'the only place I think we are seriously under-covered is South America. Though we have regular freelances in most countries, this is the area I want to look at next.'

She is openly envious of *The Times* as well she might be, for under its new editor Robert Thomson, an Australian, that paper has hugely increased its foreign coverage. Its foreign editor Martin Fletcher puts this down more to Thomson's interests than to September 11 as such. 'Since he's taken over, the number of [foreign] pages has gone up from three a day to six a day, and often eight or more. I've hired four more full-time correspondents recently.' *The Times* now has seventeen full-time overseas staffers but also ten more or less full-time 'super-stringers' and thirty-three others contracted to work for the paper. Beyond that, its internal list shows addresses or contacts everywhere from Iceland and Hungary to Peru and Cambodia. Even *The Times*, though, is dwarfed by the huge world news-gathering operation of the *Financial Times* which with its German and US editions considers itself a global paper and has no fewer than 172 reporters on its books in forty-three bureaus around the world. It is a specialist newspaper with a strong business and financial bias but its overseas reach is longer than any British newspaper in the often-recalled glory days of the 1950s or 1960s. The BBC news-gathering operation is bigger still, with 250 correspondents and reporters and forty-one bureaus which range from one person and a phone to the large, complex and well-equipped Washington newsroom. Granted, the BBC runs a World Television service, and has alongside it the World Service radio operation, which is also massive; still, compared with the tentative expeditions of *Panorama* teams in the 1950s, setting out with their aircraft tickets for New York or Kenya, this is a full global operation far bigger than ever before. Like the major newspapers, the BBC is concentrating more time and energy on the Arab world and on the Far East than it used to.

There is, at the upper end of the market, absolutely no evidence of 'dumbing down' in foreign news. Papers without huge numbers of correspondents may, like the *Independent*, emphasize the quality and writing of the people they do have; but so did the old *News Chronicle* when James Cameron worked there. At the *Guardian* they are likelier than any other paper to put long foreign stories on the front page, frequently ones away from everyone else's daily news list; they also strive very hard to 'join the dots' and run longer reads than competitors. Harriet Sherwood talks of her readers' post-September 11 'increased appetite for making sense of global events'. She is running more pieces aimed at connecting events in different parts of the world and agonizes particularly about how to make coverage of the EU more engaging – for instance, by running pan-European analysis articles about different attitudes to ID cards, or European Muslims, or fees for education. 'I could fill the foreign pages ten times over with stories of terrible things happening around the world.' She adds: 'I am also trying to encourage our writers to look for cultural, human interest and humorous stories.' Whether it is *The Times* with its expanded foreign pages, or the BBC's now heavy stream of foreign news packages, including stories deliberately selected from places mainstream news has forgotten about, there is a good case for arguing that Britain in the early 2000s is going through a golden age in overseas news reporting, just twenty years after many experienced reporters felt the trade was dying out.

The foreign correspondents themselves will continue to bitch and worry. They will dislike the idea that things are going well for them, because they are natural moaners. Certainly, they have plenty to worry about. We have already discussed the pressure of twenty-four-hour news on broadcast correspondents' ability to actually go and find things out; and the constant problem of interesting readers and viewers in apparently circular and hopeless dilemmas, whether in the Middle East or in Africa. Then there is the problem of television creating the news wherever it lands, attracting violence and protest simply because it is there. During the Genoa summit of the G8 which I attended as a BBC reporter, there were spectacularly violent anti-globalization demonstrations. The protesters knew very well that the world's cameras were there: TV reporters from Tokyo, Trondheim and Toronto were lined up in serried ranks by the old Genoese port, relaying the pictures and stories around the globe. As a result, the infuriated leaders of the world's most powerful countries decided they could only meet in future in the most remote settings – on top of a Canadian mountain, or on a sealed-off island, surrounded by US Navy patrol boats. That will be a problem for decent journalism, trying to hold political power to account, in the decades ahead. And there are other serious questions facing journalism about the behaviour of powerful governments, including the United States, to war and overseas correspondents. The embedding of correspondents in the British and US forces in the Iraq War was not judged, in the end, to have produced a gung-ho mood of itself, even if particular broadcasters waved the flag excessively from the newsrooms at home. But the war on terrorism has so far been a badly reported war, in which key questions like the whereabouts of Osama bin Laden were left to drift into the ether.

The British reporter Anthony Loyd, voted foreign correspondent of the year in 2002, recorded in *The Times* that May how the true story of a minor operation in Afghanistan was inflated by army officers into a great success against terrorists, and faithfully reported that way by journalists who were kept in the Bagram airbase and not allowed to travel independently. Three al-Qaeda terrorists in eastern Afghanistan had fired upon coalition special forces, killing or wounding two of them. A follow-up operation by US troops had apparently discovered ammunition, weapons and cave complexes. In fact, reported Loyd, a small number of armed men, probably Afghans, stumbled across six Australian SAS:

> Surprised, the men raised their weapons and were shot in the chest by the SAS. Requesting extraction, the SAS were surprised by the arrival of two Chinooks full of American paratroopers, who began searching a nearby village. By their own account, the Americans admitted that one of the two weapons they found was an ancient Lee Enfield which they took from a villager's home as a trophy. The caves they discovered had livestock in them. The incident is forgotten now.

This minor incident is nevertheless a classic example of the way British and US operations may be building up anger in parts of the world British and American citizens now hear little about. Loyd continued:

> The few British journalists who opt to stay away from Bagram and report from the field are regarded as mavericks who are 'not on side' and not to be trusted. It is shameful that so few organisations have challenged the Ministry of Defence on its information policy and removed their personnel from the pool system. Hungry for footage of 'our boys' the media has largely sold out on ethics and integrity . . . In truth the public does not know what is happening in Afghanistan today, or how British troops are being utilised. If it believes the anodyne reports of the 'pool' reflect events, as spokesmen suggest, then it is sadly mistaken.

Much the same could be said of post-war Iraq, which is simply too dangerous for many journalists. When I asked Robert Fisk about the glamorous image of the foreign correspondent's life, he was quick to admit that there were times when he sat on the balcony of his Beirut flat and watched the Mediterranean through the palm trees outside, and perhaps punched the air at the thought of a story or pictures he had got out, which had made headlines round the world, and felt life was sweet. But, he added, the life of a proper correspondent, who kept away from the pack and tried to discover what was going on for himself, was also hard, dangerous and lonely. It involves long days of uncomfortable and perilous travel in rickety cars, or being fired on. It involves food poisoning and sudden hunches which persuade you not to journey to a place of danger. 'At the end of the day, it does take its toll on you. I feel very tired sometimes. I feel angry.' But Fisk, like most foreign correspondents of real quality, is an unconvincing depressive. He quickly moves on to another story, taking a great gamble, and a terrifying drive along a road being shelled by the Israeli navy, to get vital pictures and words back to London. Afterwards saying: 'I remember sitting on that balcony thinking, we did it, we did it, we fucking did it. We took the risk and it was worth it.'

At the best that's what it is all about. They take the risk and it is worth it. *Salut*.

Two: Columnists, from Pundits to Panderers

It is like remembering your first cigarette, girlfriend, heartbreak. My first column came when I was with the *Scotsman* in the late 1980s. It was about 850 words long and appeared in the Saturday paper under the title 'Tribunes and Tyrants'. Shortly afterwards I joined *The Economist* and wrote a longer weekly column there under the name 'Bagehot' after that paper's most famous contributor. We were encouraged to argue but only within the limits of a fiercely policed liberal free-trade agenda that has been the paper's spirit since Victorian times; and we were told the hidden secret of *The Economist* and much other opinionated journalism – 'simplify, then exaggerate'. Then, a few years on, the *Independent*'s Peter Jenkins, one of the most famous columnists of his time, suddenly died and I was offered his slot, a three-times-a-week column on politics and current affairs. When I was editor I carried on writing columns for that paper. When sacked, I went off to write more columns still, for the *Express* in the middle of the week and the *Observer* at the end of the week. Next, after I joined the BBC, I wrote a weekly column of a different kind still for the *Daily Telegraph*. In one of those mad calculations columnists sometimes do on the back of an envelope, I reckoned that, by the time of writing this, and without including one-off columns or early ones, or columns written to be broadcast, I had written some 1.45 million words of newspaper columns – that is, rather more than ten times the number of words in the book you are currently holding. That is a lot of words; and some of them had several syllables. But this record, during fifteen years or so, is not impressive compared with the real word-shovellers of recent times. Bernard Levin once calculated his *Times* columns as amounting to 14 million words.

The Pundits

The most important columnists are the pundits. Some people will disagree with that. They will say they are only the most self-important ones. But the pundits are the journalists who try to influence in some way the course of public life, by putting arguments to those in power and expecting to be heard. They do not regard themselves as mere entertainers. They look to their readers as a community not as followers but listeners and participators in a wider conversation. Pundits today include Simon Jenkins, Peter Riddell, Michael Gove and Matthew Parris on *The Times*; Polly Toynbee, David Aaronovitch and Jonathan Freedland on the *Guardian*; Will Hutton and Andrew Rawnsley on the *Observer*; Matthew d'Ancona on the *Sunday Telegraph*; Don Macintyre and Yasmin Alibhai-Brown on the *Independent*; Boris Johnson on the *Spectator* and *Daily Telegraph*, and others. They are a formidable, erudite and well-informed crew. Yet the golden age of the pundit may have passed. Few individual columnists have the influence on centre-left thinking that the late Peter Jenkins or Hugo Young during the 1980s did or on the right that T. E. Utley and Sam Brittan once had.

British journalism has had great and opinionated political writing from very early on, notably in magazines and reviews. The Somerset polymath Walter Bagehot, who wrote upwards of 2,000 long articles on everything from economics and banking to Shakespeare and Cabinet reshuffles during his sixteen-year editorship of *The Economist*, was perhaps the most complete pundit of Victorian England. Other, greater prose stylists, such as Hazlitt and Cobbett, were also political columnists but attacked from the radical outside; unlike Bagehot, they had no notion of influencing Westminster directly. Some modern journalists were intelligent enough to have looked back at the great political writers of the nineteenth century and learned lessons. Hazlitt, Cobbett and Bagehot all have a remarkably clear, vigorous style and all used Anglo-Saxon words, rather than French-based ones whenever they could. They are all vivid and use direct reporting at times. They can be funny, but reserve humour for making political points. Cobbett was the most brutal of the three, and his furious invective changed direction rather a lot. He switched his mind and position several times on the most important issues, and seemed entirely unabashed; modern columnists have done the same. Hazlitt invented the critical term 'gusto' and demonstrated it in his short, jabbing sentences and sensual expressions. He is a fighting writer: one critic said of him: 'Prose needs to represent the swell, the stretch, the imprint of the moment. Every word should strike like a fist, while continuous prose should have a flexible crinkling sweep . . .'[10] And Bagehot, a Whig writer well to the right of Hazlitt and infinitely more pro-Establishment than Cobbett, matches either of them in the clarity of his amazing intelligence, building up arguments and almost playing with them in mental delight. The British journalistic tradition has been as vigorous in political polemic as in any other sphere. Many of the lessons of these writers were picked up by George Orwell and passed on through him to a spawn of later twentieth-century political writers.

Yet punditry, in the modern sense of named political writers in mainstream newspapers seeking to exercise great influence, comes from America. 'Pundit' is a corruption of the Hindu word pandit, coming in turn from the Sanskrit 'pandita', meaning scholar. It was first used in the West as an early feminist joke. Some New York housewives mocked their pompous husbands when they formed a club to debate 'the truth' in 1854 by calling them pundits. The word, still satirical, meandered its way into mainstream American-English and by the 1920s was being used as a tag for Walter Lippmann of the *New York World*, a great and long-deceased paper which invented the idea of the 'op-ed' page – the one with the pundits and often a cartoon too. After the First World War, the United States was just beginning to confront its destiny as the world's rising great power, yet most Americans were stuck in relatively ignorant, cut-off towns. Lippmann, known as the Moses of Liberalism, helped fill the gap: 'Despite rising education levels in the country, the vast majority of people outside New York, Boston and Washington had almost no access to quality information about the state of affairs in the world – with the exception of those who read Walter Lippmann.'[11] Lippmann's genius was to convince the Washington power brokers that they needed him as a conduit to the country at large, while convincing his huge readership, swollen by syndication to scores, then hundreds, of local papers, that they needed him as their eye on Washington. He became the ultimate political middleman of America's golden years. Lippmann survived well into the television age, still punditing up to the mid-1960s, but he was joined by many more – Joe Alsop, the Scots-born James Reston, then the right-wingers William Buckley, George Will and Charles Krauthammer. Because of the vast sprawl of America and the consequent need for widely sold syndicated columns interpreting Washington's power struggles to the nation, they became influential and rich in a way few British journalists could quite imagine.

Though there were regular political voices before him, notably Garvin and Hugh Massingham of the *Observer*, the first potential imitator of Lippmann in British life was Henry Fairlie. Fairlie eventually left London for Washington and died there – not rich, not powerful, but very poor and rather sad. He was a rare example of a journalist who bewitched almost everyone who came into contact with him. He was born into the journalistic purple: his father had been a journalist and died in a taxi of a heart attack after a session in El Vino's – the trade's equivalent of a Military Cross won storming a machine-gun nest. With what one friend called his 'delinquent plough-boy's grin', Fairlie was by all accounts a personally badly behaved man. His friend Alan Watkins wrote of him: 'Fairlie was a charmer, an adulterer, a drinker, often a beggar man, even (it must be said) on occasion a thief . . .'[12] His friend Peregrine Worsthorne wrote of his reckless extravagance, his gross philandering, his abysmal private life:

Fairlie, he said, ennobled in his mind the idea of political journalism because it was the only way in which he could

> justify the selfishness of a private life which often left his wife and children without the price of a pair of shoes or, far worse, the wherewithal to pay the children's school fees. He had to write like an angel so as to justify behaving like a devil. The lower he sank in debauchery the higher he aimed in his work.[13]

And those, mark it, were his friends. Fairlie, apart from a propensity to spend money he earned immediately on spontaneous parties in expensive hotels, was constantly in debt and famously arrested immediately after taking part in a high-minded debate on the BBC radio programme *Any Questions*. He was taken to Winchester prison; his wife professed herself pleased at least to know where he was sleeping that night. Fairlie eventually fled for the US after losing a libel case brought by Lady Antonia Fraser. His political journalism, first for the *Spectator* and then a variety of newspapers, brought a freshness, wit and boldness that made many forgive him his sins. He was a passionate defender of the British parliamentary system against its modish critics, and wrote a good book on the subject. He was almost equally interested, however, in American politics and had the capacity to make himself a truly influential pundit; he spoke to his friend Anthony Howard with awe and admiration about the role of the pundits in the US. But Fairlie was brought down by his unreliability. The truth is, writing a consistently good political column is ferociously hard work.

And Peter Jenkins, who came nearer than anyone to becoming the Lippmann of the British, was nothing if not a hard worker. Toothy, genial, formidably clever and well-connected, Jenkins wrote for the *Guardian*, the *Sunday Times* and – most successfully – the *Independent*. Like Joseph Alsop in Washington, he gave splendid and frequent dinner parties, and mingled socially with Labour and Social Democrat politicians, patrolling their lawns and drinking their wines as he gave advice about the danger of the unions or the need for a stronger line on nuclear defence. Jenkins was a Konigswinter journalist. Konigswinter is a tiny place just outside Bonn which, when Bonn was capital of West Germany, played host to annual conferences of British and German politicians, journalists and civil servants. These were followed by Franco-British conferences, Spanish–British conferences and there were endless meetings for pro-American British journalists too. Now the global leaders' meetings at Davos are far better known. But Konigswinter stands for the attempt to create a pan-European ruling class, a generation of opinion-formers who had left behind the enmities of the Second World War and looked to the European community. Peter Jenkins, like Hugo Young, first of the *Sunday Times* and later the *Guardian*, spoke for this fresh vision of a European Britain, anti-communist but also more socially inclusive and kinder than the American model. He was close to a succession of centre-left politicians – Anthony Crosland, David Owen, Roy Jenkins, Denis Healey – and was a great supporter of the breakaway SDP when Labour split over Europe and nuclear disarmament.

Jenkins wrote once, twice, or thrice a week, depending on the paper employing him at the time. His wife Polly Toynbee described his working practices. Writing political columns

> was a lifestyle congenial to him, with his taste for intense talk and debate, long lunches, many friends and manic fits of writing against the clock . . . The problem was juggling a large number of highly complex issues, so in the course of one day there might be . . . defence, but also a long pre-arranged lunch on prison policy, and perhaps a meeting at Chatham House about the Gulf.[14]

Jenkins, moving through Whitehall, Westminster and numberless foreign visits and summits, juggling notes and issues, learned that the American model for a columnist could not be exactly reproduced in London, even when he was managing three informed and reporterly columns a week. The problem was that without syndication you did not have the reach or influence, which was what he really wanted. He wrote in the *Guardian*, reflecting on his trade: 'A man addressing the readers of, say, 150 newspapers three times a week could see just about anybody he wanted to see in Washington, and have his telephone calls returned.' In Britain this was not true and columnists were edged out in the telephone call department by lobby correspondents, diplomatic editors and others. Nevertheless, 'there was something to learn from the manner of the American columns, their blend of reportage, analysis and editorialising.' The political columnist suffered not from too little information, but too much. 'The difficulty is to know what it means ... The writer of a political column spends a great deal of his time reading the papers on behalf of his readers, trying to make patterns out of torrents of words.'[15]

This is not only an excellent description of Jenkins's own columns, but also of the ideal political column. Columnists are not priests, but fallible hacks. To start with, their opinions are of no intrinsic interest. The reader has to be persuaded they are useful. This could be because they are simply better at expressing the prejudices and instincts of readers than the readers are themselves, and there is a market in that. But it hardly takes the national conversation forward. The best pundits are worth reading because they bring you information from the heart of power and then set it in context, in a single piece of argument which strips away the dross and detail, and helps you see what is really happening in the Foreign Office, Downing Street, the State Department or the White House. They have to glean information, a higher reporting, and then they have to process it. This bit matters, that bit doesn't. This argument is the same one they've been making for years. That bit is new. A U-turn – why? What does it mean?

Only after all that hard work has been done, might we be persuaded their opinions are of value. Then, the pundit can make the claim of any expert: I am worth listening to because of what I know, what I remember, and because of how seriously I have thought this through. Stephen Bayley, the critic, puts it well, quoting Victor Hugo, who said that imagination is intelligence with an erection: 'In a similar way, an opinion is knowledge that has been given a particular direction. Unmediated knowledge is just data, dull and meaningless. Opinions are informed patterns of thought, they are what makes knowledge valuable.'[16] You can then spit the best pundits out on political grounds for being too left wing, or right wing, or slavishly keen on a certain politician; but at least you know they are giving you something to chew on first.

Hugo Young said he was less politically connected than Jenkins. He was not a player, just an observer. He wasn't writing for the benefit of politicians. He had to talk to politicians, and officials, and found they could be excellent company, but it was always 'supping with the devil'. The columnist had to write as an outsider and discover as an insider. There was a limit to the intimacy:

I can think of no more than three politicians I've regarded as friends. Friends, in this business, are poison to the work. That's a social tic I can't shake off. For example, I've had fewer politicians in my house, for the possibly ignoble reason that I'd find it hard to be honestly disagreeable about them in print after that.[17]

It may be simply a matter of temperament: Hugo was private and fastidious, inclined to moral agonizing, while Peter was gregarious and boisterous, and inclined to argument. But talking around Whitehall and Westminster, it seems that although Hugo Young regarded himself as an outsider, and relatively friendless among politicians, they thought he was close to many of them. He never became hip-and-thigh close to a minister or party leader, as Jenkins did to David Owen (though it did not stop him describing Owen in print on a famous occasion as a megalomaniac) but he did have excellent and friendly relationships with scores of leading MPs and diplomats.

Do pundits influence them? Jenkins and Young were great ralliers of the liberal, pro-European and moderate left, who made the arguments that preceded Tony Blair's rise to power with greater force and clarity than most politicians. Jenkins certainly helped stiffen the spine of Labour right-wingers and SDP leaders on issues of nuclear defence, which he passionately supported; Young reckoned he might have tipped the balance on some civil liberties issues. You could make similar points about the influence of some liberal economic pundits, such as Sam Brittan and Peter Jay, on Margaret Thatcher, and Utley's influence on Tory attitudes to Northern Ireland. But the main political pressure is from the electorate, who are in turn not much influenced by columnists; and columnists know it. In a nice twist, one of the best warnings about the dangers of pundits taking themselves too seriously came from Lippmann himself, writing in 1940. He had, he said, an almost fanatical conviction that columnists should not think of themselves as public personages. Frank Cobb was his former and famous New York editor. 'I am not adviser-at-large to mankind or even to those who read occasionally or often what I write. This is the code which I follow. I learned it from Frank Cobb who practiced it, and abjured me again and again during the long year when he was dying that more newspaper men had been ruined by self-importance than by liquor.'[18] Yet self-importance is hard to avoid when you are courted by Cabinet ministers and invited onto radio and TV programmes to tell the world what you think. It is ruinous, and it is addictive, and I should know.

And Jenkins and Young were indeed as much part of the post-war British political establishment as any elected individual. They both died relatively early, Jenkins at fifty-eight, in 1992, waiting for a lung transplant, and Hugo Young at sixty-four, in 2003, of cancer. At Jenkins's memorial service at St Margaret's, Westminster, virtually all the non-Thatcherite political class turned up, and there was a reading from Michael Heseltine, then president of the Board of Trade. At Young's memorial service in Westminster Cathedral, the congregation included most of the Cabinet, including the chancellor, Gordon Brown: Tony Blair, who had been savaged by Young over the Iraq War, was missing only because he was with President Bush for the state visit. And Chris Patten, the Tory politician who knew both men well, praised Young for his moral denunciations: 'when our principles turned out to be made of marshmallow, when our vision was plainly a fraud, when our behaviour was motivated by cowardice, the judgement came like a mighty blow to the head'. If that isn't being part of the Establishment, punditry as laid down by Lippmann, what is?

It is about authority. Like Lippmann, Reston, Alsop and others, Young and Jenkins won their authority by hard brain-work and reporting. They went. They saw. Above all, they read. They knew the detail of policy as well as the history of the political feuds that might underpin a current argument. Now there is a degraded version of punditry which is horribly appealing and has done much to reduce its authority. The problem is laziness, and money. Few modern pundits really work at the information-gathering side of the trade, but even the few shining examples who do no longer really fit Lippmann's Establishment position. Simon Jenkins is a proper information-gatherer. He meets and asks, he visits Baghdad and he has a formidable list of Establishment friends and contacts. But he is at an angle to the Labour government, too little impressed by them to desire much mingling. Peter Riddell, also of *The Times*, works hard in the old way but is not treated by his paper as a full-time, full-throated pundit, perhaps because his views are generally consensual. Polly Toynbee at the *Guardian* is also a proper worker, a phone-hammerer and someone who actually goes out to meet the public sector workers she writes about, and who cares about facts. Andrew Rawnsley of the *Observer* and Matthew d'Ancona of the *Sunday Telegraph* are well-connected, witty and shrewd analysts of the political scene; but they are read for their information rather than their political advice. They are both taken very seriously in Downing Street. Will Hutton, of the *Observer*, is a rare bird in modern punditry: after working in the City he is economically literate but has a very clear and strong social-democratic critique of the American (and Americo-British) variety of capitalism. With the huge success of his book *The State We're In*, Hutton did achieve a status of super-pundit, though Labour ministers read him not to have their minds changed, but to make themselves feel uneasy. Over at the *Independent*, Donald Macintyre has a special authority for his exemplary self-abnegation during the Wapping dispute, when he refused offers of re-employment after he resigned until his deputy and number three in the old *Times* labour team got jobs too. This rare example of good behaviour is a mark of the man. Macintyre is both well-connected and listened to; evidence to the Hutton Inquiry in the autumn of 2003 revealed that Tony Blair's inner circle read and reacted to his column in the *Independent*.

There are political writers who avoid the pitfalls of punditry by force of their literary personality. Alan Watkins would probably resist the word literary: he presents himself to the world as a rather down-to-earth Welsh observer of political and sporting life. He is a great deflator. His columns now tend to the nostalgic and some of his stories, it is said, have been told more than once. But Watkins has the inner ear of the great stylist; he writes almost exactly as he speaks, with cadences and twists of humour that no one else in British newspapers can match. His columns teach one little about the Blair government, but for anyone who cares about the language, they are weekly tutorials in good English. A similar point can be made about Matthew Parris, the former Tory speechwriter, Tory MP, diplomat and television interviewer, who has been more prolific than any other pundit of recent times.

It is a *Times* tradition to have columnists who can range widely – politics, travel, the economy, law, sex – and Parris is by far the best current example. Where Bernard Levin first danced, in the sixties and seventies, followed by William Rees-Mogg and Simon Jenkins, Parris now walks. He is simply one of the best writers of prose on these islands, and has a huge following – why? Because he can tell a story. Because, like most people he has political views without being a party fanatic. Because he has an engaging habit of standing up for the underdog, and going against the grain – backing John Major when the know-alls wouldn't, for instance. Because his range of interest, from llamas to remote islands, Tory history to gay rights, hill-walking to comedy, is so immense. But above all, because he can write beautifully and works so very hard. His claim to authority is unusual: he asks you to assent to what he says because he is so patently decent and so likeable. In his most productive period, between September 1988 and September 2002 he wrote 3,595 articles, an average of about five a week, including a *Times* column, four or five political sketches and other commissions for a vast range of publications, including the *Sun*, the *Investor's Chronicle* and the *Spectator*. At present, having dropped his sketch, Parris is writing about three columns a week and aims to work for the national papers for not less than a pound a word. I reckon his earnings to be at about £300,000 a year when he was at full pelt, and a bit less now; but let nobody who has not tried to do it tell you this is necessarily easy money.

Parris is the leader of the pack of personal pundits – that is, the writers making general points about politics and public life, but writing deliberately as themselves, with their foibles, lifestyle and own history on display, rather than adopting the Olympian distance of the Lippmann tradition. With Parris, or David Aaronovitch of the *Independent*, or Simon Hoggart of the *Guardian*, or Suzanne Moore of the *Mail on Sunday*, the regular reader will find out about their family, gardening or shopping habits, attitudes to smoking, food, fatherhood, sex and much else alongside the political observations. It is a different and in some ways a more dangerous sell than that offered by a Hugo Young or a Simon Jenkins. The underlying assumption is that authority comes not from gathering news and views across Whitehall lunch tables or in weekend phone calls with ministers, but from the reader knowing, and therefore trusting, the columnist. Know me, know my domestic situation, and read me as a friend, someone worth trusting because of the kind of person you know I am. Now as it happens, this writer does know all these people and I can therefore say that the Parris, Aaronovitch, Moore or Hoggart that so many people read on the page, seem very like their real selves. They are not putting on a persona for the column, or if they are it is also the persona they wear at public events. Good writers all, their idiosyncratic histories, attitudes and instincts come through the writing. So as a reader, if you like the style you may well be right to trust the column. The danger, however, is obvious. The columnist has thrown him or herself far more openly into the public arena and is likely to be judged like an actor, or TV star. In a confessional culture which turns us into voyeurs, there is no hiding place for them when things go wrong, or the columnist decides he or she is bored and wants to pull the drawbridge up.

But even these people, taking risks with their private identities, do not have the heft and influence of pundits twenty years ago. Is this simply because there are too many? It may be that, though a really powerful voice always finds its audience. More to the point, the shape of British politics has rather repelled punditry. The Blair government, after its flirtation with the third way, has eschewed big ideas and ideology, and is therefore not much given to arguing about great principles. It has turned to the detail of public service reform and management, which may be more important, but rarely makes a column sing. It goes to the specialists of the think tanks and academic research for its ideas. And the Conservatives, thrashing about in search of a strategy after their 1997 defeat, simply angered right-wing pundits. On all sides, the necessary groove between thinking, politically engaged journalists and politicians has been missing. It has been replaced by the entertaining and endless soap opera of Blairites and Brownites, or the twists and turns of Tory leadership woes before the coronation of Michael Howard; and these are relatively easy to write about, but hardly convey authority. They are a little too near entertainment and a little too far from urgent argument. So, instead, many pundits have turned away from the careful and laborious mix of political investigation, analysis and exposition favoured in the Jenkins–Young era, and turned instead to shouting.

There is a role for shouting columnists. There always has been. Cobbett was a shouter. In many of his modes, particularly when it came to crime, Bernard Levin on *The Times* was a shouter. This country contains many angry people and they like to hear their anger articulated. The furious denunciations of Labour's moral decay by Melanie Phillips or Peter Oborne in the *Daily Mail*; the passionate nostalgia and pessimism about the condition of England in the columns of Peter Hitchens; the fulminations from left-wing comedians in the *Guardian* or the *Independent* . . . all these cries of pain and despair sell newspapers. But the problem with shouting about how much you hate a politician or government is avoiding monotony. Columnists hired to be angry are caught in a trap: after being angry, what do you do next, except try your level best to be angrier? In the end, you go hoarse, adjectivally if not physically. To attract attention, you have to keep upping the ante, finding ingenious new forms of abuse, or even more alarming arguments. For Peter Oborne, whose columns range from the *Spectator* to the *Mail* and *Observer*, making him probably the most widely spread columnist of the early twenty-first century, it is a trivial problem. For he is a voice of Tory England, whose ruddy face and baggy tweed jackets, and fondness for horse racing and corduroys mark him as the latest inheritor of a timeless role on the political scene. There is always a market for that. Similarly, there are a certain number of semi-official positions in the centre and left of politics, so that at any one time there will be a recognized leading left-liberal voice (currently fought out between Polly Toynbee and Will Hutton) and a leading left-Opposition voice, such as Nick Cohen. These are important niches to stand in, and there is vigorous competition to speak for the major divisions in political life, and dissent about who is really the best. But for most opinionated pundits it is almost impossible not to end up becoming an over-packaged parody of your earlier self. This has happened to Richard Littlejohn on the *Sun* and Jeremy Clarkson at the *Sunday Times*. They become trapped. They probably both have many unexpected, moderate or subtle views; but they have no market for them.

The final group of star columnists don't bother with conventional politics at all. They have the techniques of the best political columnists but have turned them to other purposes – generally, the job of provocation and causing a fuss. Nobody is better at this than Julie Burchill, who infuriated many of the *Guardian*'s readers every Saturday before moving to *The Times*. The Burchill story of shy Bristol girl who broke into journalism at sixteen for the *New Musical Express* – 'hip young gunslinger' is the phrase generally used – and became an instant star for her writing on punk with her first husband Tony Parsons before emerging as 'Queen of the Groucho Club' in London's Soho and then decamping to Brighton, is well known. Having ditched two husbands and one son, opened and killed the *Modern Review*, enjoyed a self-publicized lesbian affair with the writer Charlotte Raven, survived long periods of cocaine addiction and generally been a bad girl, Burchill has used her own life as a constant source of copy. She progresses partly through highly publicized feuds which draw many of the rest of us helplessly in as goggling, slack-jawed spectators, revelling in her verbal aggression. In medieval Scotland there was a great tradition of 'flyting', in which two poets would compete to see who could abuse the other in the most inventively obscene and damaging way; a Burchill feud offers something of the same satisfaction. She picks enemies who can fight back – Toby Young, Martin Amis, Helen Fielding. Here she is, as a taster, in the middle of a feud some years ago with the self-publicizing American feminist academic Camille Paglia:

> I know ethnicity means a lot to you. You've a wop name, so you think you're Robert De Niro. These little girls, Jewish and middle class and whatever, are too nice, too well bred to fight back. I'm not. Don't believe what you read about the English; our working class, from where I'm proud to come, is the toughest in the world. I'm not nice. I'm not as loud as you, but if push comes to shove, I'm nastier. I'm ten years younger, two stone heavier, and I haven't had my nuts taken off by academia.

Burchill's packaging of her private life has been roundly attacked as freak-show journalism, childish and inconsistent. But it is another high-wire act that depends on verbal inventiveness and great skill to sustain. Although she is simply one of the liveliest prose-producers in the land, verbal pyrotechnics will never be enough. Burchill may have some zany opinions on Stalin and may sentimentalize the working classes, but she brings a voice into public debate that contradicts the vast majority of polite, middle-class, liberal-mimsy columnists she is up against. She's part of the British story too, and more similar in her attitudes to many ordinary women than the conventional press would like to admit. Other lifestyle columnists have performed similar services. John Diamond's column about living, then dying, with throat cancer brought that part of the human experience onto the page. Because he was a gifted and funny writer, his *Times* columns did a job that two dozen earnest medical journalists could not have matched.

Michael Bywater brings to life the dancing madness of the intelligent, almost too intelligent, male mind trapped in a sea of media-ocrity. Deborah Ross's weekly self-portraits of the cheerful but slovenly wife and mother, dragging through shopping and skiving the chores, come nearer to describing how much of the country actually lives than any of the thousands of glossy improve-your-life articles stuffing the weekend papers. These are people writing against the overbearing culture of liberal politeness and material gorging, smirking and shopping. They are worth their bag of oats. Where Henry Fairlie hid his disreputable life so that he could write heroic prose about the public weal, a succession of modern columnists parade their lives in the cause of honesty. Which, in a culture of euphemism and blandness, is a necessary corrective.

It is very difficult to do, as the scores of failed imitators show. But is it worth doing? In an article attacking Burchill after a complicated feud about cocaine, involving another journalist, Deborah Orr and her husband, the novelist Will Self (and if you think this is insanely introspective, try the Grub Street of Defoe or the literary world of Dickens and Thackeray; they were just the same), Yvonne Roberts attacked the whole Burchill project. Burchill had once said that she was in showbusiness, and Roberts replied that 'the conversion of columnist from side-show to star turn blocks more imaginative and diverse solutions to how the media can woo women . . .' Writers like Burchill, she went on,

> have begun to attack the very heart of newspapers since they eat up valuable space and come cheaper than funding a network of reporters or adequately resourcing long-term investigative journalism. Somewhere along the way, a less celebrity-dazzled editor might have coaxed something a lot more powerful and long-lasting from Julie than writing as a trivial pursuit.[19]

It is the allegation about what else the money and space could have bought that bites most. Columnists have engorged space, and are easy for editors; even highly paid ones do probably cost less than running long investigations or overseas correspondents. Columns have multiplied crazily in modern British newspapers. There are columns on gardens, cheap wine and etymology, columns on bicycling, on 'my loveable children', on birdwatching and sex with strangers, columns on every form of activity and dreaming known to urban mankind. There are ghosted columns by celebrities, and columns by celebrities that would have been much better had they been ghosted. Keith Waterhouse, voted by readers of the *British Journalism Review* as the greatest columnist now writing, pointed out that these columns are now offered 'like Sunday school prizes' to minor celebs, adding, 'Mercifully, their columnising careers do not generally last long – either their agent gets too greedy or the editor tires of them, or both.' Mostly, lifestyle and celebrity columns are a form of sub-journalism that requires no reporting or finding out and often no facts. A few, a very few, columnists are witty enough to write grippingly about almost nothing at all – the old greats like Ring Lardner and Flann O'Brien and the newer ones like Michael Bywater or Deborah Ross. But behind these, lumbering desperately and wittering as they lumber, are a thousand no-hopers who somehow stumble into print, wasting many innocent readers' time.

Take a single, typical Sunday, 16 November 2003 for example. It was a laborious and grimy task but I did it. I counted the columnists in the main national papers. I excluded the pieces which were really advice columns, or writing on cookery, gardening and drinks. I found more than seventy columnists. In its main section the *Observer* had Christina Odone (British–US relations), Andrew Rawnsley (ditto), David Aaronovitch (ditto), Mary Riddell (a ministerial scandal), Euan Ferguson (this and that), Will Hutton, Nick Cohen, Richard Ingrams and Ellie Levenson. But in other sections its columnists included Barbara Ellen, Phil Hogan, Oliver James, Peter Preston, Sally O'Sullivan, John Naughton, Will Buckley, Kevin Mitchell and Ian Ridley, Victoria Cohen and Robert McCrum. Some were writing about specialist issues or were being light-hearted. Still, that makes twenty columnists in a single newspaper. The *Sunday Telegraph* had nine columnists on its pages, ranging from fact-packed essays in the higher reporting, by John Simpson and Matthew d'Ancona, to the gossip column 'Mandrake' by Tim Walker and columnists on almost nothing at all (Oliver Pritchett, Jemima Lewis). The *Sunday Times* had twelve columnists, writing on everything from recent shock-ads by Barnardo's (John Humphrys) to India Knight on the sex war and Michael Winner on restaurants. The *Independent on Sunday* had ten, including Alan Watkins and the dreadful Janet Street-Porter; relatively cash-strapped,

it tends to use its own reporters as moonlighting columnists and in
this issue ran columns by the health correspondent Jeremy Laurence
and the foreign affairs correspondent Mary Dejevsky, as well as its
main political voice, Steve Richards. The *Mail on Sunday* made do with
a relatively restrained five columnists, notably Peter Hitchens and
Suzanne Moore; the *Sunday Express* had nine, including Boy George,
Robert Kilroy-Silk, Jimmy Young and its editor Martin Townsend. In
general, the more downmarket the paper, the fewer columnists – amid
the lurid stories, the *News of the World* had only two and the same
went for the *Sunday Mirror*. And all this is before the non-London
Sundays have been taken into account: readers in Scotland, with the
Sunday Herald, or in most of non-metropolitan England and Wales,
have more columnists still clamouring for their attention.

It is a formidable babble of finger-jabbing, shrugging, winking,
frowning, hectoring verbiage and a small industry in its own right. The
Saturday papers have almost as many columnists – by some countings
more, if you include all the shopping-style pieces in their supplements
– and the daily papers organize their columns like broadside cannon-
ades, the Monday team against their rivals' Monday writers. If you
write for a broadsheet, you might be 'up against' Polly Toynbee or
Simon Jenkins. Editors struggle to get the right mix of heavy-political
and light-frothy, of older men and younger women, of long columns
and short ones. The biggest columns in *The Times* run to 1,400 words,
which is generally thought to be at the high end of the readable;
the smaller columns may be only 500–600 words. There are by my
counting upwards of 200 regular national newspaper columnists; I
guess there must be more than twice that if you add in the magazine
world and the main provincial papers. A calculation by the Downing
Street press office of columnists they might want to try to influence
found 221 of them. This is a new phenomenon. In the press of a
generation ago, there were far fewer columnists; a political notebook
there, an arts round-up here. Why? As so often there is a boring reason
and an interesting reason.

And as so often, the boring reason is 'shopping'. As today's papers
are bigger in bulk, with more sections and advertising-funded supplements, they need more specialist columnists to help fill them. So long
as the columnist has been taught a little English and is sober enough
to deliver the right number of words at the right time of the week

(not so difficult these days, with computerized word counting) he or she can fill up a block of newspaper space for months, then years, without being bothered. As Ann Leslie spotted forty years ago, many columnists do not have to go out and interview people, or check facts, or do anything much beyond spinning out an idle thought or a pet prejudice and pressing the 'send' key, followed by a monthly invoice. Advertising exists for leisure publications of all kinds; the newspaper group then has to find a way of filling in the gaps between the advertising. This is not so easy. There is a limited number of talented journalists and interesting issues. Adding another column saves the editor from thinking about what else might be put there. Columnists have found themselves in possession of this modern urban accessory after flirting with an editor at a Christmas party, or being sacked from a more responsible job, or simply because they were in an office at the right time, when it became clear there was a hole to fill. 'I've got a column' is like 'I'm a consultant'. Some years back *Private Eye* started to satirize one variant of this disease, the middle-class female journalist writing about her dumb spouse, gormless nanny and precociously interesting children in an allegedly humorous way; unfortunately 'Polly Filler', as they called her, is a great deal more entertaining and sharp than the columns she is meant to send up. It also runs a spoof column in which celebrities discuss their attitude to spoons. Again, a flick through the average broadsheet newspaper package on any Saturday morning shows that this is barely satire.

The more interesting reason is that people do not take anonymous editorials or 'leaders' as seriously as they used to. From Victorian times to the 1980s, there were few jobs as highly rated, at least by the people doing them, as leader writing. Teams of cerebral men, almost always men, in front of coal fires, taunting one another with obscure Latin or Greek quotations, translating Proust in their spare time, used the anonymous leader columns to pursue pet causes, from tariff reform to Ulster Unionism. They felt themselves to be the soul of the paper, the essence of *The Times* or the *Guardian*. They thundered. They pleaded from their secular pulpits. They were read not only by the politicians and the permanent secretaries, the bishops and university professors, but by the whole class of educated, socially aware citizens. The newspaper editorials were an important place for the national conversation to take place, well before the *Today* programme or *Question*

Time. They were the reverse of democratic. Where there was an activist, political proprietor, as at Beaverbrook's *Daily Express*, the leader team would be the voice of the boss and often have privileged access; it was a good way for a young man on the make to be seen. In other set-ups their sense of carrying the torch of C. P. Scott or the Astor tradition meant they were constantly struggling to adapt old principles to new times. The leader teams still exist, though they are more often composed of one or two people, plus executives and columnists working part-time.

Much research and good argument can still flow through an editorial. What has gone wrong for them is that readers have lost respect for the idea of anonymous or institutional authority passed down through newspaper generations. This is hardly surprising, because the papers themselves have been jerked from one owner to another. Now we know that *The Times* is a Murdoch paper, the idea of its voice reverberating essentially unaltered from Georgian times, or even from the 1920s is an absurdity. For whom does its leader team speak? The latest editor, brought in by Rupert Murdoch? The interests of News International? Or simply the bright, intelligent bunch of journalists charged with writing those leaders, who work under general instruction about the paper's positions on issues like the euro or taxation? On papers like the *Guardian* or the *Observer*, the leader teams may have a particular historical tradition, but they are writing for an audience which sprawls from soft Toryism to Trotskyism, with every variant of progressive in between; the idea that a group of anonymous writers can speak with special authority contradicts everything they stand for. Papers undergoing swift and regular changes of ownership and strategy, from the *Independent* to the *Express* and even the *Daily Telegraph*, have too recent or narrow a tradition for readers to look to them as pulpits of established truth. Only a very few papers have such a strong ideology that the whole publication can speak as one: on *The Economist* the illusion of unwavering belief is maintained with some success but hardly anywhere else. We are used to putting names to ideas, and to watching contradictions emerge as a particular writer struggles with the world; that seems more honest these days than anonymous, corporate 'lines' of opinion. Today's readers are more sceptical and consumerist than the post-war generation who turned to leaders to know what to think; they are likelier to argue back, at least mentally. The fall of the editorial and the rise of the columnists is like the collapse of late medieval Catholic dogma before a rag-tag collection of itinerant roadside preachers.

How to be a Columnist

Writing a column is easy. Most students of most courses in most universities could turn out a thousand words to a deadline, making some kind of sense. When I first began a column of my own I would reflect that I was basically writing school essays but being paid enough to live a comfortable London life for what was once worth only a squiggle of red ink and a schoolteacher's signature at the bottom. But writing a *good* column is not easy. It is fantastically difficult and only a handful of people at any one time are able to manage it. As with political cartoonists, there is visibly more demand for good columnists than there are good columnists to go around: if this were not so, there would be no badly drawn, boring cartoons and no badly written, boring columns. You may think you could have written a single column better than a particular columnist, but remember the columnist does it for a living, every week of the year, sometimes several times a week. So how is it done? There are no rules, any more than there are absolute rules about how to write a novel; the creative and clever columnist will break any rule and profit by doing so. But there are general points about this huge explosion of opinionated journalism that are worth readers, and writers, remembering.

First, a good column is not just opinion. It contains an element of reporting. I turn to the column of many of the people mentioned already because I trust them to have been lunching, phoning and talking to politicians or civil servants. As Young and Jenkins showed, a column can be a form of higher reporting – fresh information brought hot and appetizing from the lunch tables of the powerful. But unlike a news article, a column can surround the information with context and analysis; the columnist can use all the familiar tools of metaphor, historical analogy and humour to help us understand not simply what the prime minister is saying privately but why; how seriously to take it; and where it may lead him next. Most columnists don't have access to the prime minister, or perhaps anyone very powerful. But they should still be telling the readers something factual they're unlikely to know – perhaps some astonishing statistics culled from an obscure Internet site, or a vivid description of a crack house or foreign city few us of are likely to know. Neal Ascherson of the *Observer* was much mocked at times for the way he would bang on about Poland in the days of the Soviet empire; but his understanding of Eastern Europe made him a valuable columnist at a time when most British readers were fantastically ignorant of the place. Similarly, when he wrote about Scotland, or about British political culture, he had enough historical knowledge to surprise – when everyone else was analysing the social unrest of the miners' strike and the inner-city riots of the early Thatcher years as a deplorable collapse of Britain's civilized political tradition, for instance, Ascherson was able to point out that our tradition is actually quite violent: it is just that most history has sanitized it. That argument, backed up with facts and examples, was fresh information to most readers, just as much as a Cabinet minister's private views.

Simon Jenkins is best when he has been striding round some corner of rural England and come upon a sight which rouses him to anger, or when he has been abroad; he brings reporterly information with him, lays it before the reader, and sets to work upon it. Parris is best when he has been out and about – at some disreputable bar with Peter Ackroyd, or on a remote island, or in the Commons – and tells us about his experience, before he discusses what it all means. Toynbee often simply lays out figures, from official papers, that few of us know and which put a new light on poverty, or the behaviour of the trade unions, or some other public issue. Facts are the essence of a column, the fibre that makes the thing more than a dribble of opinion. When I was writing a political column, I always tried to ensure I'd spoken to relevant people, schoolteachers or City brokers or MPs, and that I'd read up on the background – a think tank report, or perhaps a book on the politics of East Africa, or some speeches in *Hansard* – before I began typing. The main reason is to avoid the deadly, airless circularity of so much opinion. Almost always, when speaking to someone with a specific skill or history, whether a fisherman or a philosopher, you see a story or issue from a different perspective. You find that, actually, the 'racial' incidents in the small town were to do with a gang feud, in which both gangs mixed Asian and white members; or that actually, the numbers dying from CJD were going down, not up; or that actually, these Serb 'paramilitaries' were merely soldiers who wanted to go home. It is the 'actually', the twist away from the expected, that makes a good column sing.

One dangerous hand-me-down way of introducing striking facts, used by a host of well-paid columnists, is to seize on something already in the press and give it your own treatment. Occasionally, if the information comes from a relatively obscure publication, or has simply been overseen in the rush of other news, it can be worthwhile; there's a shocking story in *Jewish Fortnightly* or some extraordinary fact about policing merely noted in a single paragraph in the *Telegraph*. Fair enough. But most of the time this is how idle columnists, who can't be bothered to leave their kitchen tables or air-conditioned offices, feed the insatiable need for topics to write about. And a skilled columnist, with a good eye for the audience, can do very well out of recycled cuttings. Lee-Potter in the *Mail* and Burchill both do it, and thrive. But first, the columnist has no idea whether the original story was true, or a travesty, so there is a great danger of simply giving added velocity and prominence to nonsense. And second, if the columnist has done no work other than read somebody else's work, where is the fresh thought coming from? Presumably the stock of prejudices already in the columnist's head. In general, a columnist who does no original work is a dud. A worrying number of columnists, and their editors, don't seem to realize this.

But even with interesting and unexpected facts ready to be used, a serious columnist or pundit is only half started. Every column is also an argument, a case, a piece of logic. In general, it needs to be about something that can be expressed in a single headline-sized phrase or sentence. If the columnist cannot say concisely, for instance, 'gay men have too much power in British sport' or 'it's time for Gordon Brown to leave the Treasury' or 'digital television has been a disaster' then it is likely that the column will be confused, and therefore dull. If it isn't a statement, it's a waste of time. So you either have to talk to yourself – I found the morning shower and the walk to work particularly useful – or you have to have a good features editor to talk to, honing and refining the argument until it is clear in your head. This is the hardest part of all. For the argument should strive also to be two things which are not instantly compatible. It must be consistent with what you have

said before (otherwise you will seem ridiculous to the regular reader).
And it must be fresh (otherwise, the reader will feel, yes, I *know*, you
said it last week). The most obvious way of squaring the circle is to
take a position you believe in, and have expressed before, and turn it
on a new subject. So a free-market Tory columnist might try to explain
how the market can deal with the problem of high-calorie junk food
making children fat. Or a feminist might tackle the effects of England's
World Cup rugby victory. Some of the best arguing in journalism is
of this sort – Nick Cohen in the *Observer* was an absolute stereotype of
the typical anti-Iraq War journalist, a man of the left, deeply hostile to
Tony Blair and George Bush. Yet he was in favour of the war, and
wrote exceptionally well about why, from a socialist viewpoint. The
veteran feminist Bea Campbell wrote some of her very best columns
on the subject of hooligan boys, displaying great sympathy. Another
way of dealing with the consistency/freshness dilemma is to announce
that you have changed your mind, and explain why. This can be very
effective – Peter Jenkins on his disillusionment with David Owen was
a famous example – but is to be used sparingly, for obvious reasons.
The worst way is to simply keep changing tack and hope nobody
notices. *Private Eye* will, if no one else does.

   Still, with an argument formed and the reporting or factual
background at your fingertips, the problem of structuring a column
should virtually disappear. The classic column states an argument, then
runs through pros and cons, testing the reader with the force of
evidence and brutally goring the case against; and then concludes,
telling us why this argument (about which we are now convinced) is
urgent and important and should not be forgotten. In the running
through of the argument you very often find triplets – three examples,
three counter-arguments, three facts. I have puzzled about this and
conclude that three is hard-wired into our brains as the shortest list
there is. Two facts, two quotations, two sets of numbers (see) rub up
against each other and make us look for contrast. But three gives a
spurious impression of accumulated, irrefutable evidence. Opposing
pairs are essential too, of course, to most columns. If the New Labour
soap opera had had three or four would-be leaders, Gordon and
Charles and Patricia all equally fighting it out, then it would have
been dull to write about. We need 'Tony and Gordon', just like we
need 'left and right'. Many columns that feel strongly constructed and

convincing turn out, on inspection, to be based on simple patterns of triplets and opposing pairs.

In the preceding paragraph I have used 'often', 'most' and 'many', which are regular weasel words used by – many? – most? – columnists. They give a vague sense of weighting, of evidence mulled on, even if no real statistical evidence or counting have taken place. 'Most Labour MPs'? 'Most columnists'? 'Most ordinary people'? When you reach these kinds of assertions ask yourself if the writer has counted, spoken to or in any other way assessed them. They are one example of how to disguise opinion as fact. Even having done some reporterly fact-finding, and having worked through an argument and having begun to structure the piece, the columnist will do no good without a decent sense of how to use English unfairly. The cheer-words (decent, fair, reasonable, fresh, open, clear, brave) and the boo-words (biased, sordid, odious, tyrannical) must be carefully assembled, to be rained down on the reader like rocks from an ambush. The arguments of your enemies may be brutally simplified and then exaggerated in the most ludicrous possible manner; though the best columnist is the one who takes the best opposing argument, expressed best, and still beats it. The weak points in your own case will be acknowledged but briskly skipped over. And you will bring the reader through your argument with a basic sense of rhythm – short sentences punctuated by longer ones; stabbing syntax – plenty of dashes. And in defiance of teachers, many sentences starting with 'and'. But others will have 'but'. Or 'or'. Verbs being optional.

Good columnists, like good writers generally, have personal rhythms, which I have noticed are similar to their speech rhythms and probably therefore to their rhythms of thought. Bagehot wrote once that the knack was to write like a human being: 'legibility is given to those who ... are willing to be themselves, to write their own thoughts in their own words, in the simplest words, in the words wherein they were thought'. And he practised what he preached: his colleagues noted that in old age he wasn't at all grand but was working hard at being conversational and putting things in common speech; he would search out and use expressive, useful colloquialisms, including new American words. This is probably why Bagehot is so very unusual among Victorian columnists in still being easy and entertaining to read today. Ideally any powerful columnist will be easy on the ear and eye.

But it takes a lot of work and sweat to be clear. Hugo Young was a great columnist but his less-good work could read as if it had been originally written in German, and poorly translated. Ed Pearce, once of the *Telegraph* and now of *Tribune*, can write like a punk-teenage Carlyle[20] and Peter Preston, a great editor of the *Guardian* and a man crammed with interesting knowledge and views, is not a great columnist simply because of his difficult, spasmodic sense of rhythm.

Ever since Orwell pointed it out, journalists have accepted that a word-hoard based on Anglo-Saxon, with its earthier, more basic grip, is better than a Latinate-Francophone vocabulary. From Cobbett to Churchill, the most moving and urgent prose in English has turned to the shorter, more pointed words of the peasants and used them against the multi-syllabic officialese that began with Norman clerks and continues in government English even today. Reading hundreds of columns, it is immediately obvious whether or not the writer understands this simple rhetorical truth about the language. Boris Johnson is particularly good about it. But there are other tricks which seem to work. Columns which start with a strong sensual image – colours, weather, food, smells, a woman roaring with laughter or the cost of a bottle of wine – attract the eye in a way the cleverest abstract sentence will not. The opening needs to work immediately: it should affront readers, or make them laugh, or puzzle them in an engaging way. I rarely rewrite, but often go back to the first few sentences time and again. The ending may well pick up on the opening image or thought. You should 'bite the tail': it gives a satisfying sense of completeness. Between the column's nose and tail, there should be some numbers, but no more than three or four. No quotation should last longer than ten short newspaper lines. No columnist should ever mention another one. All right – I am indulging in self-parody. But there are *not* as many ways of writing a good column as there are columnists; basic bundles of English work time and again, just as most music is built up with basic chords. The good columnist packs in fact, anecdote, argument and striking imagery in a thousand words, carefully mixed, time and time again. To do this well is one of the most enjoyable things in public life, and also one of the most rewarding.

Foreign correspondents and columnists are the acknowledged aristocrats of modern journalism. How can this be? The two wings of the trade seem so very different. The foreign correspondent is 'out there'; the columnist is classically 'in here'. It would be a statement of barbarity to say there were too many foreign correspondents – how can we not want as many eyes on the outside world as the industry can buy? But it is a statement of plain fact that we have too many columnists. Foreign correspondents are hired to report, columnists to opine. It would be easy to conclude that foreign correspondents are benign journalism at its best (that is certainly what they think), while the sprawl of pundits and lifestyle columnists is evidence of social sickness, the journalism of the fascinatingly whorled navel. Foreign correspondents, one might argue, rise in numbers and status when a society is outward-looking and interested in the world; columnists thrive in a society grown flabby, bored and selfish. I hope I have shown that the truth is not so simple. Journalism is never about simply reporting bald facts. It is about assembling them into a coherent story, which in turn often asks us to feel some emotional reaction. Foreign correspondents are often driven to conclude, to point out, to express anger or pity . . . in short, to start behaving like columnists. Good columnists, meanwhile, must be reporters too, going out into the world, if not physically then at the very least strapped to a powerful search engine. Robert Fisk finds his opinions bubbling so hot that he now doubles as a columnist. Ann Leslie, who gave up writing columns because she didn't know enough about the world, now finds that her years of travelling allow her to write in a style that can be both opinionated and convincing. Among columnists, Oborne may travel to Afghanistan, Simon Jenkins to Iraq; while earlier columnists, such as Peter Jenkins criss-crossing America and Germany or Neal Ascherson in Eastern Europe, have behaved like roving reporters.

And that is the word that counts. Reporters are what journalism is about. Great foreign correspondents are reporters who shape the chaos of the world into stories that make sense. Great columnists are reporters of political life and dramatic life, with the licence to use the techniques of fiction and rhetoric to tell us what they believe is happening. Never mind the arguments about ownership and regulation. A journalism which is based on vigorous, honest reporting is in good health; one which is not is in decay. It's as simple as that.

Epilogue

Predicting the future of journalism is a mug's game. Papers which have now died once seemed unstoppable. Others seemed doomed, but have thrived. There was once a general view that the *Guardian* and *The Times* would have to merge to stay in business. Rupert Murdoch assured David English that there would soon be only three national papers left in Britain – *The Times*, the *Daily Mail* and the *Sun*. Hugh Cudlipp held the first edition of Murdoch's *Sun* aloft and derided it as a disaster. In the 1940s senior BBC executives decided there was no future in trying to put news on television. Others, a little later, thought the *Today* programme could only work if it was kept light and jokey. The owner of the *Financial Times* sold it after the Second World War because it was obvious that capitalism was doomed. More recently, there was a plan to turn the *Observer* into a glossy magazine since it was clearly fated to continue losing sales as a newspaper; it is now a rare success story. My favourite example of crystal-ball gazing comes from one of the greats of the industry, R. D. Blumenfeld, a long-standing editor of the *Daily Express*, who predicted in 1933 that the press of fifty years later would be less salacious, less biased and would have solved the distribution problem, because 'every newspaper will have its own aerodrome'.

So let us tread warily. Some of today's papers will not survive. Other papers and programmes unknown now will be favourites in the future. The Internet will continue to rise as a source of news; it will continue to merge with what we now call television. And the British journalist?

We have become caricatures and must do something about it. We are often seen as strawberry-nosed voyeurs, liars, drunks and cynics. This is nobody else's fault. We cannot blame evil tycoons or proprietors, since their influence has actually grown less, or the politicians and regulators, since we spend much of our time trying to keep both off our backs. We cannot blame the playwrights, cartoonists or Rory Bremner. Nor can we blame the public for any falling-off in quality in journalism, since the public is in general better-educated than ever. If sales of good quality books, and music, and theatre tickets are all going up, and if people are leaving school with good exam results, and if the proportion of people going to university is rising fast, then we can hardly accuse readers and viewers of dumbing down. Some editors and journalists loudly deny there has been a falling-off. They point out that the sheer quantity of daily journalism produced in Britain is not only great, but is greater than at many times in the past. It was once said that an editor is someone who sorts the wheat from the chaff; and then prints the chaff. But people have been complaining like that since the days of Daniel Defoe.

When was the age of gold? Was it in Victorian England, when the broadsheets were dreary Establishment notice boards and the popular papers were lurid, bloodthirsty records of murder and rape? Was it between the wars of the last century, when gossip columnists rose to power, and circulation-boosting stunts were invented, and most papers thought Hitler wasn't much of a threat, and the BBC was allowed to report nothing that had not been reported by agencies already? Was it after the Second World War, when the papers were thin and meagre? Or in the 1960s when sex journalism returned through the Sunday papers, and TV journalists learned the tricks of emotionalism? Or the 1970s, when Murdoch's *Sun* appeared and old Fleet Street teetered on the edge of industrial collapse and people of the quality of Harry Evans had to quit the British trade? Or the 1980s, when the modern *Daily Mail* really got into its stride, and the old lobby system of secretive briefing enjoyed its Indian summer? What was so great about the past and what is so bad about now?

Indeed, you could argue that British journalism is about to enter a golden age in this new century. After all, it is now a trade almost entirely composed of university-trained graduates, policed by watchdogs, which still sells far more papers and makes more broadcast news bulletins than any comparable European rival. With the Internet, it has access to more information, faster, than journalism has ever had before. Because modern communications are so fast and so easy to use, it is probably harder to lie in journalism than it used to be, too. There are individual scandals, such as the *New York Times* saga, when a leading reporter was caught making up stories. But if you bother to go back and read the scams and lies of American or British journalism a century ago, that's hardly a modern vice. True, journalists at the bottom are badly underpaid and undervalued and journalists at the top are overpaid and overrated. But as I've shown, that was always true.

Even so, in the end, I believe there are serious problems in British journalism that everybody needs to talk about, and rather more openly than we have done. Every twist and mistake of a senior politician is pored over and pointed at. But when newspapers get it wrong or TV reporters make a bad call, we mostly get away with it. There's no mystery there: we are the self-appointed referees of modern life and we are not greatly inclined to blow the whistle and send ourselves off the field. So, what are those problems?

The first problems are about trust. If politicians have issues of trust so, by God, do journalists. Our problem is less direct lying than slimy misrepresentation. Some hyping is inherent in journalism. The world is complicated, confusing and many-sided: to produce a story, much of the complexity has to be stripped away. Otherwise you have a jumble that repels interest. Still, how many quotes by anonymous experts or sources are invented, or at least 'improved'? Every day of the week I read stories about subjects I have followed and find myself uneasy or suspicious about off-the-record assertions which just seem too neat, too convenient. How often has the reporter gone through a long interview and stripped out a few words, junking all context and balance, to produce a deliberately misleading effect? I have become just as suspicious about numbers and statistics.

Journalists are seen as untrustworthy particularly by sources or victims – the ordinary people caught up in news stories who are promised friendly help by the reporter and then find themselves brutally caricatured and savaged; or who are assured that something is off the record when it is not; or who are vaguely promised money which never actually materializes. The honest advice I would give a friend or family member pursued by a journalist is to say nothing at all at first, and then to weigh every word against the chance of it being twisted before making a statement. My hypocrisy is that I am on the other side in professional life. Not only do I know the pressure to produce a story, to 'deliver', I am also well aware that the public is not innocent, but has its share of greedy narks who think national newspapers are a better-odds version of the National Lottery.

Another part of the trust problem is our reluctance to correct stories. This is hard-wired into journalism. We like to think of 'the story' as a single, clear event, a few minutes of airtime or a few inches of print – self-standing, almost pure. It's done one day, and the next day is blank, fresh, waiting for a new story. Yet in the mess and confusion of life, hardly any stories are like that. They are dabs, or splashes, of a picture, constantly needing to be rubbed out, amended, added to. They are unreliable fragments of longer shaggy-dog tales. Very few stories are simply statements of fact that lead nowhere. So correcting them, adding to the reader or viewer's knowledge, ought to be a regular daily act. The customer ought to be assumed to know that what we say about a speech, a political stunt, a murder or a new strain of a virus is tentative, not final, and will need correction. Instead we have the habit of leaving loose ends everywhere. We don't go back often enough and ask: were we right; what actually happened next?

After problems of trust, there are, just as serious, problems of tone – above all, exaggeration. If there is a medical doubt about something, we cry plague. If there is a small rise in the possibility that some habit or product, in excess and in some people, may cause cancer, then hysterical shrieks of instant warning erupt on the front pages. If there are questions about a politician's motives, personal behaviour or honesty, we tend to treat him as the moral equivalent of a serial killer and turn to the facts later. Closely allied to our habit of exaggerating dangers and depravity, we now have a culture of completely implausible self-righteousness. It may not be a major national problem but it is not pretty. The classic *Mail* headline which begins 'Is this the Most Evil/Depraved/Shocking . . .?' can almost always be answered 'actually, no'. The tabloids pretend to quiver in shock about absolutely normal, if regrettable, human behaviour – adulteries, marital break-ups, petty deceits. Neither the journalists writing the stories, nor presumably the regular readers reading them, are actually shocked. Mostly it is just a minor buzz of titillation or Schadenfreude.

Very close to this is general emotionalism. We wring the facts to get the biggest emotional impact. This used to be called tabloid journalism, and indeed you found it on the front page of the *Mirror* a lifetime ago. But it has spread, just as the cult of celebrity has spread from being just a few stories in gossip columns to taking over whole papers. The idea of news has altered. It stopped being essentially information and became something designed to produce – at all costs, always – an emotional reaction, the more extreme the better. Shock; eroticism; fear; laughter; anger . . . a paper which could produce a ripple of reactions from page to page could not fail. The red-tops are now a multicoloured bouquet of sex and anger. The grief of a parent, or the guilt of a convicted drug trafficker, is news even if it is completely unsurprising. The upmarket papers are being lured in, too. The *Observer* exists for people who are more liberal and urban than the classic *Mail* or *Express* readers, but it is now a more emotional paper, searching out stories about tragic lives and deaths, honour killings and betrayals. Part of the *Independent*'s recent revival is simply about going tabloid in size, but it has also used highly emotional front pages to pose questions about the Iraq War, or migration.

You could say that this is simply journalism reflecting modern Britain, as it always does. We have become a more emotionally open, or soppy, country. We expect to be moved as much as informed. We make sense of our lives not through politics or class, but through tales of personal redemption, pitying ourselves and blaming anonymous others. Our press reflects this just as it reflects our dazed consumerism. So what? Perhaps there is nothing to be done. If this is what works for British people now, who are journalists to worry?

The trouble is, it isn't working. Newspaper sales have crashed over the past three decades. Paid-for nationals are a million down in the past five years. The audiences for mainstream TV bulletins have fallen too, and the new twenty-four-hour digital news services have not filled the listening and viewing gap. If you live your life without news, then you become a kind of political zero, with no grip on the world around you. News is the nervous system of urban humanity. It is the fresh air of democracy. Robin Dunbar from Liverpool University argues that bad news, or a lack of news, could even effect the fate of the planet. If people are not able to follow, sustain and interrupt complex arguments, they will give up trying to understand and influence the world around them, whether it be wars in the Middle East, cloning or global warming:

Essentially, more and more people will give up thinking and following these issues and leave them in the hands of eloquent experts – scientists, politicians and others – who will take on the roles of shamans. That is scarcely a healthy development.

Many of us still measure out our lives not as a poet said, in coffee spoons, but in news. The hourly murmur on the radio; the urgent television; the large, angry letters of the front pages – these surround us. This idea that we can explain things, perhaps even explain our lives, by upending a torrent of information over our heads may seem odd. But if the news is well made, if it faithfully reflects the big facts of the world around us, then it can empower us. I am writing this on a dark winter morning, with heavy rain beating down. I know, because of the news, that this has been one of the wettest and warmest winters in recent history. English towns are flooded. Where, perhaps, my great-great-grandmother would have reacted to similar floods by seeing them as a judgement by God on wicked people, I believe they are caused by global warming. I also think global warming is caused by human activity – not wickedness, exactly, but our biological success as a species which consumes and burns so much carbon. When I buy food, I know a bit about where it came from. When I wait for the bus to work, I know about the rows over transport congestion. These things can feed back into my conversation with friends and families, our little campaigns, our votes. Without well-made news we all weigh less. So the fall in newspaper sales and bulletin viewers, if it is caused by avoidable failures in journalism, matters.

The last question is: what can be done? The solution is in the brains and hands and soul of the British journalist, and nobody else. That may not seem an inspiring thought. But the good news is that journalism is an infinitely suggestible and flexible trade. Often in its history a single paper or a single editor has had a huge ripple effect – a Northcliffe, a Russell, a Dacre, a Dimbleby changes the way hundreds or thousands of others do their work. When it comes to some of the trust issues described above, we can already see the shrewder editors reacting. Quite a lot of papers have recently appointed ombudsmen or readers' representatives. Associated's free *Metro* papers are deliberately high on straight reporting and low on emotionalism and are doing well. The *Guardian* has issued fresh instructions about on-the-record quotes after Lord Hutton's report, while the BBC itself thoroughly overhauled its procedures.

If it becomes accepted in the trade that a loss of trust and an increasingly hackneyed emotionalism are actually losing readers, then the owners and practitioners of journalism will react. They need to. People talk about tabloid newspapers as 'the comics'. It was a term that came in during the 1980s and is an eloquent one. Because comics are old hat. The real ones, the coloured strip-stories of urchins and cowboys, are out of business. They simply do not compete when up against scores of TV channels. We are seeing the first signs of the same thing happening to the tabloid 'comics' too. The *News of the World*, arguably the pioneer of this, has seen its sales crumple to a fraction of where they were in the long-lost days of the sixties when it was still packed with real news too. The *Sun*, though it has the benefit of being the market leader, is in steady decline, one day full of bare breasts, the next of heavy political analysis. The worst example of daily tabloid collapse, though, is the *Mirror*. The loss of its reputation for authority and commitment has been followed by a catastrophic fall in circulation. It tried to head upmarket but its editor was quickly hauled back by the management and told to return to the celebrity agenda. It is much easier and quicker to get down the slope than climb it and it would take ten or fifteen years of steady rebuilding and nerves to allow the *Mirror* to return to its old authority, if it ever could. The *Daily Star* bucked the trend for a while, by concentrating ruthlessly on people on telly, and virtually giving up traditional reporting. But it is in trouble too, just like the *Express*.

And the *Star* has a message for the whole trade, the message that I finally believe is the most important of all. It was much mocked when the *Daily Telegraph* media team outed its in-house fictional byline, 'Tony Leonard'. The *Star* used this name to cover up the fact it was not sending its own journalists to key events like the Soham murder trial, or to Westminster, or the City, or indeed anywhere much. Tony Leonard became the most prolific journalist in Fleet Street history, with 818 stories for the *Star* during the first eleven months of 2003. But he has many colleagues. The truth is, across the industry, we have seen a huge increase in 'here's one I made earlier' journalism, the journalism of people sitting in front of screens in airless offices on the outskirts of towns, under the lash to be 'productive' – that is, to churn out repetitive stories by rote, lifted from rivals or from the Internet or press agencies, and massaged to fit that paper's particular audience. Office-bound journalists are vulnerable to the PR machines, the con men, the special interest groups and above all errors that have been trapped in electronic or paper files. This is why so many papers, from the upmarket to the downmarket, carry the same stories, often treated in the same bland way. The police helmet is being reduced in size? Find six other national icons and photo-reduce them. Some radio star is pissed again? Look out his earlier escapades and trot them out yet again.

Journalism needs the unexpected. It needs the unpredictability and oddness of real life. That means it needs real reporters. There is no better protection against the special pleading and salesmanship of the PR machines than decently paid and experienced journalists, trusted inside their organizations to use their judgement. Time and again, newspapers have been saved by the scrupulous health correspondent who refuses to take a scare at face value; or the science correspondent who manages to show shades of grey in a controversial and complicated story about genetic research; or the interviewer who is big enough not to grovel to the agent's agenda; or the political correspondent who points out that a much-hyped poll is based on too narrow a sample to be given prominence. It goes for the general reporters too – the people who go back to the source of hysterical-sounding quotes, and discover that she was misrepresented, or didn't quite mean it that way; and those who stay in the office and make yet another last check-call, discovering that things were not as first said. 'We're calling this the work of Muslim extremists. Is that OK?' says the night editor. 'Well actually no, not necessarily . . .'

So the most important thing is to hire more reporters – front-line people who are inquisitive, energetic and honest. For all its many faults, detailed earlier in this book, at least the *Daily Mail*, one of the rare commercial success stories of today, does invest in reporting. It pays more and hires more and sends more people around the country. And, whether you like what they bring back or not, it shows. Tomorrow's reporters will have chaotic but interesting lives. Journalism will mess up their relationships, keep them poorer and less secure than they might be elsewhere, and give them an obscure and secret buzz no one outside the trade will ever really understand. But if they do it well, they will be central to the health of the people.

As for me? Well, I'm still a hack, still in love with the trade that I hate. Sometimes it seems a rotten job; but it's better than all the other ones. On good days, it's heaven. On the bad ones, I remember James Cameron:

> The spectacle of the conscientious journalist bemoaning the shortcomings of his profession is both pitiable and platitudinous, like that of the rueful whore. His condition may be unfortunate but it is hardly irremediable; the journalist who feels that the methods of the organisation that pays him are a doleful burden upon his principles can as a rule resolve his dilemma: he can stop taking their money, and get out.

Notes

1. The Snobs and the Soaks

1. Edward Frank Caudlin, *Teach Yourself Journalism*, English University Press, 1951.
2. Quoted in Ian Hargreaves, *Journalism, Truth or Dare?*, OUP, 2003.
3. See R. M. Wiles, *Freshest Advices*, Ohio State University Press, 1965.
4. This and the foregoing about bribes comes from Stephen Koss's monumental study, *The Rise and Fall of the Political Press in Britain*, Hamish Hamilton, 1981, 1984.
5. Quoted in Alan J. Lee, *The Origins of the Popular Press, 1855–1914*, Croom Helm, 1976.
6. See Louis Heren, *The Power of the Press*, Orbis, 1985.
7. Quoted in Oliver Woods and James Bishop, *The Story of The Times*, Joseph, 1983, also in Heren, *The Power of the Press*.
8. *The History of The Times: The Tradition Established 1841–1884*, The Times, 1939.
9. Heren, *Power of the Press*.
10. Ralph Straus, *Sala, Portrait of an Eminent Victorian*, Constable, 1940.
11. G. A. Sala, *Life and Adventures*, 3rd edn, 1895.
12. See Prologue, Koss, *The Rise and Fall*.
13. Alan J. Lee, *Origins of the Popular Press*.
14. See Prologue, Koss, *The Rise and Fall*.
15. Kennedy Jones, *Fleet Street and Downing Street*, Hutchinson, 1920.
16. R. J. Minney, *The Journalist*, Geoffrey Bles, 1931.
17. Alan J. Lee, *Origins of the Popular Press*.
18. Tom Clarke, *My Northcliffe Diary*, Gollancz, 1931.
19. R. J. Minney, *The Journalist*.
20. Quoted in Jeremy Tunstall, *Newspaper Power: The New National Press in Britain*, Oxford, 1996.
21. Tunstall, *Newspaper Power*.

22. Tunstall, *Newspaper Power*.
23. Bernard Ingham, *Kill the Messenger*, HarperCollins, 1991.
24. From 'An Outpost' by J. B. Priestley, in *The Book of Fleet Street*, ed. T. Michael Pope, Cassell, 1930.
25. Phillip Knightley, *A Hack's Progress*, Jonathan Cape, 1997.
26. Barry Norman, *And Why Not?*, Simon & Schuster, 2002.
27. From *Strangers within the Gate* by George Blake in Pope, *Book of Fleet Street*.
28. Duff Hart-Davis, *The House the Berrys Built*, Hodder & Stoughton, 1990.
29. Glenton and Pattison, *The Last Chronicle of Bouverie Street*, George Allen & Unwin, 1963.
30. From Christopher Hitchens's introduction to Evelyn Waugh's *Scoop*, Penguin, 2000.
31. Michael Frayn, *Towards the End of the Morning*, Faber & Faber, 2000.

2. What is News?

1. Jon Silverman and David Wilson, *Innocence Betrayed*, Polity Press, 2002.
2. Quoted in Thomas Boyle: *Black Swine in the Sewers of Hampstead*, Hodder & Stoughton, 1990.
3. The story is fully told in *Black Swine in the Sewers of Hampstead*.
4. S. J. Taylor, *The Great Outsiders*, Weidenfeld and Nicolson, 1996.
5. See Taylor, *Great Outsiders*, and also Tom Clarke, *My Northcliffe Diary*, Victor Gollancz, 1931.
6. *The History of 'The Times'*, Vol. IV, Printing House Square, 1952.
7. From the *New Clarion*, quoted in Engel, op. cit.
8. In *The Book of Fleet Street*, ed. T. Michael Pope, Cassell, 1930.
9. Pope, *Book of Fleet Street*, essay by James Bone, 'Stunt'.
10. In Phillip Knightley, *A Hack's Progress*, Jonathan Cape, 1997.
11. Duff Hart-Davis, *The House the Berrys Built*, Hodder & Stoughton, 1990.
12. See T. S. Matthews, *The Sugar Pill*, Gollancz, 1957.
13. Matthews, *Sugar Pill*.
14. *British Journalism Review*, Vol. 15, No. 1.
15. See *Health in the News*, published by the King's Fund.
16. Michael Diamond, *Victorian Sensation*, Anthem Press, 2003.
17. Chippendale and Horrie, op. cit.
18. The *Spectator*, 28 February 2004.

3. The Dirty Art of Political Journalism

1. Ruth Dudley Edwards, *Newspapermen*, Random House, 2003.
2. See Andrew Sparrow, *Obscure Scribblers*, Politico's, 2003.
3. T. F. Lindsay, *Parliament from the Press Gallery*, Macmillan, 1967.
4. See Sparrow, *Obscure Scribblers*.
5. See Sparrow for this debate, *Obscure Scribblers*, pp. 12–14.
6. Sir John Hawkins, *Life of Johnson*, 1787.
7. Alastair Campbell, speech to Media Correspondents Association, October 2001, reprinted in *British Journalism Review*, Vol. 13, No. 4.
8. Interview with Geoffrey Goodman, *BJR*, Vol. 13, No. 4.
9. See Michael Cockerell, Peter Hennessy and David Walker, *Sources Close to the Prime Minister*, Macmillan, 1984.
10. Campbell speech to Media Correspondents Association.
11. The best digestible account of all this is in John Rentoul's *Tony Blair: Prime Minister*, Warner, 2001.
12. From Gavin Astor et al., *Fleet Street: The Inside Story of Journalism*, Macdonald, 1966: essay, 'Parliamentary Men' by Geoffrey Wakeford of the *Daily Mail*, chairman of the lobby 1956–7.
13. Both quotes from Bernard Ingham, *The Wages of Spin*, John Murray, 2003.

4. Lord Cooper and his Children

1. The story of the founding of the *Independent* has been recounted in detail by Nicholas Garland, the cartoonist, by Michael Crozier (*The Making of the 'Independent'*, Gordon Fraser, 1988) and by Stephen Glover in *Paper Dreams*, Jonathan Cape, 1993.
2. Richard Stott, *Dogs and Lampposts*, Metro, 2002.
3. Interview with author.
4. T. S. Matthews, *The Sugar Pill*, Gollancz, 1957.
5. All quotes from Bill Deedes, *Dear Bill*, Macmillan, 1997.
6. Penny Junor, *Home Truths: Life Around My Father*, HarperCollins, 2002.
7. From S. J. Taylor, *An Unlikely Hero: Vere Rothermere and how the 'Daily Mail' was Saved*, Weidenfeld and Nicolson, 2002.
8. Peter Chippindale and Chris Horrie, *Stick it up your Punter!* Heinemann, 1990.

9. Stephen Glover, *Paper Dreams*, Cape, 1993.

10. Ruth Dudley Edwards, *Newspapermen*, Secker & Warburg, 2003.

11. Arthur Christiansen, *Headlines All My Life*, Heinemann, 1961.

12. All quotes from Harry Evans, *Good Times, Bad Times*, Weidenfeld and Nicolson, 1983.

13. *Nicholas Tomalin Reporting*, ed. Ron Hall, Andre Deutsch, 1975.

14. Phillip Knightley, quoted in the *Observer*, by Patrick Weever, 6 July 2002.

15. Nicolas Coleridge, *Paper Tigers*, Heinemann, 1993.

16. Penny Junor, *Home Truths*.

5. Into the Crowded Air

1. Vin Ray, *The Television News Handbook*, Macmillan, 2003.

2. Grace Wyndham Goldie, *Facing the Nation: Television and Politics, 1936–1976*, Bodley Head, 1977.

3. Wyndham Goldie, *Facing the Nation*.

4. Robin Day, *Day by Day*, William Kimber, 1975.

5. Wyndham Goldie, *Facing the Nation*.

6. See Michael Brunson, *A Ringside Seat: The Autobiography*, Hodder & Stoughton, 2000 and Kate Adie, *The Kindness of Strangers*, Headline, 2002.

7. Richard Lindley, *'Panorama': Fifty Years of Pride and Paranoia*, Politico's, 2002.

8. Lindley, *'Panorama'*.

9. Ray, *Television News Handbook*.

10. *Financial Times Magazine*, 4 October 2003.

11. Brunson, *Ringside Seat*.

12. From Jack de Manio, *To Auntie with Love*, Hutchinson, 1967.

13. *Today* references come mainly from Paul Donovan, *All our Todays*, Jonathan Cape, 1994; Tim Luckhurst, *This is Today*, Aurum, 2001 and Sue MacGregor, *Woman of Today*, Headline, 2002.

14. Wyndham Goldie, *Facing the Nation*.

6. Two Aristocracies

1. See Rupert Furneaux, *News of War*, Parrish, 1964.

2. *New Statesman*, 13 May 2002.

3. John Simpson, *Strange Places, Questionable People*, Macmillan, 1998.

4. The story is told in the bible of foreign-correspondent literature, Phillip Knightley's *The First Casualty*, Prion Books, 2000.

5. Christopher Mayhew & Michael Adams, *Publish it Not . . . The Middle East Cover-Up*, Longman, 1975.

6. John Pilger, *Heroes*, Jonathan Cape, 1986.

7. Kate Adie, *The Kindness of Strangers*, Headline, 2002.

8. Don McCullin, *Unreasonable Behaviour*, Vintage, 1992.

9. Godfrey Hodgson, in *The Historical Journal of Film, Radio and Television*, Vol. 20, No. 1, March 2000.

10. Tom Paulin, *The Day-Star of Liberty*, Faber, 1998.

11. Eric Alterman, *Sound & Fury*, HarperCollins, 1992.

12. Alan Watkins, *A Short Walk Down Fleet Street*, Duckworth, 2000.

13. Peregrine Worsthorne, *Tricks of Memory*, Weidenfeld & Nicolson, 1993.

14. In *Anatomy of Decline: the Political Journalism of Peter Jenkins*, ed. Brian Brivati and Richard Cockett, Cassell, 1995.

15. *Anatomy of Decline*, the *Guardian*, 3 June 1977.

16. Stephen Bayley, *A Dictionary of Idiocy*, Gibson Square Books, 2003.

17. Hugo Young, *Supping with the Devils*, Atlantic Books, 2003.

18. See Karl E. Mayer, *Pundits, Poets and Wits*, OUP, 1990.

19. The *Independent*, 11 June 2000.

20. This is not intended to be a compliment.

Index

JOHN SERGEANT

Give Me Ten Seconds

PAN BOOKS

For thirty years John Sergeant worked for the BBC, latterly as Chief Political Correspondent. He then became Political Editor of ITN. *Give Me Ten Seconds* is his riveting, frequently hilarious and often touching autobiography. In it, he takes us from his rather curious childhood to his early years as a reporter on the *Liverpool Post*, and thence to the BBC. Memorably handbagged by Mrs Thatcher on the steps of the Paris Embassy following her failure to retain the leadership of the Conservative Party, Sergeant has been the man on the spot at most of the major news stories of the last twenty years. His mordant wit, keen sense of the absurd and acute powers of analysis pervade the book. He has a wealth of funny anecdotes featuring the key political figures of our time and his understanding of the labyrinthine workings of Westminster – and Broadcasting House – is second to none.

'An all-time rip-roaring read'
Independent on Sunday

'This intriguing autobiography covers the author's broadcasting life and snapshots from an extraordinary family history. Sergeant is neither self-deprecating nor boastful . . . as moving as John Mortimer's memoirs, *The Summer of a Dormouse*'
The Times

'Excellent'
Daily Telegraph

OTHER BOOKS

AVAILABLE FROM PAN MACMILLAN

JOHN SERGEANT
GIVE ME TEN SECONDS	0 330 48490 7	£7.99
MAGGIE	1 4050 0526 2	£20.00

JOHN SIMPSON
A MAD WORLD, MY MASTERS	0 330 35567 8	£7.99
THE WARS AGAINST SADDAM	0 330 41890 4	£7.99
NEWS FROM NO MAN'S LAND	0 330 48735 3	£7.99

TOM WOLFE
THE NEW JOURNALISM	0 330 24315 2	£8.99

All Pan Macmillan titles can be ordered from our website,
www.panmacmillan.com, or from your local bookshop
and are also available by post from:

Bookpost, PO Box 29, Douglas, Isle of Man IM99 1BQ
Credit cards accepted. For details:
Telephone: +44 (0)1624 677237
Fax: +44 (0)1624 670923
E-mail: bookshop@enterprise.net
www.bookpost.co.uk

Free postage and packing in the United Kingdom

Prices shown above were correct at the time of going to press.
Pan Macmillan reserve the right to show new retail prices on covers
which may differ from those previously advertised in the text
or elsewhere.